Security Without Nuclear Weapons?
Different Perspectives on Non-Nuclear Security

Security Without Nuclear Weapons?

Different Perspectives on Non-Nuclear Security

Edited by
Regina Cowen Karp

OXFORD UNIVERSITY PRESS
1992

Oxford University Press, Walton Street, Oxford OX2 6DP
Oxford New York Toronto
Delhi Bombay Calcutta Madras Karachi
Kuala Lumpur Singapore Hong Kong Tokyo
Nairobi Dar es Salaam Cape Town
Melbourne Auckland Madrid
and associated companies in
Berlin Ibadan

Oxford is a trade mark of Oxford University Press

Published in the United States
by Oxford University Press Inc., New York

© SIPRI 1992

British Library Cataloguing in Publication Data
Data available

Library of Congress Cataloging in Publication Data
Data available
ISBN 0–19–829143–4

Typeset and originated by Stockholm International Peace Research Institute
Printed in Great Britain
on acid-free paper by
Biddles Ltd, Guildford and King's Lynn

for Joshua and Madeline
and their world

Contents

Preface

This is the second book of a two-volume project entitled 'Security Without Nuclear Weapons?'. The first book is a study of how states have responded to the existence of nuclear weapons. The present study explores what non-nuclear security is, how existing thinking about international security needs to change and what the opportunities for and constraints on nuclear abolition might be. This is not a book on nuclear disarmament. Rather, it is about non-nuclear security in a world of states.

The contributions to this book were written before the end of the cold war had been universally acknowledged and before recent US and Russian agreements to make substantial cuts in their respective nuclear arsenals. While these agreements are to be welcomed, the debate about a future international security order and the role of remaining nuclear weapons in national security strategies is only beginning. As we think of the post-cold war future, the security themes and issues discussed by the authors of this book are of primary relevance.

Acknowledgements

My gratitude is due to all contributing authors especially for their advice and willingness to engage in an intellectual 'process utopia'. I also wish to thank the members of the project advisory group, whose critical guidance has been invaluable throughout the project: Professor Dr Kurt Biedenkopf (Germany), Dr Barry Buzan (UK), Bischof Dr Christoph Demke (Germany), General George Fricaud-Chagnaud (France), Professor Andrey Kokoshin (Russia), Professor Joseph S. Nye, Jr (USA), Dr Sergey Rogov (Russia), Professor Yoshikazu Sakamoto (Japan) and Professor Jack Steinberger (Switzerland).

A large debt is owed to Dr Walther Stützle, former Director of SIPRI, who encouraged this endeavour and offered much valuable insight. My gratitude is also due to Stephen I. Griffiths, Andreas Behnke and Irving Lachow. I am especially thankful to Don Odom, my editor at SIPRI, for his excellent editorial work.

Finally, I owe a great debt to the generous love of my husband Aaron.

Dr Regina Cowen Karp
Project Leader
August 1992

Foreword

It is unusual that a book, conceived and written before a period of fundamental and encompassing change, would be so relevant by the date of its publication. Indeed, the themes of the Security Without Nuclear Weapons? project which are reflected in this book (the second volume of the project) are perhaps more relevant today than when they were initially conceptualized. During the course of this forward-looking and future-oriented study, the unthinkable has not only become possible, but also the possible has become highly probable.

The end of the cold war and the disintegration of the Soviet Union raises fundamental questions about the future of international security. As an academic community, we are challenged to reappraise our thinking about the sources of war and peace. While no one knows the exact shape the future will take, there is a responsibility to engage in serious debate about a possible security order that does not rely on nuclear weapons for enforcement.

During the past 40 years or so, nuclear disarmament has often been called wishful thinking, because the proposals for achieving it generally have ignored the rightful security interests of states. This book represents a departure from this traditional approach. Its aim is to explore how states might be able to move progressively to fewer and perhaps even zero nuclear weapons *without* sacrificing security. The contributors to this volume do not anticipate that this process towards nuclear abolition will be easy or without controversy. They identify problems of universality, verification, compliance and stability.

Still, it is noteworthy that—in light of the fundamental changes that have taken place both in world politics and in the East–West context—the aforementioned problems can be addressed in a meaningful and credible way. The cold war is over and the Soviet Union no longer exists. These changes provide unprecedented opportunities to investigate the possibilities for a different kind of international security, free from nuclear weapons.

There are also political, moral and military imperatives to seek security without nuclear weapons. Nuclear weapons clearly belong to a past concept of security. They are not an adequate means to respond to new realities, threats and challenges.

The conclusions and findings of this study are commended not only to students of politics but also to politicians who must take the bold decisions which will shape the security of tomorrow.

Dr Adam Daniel Rotfeld
Director, SIPRI
August 1992

Abbreviations and acronyms

ABM	Anti-ballistic missile
ACDA	Arms Control and Disarmament Agency
AEC	Atomic Energy Commission
ALCM	Air-launched cruise missile
ANZUS	Australia–New Zealand–United States (alliance)
ASEAN	Association of South-East Asian Nations
C^3I	Command, control, communications and intelligence
CBM	Confidence-building measure
CFE	Conventional Armed Forces in Europe
CSCE	Conference on Security and Co-operation in Europe
CTB(T)	Comprehensive Test Ban (Treaty)
CWC	Chemical Weapons Convention
Enmod	Environmental modification
Euratom	European Atomic Energy Community
GRIT	Graduated Reciprocation in Tension Reduction
IAEA	International Atomic Energy Agency
ICBM	Intercontinental ballistic missile
ICJ	International Court of Justice
INF	Intermediate-range nuclear forces
INFCIRC	IAEA Information Circular
JCS	Joint Chiefs of Staff
MAD	Mutual assured destruction
MIRV	Multiple independently targetable re-entry vehicle
MSC	Military Staff Committee
MTCR	Missile Technology Control Regime
MW	10^6 watts
NATO	North Atlantic Treaty Organization
(N)NWS	(Non-) nuclear weapon state(s)
NPT	Non-Proliferation Treaty
NWFZ	Nuclear weapon-free zone

OPANAL	Agency for the Prohibition of Nuclear Weapons in Latin America
OSI(A)	On-Site Inspection (Agency)
PAL	Permissive action link
PNE(T)	Peaceful Nuclear Explosions (Treaty)
PTB(T)	Partial Test Ban (Treaty)
R&D	Research and development
RERTR	Reduced Enrichment for Research and Test Reactor
RV	Re-entry vehicle
SCC	Standing Consultative Commission
SDI	Strategic Defence Initiative
SLBM	Submarine-launched ballistic missile
SLCM	Sea-launched cruise missile
SNF	Short-range nuclear forces
START	Strategic Arms Reduction Talks
TLI	Treaty limited items
TTB(T)	Threshold Test Ban (Treaty)
UNCITRAL	United Nations Commission on International Trade Law
UNESCO	United Nations Educational, Scientific and Cultural Organization
URENCO	Uranium Enrichment Company
SWU	Separative work unit
WTO	Warsaw Treaty Organization

1. Introduction

Regina Cowen Karp

I. Competing security perceptions: strategy, disarmament and peace research

More than 30 years ago, William T. R. Fox observed that 'rational political action consists in achieving the best possible reconciliation of the desirable and the possible'.[1] Thinking about security without nuclear weapons, the subject of this book, is an attempt to reconcile the desirable objective of nuclear disarmament and the realities of the still anarchic international system.

Strategists and nuclear disarmers have been kept apart by profoundly opposing assessments of the nature of interstate politics and the desirability of nuclear disarmament. One of the objectives of this book is to bridge the intellectual chasm that has persisted for most of the post-war era between these two schools of thought.[2]

Conventional strategic wisdom and nuclear strategies leave little intellectual space for considerations of international security that do not readily accept the fundamental and immutable role of nuclear weapons. Indeed, the strategic community has consistently dismissed nuclear disarmament as a fanciful idea, realistic only if the world were a different place, where conflict between sovereign states no longer existed, where perhaps sovereign states themselves had been superseded by world government. For nuclear strategists, the challenge was not to explore alternative security arrangements but to cope with the challenge of the nuclear revolution itself. They saw nuclear disarmament as advocacy of a better world but one that essentially ignored the power-political foundations of the present. Visions of a future international order were thus regarded as utopian, respectable in their aspirations for a conflict-free environment but unworkable because they did not at all, or insufficiently, address the conflict-prone nature of existing state relations.

Advocates of nuclear disarmament and peace researchers concerned about the dominant role of nuclear weapons in international security freely admit that they have a vision of a world in which nuclear weapons have been abolished. They foresee the creation of co-operative relations between states and regard the existence of nuclear weapons and the persistent threat of nuclear war as an obstacle to achieving this goal. While many strategists would agree that nuclear

---

[1] Fox, W. T. R., 'The uses of international relations theory', ed. Fox, W. T. R., *Theoretical Aspects of International Relations* (University of Notre Dame Press: Notre Dame, Ind., 1959), p. 46.

[2] How states have reacted to the existence of nuclear weapons, is the subject of the first project book. See Cowen Karp, R. (ed.), *Security With Nuclear Weapons? Different Perspectives on National Security* (Oxford University Press, Oxford: 1991).

stockpiles are too high and that the proliferation of weapons of mass destruction poses a serious threat to international security, nuclear disarmers and strategists differ in two important respects. They have a very different appreciation of the relationship between nuclear weapons and international security and of the forces that shape international relations. For strategists, the East–West conflict and the cold war dominate all other security concerns. Threats are assessed in terms of their impact upon East–West relations. Nuclear weapons and a policy of assured destruction stabilize the relationship and are regarded as essential for deterring war between the nuclear-armed protagonists. Nuclear disarmers and peace researchers by and large do not believe that nuclear weapons stabilize East–West relations, nor are they viewed as essential in deterring war. They most certainly do not believe that nuclear weapons should be the all-informing and all-organizing principle of international security.

As strategists dismiss visions of an alternative future without nuclear weapons, peace researchers and nuclear disarmers dismiss the constraints the existing international system might impose on realising their visions. To them, the goal of a nuclear weapon-free world is defined as a global aim of such necessity and urgency that it subordinates all other political concerns. Comparatively little attention is devoted to the processes by which the goal of nuclear disarmament could be attained. In fact, nuclear disarmament is often portrayed as easily achievable. The primary ills of the world are ascribed to the recalcitrance of politicians and not, as the strategists would have it, to the anarchic nature of the international system and the forces of power politics that govern relations between states.

While strategists want to cope with the security dilemma, avoid military imbalances and maintain crisis stability, nuclear disarmers believe that the very acts of doing politics with nuclear weapons carries unacceptable risks of misperception and miscalculation, perhaps bringing about the very situation of war they want to avoid. Nuclear strategy is therefore conceived as a fundamentally dysfunctional exercise that should be abandoned before the world runs out of luck and is plunged into a nuclear holocaust.

Neither school of thought is as monolithic as they often describe each other. Not every one in the strategic community subscribes to a narrow, military understanding of security and by no means do all peace researchers believe that nuclear disarmament is a panacea from which all other solutions for conflict resolution would flow. Both schools have critics in their own ranks. The important point though is that criticism within focuses on excesses rather than principles. Thus the field of strategic studies has produced a vast array of literature critical of the conservatism for which it is often best known, but has failed to offer alternatives to a deterrence-based security strategy. Peace research as an academic discipline has matured, is no longer exclusively concerned with disarmament and recognizes political constraints but not to the extent that nuclear weapons have become acceptable means of policy.[3]

The tragedy is that neither school was able to predict the fundamental political changes that have taken place since the fall of the Berlin Wall in 1989. The strategists had become captives of deterrence thinking, focused on the Soviet Union as the permanently hostile adversary. When the Soviet Union ceased to exist and their intellectual referent collapsed, the field of strategic studies was immediately deprived of of its primary cause and objective. Strategic studies, if it is to survive at all, has to recognize that military balances are not the only barometer attesting to the state of international security and that political change was not the result of military imbalances and power-political manœuvring but a consequence of domestic change in the Soviet Union.

Neither can peace research take the credit for anticipating the radical political changes of the late 1980s and early 1990s. Its advocacy of nuclear disarmament as the means for political change prevented it from recognizing that such change could come about quite irrespective of vast nuclear arsenals. The peace research focus on nuclear weapons rather than on the politics that underpin the thinking about these weapons had put the cart before the horse. Thus both schools had got it wrong.

While these failures to foresee fundamental political change are recognized, the world is still a long way from a comprehensive re-evaluation of the new security situation. However, it is clear that nuclear deterrence as the principal feature of international security cannot survive. In order to understand why it has played such an extraordinarily formative role in international security, it is necessary to reflect upon the way it was conceived and the powerful hold it has exerted over policy.

II. Nuclear weapons and nuclear deterrence

Nuclear deterrence is not merely a security strategy, it is a whole way of thinking about security. The intellectual path chosen by the strategists of the 1950s and early 1960s was to embrace nuclear weapons in their perceptions of international security and in the policy choices they offered. In the process, these strategists were instrumental in creating a specific understanding of nuclear deterrence and its diplomatic and military requirements. This particular understanding of nuclear deterrence comprises a series of interrelated assumptions about the nature of world politics, the characteristics of post-war international relations, the primary sources of threat and the utility of nuclear weapons for organizing international security. In combination, these assumptions reflect a distinct perception of world order and the necessity to shape this order through nuclear deterrence.

[3] For an excellent review of the state of the discipline, see Nobel, J. (ed.), *The Coming of Age of Peace Research: Studies in the Development of a Discipline* (STYX Publications, Groningen: 1991).

Early nuclear strategists did not worry about whether or not to incorporate nuclear weapons into national security planning. That nuclear weapons existed was a fact. The questions strategists posed were not focused on how to make nuclear weapons irrelevant or how to prevent the nuclearization of international security. Instead, the questions concerned how to utilize nuclear weapons to avoid nuclear war and to advance political interests. Certainly, these were fascinating questions. For the first time in human history man had created a weapon capable of destroying civilization. Much had to be learned about how to harness such destructive capability for purposes other than warfare.

The works of Bernard Brodie, Herman Kahn, Albert Wohlstetter and Thomas Schelling set the intellectual parameters and significantly shaped the course of the nuclear debate. What was learned about nuclear deterrence was in large part determined by how this learning process advanced and by who the learners were. Although not confined to the RAND Corporation in California, most thinking about how deterrence might work and the kinds of forces that might be required to successfully deter a nuclear war emerged from RAND. There, a small group of people of diverse professional backgrounds and necessarily all new to the subject of nuclear war avoidance explored the meaning of the nuclear revolution. Their explorations were guided by a particular understanding of world order and their expectations about the role of nuclear weapons within it were shaped by that understanding.[4]

In essence they were all realists. To them, world politics was about states struggling for power, balancing each other through a continuous struggle to improve their relative position *vis-à-vis* one another. The world was thus a dangerous place where military balances mattered and where the successful jostling for military advantage could decide a country's fate. The international situation in the 1950s and early 1960s gave credence to this pessimistic outlook. The cold war was at its peak, the division of Europe appeared to be permanent, and spheres of influence had been established and were jealously guarded. The Soviet Union was regarded as the implacable foe, driven to aggressive expansionism by its communist ideology. The Soviet Union was fast catching up with growing arsenals of nuclear and thermonuclear weapons, and Western Europe was held to be vulnerable to Warsaw Pact conventional attack. For realists, the post-war political situation posed stark choices. The United States was either going to succumb to growing Soviet power or it was not. What strategists were looking for was a security strategy that would counterbalance growing Soviet nuclear capabilities and thwart Soviet political intentions.

Nuclear deterrence fit well into this political environment. A policy that deliberately threatens annihilation of the enemy must surely deter even the most ardent foe. The threat of annihilation seemed to be an appropriate response to the dangers that were likely to come from the Soviet Union. It was a realist

---

[4] See Baylis, J. and Garnett, J. (eds.), *Makers of Nuclear Strategy* (Pinter Publishers: London, 1991), especially the introduction.

response to the power politics of the nuclear age and nuclear weapons became part of a realist perception of international relations.[5]

III. Security without nuclear weapons?

The preoccupation on the part of strategists and policy-makers with nuclear weapons—because they think these weapons are essential—and on the part of peace researchers—because they think they are non-essential but dangerous instead—has led to a perpetual polarization of the international security debate. In comparison, far too little attention has been given to a sober exploration of the feasibility of security without nuclear weapons. Realist assumptions about the anarchic international system and the necessity to mitigate its effects with the weapons of the age have dominated 40 years of scholarly discourse as though peace could only be maintained by accepting a nuclear weapon-based definition of security. The question of whether nuclear disarmament could be desirable and achievable in an anarchic international system has never been seriously addressed. Anarchy meant power politics and made the pursuit of nuclear deterrence imperative; for peace researchers, anarchy was not to be analysed but to be overcome.

The contributors to this book do not constitute a third 'option'. Instead, they build upon both strategy and disarmament. From strategy they accept the anarchic nature of the international system and the need of states for security but question strategy's nuclear deterrence logic. From disarmament they welcome the desirability of no nuclear weapons but do not subscribe to its disregard for political constraints.

Because the processes of professional socialization into pro- and anti-nuclear camps have been so successful, the task of thinking about security without nuclear weapons—let alone exploring how it could be achieved—is far from simple. In seeking an answer to these questions, two intellectual pitfalls loom large.

First, if we proceed as true realists, that is if we assume that states are in a Hobbesian state of nature compelled to counteract a perceived security dilemma with the weapon of the age, our enquiry into the possibility of non-nuclear security would be concluded very quickly. We would find that this kind of security was neither feasible nor desirable since the Hobbesian view provides us with a static account of state relations, explaining past, present and future. In order to avoid the Hobbesian pitfall of international anarchy as the primary determinant of state behaviour, traditional realist understanding of international security has to be broadened, allowing for other explanations of international stability to be included. Nuclear deterrence then becomes only one possible explanation of and prescription for security.

The second pitfall concerns idealist assumptions about how non-nuclear security might be achieved. It would be wrong to assume that a broader con-

---

[5] Vasquez, J. A., *The Power of Power Politics: A Critique* (Frances Pinter: London, 1983).

ception of international security makes it easier to achieve the goal of nuclear abolition. A debunking of realism alone will not lead to a world without nuclear weapons. States have genuine security interests. It is therefore crucial not to confuse alternative explanations of the present with the likelihood and possibility of putting security on a non-nuclear footing in the future. Different interpretations of the present may widen the spectrum of different possible futures but these futures may not be non-nuclear. It is not enough to hope that non-nuclear security might somehow come about. It needs to be pursued deliberately.

None of the authors in this book suggests that ridding the world of nuclear weapons is going to be easy. While rejecting the intellectual strait-jacket of realism, they do not believe that nuclear disarmament is just around the corner. Nor do they believe that there is one single solution to the nuclear predicament. Indeed, by accepting the existence of international anarchy (but not the realists' nuclear prescriptions) the authors also accept that nuclear abolition can only be achieved with and through the consent of states.

If our analysis of non-nuclear security has to begin from where the world is today—that is, in a condition of international anarchy—how can nuclear weapons be abolished? Can states transcend the dogma of nuclear realism and provide security for themselves without relying on nuclear weapons? Can we as scholars think of security in non-nuclear terms and envision the requirements for a totally different kind of security? Furthermore, how will it be possible to get there? Since there is neither a consensus on how to think about non-nuclear security nor an agreed road-map towards it, it is appropriate to begin our exploration with an enquiry into the intellectual task of thinking about nuclear abolition.

Beyond nuclearism

In chapter 2 Ken Booth and Nicholas Wheeler challenge the conventional wisdom that the foremost task of the nuclear age is to make nuclear deterrence work. The assumption that informs this conventional wisdom is that nuclear weapons have become part of the structure of the international system. In other words, nuclear weapons are here to stay, cannot be disinvented and the world must therefore learn to live with them as best it can. The prescription that flows from this assumption is to avoid the 'fictional utopia' of nuclear disarmament. War avoidance through robust deterrence policies holds the answer to the nuclear problem for the majority of strategic thinkers.

It is an indisputable fact that nuclear knowledge and know-how cannot be erased or recaptured. In this sense, Bernard Brodie was right in saying that 'the rigidity lies in the situation not in the thinking'. Booth and Wheeler argue that over time the thinking about security has become as rigid as the situation it aims to describe. The authors suggest that the often casual dismissal of the question of nuclear abolition on the part of 'serious' scholars and policy-makers attests more to persistent intellectual hegemony than to reflective debate. Chapter 2, then, is an attempt to think of international security in non-nuclear terms.

This effort is far from naïve. History provides pertinent examples of dramatic changes in thinking, 'if enough people in the right place and with relevant power want radical change'. If de-colonization had been proposed in the late 19th century, if European union had been envisaged in the 1930s, or if the fall of the Berlin Wall and the subsequent collapse of the Soviet empire had been forecast in early 1989, these transformations almost certainly would have been written off as 'fictional utopias'—wishful thinking at its best. Yet all these processes and events have taken place, each bringing about radical transformation of existing world views. These same developments attest to the fact that seemingly permanent fixtures of the international system can be changed, that mankind is not condemned to perpetuate structural conditions. Booth and Wheeler recognize that critics might argue that nuclear weapons are fundamentally different, in a category of their own, and that a comparison between European unity and nuclear abolition is flawed. The authors reject this criticism on the grounds that the issue is not one of deciding which event is more important but to acknowledge that to treat any possible development in international relations as 'unthinkable' is itself flawed. The 'unthinkable' should not be excluded from serious debate because it appears to be unrealizable today. It cannot be the function of scholarship to resign itself to an endorsement of an intellectual status quo. Instead, scholars should also explore the continued necessity for and legitimacy of nuclear weapons in post-cold war international politics.

Would the abolition of nuclear weapons lead to perfect security? Booth and Wheeler do not see nuclear abolition in the context of a perfect world providing perfect security. Rather, 'the aim is to discuss the feasibility of reducing insecurity at progressively lower levels of nuclear weapons until a level of zero nuclear weapons is achieved'. Total security in the sense that no state feels threatened and that no state is in a position to threaten another cannot exist as long as we envisage a world of states, a world that is recognizable to us.

To Booth and Wheeler, the missing link between realist interpretations of anarchy and utopian prescriptions of nuclear abolition is a reappreciation of international politics and its crucial role in achieving non-nuclear security. The key that links the present to a radically different future lies in a transformation of the politics that relate states to one another. If we want to achieve non-nuclearism, we must focus on processes that will help create a 'non-violent conflict culture'. Booth and Wheeler suggest thinking about nuclear disarmament in terms of 'process utopias'. Seen as 'benign or pacific trends' process utopias are a useful concept with which to address the problems that lie between today's nuclear weapon-armed world and one that bases its security on other principles.

If nuclear disarmament is conceived as a process instead of the quick and radical change advocated by traditional disarmers, the proposition to move towards nuclear abolition becomes far more realistic. The objective of disarmament is maintained while it is recognized that it can only become reality through processes that have their foundation in what is possible. The process-utopian approach has many advantages, among them a time-frame that is not linked to a rigid timetable. The approach is not concerned with devising the details of a nuclear-disarmed world. Indeed, the crucial difference between process utopia on the one hand and traditional realist and disarmament approaches on the other is that a process-orientated approach does not dogmatically prescribe what is impossible or what is possible now but aims to pursue its goal step by step.

What are the chances that this approach can lead to nuclear abolition? To the process-utopian, this is the wrong question to ask. Nuclear weapons are not going to become irrelevant to the powers that have them or to those who want to possess them if the question is perceived to address present political conditions. Political relations between states need to change, a basic willingness to progressively diminish the role of nuclear weapons must exist if nuclear disarmament is to become a reality. Thus the meaning of disarmament feasibility will change over time. What appears to be unfeasible today may be achievable at a future time. The process-utopian approach encourages the development of a more dynamic understanding of what is feasible in world politics. Nuclear abolition can be achieved if prevailing pro-nuclear processes are progressively redirected towards it.

Now that the cold war is over, there is a great opportunity to reassess what it was about. The lessons about the utility of nuclear weapons in keeping the cold war peace may upon reflection no longer appear to be as compelling as they once were. Historical and cultural factors relevant to keeping the peace may appear to be more credible than the narrowness of the nuclear equation. The recognition that general war is becoming obsolete for reasons other than the 'successful' management of the nuclear balance may capture the collective imagination about a future world order more than a continued debate about deterrence requirements. Given the problems in Eastern Europe and in the former Soviet Union, and the dangers of nuclear proliferation in crisis-prone regions, a strategic debate focusing on nuclear weapons rather than on international security problems would appear to be sadly out of touch.

The proposed process utopia offers the prospect of a new kind of strategic debate, one which addresses the disutility of nuclear diplomacy and focuses political effort on creating security regimes and security communities. Booth and Wheeler, however, caution the optimist. States will not be quick to develop a shared sense of security, nor will all states progress towards peaceful relations at an equal pace. The authors argue that the pace is not what matters. What matters is the direction in which international politics in the post-cold war era evolve. The list of obstacles to nuclear abolition is long and we do not know at present how to overcome a great many of them. What is important is the recognition that unless this process is consciously and deliberately embarked upon—step by step—a strategic culture which purports 'that there is no stronger basis for the coexistence between peoples than genocidal fear' will continue to be legitimized.

Towards non-nuclear security: costs, benefits, requisites

In chapter 3, Erwin Häckel examines the economic arguments for and against nuclear disarmament. The basic thrust of his contribution is that economics is 'an exercise in the evaluation of alternative decisions, measured in terms of comparative advantages or disadvantages flowing from the use and allocation of resources'.

Häckel argues that none of the nuclear powers regard economic cost as a decisive argument against the maintenance of a military nuclear capability. Economic considerations sometimes play a role during force modernization debates but cannot overturn the earlier principal decision to become a nuclear power. The economic burden a country bears for its nuclear weapon forces is relatively small and supports the argument that nuclear weapons represent a very cost-effective allocation of resources. The author does, however, add a note of caution. The total cost of nuclear weapons is inevitably more than the core cost for the nuclear warheads themselves. In order to effectively exploit the destructive power of nuclear weapons, a country must maintain a nuclear weapons programme, relying on a variety of delivery systems and associated military infrastructure. Hence only industrially developed countries 'willing and able to support a large military force can afford nuclear weapons'.

Häckel observes that the utility of nuclear weapons in military planning has declined. Nuclear weapons are not uniformly useful irrespective of the military contingency. Military missions previously reserved for nuclear weapons have become progressively de-nuclearized, especially with respect to air-defence and field artillery missions. Technological advances in conventional armaments have resulted in the replacement of nuclear warheads with conventional ones, further limiting the efficiency of nuclear weapons. Furthermore, the lessons from the experience from the wars in Vietnam, over the Falkland/Malvinas Islands and in Afghanistan suggest that nuclear weapons are not useful in determining the course and outcome of conflict, lessons which have gradually increased a perception of nuclear weapon disutility.

A corollary to the decline in utility of nuclear weapons is the maintenance of sizeable conventional forces by nuclear weapon-armed countries. A country with military ambitions, Häckel argues, does not rely on its nuclear forces alone but also must maintain 'the large expenditure associated with conventional armaments'. The record shows that nuclear weapons cannot be a substitute for conventional arms.

Häckel suggests that these factors work against the proliferation of nuclear weapons to countries that do not have the financial resources and industrial infrastructure required to sustain a mix of nuclear and conventional forces. Hence nuclear weapons are unattractive to all but a few developing countries. It is, however, these countries to which nuclear weapons might present 'an optimal choice towards the synergistic utilization of available resources for national security purposes'.

Häckel is especially concerned about threshold or near-threshold countries that already command large military establishments and possess an indigenous defence industry, a flourishing civil nuclear programme and sophisticated military equipment which may be used for nuclear delivery. For such countries, the additional economic burden that comes with a nuclear capability might not be difficult to shoulder.

Häckel's analyses of the cost and benefits of having nuclear weapons and the prospects for nuclear proliferation lead him to argue that nuclear disarmament cannot be about the abolition of nuclear weapons alone but must encompass the abolition of the many facilities and capabilities related to the operation of nuclear weapons. The author does not, however, see nuclear disarmament as imminent and rejects the idea of a grand treaty. He believes it to be more realistic to envisage a process of nuclear abolition which in the first instance should aim to include measures to decrease nuclear military missions and areas of nuclear deployment.

The challenge to Häckel is to focus on measures that decrease the perceived security relevance of nuclear weapons. Accordingly, security dependence on nuclear weapons should steadily be reduced until the benefits believed to derive from nuclear possession have become marginal. This marginality may not lead to zero nuclear weapons. The author argues that new understanding about what makes for war and peace has to develop to make nuclear abolition reality. Thus countries need to be able to perceive a range of security choices. If the only choice for international stability is acceptance of 'power, unequal status and a modicum of intimidation, . . . the persistence of nuclear weapons is the price to pay'.

Legal issues concerning the feasibility of nuclear weapon elimination

Julie Dahlitz explores the role international law could play in helping states to rid themselves of nuclear weapons in chapter 4. The primary role of international law, the author argues, is to provide the legal framework within which nuclear abolition might be achieved and the legal method that guides the process. In this sense, international law is first and foremost seen as buttressing political will. Dahlitz however also suggests a more creative role for international law developing out of legal reforms that make it more attractive for states to employ the law for arms control and disarmament.

Dahlitz is especially concerned about the poor state of existing international law in the security area. When embarking on a process leading to non-nuclear security, states, cautious to safeguard national security during the transition period, will need to be confident that norms they adhere to and rules they follow are effective, that disputes about commitments can and will be settled peacefully and that treaties ratified are unambiguous. In this sense, the law governing a process of nuclear elimination should not be a matter of casual and unpredictable status, but clear in its wording, intent and implementation. Since international law is 'a socially created tool for achieving desired purposes' acquiring authority from those who make it and those who accept it, it is clear that its evolution can only be advanced by states themselves. How then should international law develop in the security field?

Dahlitz suggests that it should evolve to stimulate and accommodate the changes in international relations necessary for nuclear abolition. The evolution of the law then becomes part of a general transformation of the international system towards the acceptance of a non-nuclear security order. Dahlitz foresees not only the conclusion of new treaties but also a reformulation of 'the theoretical structure of the law so as to conform with its contemporary function'. During the post-war era international law as it relates to security matters developed in a politically hostile environment. Thus a deliberate effort needs to be made on the part of states to create laws, through custom and treaties, that more closely reflect co-operative endeavours.

The author argues that, despite its present shortcomings, the law as it exists offers much to build upon, especially during the early phases of a disarmament process. Existing bilateral and multilateral arms control treaties may serve as prototypes of more comprehensive ones in the future. International and regional organizations could expand their co-operative efforts and especially the United Nations could take a more active role in the security area.

Perhaps more difficult, according to the author, is the theoretical development of international law where she observes 'a profound resistance to reappraising the basic tenets of the theory of international law, for fear that to do so might undermine the existing fragile consensus which is so valuable, despite its questionable foundations'. Without appropriate legal theory, states will remain reluctant to enter agreements curbing their sovereignty over national security. The law must assure states of the methods by which it will be interpreted and implemented. If it fails to do this, confidence in the law is eroded.

In a process of nuclear reductions and eventual zero nuclear weapons, international law can provide structure, transparency, predictability and universality. But, Dahlitz asserts, the legal mechanisms must themselves become transparent and predictable. In other words, legal tools and methods will have to evolve in order to match the task at hand.

Thinking about no nuclear forces: technical and strategic constraints on transitions and end-points

Chapter 5 by Paul White, Robert Pendley and Patrick Garrity considers how technological developments might encourage or impede processes of denuclearization. The authors argue that the emergence of nuclear weapon technologies and their integration into politics conformed to an existing pattern of relationships between politics and technology. Hence 'international power and status continued to flow from such factors as a nation's relative conventional military capabilities, economic production capacities and creative potential, and not just nuclear weapons'. This observation notwithstanding, the authors argue that the fear of nuclear war and the deterrence theories that developed gave this new military technology a very special place in international security. What are the technical issues involved in weaning international security from nuclear weapons?

The authors envisage a process of denuclearization in which the interaction between technology and politics might provide a permissive/non-permissive environment for nuclear abolition. In the first instance, they foresee the successful implementation of the 1991 START (Strategic Arms Reduction Talks) Treaty, providing the foundation for cuts to moderate numbers of some 3000 nuclear weapons. At this level, force cuts would begin to have a major impact on flexibility and target coverage. The nuclear forces of the United States and Russia would have declined to levels that make the inclusion in arms control talks of the secondary nuclear powers imperative. Proliferation of nuclear technology would begin to appear as a security threat of the first order and states could no longer remain sanguine about the proliferation of advanced conventional technologies. The deployment of limited anti-ballistic missile defences may gain credibility, especially against a small nuclear attack. The safety of remaining nuclear systems must be assured.

Going from moderate to small numbers of around 1000 nuclear weapons would, the authors suggest, require a substantial redefinition of the concept of deterrence. The lines between what makes for a great power and between nuclear and advanced conventional weapons would begin to blur. The power constellation between five states having equal numbers of nuclear weapons would most likely change, providing room for new and perhaps shifting alignments. Deployment of defences against nuclear attack could become critical in determining military stability.

Moving to very small nuclear arsenals would require a far-reaching transformation of the international system. States would have to be confident that their security is safeguarded, that the possibility of cheating on agreements is marginal and that verification procedures are functioning efficiently. States would also want to see effective control over conventional armaments in place in order to forestall conventional break-out options. The authors argue that with nuclear reductions, a rethinking of conventional strategies, away from offensive deployments, would be necessary.

As the world approaches a condition of zero nuclear weapons, agreement will have to be found on what precisely 'zero' means. In addition to warhead destruction, should it include all materials and facilities related to nuclear activities? The then existent security system must be able to cope with the threat of hidden nuclear weapons and a clandestine capability to reintroduce nuclear weapons.

Overall, the authors feel that the technical challenge of nuclear elimination is formidable and that emerging technologies, especially those of dual-use, are likely to impose constraints upon states' willingness to pursue nuclear abolition. Technologies such as those continuously emerging through the communications revolution do provide transparency and may act as incentives to reduce nuclear weapons to low levels. The final step towards zero, however, must remain a political decision.

Verification of nuclear weapon elimination

Chapter 6 by Patricia Lewis notes the enormous progress made in recent years in verifying compliance with arms control treaties. On-site inspections and challenge inspections have become almost routine. At the same time, improvements in the political sphere have reintroduced the concept of 'reasonable sufficiency' to countries' approaches to verification. The greater extent to which verification can now be implemented has, however, also highlighted the substantial cost involved.

The verification regimes that are in place with the INF and START treaties are useful and can be built upon with respect to broadening their scope. Lewis makes the crucial point that for verification purposes, it is far easier to verify the absence of missiles than agreed limits. If a certain class of missiles is no longer permitted to exist, all related facilities will also have to be disbanded, making it well nigh impossible to reproduce a missile of that class clandestinely. Thus verifying the INF Treaty was easier than verification of the START Treaty.

Very small numbers of nuclear weapons raise verification demands dramatically. All remaining nuclear weapons would have to be declared and secondary and threshold nuclear powers would have to be involved. Production, storage and deployment facilities would have to be monitored very stringently using national technical means, on-site inspections and perimeter portal monitoring.

Going to zero nuclear weapons quickly rather than maintaining small arsenals for an indefinite period is easier to verify and less costly. Lewis argues that the technicalities of a global verification system monitoring the whereabouts of a few nuclear weapons would be so costly and perhaps not sufficiently efficient that greater confidence in a verification regime could be achieved at zero than at any level close to it.

If states should seriously consider moving towards nuclear abolition, investment in verification should be made now. Verification can act as a confidence-building measure, lead to greater openness and its successes built upon more ambitious arms reduction efforts. The sooner this is achieved, Lewis argues, the fewer the chances of hidden activities being discovered at a later stage when a few nuclear weapons could make the difference between nuclear and non-nuclear security.

Nuclear weapon elimination: fissile material and warheads

The technical processes necessary to achieve a cut-off of fissile material production, the dismantlement of nuclear warheads and the accounting of fissile material already produced are the subject of chapter 7 by Frank von Hippel.

A cut-off of fissile material production would involve a halting of plutonium and weapon-grade uranium production and a destruction of all production facilities. While the existing International Atomic Energy Agency (IAEA) safeguards should be extended to cover nuclear reactors, their fuel cycles and any separated plutonium in all countries, the possibility of plutonium diversion cannot be ruled out. Small diversions could be hidden in measurement errors and von Hippel explains that, over time, there may be enough plutonium accumulated to make several nuclear warheads.

As regards weapon-grade uranium, verifying a production cut-off is some-what simpler since most uranium produced is of low-level enrichment. More problematic is enrichment through nozzle, centrifuge and laser technologies. Such facilities would have to be identified and their activities halted.

Von Hippel foresees no technical difficulties associated with warhead dismantlement and suggests the dilution of highly-enriched uranium recovered from warheads with natural or depleted uranium. Plutonium could be burned off under safeguards or disposed of with other radioactive waste.

A major problem for verifiable nuclear abolition stems from uncertainty regarding the amount of fissile material that has already been produced. According to von Hippel, we do not know and cannot ascertain with certainty how much fissile material has been produced over the past decades, thus we cannot *prove* the existence of a nuclear weapon-free world. He suggests, however, that this proof might not be necessary if co-operative security arrangements have replaced nuclear weapons in international security.

The end of superpower nuclear arms control?

Chapter 8 by Lynn Eden explores the conditions that might make the elimination of nuclear weapons feasible in the United States and the Soviet Union/Russia. The author identifies the primary actors in the arms control processes in both countries and analyses their roles in shaping the purposes and policies of nuclear arms control.

In the case of the United States, Eden argues, arms control proposals must have the support of the President, Congress and the military. In recent years, primarily as a result of budget pressures and a reduced Soviet threat, traditionally existing coalitions of interests in favour of arms control and force modernization have been breaking apart. No longer does congressional and military support for arms control policy appear to be linked to concurrent approval of new nuclear weapons. Domestic economic constraints and the perception of a more benign international environment are eroding the traditional premises for arms control. Eden suggests that under these conditions, large nuclear cuts are possible.

In her very thoughtful analysis of the arms control process in the Soviet Union (the chapter was written prior to the country's breakup), Eden argues that the military played a significant role in shaping arms control policy, a role enhanced by their virtual monopoly on military expertise. As in the USA, arms control processes did not impede force modernization programmes. A break with traditional approaches came with Mikhail Gorbachev, whose across-the-board arms control initiatives, coupled with a shift in domestic political coalitions, reduced the power of the military significantly. Future arms control possibilities will greatly depend on how the transition period to a post-Soviet order in the region is managed. If, however, economic reforms and democratization continue, a readiness to enter negotiations for deep nuclear reductions is likely to emerge.

Although Eden does not see nuclear abolition on the agenda, she does not discount its feasibility. First and foremost, nuclear abolition would require skilful political leadership at the highest level. The interplay between a continuously benign international environment and domestic bargaining processes would have to be such that a domestic consensus could be mustered in support of nuclear disarmament. The recently achieved break with traditional domestic coalition building suggests that much more radical nuclear reductions can be achieved without leading to force modernization.

Nuclear proliferation and the elimination of nuclear weapons

George Quester explores two questions in chapter 9. First, he asks what the experience in halting nuclear proliferation can tell us about a nuclear weapon-free world. Second, he asks what might be the proliferation problems in such a world.

The author notes that proliferation has not occurred on as grand a scale as realist assumptions about the international system had postulated. Nevertheless, achieving deproliferation and eventual elimination of nuclear weapons may well depend on the lessons nations have learned from the experience with these weapons. If nuclear weapons are seen to have been useful for whatever reasons, incentives to proliferate will persist and nuclear elimination will be that much more difficult to achieve.

However, a majority of countries are party to the 1968 Non-Proliferation Treaty (NPT) demonstrating clearly that they do not regard nuclear weapons as useful. But Quester suggests that a drastic reduction in the arsenals of the nuclear stockpiles that now exist is necessary to enhance non-proliferation efforts and strengthen the NPT regime by inducing threshold countries to relinquish their nuclear capabilities. The counter argument to a process of nuclear reduction and elimination by emulation rests with the realist assertion that power, where it is seen to recede, will be replaced. Quester argues that, in light of the many dramatic political changes we have witnessed recently, we simply cannot know how relevant traditional assumptions about state behaviour will turn out to be. The post-cold war world is not the world of the 1920s and 1930s. The rise of liberal democracy makes a general demilitarization of security possible.

Turning to proliferation threats in a nuclear disarmed world, Quester sees one of the foremost threats emerging from the then still existing knowledge of how to make nuclear bombs. This problem is compounded by the difficulty of reliably accounting for fissile material. In such a situation should the international climate worsen, suspicion as to who has what capabilities might arise quickly. Quester suggests that in order to avoid such an outcome, greater stability might be achieved with small submarine-based deterrent forces since 'the fears of cheating and the temptation to cheat can translate all too quickly into fears and temptations of surprise attack or preventive war'.

The role of hegemonies and alliances

In an anarchic international system, hegemonies and alliances have served to counter the security dilemma. In chapter 10, Harald Müller asks how nuclear elimination would impact upon the traditional function of hegemonies and alliances.

Hegemonies provide security for its members against each other, alliances provide security from external threats. Both hegemonies and alliances are voluntary arrangements in which members either benefit from the superior resources of the hegemon or, as with alliances, achieve security benefits through pooling their defence resources. Nuclear weapons, Müller argues, do not play a dominant role in hegemonies. The hegemon's resources are already vastly superior and a successful hegemony in which the hegemon provides security freely does not rely on nuclear compellence. If the hegemon were to use instruments of compellence, nuclear or otherwise, the voluntary nature of the hegemonic order would be jeopardized, threatening the entire security arrangement. Where nuclear weapons exist within a hegemonic region, they primarily have an intra-hegemonic order or stratification function but not a security role. Under non-nuclear conditions, a hegemony could continue to flourish were it not, as Müller argues, for other structural weaknesses which tend to push hegemony towards empire. *cf Gilpin*

In alliances, nuclear weapons play a far more central role. They are believed to counter an external threat and they are often the principal balancing tool employed by an alliance. If alliances were to abandon their reliance on nuclear weapons as the ultimate guarantor of security, the condition of the international environment will be crucial in determining the future of alliance relationships. Müller argues that in a high-threat environment, 'non-nuclear alliances . . . are improbable as stable security arrangements. They are more likely to be transitional stages, tending towards nuclearization'. Although a low-threat environment suggests a more promising future for a non-nuclear alliance, the possibility of reversal from low to high threat is ever present and might make it prudent for an alliance to maintain at least some nuclear capability. Thus non-nuclear security can only be maintained in a non-reversible, low threat environment.

Müller suggests that to achieve this benign environment, security *regimes* must be created which address 'grievances, sources of misperception and the military postures of states in the most comprehensive way possible'. Regimes in the security field should aim to increase transparency and predictability based on agreed principles, norms and rules. There should be a series of interlocking regimes which together make a reversal of non-nuclearity unnecessary. In order to function effectively, security regimes must be comprehensive, unambiguous and global. Müller argues that regime-building should begin with what is possible. Regimes aimed at achieving non-nuclear security would thus build upon the shared interests of states with their effect on security perceptions cumulative over time. Müller foresees a long time-frame for successively proceeding to non-nuclear security especially since regimes have to grow organically within every region and must be established issue-by-issue. In the long run, non-nuclear enclaves will have little chance to survive in a hostile environment, hence 'non-nuclearism . . . must encompass the globe, or it will have no future at all'.

Minimum deterrence and nuclear abolition

In chapter 11, Nicholas Wheeler explores the concept of minimum deterrence and the role it may have in providing security at relatively low nuclear force levels. Wheeler observes that there is no consensus on what constitutes minimum deterrent forces and the political and military function they should have. Most commonly though, minimum deterrence is seen as a return to MAD, relinquishing counterforce strategies and the multiple warhead missiles that support them.

Critics of minimum nuclear deterrence muster three objections. First, at very low numbers, a state might be tempted to cheat, gaining unilateral advantage at the expense of the common enterprise. Second, either side's assured destruction capability may become vulnerable to technological innovation. Third, small nuclear forces would mean inflexible forces, robbing policy-makers of all but countercity targeting options. Wheeler rebuts these objections.

He suggests that confidence building measures in the nuclear field coupled with measures that increase military transparency can go a long way to reassure the superpowers that no militarily significant cheating is taking place. In order for these measures to be credible, Wheeler argues that they must be preceded by an acceptance of common security instead of strategic superiority. With common security as the principal pillar of the post-START strategic relationship, technological innovation for unilateral advantage must be constrained. As first steps, Wheeler suggests a comprehensive test ban treaty (CTBT), curbs or bans on flight testing and a strengthening of the 1972 Anti-Ballistic Missile (ABM) Treaty. The problem of military inflexibility with small nuclear forces, Wheeler asserts, may not be a problem at all since 'no one knows what is necessary for effective deterrence'. In any case, the pressures which in the past have led to counterforce options, such as extended deterrence requirements and Warsaw Pact conventional superiority, are waning or already absent.

Although Wheeler regards moves towards minimum deterrence as an essential step in reducing the vast nuclear arsenals of the superpowers, he worries that the processes of reaching a consensus might legitimize nuclear forces at lower levels and endorse the concept of deterrence indefinitely. Moreover, as long as nuclear weapons are seen as useful by states who have them, levels at which they are being kept do not address the fundamental problem of nuclear proliferation. Even at a minimum deterrence level, nuclear forces would remain an expression of the self-help nature of the international system and a legitimate instrument to counter the security dilemma. Wheeler questions the merit of minimum nuclear deterrence as a developmental end-point, foreseeing the virtual impossibility of replicating minimum deterrence postures among adversaries in the developing world.

Nuclear weapons cannot be accepted as a remedy for security problems in the developing world and Wheeler suggests the development of regional security policies as the only alternative to proliferation. Such policies should aim to foster security co-operation between states and encourage democratic processes within. As a long-term goal, the establishment of security communities modelled on the West European experience should be pursued. Minimum deterrence then is no alternative to the nuclear predicament. The threat of nuclear proliferation makes these weapons a global phenomenon. Concepts of smaller nuclear forces send important signals but do not give answers.

IV. Is non-nuclear security feasible?

Throughout the nuclear era strategic policy has been based on two related beliefs. First, that the invention of nuclear weapons in an anarchic international system compels states to acquire these weapons. Second, that nuclear disarmament under conditions of international anarchy is impossible and, should it ever become possible, would be dangerously destabilizing. Strategic logic thus postulates that security in the nuclear age can only be found through the ultimate threat of mutual annihilation. In a nutshell, anarchy makes nuclear weapons (once invented) necessary and anarchy justifies their continued existence. This is tantamount to saying that as far as international security is concerned we have truly reached the end of history and security will have to remain nuclear-based. It is also tantamount to abdicating from critical reasoning. This book poses three intellectual challenges.

The first challenge to the nuclear belief system lies in a recognition that mankind has an obligation to exercise choice in the way it shapes its future. Realists tell us that there is no choice and if there was, we should not exercise it because we do not have all the answers to nuclear disarmament ready now. Thus the 'right' choice is not to choose. The question that must be asked is why we should abide by this prescription when we would not take it seriously regarding any other human activity.

This assumption clearly is mistaken. Civilization does not advance because of perfect knowledge, but through processes of learning. It is this learning process that has given us our values and norms and their refinement holds our future. Of course, not everything that happens is learned, nor does it need to. Learning is not about accumulating information but about choice within the context of an existing civilization framework. Our capacity for choice does not depend on our ability to pin down the last consequential detail. Indeed, if perfect knowledge for any human enterprise could be obtained, we could conceive of a grand plan in which everything had its assigned place. Should the fact that we cannot have such a plan reconcile us to the possible fate of nuclear annihilation? On what grounds should we accept this fate?

Realists speak of nuclear management techniques that will make deterrence safe and provide security. They paint a spectre of instability for all attempts to do otherwise. Yet the basis of their pro-nuclear argument is thin. It rests entirely on the assumption that nuclear management can be made to work indefinitely. This requires no greater leap of the imagination than nuclear disarmament. The lack of perfect knowledge for which they fault those exploring alternative security futures is not recognized as the decisive flaw in their own argument.

The future of nuclear weapons then comes down to choosing between different kinds of risk, those of nuclear perpetuation and those of nuclear abolition.

The second challenge posed in this book regards the process of disarmament itself. Much of the persuasiveness of realist thinking stems from the assumption that those who wish to get rid of nuclear weapons want to do so quickly and without due regard for the complexity of the existing security situation. This is certainly true for most disarmament activists. The present volume, however, shows that it is possible to discuss the question of nuclear disarmament, not in ignorance of security concerns but shaped by these very concerns.

It has to be recognized that international security *can* be differently conceived. What makes this reconceptualization possible is the book's focus on nuclear disarmament *processes*. These processes must of necessity build upon where we are today, because that is where we are; and, these processes must build on the consent of states, because it is *security* we are trying to maintain. This approach to non-nuclear security makes for a gradual progression towards this goal. Speed is not our concern, security is.

Nuclear disarmament perceived as a security-building process is fundamentally different from disarmament advocates' or realist views of the future of the international system. The security problems discussed in this book do not suggest an easy road to non-nuclear security. Nor will progress towards this goal proceed at an equal pace everywhere. Each step will pose new questions about how to proceed. Trying to forecast all the answers is impossible.

The third challenge that emerges in these pages is the paucity of existing security thinking based on deterrence. The end of the cold war, the unification of Germany and the demise of the Soviet Union have turned this thinking upside down. Without the cold war and the Soviet state, deterrence as the organizing framework for security has collapsed and with it the cold war bilateralism. Those who want to maintain deterrence fail to understand the significance of these changes and the irrelevance of deterrence for anything else but traditional East–West security concerns.

Deterrence legitimizes the continued existence of nuclear weapons without providing the tools to address new security problems. Negotiations towards ever smaller nuclear arsenals should be encouraged but numbers of nuclear weapons are not as important as the principle of deterrence that is being perpetuated. As long as we accept deterrence we implicitly endorse nuclear proliferation.

If instead we accept that we have a choice about the future shape of international security, understanding the necessity for gradualism and recognizing the need for a different approach in light of the vast political transformations taking place, we can begin to debate the intellectual agenda in this volume.

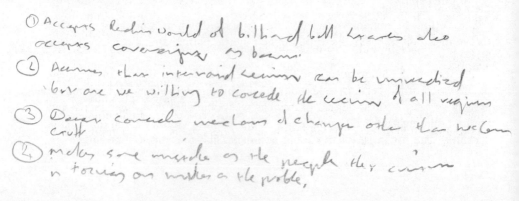

2. Beyond nuclearism

Ken Booth and Nicholas J. Wheeler

I. Introduction

Thirty years ago Herman Kahn invited strategists to think the unthinkable—to speculate in a systematic way about the use of weapons of mass destruction in war. It did not prove to be an insurmountable challenge. Nuclear war fighters eventually proliferated. Kahn had got it wrong. The most demanding intellectual challenge for strategists—the real 'unthinkable'—was (and remains) the contemplation of a world without nuclear weapons. The very idea confronts almost all mainstream theories and assumptions about state and human behaviour.

II. Fictional utopias

The problem of reaching and implementing a global elimination of nuclear weapons has received rather limited investigation, even from those individuals and groups committed to anti-nuclear politics. Some have thought nuclear weapons such an abomination that getting rid of them is enough in itself and that whatever follows cannot be worse. Other advocates of nuclear disarmament have focused their efforts on what might be achieved in their own country or region, while postponing their concern about distant global prospects. A systematic investigation of a world without nuclear weapons could not be expected from pro-nuclear opinion, since the latter grouping has believed that global elimination is neither desirable nor practical.

The genuine intellectual challenge facing analysts is to imagine a 'real' world in which states will come to agree to abolish all nuclear weapons. It is of course possible, without much difficulty, to conceive global abolition of nuclear weapons in a perfect world, one in which everybody is good or which has institutions so foolproof that all potential transgressors will be deterred or controlled at an acceptable cost. Although such a world could be imagined, it would not be helpful—it would not represent the real world in which everybody is not good and no human institution is free of the risk of being undermined by antisocial behaviour. Schemes based on unrealistic expectations can sometimes be interesting but they are always premature. They are likely to provoke the sort of comment Henry IV is supposed to have made about an ambitious scheme for reorganizing the world community: 'It is perfect', the King said, 'perfect. I see no single flaw in it save one, namely that no earthly prince would ever agree to it'.[1]

In what is still a recognizable world of international relations, earthly princes and students of earthly princes have been almost unanimous in dismissing as unrealistic the goal of global nuclear disarmament. There have been ritualistic calls for total abolition from the leaders of states which do not possess such weapons themselves, while superpower leaders, for propaganda reasons, have occasionally associated themselves with the idea of general and comprehensive disarmament. But for the most part world leaders have not believed that total nuclear disarmament is a serious strategic prospect. There have been two notable exceptions in recent years. The first was the call in January 1986 by President Mikhail Gorbachev, whose disarmament credentials are much better than most, for the elimination of nuclear weapons by the year 2000. The second was President Ronald Reagan's rush of disarmament blood at Reykjavik in October 1986. However, these are the exceptions that prove the rule. Reagan's advisers quickly corralled the wayward President, while Gorbachev had come by 1989 to recommend a strategy based on minimum deterrence. It quickly became superpower nuclear business as usual, only somewhat less so in view of the strategic arms reduction treaty (START) negotiations. The present policy-makers of the nuclear powers have in practice accepted that nuclear weapons will be maintained as long as there are sovereign states.

The standard opinion of earthly princes was clearly expressed by former President Richard Nixon, when he offered the US foreign policy establishment his verdict on Reagan's performance in Iceland: 'At the Reykjavik summit, the Reagan Administration undermined public support for nuclear deterrence by advocating the idea of eliminating all nuclear weapons. We must renounce the Reykjavik rhetoric in unequivocal terms and explain to Western publics the realities of the nuclear age'.[2] Such is the policy-maker's view in a nutshell: talk of eliminating all nuclear weapons must be regarded as 'rhetoric', since the perceived 'realities' are that nuclear weapons deter both nuclear and conventional war, and cannot be disinvented. A slight variant of this theme was offered by James Schlesinger, a former Director of the US Central Intelligence Agency (CIA), Secretary of Defense and Secretary for Energy. Commenting on the Reykjavik summit meeting under the heading 'The dangers of a nuclear-free world', Schlesinger argued that given the 'imprint of nuclear capabilities on our minds, to seek total nuclear disarmament is to seek a goal as risky as it is impractical'.[3] However, he did add one qualifier: 'Nuclear arsenals are going to be with us as long as there are sovereign states with *conflicting* ideologies'.[4] A world of liberal democracies, he presumably meant, would be a recipe for the safe elimination of all nuclear weapons. More recently Federal Chancellor

[1] Quoted in Garnett, J., 'Disarmament and arms control since 1945', ed. L. Martin, *Strategic Thought in the Nuclear Age* (Johns Hopkins University Press: Baltimore, Md., 1979), p. 216.
[2] Nixon, R., 'American foreign policy: the Bush agenda', *Foreign Affairs*, vol. 68, no. 1 (1988/89), pp. 208–209.
[3] Schlesinger, J., 'The dangers of a nuclear-free world', *Time*, 27 Oct. 1986, p. 15.
[4] Schlesinger (note 3), p. 15 [emphasis added].

Helmut Kohl has described the call for a nuclear weapon-free world as a 'utopian demand', and those who propose it as 'the great simplists'.[5] A British policy-maker involved in nuclear decisions has said: 'I'm arguing that we've got to try and make stable deterrence work for the rest of history'.[6] This latter statement is a perfect expression of what might be called 'structural nuclearism': the case for nuclear weapons is seen to lie not in the need to counter particular threats, but in the strategic logic of the international system.[7]

Turning from earthly princes to the students of earthly princes, we see among the mainstream writers about international politics and arms control the same negative attitude to the desirability and practicality of global nuclear disarmament. This viewpoint was expressed with great clarity by the prestigious Harvard Nuclear Study Group in the early 1980s. Its authors wrote:

We are left, therefore, with our imperfect selves, imperfect nations, and imperfect relations among them. And it is upon this imperfect structure that the capability of waging infinitely destructive nuclear war has descended. Humanity has no alternative but to hold this threat at bay and to learn to live with politics, to live in the world we know: a world of nuclear weapons, international rivalries, recurring conflicts, and at least some risk of nuclear crisis. *The challenge we face is not to escape to a fictional utopia where such problems do not exist.* It is to learn how to live with nuclear weapons in ways that are successfully safer and in which the freedoms won by men and women are kept secure and can grow.[8]

Later in the book, the Harvard Group labelled as 'atomic escapism' the idea that nuclear weapons will one day disappear. 'They will not', the Group emphasized; consequently, 'mankind must learn to live with them if we are to live at all'.[9] Clearly, the Group believed that mankind would be able to live successfully with nuclear weapons, indefinitely, if the Harvard prescriptions were followed.

The views of the Harvard Nuclear Study Group undoubtedly represent the voice of the overwhelming majority of those in the academic field who have addressed the question of nuclear weapons. This academic 'hegemony' has been evident since Bernard Brodie, within months of the dropping of the first atomic bombs, declared that the world had entered the age of deterrence.[10] The reasons for the development of this mind-set were partly the result of the professional socialization of academics into the 'strategic studies community', and

[5] Quoted in Kent, B., 'Moulding a Pax Europa', *The Times*, 14 June 1990, p. 14.
[6] Quoted in Miall, H., 'New visions, new voices, old power structures', ed. K. Booth, *New Thinking about Strategy and International Security* (HarperCollins: London, 1991), chapter 12.
[7] This is an extension of Lifton and Falk's definition of 'nuclearism': 'By nuclearism we mean psychological, political, and military dependence on nuclear weapons, the embrace of weapons as a solution to a wide variety of human dilemmas, most ironically that of "security"'; see Lifton, R. J. and Falk, R., *Indefensible Weapons: The Political and Psychological Case Against Nuclearism* (Basic Books: New York, 1982).
[8] Carnesale, A. *et al.* (the Harvard Nuclear Study Group), *Living with Nuclear Weapons* (Harvard University Press: Cambridge, Mass., 1983), p. 19 [emphasis added].
[9] Carnesale, A. *et al.* (note 8), p. 253.
[10] This is the theme of Brodie's contribution in Brodie, B. *et al.*, *The Absolute Weapon: Atomic Power and World Order* (Harcourt, Brace and Co.: New York, 1946).

partly because the thinking about nuclear deterrence and its associated view of the world was congenial to policy-makers, especially those in the United States. This view prevailed because the dominant group saw no alternative. Nuclear weapons had been irrevocably invented, and they created their own reality. As Brodie himself said, 'the rigidity lies in the situation, not in the thinking'.[11]

The expert opinions cited above underline the difficulty of the task of those who wish to wean international politics from a dependency on nuclear weapons. But such negative views are not confined to experts; they are shared by the majority of people in the nuclear weapon states. On the whole, public opinion in these countries has been satisfied with their national 'nukes', although not necessarily in the number or the type of weapons possessed. If this is really the case, why should time be spent discussing a 'fictional utopia' when so many urgent issues clamour for attention?

III. Confronting the unthinkable

Much of the talk about global nuclear disarmament is unhelpful. Some anti-nuclear opinion is obviously wishful thinking, while insincerity is the norm in the pro-disarmament propaganda of cynical governments. But because an idea has mostly attracted wishful thinking and propaganda, it does not follow that it is beyond the bounds of serious and practical thought. There was a time when talk about the breaching of the Berlin Wall could be categorized as merely wishful thinking or propaganda. Yet the unthinkable occurred, literally overnight. Such transformations can occur if enough people, in the right place, change their minds.

To what extent, therefore, should the criticism that global nuclear elimination is a 'fictional utopia' be accepted. Put another way, just how utterly removed from the real world is such an idea? Furthermore, even if an idea can be characterized as 'utopian' (i.e., outside what is today thought to be politically possible), might there be a case for thinking and acting as if it were not? This chapter argues that the answers to these questions are more complicated than the policy-makers referred to above imply.

First, it is desirable on several grounds to confront the assertion that the contemplation of a world without nuclear weapons is no more than wishful thinking or propaganda, or speculation about a fictional utopia. The latter in particular implies that the subject should be beneath the concern of anybody who would want to be considered a serious scholar. This is equivalent to throwing down an academic gauntlet. It is a form of intellectual blackmail whose purpose is to delegitimize strategic thinking outside the mainstream framework. By using a label like 'fictional utopia' the Harvard Nuclear Study Group are, in effect, warning those who would take seriously the idea of global nuclear elimination that they had better desist, or otherwise they will be dismissed as naïve. It is intellectual 'ghettoizing' by negative labelling. This

---

[11] Quoted in Kaplan, F., *The Wizards of Armageddon* (Simon & Schuster: New York, 1983), p. 342.

chapter challenges such academic hegemony, even while admitting that global nuclear elimination is not feasible over the near- or even medium-term.

History shows that it is not naïve to confront ideas mainstream opinion considers unthinkable, because fictional utopias do in fact sometime materialize. The idea of European political unity in the 1930s would surely have been dismissed as propaganda, wishful thinking and a fictional utopia by the realists of the day. They would have argued that the history of Europe had been one of national rivalries and war, and that periods of co-operation had been temporary. So it had been and so it would be. A half of a century later, however, the achievement of European political unity may be within the realm of practical politics.

Similarly, the idea of eradicating colonies in the 1890s might also have been described in similar words: propaganda, wishful thinking and fictional utopia. Realists would have argued that the history of the world had been one of imperialism and war; that great powers possess colonies; that weakness attracts power; and that colonies produce wealth and prestige. In short, colonies were seen as functional and legitimate. So it had been, and so it would be. Within 50 years of such thinking, decolonization had come within the realm of practical politics; and within 70 years almost all colonies had achieved independence. An established feature of relations between states was no longer functional and had been delegitimized; along with it, the notion of 'great power' had been readjusted. Clearly, what is politically possible within the arena of international politics can expand: if enough people in the right place and with relevant power want radical change, it can occur. Ideas have their time. Yesterday's fictional utopia can become today's fact of political life.

An immediate question remains: does the contemplation in the 1990s of the global elimination of nuclear weapons belong to the same category of fictional utopias as the idea of European political unity in the 1930s or decolonization in the 1890s? Or is there a category difference? Does nuclear abolition impact *more essentially* on the very nature of statehood, independence, great powerness or on the character of the game of nations? Some comparisons are close. Like the prospects of European unity and decolonization, the abolition of nuclear weapons impacts directly on ideas and feelings about sovereignty, national autonomy, prestige and security. But what may be considered a category difference is the fact that nuclear abolition involves the decision by governments to rid themselves of their most destructive weapons. This has never before been tried by states. But is this singularity sufficient in itself to justify the termination of further discussion about nuclear abolition? Even if there is a category difference between nuclear abolition on the one hand and the history of European political unity and colonialism on the other, the latter cases do at least support the general point that the 'unthinkable' can happen in international politics, and within one human lifetime. Furthermore, the 1990s may be particularly opportune for confronting the unthinkable. As the 1990s begin, there is a general consciousness that a revolutionary period in international politics is underway and that the world is faced with the reality of fundamental change.

Recent events will have both a negative and positive impact on thinking about nuclear abolition. The negative implication arises from the fact that better can be worse. With the decline of the fear of superpower war, people naturally tend to ignore the problem of nuclear weapons. As a result, the decline of the Soviet threat and the growth of East–West co-operation has led to a loss in the support for those organizations in the West committed to nuclear disarmament. Nuclear issues, at least for the moment, have become less central in domestic political debates.

There is a different problem in the Soviet Union. Since mid-1989 President Gorbachev has backed away from his 1986 vision of a nuclear weapon-free world by the year 2000; instead, he has talked about moving towards minimum nuclear deterrence. This backtracking might continue. It is even conceivable, if Soviet conventional military forces decline significantly in relation to those of the Soviet Union's putative adversaries, that the Soviet military leadership will demand greater reliance upon nuclear weapons in order to compensate for conventional weakness. As the Warsaw Treaty Organization is buried, Soviet strategy could be reborn in the guise of a NATO-like flexible response.

There are also negative trends outside of the East–West relationship. The spread of ballistic missile technology and chemical weapons in the Third World, and the continuing anxiety about the proliferation of nuclear weapons to unstable regions and leaders, will give pause to any existing nuclear power contemplating ex-nuclear status. As the cold war faded, the metallurgic imagery rationalizing the continued possession of nuclear weapons in the West quickly shifted from the iron curtain to tin-pot dictators. The invasion of Kuwait by Iraq in August 1990 violently emphasizes this point.

Against these negative trends, two important positive ones are also evident.

1. There is the prospect that nuclear weapons will become increasingly regarded as irrelevant factors in the daily business of international politics. In the end, it may be that the increased likelihood of this possibility—rather than the force of any argument that nuclear weapons are immoral or dangerous—will be the most potent factor leading to decisions about the reduction and eventual abolition of these weapons. Like colonies, nuclear weapons could cease to be functional and legitimate. If this proves to be the case, the nuclear world may yet end not with a bang but with a whimper. Progress in this direction will be helped by the psychological spill-over from the successful trends (provided they continue) in the complex and vexed issue of chemical disarmament.

2. More immediately important, new thinking on the subject of nuclear disarmament may develop as a result of the ending of the cold war. To date, the issue of denuclearization in the West has been tied up with loyalty tests of one sort of another. As a result, the scope for rational discussion has been considerably circumscribed. Even those of a liberal disposition in the West, and

particularly in the United States, have been reluctant about engaging in the nuclear versus non-nuclear debate: to admit to supporting nuclear disarmament during the cold war was often interpreted as being equivalent to admitting being soft on communism. Taking such a stance was a certain disqualification for any academic seeking a post in Washington. The same was true, in reverse, in the Soviet Union. Instead of open-minded discussion about nuclear weapons, there were loyalty tests and dialogues of the deaf.

The iron curtain put us all behind the wire, psychologically and intellectually speaking. The cold war helped to compound old ways of thinking not only about foreign and defence policy, but also about domestic politics. And the old ways on both sides of the wire were mutually reinforcing: propaganda provoked propaganda, pro-nuclear postures triggered pro-nuclear postures and nationalism stimulated nationalism.

It is, of course, unlikely that the experience and ending of the cold war on its own will do for the theory and practice of global nuclear abolition what the experience and end of the World War II did for European unity. Even so, the period 1985–89 should significantly expand our ideas about what is possible in international politics. We have witnessed the unthinkable in Eastern Europe. In the security realm there is a remarkable contrast between the new agenda of the early 1990s and the concerns of the Reagan–Brezhnev period. A decade ago denuclearization and defensive defence were unheard of or were identified with fringe activists. They are now at the centre of the security agenda. Recent events show that radical change is feasible.

The history, let alone the results, of the cold war have not been assimilated. As re-evaluations of the past take place, and the old adversaries work out new political and economic arrangements, different perspectives will be created on the civilization-threatening destruction that was perfected in order to keep apart the political systems of West and East. Re-evaluations of history and the continuing spread of new thinking about security could become mutually reinforcing, just as cold warism and deterrence ideology were mutually reinforcing. The northern hemisphere has become a test tube for a new kind of international politics. As a result, what for decades has been unthinkable—the practical contemplation of nuclear abolition—can now be placed within the framework of strategic futures about which serious scholars can talk.

IV. Balancing risks

For many people, the question of what to do with nuclear weapons is primarily a matter of morality. Nuclear weapons are deemed to be absolutely abhorrent and so must be absolutely eliminated. Nuclear pacifists, like other pacifists, do not give the last word to possible political consequences. They attempt to live by absolute moral standards: no violence in any circumstances, or—somewhat less tidily—no weapons of mass destruction. The pacifist tradition is a long and honourable one but it is not one that has attracted majority opinion in any country. For most people the defence issue—whether it pertains to nuclear or conventional weapons—is one of balancing risks. Is there more security in a world of many or of zero nuclear weapons? If nuclear abolition is achieved, what are the risks of cheating, nuclear blackmail or major conventional war?

Before discussing relative risks two clarifications are necessary.

1. It is misleading to talk about a 'post-nuclear' or 'non-nuclear' world as a possible future state of being. Nuclear weapons have been invented, and, realistically speaking, this knowledge can never be lost. Thus, the world will always be a 'nuclear' one. But, although nuclear weapons cannot be 'disinvented', they can be physically eliminated and nuclear 'strategies' can be rejected.

2. The chapter is not based on the assumption that the abolition of nuclear weapons, if achieved, would bring about a complete end to insecurity. In this regard, we are in agreement with the Harvard Nuclear Study Group when it argues that an escape into 'mythical worlds of perfect security' is not possible.[12] This chapter assumes that perfect security is inconceivable: all individuals and societies must live with some insecurity. Therefore, no attempt is made to design a blueprint for perfect security in a non-nuclear world; instead, the aim is to discuss the feasibility of reducing insecurity at progressively lower levels of nuclear weapons until a level of zero nuclear weapons is achieved.

Risk assessment in international politics is notoriously difficult. For example, there is the temptation to engage in wishful thinking or to make predictions which simply produce psychologically satisfying conclusions.[13] It is tempting for pro-nuclear advocates to compare the alleged nuclear stability of the past 45 years with the hypothesized instabilities of a world without nuclear weapons. Closer examination reveals a more complex picture. 'Nuclear weapons have kept the peace' is a familiar refrain, but this assertion overlooks several tense crises as well as what must be considered the good fortune of the nuclear powers in avoiding the potentially catastrophic interlocking alerts which could have led to a 'nuclear Sarajevo'.[14] No-one can logically argue that nuclear deterrence has 'worked': all that can drawn from the post-war record is that it has not failed. But it might have. Furthermore, in the maintenance of whatever 'peace' has existed since 1945, perhaps other factors were more important than nuclear weapon capabilities. Facing an indefinite future, the most prudent conclusion is that the past was merely prologue. This means that even if nuclear deterrence has not failed for 45 years, it does not follow that it will continue to work forever, through all of the possible ups and downs of international relations: 'Those who are cheered by forty-odd years of tenuous peace resemble

---

[12] Carnesale *et al.* (note 8), p. 254.

[13] Robert Jervis provides a particularly good analysis of this problem. See his *Perception and Misperception in International Politics* (Princeton University Press: Princeton, N.J., 1976), especially chapter 10.

[14] Bracken, P., *The Command and Control of Nuclear Forces* (Yale University Press: Conn., 1983), p. 2.

the man falling off the Empire State Building saying "so far, so good" as he passes the fortieth floor'.[15]

The post-war record suggests that nuclear weapons have proved, and are likely to continue to prove, to be marginal in determining the great waves of history. The rise and fall of communism is revealing in this respect. Communism spread into Eastern Europe in the late 1940s in face of a hostile US atomic monopoly, and communism collapsed in the late 1980s despite an immense Soviet nuclear capability. Nuclear deterrence does not stop history, although its breakdown could bring it to an end.

Established strategic theory has often broken down in the past. Today pro-nuclear opinion assumes that stable deterrence can be made to work indefinitely. This results in a unusual paradox. It is strange indeed that nuclear strategists, those who most pride themselves on being hard-headed realists, can be so sanguine about survival in a world of permanent nuclear weapons and proliferating nuclear powers. Realists claim to base their philosophy on an understanding of the tough and gloomy path of human history, and the recognition of the dark side of human nature; yet they, above all, believe that nothing can go catastrophically wrong with an order founded on nuclear deterrence. This belief constitutes a realist fiction.

The strengths and weaknesses of nuclear deterrence were well rehearsed in the debates about defence in the West during the 1980s. This chapter, therefore, focuses on the main criticisms that have been addressed concerning two nuclear futures: one with nuclear weapons and the other after these weapons have been abolished.

The anti-nuclear weapon arguments (see table 2.1) are familiar because of the airing they were given during the new cold war of the early 1980s. In contrast, the criticisms of the abolition of nuclear weapons (see table 2.2) are less familiar; they only resurfaced (and then briefly) after the October 1986 Reykjavik summit meeting which placed a 'nuclear free' world, for a moment, on the superpower agenda.

The two sets of anxieties—the anti-nuclear and the pro-nuclear—underline the point that there is no risk-free future (see above). Whether or not particular capabilities exist, the world will still be actually or potentially one of nuclear weapons, with all of the risk of catastrophe which that implies. The future only offers different balances of insecurity.

The list of criticisms of nuclear deterrence (table 2.1) are a reminder that best-casing the pro-nuclear argument (on the basis of limited conclusions to be drawn from the last 45 years) while worst-casing the anti-nuclear argument (table 2.2) (on the basis of conceivable but not guaranteed outcomes in a nuclear weapon free-world) should be avoided. To restore the balance, the argument should be turned around. More explicit consideration should be given

---

[15] Those attracted to this analogy are described as 'pessimists' by Betts; see Betts, R. K., *Nuclear Blackmail and Nuclear Balance* (Brookings Institution: Washington, DC, 1987), pp. 1–2.

Table 2.1. The main criticisms of a reliance on nuclear weapons and deterrence

---

1. Nuclear weapons are uniquely destructive.

2. Modern technology is such that a crisis could become a catastrophic war in hours rather than days.

3. Nuclear strategy allows no scope for breakdown, since it cannot convincingly be demonstrated that a nuclear war can be kept limited.

4. The nuclear arms race has been divorced from politics and has itself been an independent source of mistrust and danger.

5. Nuclear winter is the ultimate worst case in strategic thinking.

6. The possession of nuclear weapons by any state legitimizes proliferation elsewhere.

7. If the goal of zero nuclear weapons is not pursued there is always the danger that strategic logic will tend to push towards the irrational logic of nuclear war-fighting.

8. Nuclear weapons are immoral.

9. Nuclear weapons are illegal.

---

to those aspects of the balance of nuclear terror that have been the most dangerous and to the advantages of nuclear weapon elimination.

One danger in particular should be emphasized as we contemplate an indefinite nuclear-armed future: the danger of proliferation. It is almost universally agreed—even by supporters of nuclear deterrence—that a world of many nuclear powers would be a more dangerous world. In the light of the proliferation risk, even what in 1991 seems to be the radical step of moving towards very deep cuts in strategic forces (minimum deterrence) does not go far enough. Minimum, like maximum deterrence, legitimizes the possession of nuclear weapons as the 'ultimate guarantors of sovereignty'. While this is the nuclear creed for the powerful and secure, the pressures for nuclear acquisition among some of the less powerful and less secure will remain. The problematic notion of minimum deterrence cannot therefore be adopted as a logical endpoint for present moves towards denuclearization.

Even from this brief discussion it should be evident that the problem of trying to understand and balance risks is enormously complex. It involves the vagaries of human psychology. Why is it, for example, that most people in the nuclear weapon states have not feared nuclear war as much as some other possibilities? For many, the fear of nuclear war has been less powerful than the fear of foreign domination (or even the fear of lower living standards as a result of the disruption of supplies of oil). The longer it is believed that nuclear weapons 'work', the more difficult it will be to change such attitudes. But there are three possibilities which might revise popular ideas about nuclear risk.

1. People might come to accept a revisionist history of nuclear weapons. A new 'common sense' might emerge which recognizes that while nuclear weapons have not failed, they have not actually 'worked'. To the extent there has been stability in the past, it will be seen as having been the result of factors other than nuclear deterrence.

Table 2.2. The main criticisms of the abolition of nuclear weapons

---

1. Nuclear weapons cannot be disinvented, and thus the knowledge that these weapons might reappear on the world scene would create an atmosphere of continuous and ultimately unbearable mistrust.

2. There would be permanent edginess about cheating.

3. Nuclear abolition would create a crisis-unstable international environment.

4. Nuclear abolition would make the world safe for conventional war.

5. Without the nuclear weapon framework, serious conventional arms races would ensue.

6. There is always a danger of the rise of an ambitious leader who would overthrow the system by arming with nuclear weapons and threatening war.

7. Conflicts are bound to arise at some point, and they will inevitably become nuclear, as both sides seek unilateral advantage by rearming.

8. The abolition of nuclear weapons would leave some countries with chemical or biological weapons, and some large populations at a geopolitical advantage.

9. The verification requirements of a global elimination scheme would be enormous, so the costs and manpower demands might be comparable with existing nuclear weapon programmes.

---

2. Popular attitudes might change as a result of disaster, as has happened so many times in the past. A small nuclear war would obviously have a chastening effect, as would a series of major accidents involving civilian nuclear power.

3. There is also the possibility that attitudes could change as a result of a different strategic debate. The most important work so far to argue the case for nuclear elimination in terms of strategic discourse is Jonathan's Schell's book, *The Abolition*.[16]

V. Post-existential deterrence

Despite being the most thought-provoking single attempt to tackle the problem of global elimination from the strategic perspective, *The Abolition* has not received serious attention from academic strategists, let alone policy-makers. After publication, it was conspicuously ignored by professional journals which normally would have reviewed such a book, particularly given the author's fame. The latter might have been the problem. It is possible that *The Abolition* was ignored as a result of a mixture of professional envy at the success of Schell's earlier best-seller, *The Fate of the Earth*,[17] and professional scorn at its message (the book proposed world government as the solution to the nuclear weapon problem). The strategic community did not take kindly to an author who seemed to be a simple utopian, and a best-selling popularizer. This neglect of the subsequent book was unfortunate. Although *The Abolition* now appears somewhat dated in the urgency of its tone, it none the less deserves careful attention. It remains the one comprehensive strategic case for nuclear weapon

[16] Schell, J., *The Abolition* (Picador: London, 1984).
[17] Schell, J., *The Fate of the Earth* (Picador: London, 1982).

abolition. In this sense, it is an agenda-setting work in a period when radical denuclearization is being considered.

The Abolition is divided into two parts. Part I provides an excellent diagnosis of the nuclear predicament. The two most 'shocking' features of the balance of terror, in Schell's opinion are: (*a*) the very short lead-time if matters go wrong in a crisis between the decision to use nuclear weapons and their arrival on enemy territory; and (*b*) the extreme price which has to be paid if a nuclear war takes place. Given the dangers of living in such a world, Schell argues that the elimination of nuclear arsenals is imperative. Recognizing (unlike in his previous book) that world government is not feasible, he sees the challenge as trying to ensure a stable nuclear weapon-free condition in a world of competing state sovereignties.

Through traditional strategic reasoning, Schell argues in Part II that the abolition of nuclear weapons is a logical and desirable goal. At the heart of this approach are the twin pillars of all contemporary strategy, deterrence and rationality. But Schell gives them a new twist. A major plank in the realist critique of complete nuclear disarmament has always been the argument that after abolition clashes between states would always carry the risk of nuclear rearmament (and that if such a race began it would be highly destabilizing). Schell counters this head-on by making the mutual threat of nuclear rearmament the essential underpinning of his strategy for a nuclear weapon-free security system. He labels it a 'deterred state', a condition of 'weaponless deterrence'.[18] As long as states realize that any attempt to rearm will provoke all the dangers of living in a world of nuclear terror, they will be deterred form taking the decisive step. Such a nuclear weapon-free condition, he argues, would be preferable to the existing situation because it would mitigate the two most 'shocking' features of nuclear deterrence cited above. For Schell the very fact that nuclear weapons cannot be disinvented is the key to nuclear weapon abolition, not its enduring obstacle.

Parity in the capacity for nuclear rearmament is the foundation for order in Schell's thesis: that is, states will not abrogate an abolition agreement because they know it will be countered at some point. Abrogation would be self-defeating. War would not become any more attractive since the mutual threat of nuclear rearmament will induce a healthy caution.

Although Schell's thesis about deterrence by the threat of rearmament is an original one, its intellectual origins can be traced back to two pioneering US strategic thinkers, Thomas Schelling and Bernard Brodie. The former argued in his classic book *Arms and Influence* that the key problem for a disarmed world would be stability.[19] For Schelling, since every condition of disarmament is a potential situation of rearmament, there is a requirement for what he called 'rearmament parity'.[20] Schell's thesis also seems to draw on the thinking of Bernard Brodie. In *The Absolute Weapon*, Brodie argued that there were two

[18] Schell (note 16), p. 97.
[19] Schelling, T. C., *Arms and Influence* (Yale University Press: New Haven, Conn., 1966).
[20] Schelling (note 19), pp. 248–51.

aspects which overshadowed all others about the atomic bomb: it existed and it was enormously destructive.[21] Brodie was of the view that a potential attacker would be deterred from using nuclear weapons, provided that there was an assurance that the assaulted state would retaliate at some point in the future, even if there was a delay of days or weeks. The threat of retaliation would ensure that the nuclear world would be a stable one. This proposition is central to *The Abolition*. Schell illustrated it by arguing that if the White House had known that Japan had been close to making a bomb in 1945, and that it would have been capable of retaliating against the United States a few weeks after any US atomic attack on Japan, then it is doubtful whether President Truman would have ordered the attack on Hiroshima.[22]

According to Schell, the mutual threat of nuclear rearmament means that after an abolition agreement the world could expect the benefits of nuclear deterrence without the dangers resulting from the possession of operational nuclear arsenals.[23] He accepts, like the critics of nuclear abolition, that a non-nuclear world can never be achieved because the knowledge of nuclear weapons cannot be lost; but, rather than bemoaning this fact, he argues that it can be used as the foundation for a global disarmament system.

It should be evident from this brief introduction to *The Abolition* that in some sense Schell is more of a fundamentalist about nuclear deterrence than the deterrence theologians themselves. The latter have elaborated since the late 1940s complex theories by which it was hoped to translate nuclear weapons into political stability; Schell himself is so impressed by the potential stabilizing properties of the threat of nuclear destruction that he considers that states can have the stabilizing benefits of the weapons without actually possessing the weapons themselves. Their deterrent value lies not in their physical presence but in their capacity to be remade. 'I exist, therefore I deter' is how the concept of existential deterrence (the philosophical basis of the trend towards minimum deterrence) has been described.[24] I deter therefore I do not need to exist is Schell's assumption for the abolition. His argument therefore pushes existential deterrence to its logical conclusion, a condition which might be called post-existential deterrence.

[21] Brodie, B. *et al.* (note 10), p. 52.

[22] Schell (note 16), p. 134.

[23] The current situation in the troubled Indian sub-continent would seem to give empirical support to Schell's case. Each additional day there is no nuclear war between India and Pakistan is a testament to 'weaponless deterrence'; each additional day there is no major war between them is a testament to the obsolescence of major war; and each additional day they remain democracies and do not fight is a testament to the peaceful propensities of democracies.

[24] The phrase 'existential deterrence' was coined by McGeorge Bundy. See Bundy, McG., 'Existential deterrence and its consequences', ed. D. Maclean, *The Security Gamble* (Rowman and Allanhead: Totowa, N.J., 1984), pp. 3–13. See also Freedman, L., 'I exist; therefore I deter', *International Security*, vol. 13, no. 1 (summer 1988), pp. 177–95.

VI. The mechanics of nuclear weapon abolition

In the *Fate of the Earth*, Schell looked towards world government as the way out of the nuclear predicament; in *The Abolition*, the key is strategy. The world government approach was based on the assumption that war would exist as long as there were sovereign states, and that nuclear weapons could not be abolished without changing the political organization of the world. Realists have always rejected world government as impractical and undesirable. They have viewed the world as being dominated by states interacting in a system which has promoted self-help behaviour, including the threat and use of force. Whereas adherents to the world government school of thought attempt to take the instruments of force out of the hands of states, realists believe that nuclear weapons have to be managed through the creation of a stable balance of terror between responsible states. Realists reject nuclear disarmament on the grounds that verification and compliance with such a ban would be impossible, and contend that the instabilities of nuclear disarmament would have the perverse effect of increasing the risk of nuclear war.

In *The Abolition*, Schell leaves world government aside and provides an agenda for thinking about the risks of nuclear elimination in a recognizable world of international politics. He offers a range of interesting counter arguments to the stock objections to nuclear disarmament, such as the problem of cheating, and the contention that abolition will increase the likelihood of conventional war and thus the chances of nuclear re-armament and possibly nuclear war itself.

Some might think that an increased risk of conventional war is worth accepting because the destructiveness of war following abolition (even if it becomes a nuclear war) will be significantly reduced when compared with the potential destructiveness of war given the existing capacity for overkill. This is not Schell's case. He does not weigh the possibly increased likelihood of major conventional war against the lesser consequences of such a war; his argument instead is that nuclear abolition will not increase the likelihood of conventional war. He believes that all war has been rendered obsolete by the invention of nuclear weapons (whether or not such weapons continue physically to exist).

What is crucial for a stable condition after abolition is an equal capacity to rearm. No state should be in a position to disrupt another state's capacity for nuclear rearmament by a conventional or nuclear first-strike (conceivable if a state has succeeded in hiding some bombs away). Were a condition of rearmament parity to occur, Schell believes that a situation of stable post-existential deterrence would exist. This raises the question: Why not go all the way and abolish conventional forces? Schell opposes this; he recognizes that some danger of war remains in a context of sovereign states; consequently, states will have to be allowed to maintain conventional forces. But he argues that such forces should be restructured so that they can be employed only in defence of national territory. By adopting a non-provocative defence posture, a conventional arms race should be prevented and aggression ruled out.

As a further safeguard to protect a disarmed state's capacity for nuclear rearmament against a pre-emptive strike, Schell suggests that it would be valuable to build non-nuclear strategic defences. With robust strategic defences in place, a violator of the abolition regime would have to weigh the prospects of its small and clandestine arsenal of nuclear weapons succeeding against the strategic defences of its proposed victim.

Schell considers that it is crucial that the level of inspection permitted under an abolition agreement be related to the level of capacity for re-armament. The more intrusive the verification, the greater the confidence of states in the stability of the agreement, and the longer the lead-time before any possible nuclear breakout. No state could ever be absolutely confident that others had not cheated, but the dangers of cheating can easily be exaggerated in Schell's opinion. He wonders whether a cheater would dare risk showing his hand since others might also have cheated, and on a greater scale. In any case, cheating need not be for aggressive purposes; it might simply be a hedge against cheating by others. A defensive cheater such as this will never want to reveal his stocks, unless threatened. Furthermore, few if any states would want to be exposed as having deliberately cheated, after signing a major international agreement. The risks to any cheater of exposure would be considerable, and the costs in international standing even greater.

What about nuclear blackmail? What about the possibility of a state cheating, threatening another state and finding itself to be the only country with a stockpile of nuclear weapons? Schell dismisses the significance of this worst-case scenario, in which all the inhibiting mechanisms of the abolition agreement will have been overridden. He returns to the argument that if all states know that aggression will lead—albeit with a time lag—to crippling counter-retaliation, then deterrence will be as firmly in force as it is believed to be today. Any would-be blackmailer would know that today's victim could be next month's avenging state with a nuclear arsenal. Other former nuclear powers would also rearm, and might align with the victim, thereby creating a much more dangerous strategic environment. Nuclear blackmail does not prosper in today's world of existential deterrence, and, by Schell's logic, there is no reason to suppose it would in a post-existential world.

Schell does not assume that a nuclear weapon-free but conventionally armed world would necessarily be trouble-free; but his plea is that we compare the risks of a world after abolition with one dominated by no prospect other than the existing balance of nuclear terror. Schell sees the great benefit of abolition as the revolution in stability which is made possible by the much longer lead-times which would exist between any decision to employ nuclear coercion and the possibility of nuclear war. A prolonged period (it is now minutes) would give the parties time to pull back from the brink of catastrophe. Given that he believes that what we have called post-existential deterrence would be unlikely to fail, Schell argues that the foundations would have been created for a more satisfactory international community.

Schell's thesis is interesting because his arguments are based on the concepts and assumptions of political realism and strategic studies. He turns these ideas on their heads, however, and produces verdicts which most strategists have considered to be dangerous delusions. For this reason alone, *The Abolition* should be regarded as an intellectual *tour de force*. It makes a case for considering global nuclear elimination not as a fictional utopia but as a realistic strategic option.

VII. Critique of *The Abolition*

Despite applauding much in *The Abolition*, is it necessary to point out that aspects of the argument are badly flawed. The main problem is that the book is essentially apolitical. This has been a common problem in the debate about nuclear disarmament, just as it has been in much mainstream theorizing about nuclear deterrence. Any project seeking to legitimize the idea of security without nuclear weapons must give due attention to the politics of abolition, both in the domestic and international contexts.

At the root of Schell's thesis is an assumption that nuclear abolition is possible without prior political accommodation between antagonistic states. In some unspecified fashion, the major states in Schell's world will suddenly decide on the need for a grand treaty which will bring about abolition in one great stride. The vexed problem of the transition is ignored. It is paradoxical that Schell, who talks about international politics as akin to a Hobbesian state of nature frozen in place by the invention of nuclear weapons, could expect states to come together and eliminate the most destructive weapons ever invented—moreover weapons which have often been described as the 'ultimate guarantors of national independence'. It would surely be out of character for governments conceiving the 'real world' in pessimistic Hobbesian terms to put their faith in weaponless deterrence, conventional defence and the process of conflict resolution. There is therefore a sharp disjunction between Schell's abolitionist prescriptions and his realist description of the problem.

It is erroneous—contrary to both theory and record—for Schell to assume that the abolition of nuclear weapons will not depend upon significantly different political relations between states. Implicit in Schell's argument is the idea that governments would need to be convinced that all of the states in the international community would be equal in their unwillingness to hide or make nuclear weapons; explicit is the idea that they would be equal in their ability to rearm if necessary. Despite this Schell disregards the fact that such a consensus appears to be impossible between states which are adversaries and unlikely between those who are suspicious towards their neighbours (in a condition of a 'security dilemma'). But different international circumstances can exist, where there is neither a state of war nor a security dilemma; here very different political potentialities arise. In Western Europe, Scandinavia and North America, for example, there exists the potential realization of Kant's vision of a world of democratic states conducting their relations in a way in which war is not only unacceptable, it is just about unthinkable. Anarchy and international security are not conceived among these states to be incompatible. The international politics of these states have become war-free not as a result of the centralization of power (the world government prescription) but as a result of the development of a 'non-violent conflict culture'.[25]

Benign forms of international politics are therefore possible; they are realistic options, not simply the products of utopian dreaming. Whether such 'security communities' will spread across the world is another matter, and even if they do the crucial problem remains of different regions evolving at different rates. While the world is finding out whether a global non-violent conflict culture is possible or not, it is likely that nuclear abolition must proceed like a convoy—at the pace of the slowest unit. Even so, in security communities we can at least glimpse the potential of war-free relations between states in the context of anarchy.

The apolitical character of Schell's argument is evident both in general themes and on particular points.

1. In order for states to put faith in 'weaponless deterrence', there must be an assumption of a universal 'strategic man' characterized by rationality and reasonable goals. But Schell ignores the possibility of 'crazy' leaders who are beyond deterrence, who may be willing to gamble all in the hope of gaining a major objective. This criticism, of course, could be addressed with equal force to the advocates of traditional deterrence theory.

2. A stable post-abolition world will require the maintenance of a legitimate international order (see below). Schell neglects the role of reassurance, and confidence- and security-building measures in maintaining order. His technical arguments about rearmament parity squeeze out the vital role of politics in a post-abolition world.

3. Schell exaggerates the prospects for the creation of a mutually satisfactory verification regime between sworn enemies. If verification is to be conducted by an international institution such as the International Atomic Energy Agency (IAEA), states in hostile relationships would have to be reassured that they were not putting themselves under any disadvantage. The Israeli anxiety about an Iraqi nuclear reactor (under IAEA safeguards) which resulted in the pre-emptive strike in 1981 underlines the seriousness of this problem. Even if verification could be achieved between hostile states, mistrust and rumour would have fertile soil.

4. Schell does not address the possibility that some states might refuse to join an abolition agreement. The unwillingness of threshold nuclear states to join

---

[25] Buzan, B., 'Is international security possible?', ed. K. Booth (note 6), chapter 1; and Jahn, E. et al., *European Security: Problems of Research and Military Aspects,* Copenhagen Papers no. 1 (Centre for Peace and Conflict Research, University of Copenhagen: Copenhagen, 1987), p. 22.

the 1968 Non-Proliferation Treaty (NPT), despite the pressure of the existing signatories, emphasizes this problem. Consequently, it would seem that an abolition agreement requires, as a basic prerequisite, a consensus among the existing nuclear powers, the threshold powers and any believed to be potential nuclear powers. How likely is such consensus? Without it the agreement is perhaps fatally weakened from the start. Schell simply assumes an agreement would be possible and satisfactory.

5. Schell's thesis ignores the domestic political context. He argues that post-abolition stability rests on the conviction that all the potential nuclear powers would be equal in their ability to rearm and to hide nuclear weapons. But the international system of sovereign states is made up of many societies with different domestic capacities, and some states would be much better at conceal-ing nuclear weapons than others. This is another situation likely to create fear and uncertainty, mistrust and rumour.

6. Schell's thesis constitutes a charter for post-existential proliferation. While arguing that nuclear proliferation is a terrifying prospect, it seems to be implicit in his argument that the proliferation of the capacity to make nuclear weapons is a necessary and legitimate part of a stable abolition regime. (This is a post-existential version of Waltz's neo-realist justification of nuclear proliferation as a source of international stability.) But would a world of many near-nuclear powers be stable or an arena for mistrust? The recent experience of the Indian sub-continent could support both arguments.

In evaluating Schell's thesis overall, much will depend upon how one chooses to calibrate the dangers of the present situation. If existing nuclear deterrence is believed to be stable, why should nuclear weapon states face the risks of aboli-tion? Schell anticipates this argument by concluding his book with the claim that 'weaponless deterrence' gives us time to stop the slide into mass destruction should deterrence fail. Earlier in the book he argued that weapon-less deterrence would lengthen the lead-time between decision and destruction from minutes to 4–6 weeks, and, eventually, to months or even years. The prize which abolition gives, therefore, is time for cool heads to prevail in a crisis before nuclear weapons are used in anger. He thereby reveals his faith in human rationality and his assumption that all war is irrational in a world which will always be able to conjure up the threat of nuclear catastrophe.

Schell assumes that weaponless deterrence will be successful because every-one knows that any aggression will be followed by retaliation (similar to the 1946 Brodie argument). But it might be small comfort for the surviving citizens of the Soviet Union, the United States, Britain, Israel—or any other country for that matter—to know that their government would sometime carry out a retaliatory attack after millions of their fellow citizens were already dead as a result of a renegade state breaking the abolition agreement and stealing a nuclear march. Schell would counter this by arguing that an abolition agree-ment would never break down if it were properly designed. There is nothing unfamiliar in this argument except the time-scale. The issue of retaliation after receiving a first strike, and the belief that deterrence will never break down, have been central to the debate about nuclear deterrence for nearly 40 years.

The weight of the preceding argument strongly suggests that the abolition of nuclear weapons will require a major transformation in international relations. Neither a political quick-fix in the form of a grand treaty nor a technical quick-fix in the form of an extremely promising verification scheme will suffice. Such quick-fixes in relation to nuclear disarmament are the equivalents of deterrence theory and the Strategic Defense Initiative in relation to the balance of terror; they are theoretical and technical gadgetry removed from politics. Politics is often the missing element in thinking about nuclear weapons—or their abolition. The transition to a condition of potential abolition requires major but not inconceivable changes in relations between states. Of course, no one knows whether or not it will be possible to achieve a war-free world, but considering Western Europe's evolution during the past 50 years (1940–90), from a Hobbesian state of war to a peaceful republican community, it does not seem impossible.

Schell attempts to combine realism with utopianism, but he does it in a crude fashion. It is unpromising, to say the least, to contemplate his abolition scheme under what he characterizes as Hobbesian conditions.[26] But does he accurately characterize these conditions? Actually what he offers is a curiously static view of the world, one which unhelpfully ignores what is realistically possible in world politics. To be realistic, our thinking requires a dynamic not a static interpretation of present conditions. As a result, Schell's apolitical approach actually overlooks those progressive aspects at work in contemporary world politics which are leading to the obsolescence of major war as an institution of international society; as confidence in such a trend grows, one spin-off could be growing support for the abolition of nuclear weapons.

Existing security communities have already effectively abolished war within them, while security regimes promise to constrain the more brutal forms of traditional power politics; these developments are feasible without the institution of world government. Perhaps in reaction to the criticism he received for his world government prescriptions in *The Fate of the Earth*, Schell overcompensated by unduly emphasizing the Hobbesian interpretation of international politics. In so doing he ignored the considerable potentiality for improved security within a condition of anarchy. Ultimately, Schell is not enough of a realist (in common-sense terms) to see that the problems of the transition cannot be wished away and that political accommodation is necessary before abolition. At the same time he is too much of a realist (philosophically) to appreciate the inadequacy of the pessimistic Hobbesian interpretation of world politics. It is ironic that Schell, who considers the realization of the Kantian project of a non-violent world to be the ultimate objective of human endeavour, should have failed to see more of it at work in contemporary international relations.

[26] Schell (note 16), pp. 93–96.

VIII. Grand treaties or process utopias?

The achievement of nuclear weapon abolition requires a political transformation in relations between states, but not one as revolutionary as is required by
the world government school of thought. It would involve something
comparable to Western Europe's transition from a state of war to a security
community taking place in all the other major areas of regional conflict. A long
time-scale is therefore unavoidable. Schell, however, assumes that a grand
treaty would be enough; this chapter argues that there is no alternative to a
prolonged transition. The road to abolition will require many small steps, not
one big jump.

In disarmament theory, the name of Philip Noel-Baker has been most associated with the rejection of gradualism, and support for a comprehensive treaty to
settle the matter once and for all. Noel-Baker has characterized gradualists as
assuming that what is 'gradual' is therefore 'realistic', that is 'practical politics
and likely to produce a real result'.[27] He argues that this is not obviously the
case, even in theory. After referring to the adage 'who travels slowly travels
safely', he writes: 'But *not* if you are in a Russian forest in a horse-drawn
troika, with a pack of wolves howling at your heels. And that will be the
situation of the nations of the world so long as the stockpiles of nuclear
weapons exist'.[28]

Gradualism was not realistic in Noel-Baker's opinion; he dismissed it as
defeatist. In its place, he suggested: 'Only a bold scheme of drastic disarmament promising fundamental changes in the conduct of international affairs,
will evoke the popular support required to persuade the politicians to carry it
through'.[29] All or nothing is preferable, in Noel-Baker's view, to the inevitable
nothingness of gradualism.

The radical approach to disarmament epitomized by Noel-Baker has been
called the 'armaments-first approach' by J. David Singer.[30] It is based on the
idea that political tensions can only begin to be reduced when the disarmament
process begins. The weapons can be reduced gradually, as Singer recommends
and as was the case with Charles E. Osgood's famous GRIT (Graduated
Reciprocation in Tension Reduction) scheme or Sohn's scheme base on disarmament zones.[31] The aim of such approaches is to produce an armaments race
in reverse. Such gradualist approaches have been rejected by other proponents
of the armaments-first school; instead they accept the injunction of Maxim

[27] Noel-Baker, P., 'Gradualism is not realistic', eds W. Epstein and T. Toyoda, *A New Design for
Nuclear Disarmament* (Spokesman: Nottingham, UK, 1977), p. 269.

[28] Noel-Baker (note 27).

[29] Noel-Baker (note 27).

[30] Singer, J. D., *Deterrence, Arms Control and Disarmament: Toward a Synthesis in National Security
Policy* (Ohio State University Press: Columbus, Ohio, 1962), chapter 7, pp. 167–91.

[31] Osgood, C. E., *An Alternative to War or Surrender* (University of Illinois Press: Urbana, Ill., 1962);
Sohn, L. B., 'Zonal disarmament and inspection: variations on a theme', *Bulletin of the Atomic Scientists*,
vol. 18 (Sep. 1962).

Litvinov in the inter-war years that 'the way to disarm is to disarm'. This was Noel-Baker's view, and it was implicitly Schell's view in *The Abolition*.

Singer identified two other approaches to disarmament, both of which fall in the gradualist school.[32] One is the 'tension-first approach'.[33] This is the UNESCO idea of ameliorating conflict by concentrating on the minds of men. It is argued that through education national attitudes can be changed, and with it tension reduced between nations. If tensions are reduced, the need for armaments will disappear. Singer himself saw little merit in this approach, since it could only be expected to have any effect over the very long term, being based on the hope of changing deeply held attitudes in a multicultural world and in an international system prone to conflict. The alternative gradualist school he called the 'political settlement approach'.[34] This is somewhat similar to the tensions approach but is identified with the realist rather than the behavioural school of thinkers about disarmament. Such an approach has been reflected in the writings of Hans J. Morgenthau, George Kennan, Salvador de Madariaga and Walter Lippmann. It is their view that the way to break into the armaments–tension circle is by first dealing with what are believed to be the underlying political problems; as Lippmann put it, 'the powers will not and cannot disarm while they are in conflict on vital issues'.[35] Singer sees little merit in this approach, mainly because it ignores the role of weapons in threat perceptions; that is, it does not give due recognition to the extent to which the process of weapons acquisition itself exacerbates mistrust between states.

Despite Singer's arguments, the case for gradualism in practice would seem to be overwhelming. Short of a major catastrophe, such as a small nuclear war, it is difficult to imagine a 'bold scheme' on the lines suggested by Noel-Baker energizing publics across the world and radicalizing governments. But a start has to be made somewhere, and Singer makes an important point in stressing the role of weapons in threat perception. They play a decisive role in perpetuating the security dilemma, which is a problem whose overcoming should be at the forefront of any strategy aimed at changing the balance of risks and reducing tension. The sensible approach, pragmatic yet progressive, is to combine the essential features of Singer's three approaches—tension reduction, political settlement and sensitivity to the security dilemma. In order to put these ideas together in such a way as to inject a distinct bias in behaviour towards a condition of stable peace[36] it is useful to think in terms of 'process utopias'.

A useful distinction has been made by Joseph Nye between 'end-point utopias' and 'process utopias'.[37] Most utopian visions, according to Nye, point

---

[32] Singer (note 30), pp. 172–79.

[33] Singer (note 30), pp. 177–89.

[34] Singer (note 30), pp. 177–89.

[35] Quoted in Singer (note 30), p. 177.

[36] 'Stable peace' is a condition in which war is thought unlikely not because of the threat of mutual annihilation but because of mutual satisfaction with the prevailing political situation; see Boulding, K., *Stable Peace* (University of Texas Press: Austin, Tex., 1979), pp. 3–29.

[37] Nye, J., 'The long-term future of deterrence', ed. R. Kolkowicz, *The Logic of Nuclear Terror* (Allen & Unwin: Boston, Mass., 1987), pp. 239–47.

to what are considered to be a better set of future conditions. Ideas about general and comprehensive disarmament or world government are of this type. In a sense, history comes to a stop when end-point utopias are reached. This chapter rejects such an approach: it sees history as an evolutionary process, not an eschatological story with a denouement; it does not accept that radical end-points are attainable in a foreseeable time-scale; and it is presently agnostic about future structural possibilities. So, rather than getting distracted by discussion of unprovable and controversial future states of being, this chapter maintains that the most productive approach to the problem of nuclear weapon abolition is to think in terms of process utopias.

Nye has defined 'process utopias' as benign or pacific trends, with the end-point being uncertain.[38] The process-utopian takes modest, reformist steps in order to make a better world somewhat more probable for future generations. What exactly that better world will look like must be settled by future generations, when the possibilities and new problems become clearer. We cannot now see far enough ahead. For the moment we can only identify sets of goals and attend to the major issues at hand. This means, in practice, mitigating the effects of the new instabilities occurring as the cold war recedes, and taking every advantage of the new opportunities to place security on a sounder footing. If, each year, the nuclear risks can be lowered a little more than the previous year, the threat will eventually be eliminated.

The immediate objective towards which benign and pacific efforts should be directed is encapsulated in the idea of a 'legitimate international order'.[39] Such an outcome would result in states having a justifiably high expectation that there would not be major war, and that in the peace that prevails their core values will not be under threat. If the major powers are basically satisfied, it will ensure that none need express its dissatisfaction by a threatening foreign policy. To many the idea of a legitimate international order might not be a compelling vision—compared, for example, with complete nuclear disarmament—but it is the only 'utopia' realistically on the agenda within the next decade or so. If a predictable peace could emerge in that time-span, based on stable political attitudes rather than the insecurity of fear, then a future generation could start thinking practically about those possibilities that now seem to be only dreams.

Those who try to bring about new worlds too quickly can easily become discouraged. One of the advantages of the process-utopian approach is that nobody expects heaven tomorrow—or even ever—and that set-backs are taken for granted. Moreover, because movement towards a legitimate international order must be incremental and across a broad front, many different people and organizations will likely be involved. The process-utopian approach is social, cultural and educational, as well as diplomatic and strategic. The goal will not

[38] Nye (note 37), pp. 245–47.
[39] See Kissinger, H., *A World Restored: Metternich, Castlereagh and the Problems of Peace* (Houghton Mifflin: Boston, Mass., 1957); and Jervis, R., 'Cooperation under the security dilemma', *World Politics*, vol. 30, no. 2 (Jan. 1978), pp. 167–214.

be achieved unless people believe that it is possible, and so there must be consciousness-raising, as well as changes in policies. The present period is a particularly promising time to promote process-utopian ideas, including radical nuclear disarmament. The process utopia approach discourages us from pressing too strongly at the present time for particular structures for security at increasingly low levels of nuclear armaments? (since by the time it comes about a very different world will exist); instead, the process utopian approach encourages us to pursue those processes that every year promise more security than the year before. As a result of such processes, relations between states will be transformed. Eventually a set of inter-relationships might be created in which the members of the international community feel that the balance of risks is such that radical nuclear disarmament is an uncontroversial step.

IX. Towards an anti-nuclear non-violent conflict culture

For nuclear abolition to become feasible (defined in terms of political accept-ability and technical practicality) it has been argued that a major transformation is required in the way states—and particularly major states—relate to each other. Whether or not this will be the course of future events is not known, but the above discussion leads to the conclusion that it would be premature to cat-egorize the idea of a global security community as impossible; at this point in world politics, it is particularly regressive to ignore the potentiality for improved security within a condition of anarchy. Security regimes (see below) can constrain traditional power politics, while security communities effectively abolish war within them. Progress in these directions, it has been suggested, is best furthered by Nye's process utopia approach.

In order to think systematically and practically about nuclear abolition we need an organizing idea; it would give a sense of direction and a standard for assessing feasibility. For want of a snappier label, this chapter suggests that the problem be approached in terms of an 'anti-nuclear non-violent conflict culture' (an extrapolation of the concept introduced earlier). It is necessary to define each of the components of the idea: (a) 'culture' implies patterns of and for behaviour which are relatively lasting (compared, for example, with 'policies'); (b) 'conflict' implies that these recurring patterns of behaviour cannot rule out disharmony; indeed, the expectation is that, given the historical record, struggle and dispute will remain part of the human political condition; (c) 'non-violent' refers to the idea that war will be ruled out as a legitimate instrument of policy (because disharmony will exist, defence against attack will be allowed);[40] and (d) 'anti-nuclear' implies strategic behaviour committed to the delegitimization, non-proliferation and destruction of nuclear weapons.

---

[40] The preferred mode for this defence posture is non-offensive defence. For a very brief overview of its main ideas (at a time when people were still largely thinking in bipolar terms), see 'Non-offensive defence', a special issue of the *Bulletin of the Atomic Scientists,* vol. 44, no. 7 (Sep. 1988).

The development of an anti-nuclear non-violent conflict culture does not require conditions of perfect harmony or the establishment of a world government. But it does require legitimate mechanisms for change (common rules, norms, principles and decision-making procedures).[41] Progress in the evolution of these mechanisms will be the test of the feasibility of improved security with fewer and fewer (and ultimately zero) nuclear weapons. This process can begin (indeed it has already begun) without the parties knowing with any certainty how the end-point might look. Although we cannot now work out how to get rid of the last few hundred nuclear weapons—and especially the last few dozen—this is not a justifiable reason for not proceeding downwards. This can be argued with confidence because when and if the international community does get down to a few dozen nuclear weapons, it will—by definition—be a world in which a significant political transformation will have taken place. A world of near zero nuclear weapons cannot possibly be 'like' the world of today. World politics will have moved far beyond the post-cold war into a condition of an anti-nuclear non-violent conflict culture.

The question immediately arises whether it would be possible to have a *pro-nuclear* but non-violent conflict culture. The supporters of nuclear deterrence obviously think so, and would point to the successful 'peace' in Europe since 1945. Indeed, they would declare that a successful pro-nuclear non-violent conflict culture already exists. Furthermore, some supporters of common security and non-offensive defence also believe that there is no incompatibility between such ideas and the existence of nuclear weapons, albeit at 'minimum' levels.[42] This view is sustainable in practice as long as one believes that nuclear weapons 'work' by bringing stability, and that widespread proliferation is a solution and not a problem. In contrast, one theme of this chapter is that nuclear weapons, by their nature, are offensive devices of mass destruction which feed the security dilemma, and which are likely, slowly, to proliferate to a larger number of states; and whatever the record of the recent past, there can be no guarantee that nuclear stability will continue indefinitely. A pro-nuclear non-violent conflict culture would be one of unstable rather than stable peace, to adopt Boulding's distinction.[43] 'I exist therefore I might be used' is both the strength and the weakness of nuclear deterrence. A stable non-violent conflict culture would have to be anti-nuclear. Nuclear weapons are the one necessary ingredient in nuclear crises and nuclear war.

Is it feasible, then, to abolish nuclear weapons entirely? The problem with this question is that it is static, and in the present tense. An answer in the present tense is easy but not complete. It can be said with complete confidence that total nuclear abolition is not now thought politically desirable or practically possible by those with the power to carry out such a policy. However, neither

[41] See Stephen D. Krasner's now standard definition of 'regimes' in 'Structural causes and regime consequences', *International Organisation*, vol. 36 (1982), pp. 185–206.

[42] See Buzan, B., 'Common security, non-provocative defence, and the future of Western Europe', *Review of International Studies,* vol. 13, no. 4 (Oct. 1987), pp. 265–79, esp. pp. 269–70.

[43] Boulding (note 36).

the basic question nor the answer should be conceived statically, because 'feasibility' is a circumstantial quality. If we think of feasibility in a dynamic fashion, the picture changes. Whereas total abolition is clearly not feasible at present, what is feasible is the opportunity to pursue a variety of anti-nuclear policies which, in turn, will help shape a different context; as different contexts materialize, questions about the future feasibility of nuclear abolition may lead to different replies. Some of the anti-nuclear policies now being implemented will directly focus on the limitation of nuclear weapons, such as the search for major reductions through the START process. Others will not be directly nuclear in their content but are significantly anti-nuclear in their meaning; they promise to help reshape strategic cultures and the role of nuclear weapons in them. The moderation of ideology as a factor in East–West relations, the spread of democracy in Eastern Europe and the triumph of capitalism will all have a major impact on the way former adversaries behave towards each other. These trends improve the prospects for the benign political transformation discussed earlier. There are, of course, adverse possibilities, which would further slow down the anti-nuclear convoy; in early 1991 the prospect of a nuclear weapon-armed Iraq was very much on people's minds.

'Feasibility' is therefore a circumstantial and dynamic quality. While it can be stated categorically that nuclear abolition is not feasible in any immediate time-scale (up to 10 years) it can be stated with equal force that it is now feasible to pursue a variety of policies which could lead within a few years to a situation in which nuclear weapons will be fewer and less central to the conduct of international relations. Instead of trying to determine 'feasibility' statically, we have a new version of the old conundrum: When does a collection of grains of sand become a heap? Translated into our present problem it becomes: When does a collection of policies and developments which are anti-nuclear in their effect become a definite 'heap'—a genuine anti-nuclear non-violent conflict culture? The answer to this question, in theory, cannot be known in advance. This is because the answer must partly be subjective (do people *feel* secure about the developing anti-nuclear heap?) and because it will never be be brought about unless enough people think such an outcome—or at least progress towards it— is desirable. Unless there is a positive prescriptive element in what we say on the subject of 'security without nuclear weapons' the exercise will be self-denying.

In summary, what is the answer to the question: Is the abolition of nuclear weapons feasible? At present the complete abolition of nuclear weapons is not thought to be feasible. However, a variety of anti-nuclear policies thought to be desirable are combining with general trends in political and economic affairs to create a situation in which progress towards an anti-nuclear non-violent conflict culture is feasible. If enough people come to feel predictably secure at lower and lower levels of nuclear weapons, then the necessary if not sufficient conditions would have been created in which total abolition might then be seen as both desirable and practical.

X. Knowledge and theory building

The above discussion points to the conclusion that consideration of the feasibility of security without nuclear weapons should pay more attention to the neglected study of the politics of security co-operation rather than the traditionally narrower concerns of nuclear disarmament. In effect, the conventional train of thought about the problem of nuclear weapons should be turned on its head, much in the way Johan Galtung turned peace research on its head in the 1960s. (Instead of the traditional focus of peace research on the causes of wars, which then led to ideas about organizational and other mechanisms to stop further outbreaks, Galtung recommended that research focused on the conditions of peace; this led in turn to consideration of issues such as 'structural violence' and prescriptions aiming at 'positive peace'. The problem of the eradication of war, from this perspective, was transformed into the problem of creating the conditions for positive peace). By analogy, those interested in creating security without nuclear weapons might profitably re-focus their efforts from the narrow military dimension (such as disarmament schemes) to the broader political dimension (such as security regimes). Instead of concentrating on nuclear deterrence, which might be described as the highest manifestation of structural nuclearism, we should instead focus on the processes which might produce 'just defence' (in both meanings of the term).[44]

The creation of an anti-nuclear non-violent conflict culture is only partly concerned with the traditional issues of abolitionists (as represented by Schell and Noel-Baker). If progress in an anti-nuclear direction is conceived as a cultural problem rather than one of disarmament, it becomes apparent that such issues as the spread of democracy, the promotion of human rights, the search for economic justice, the research into and application of conflict resolution techniques, and the growth of non-offensive defence schemes are all crucial anti-nuclear strategies. Disarmament negotiations will often be the front line in the struggle, but the outcome will essentially be determined elsewhere. Structural nuclearism will not be brought down simply in the trenches of disarmament conferences but, more likely, by indirect means.

The application of process-utopian approaches across a broad front could have the effect of making nuclearism increasingly irrelevant in the daily business of the world. While the strategic logic of an anarchical system will remain, there may nevertheless come a point at which the existing nuclear powers will feel confident enough to decide that there is nothing to be gained by the continued modernization of their increasingly small arsenals of increasingly symbolic weapons. It may then be possible to agree upon a treaty which will formalize the behavioural reality, namely the arrival of an anti-nuclear non-violent conflict culture. As was argued earlier, nuclear weapons cannot be

---

[44] 'Just Defence' is the name of a British organization committed to 'international security and the building of a stable peace' based on the right of self defence, non-offensive defence principles, denuclearization and the Charter of the United Nations. It looks to the emergence of an international consensus on defence policy organized around Just Defence principles.

'disinvented' but they can be destroyed: more to the point, nuclear strategies can be unlearned. Strategic cultures can change.

One of the most important (and unpredictable) processes of future change is cultural learning. Obviously, the knowledge and experiences that will be gained over the next 10 to 20 years cannot be known in advance. What policy-makers and publics will be thinking is an unknown; however, some choices can be made now to help shape future thinking. In the realist world of militarized power politics (which dealt with Hitler and survived the cold war) threats were met with counter-threats, hostile military buildups with arms races and threatening alliances with counter-alliances. But realism is increasingly recognized to be a shop-worn ideology. It was, as Joseph Nye has written, a 'useful first approximation' of international theory, but it 'does not take us very far'.[45] Indeed, it takes us less far as time advances, for the world it purposed to explain (and prescribe for) has changed in significant respects. As a different world political context develops, so must our theories. Just as realism must be transcended, so its strategic game must be adapted for a different context. The question now becomes: which strategic game, and new rules, should be learned for a world of complex interdependence, presently characterized by the triumph of capitalism, the emergence of multipolar political and economic structures, the continued possibility of major war but its functional obsolescence, and the growing sense of ecological crisis?

Strategy, like war, is a cultural phenomenon. The 1930s and the cold war led to nuclearism and power politics; civilization-threatening weapons of mass destruction became respectable. Whether or not this can be changed is not clear. Many believe that it cannot, but what is feasible is not determined, it is open-ended. What can be learned can also be unlearned. At this time of flux in world affairs it is open to those who are dissatisfied with traditional power-political explanations and prescriptions to try to help write the new rules for a different era for people and nations.

The evolving processes and structures of world politics have been creating a new agenda. This includes (admittedly on its outer fringes) the possible consideration of the total abolition of nuclear weapons. Gorbachev put abolition on his agenda in 1986, and the Reykjavik summit meeting unexpectedly endorsed it. However, the interlude in Iceland proved to be significant rather than serious; it was significant in the sense that the leaders of the superpowers imagined the desirability of the ultimate zero option, but it was not serious because there was little contemplation of the problem of controlling the risks and fears of people and governments on the way down to zero. Reykjavik did not spark the interest of the arms control community in the idea of a nuclear weapon-free world. Indeed, the overwhelming response was one of complete scepticism. Nevertheless, from within the disparate communities of arms con-

---

[45] Nye, J., 'Nuclear learning and US–Soviet security regimes' (Paper delivered at the 1986 annual meeting of the American Political Science Association, Washington DC, revision of 17 Sep. 1986), quoted in George, A. L. *et al.*, *US–Soviet Security Cooperation. Achievements, Failures, Lessons* (Oxford University Press: New York, 1988), p. 6.

trollers, disarmers, strategists and peace researchers there are some books, chapters and papers which are helpful. These might be visualized as coral reefs, incrementally building up around certain ridges on the seabed; as yet they hardly break the surface of mainstream thinking about strategy, but they do have the potential to form a solid island of knowledge and theory on which practical (process-utopian) policies can be built. This section outlines a research agenda on which time and resources should be concentrated in order to help us think about controlling the risks of moving towards nuclear abolition. It is difficult to place the separate items in order of research priority; what is apparent is that they fall into two categories: first, critiques of traditional analyses and prescriptions; and second, the search for alternatives. Progress towards an anti-nuclear non-violent conflict culture requires knowledge and theory building in both areas.

Revising the past

The problems of nuclear strategy. Nuclearism went into crisis in the early 1980s. It proved not merely to be an 'artificial' crisis, as was claimed by pro-nuclear opinion, but fundamental. Nuclear strategy hit the dead-end that Brodie had foreseen in the mid-1950s.[46] Confidence in the rationality and morality of nuclear doctrine has been badly shaken. Ideas about the strategic game for the post-cold war world of complex interdependence will be greatly affected by the 'lessons' we think we should learn from the recent past. These are now being re-evaluated in the nuclear field.

The myth of nuclear diplomacy. The 1980s helped to undermine the notion that nuclear capabilities are weapons in the traditional sense. The decade revealed their lack of political leverage, as the superpowers failed to translate nuclear war-fighting capabilities into diplomatic success. At the same time it could be seen that economic power created leverage, not nuclear overkill. Accumulating research shows that nuclear threats, whether implicit or explicit, have not been as significant as once was thought.[47] The momentum of such ideas will have an important impact on the way people think about the risks of moving towards zero.

The disutility of major war. There is a growing consensus that major war is becoming obsolete.[48] Most of the many wars that have taken place since 1945

[46] Freeman, L., 'Wither nuclear strategy' in Booth (note 6), chapter 3.
[47] See, for example, Halperin, M. H., *Nuclear Fallacy. Dispelling the Myth of Nuclear Strategy* (Ballinger: Cambridge, Mass., 1987); Bundy, McG., *Danger and Survival: Choices about the Bomb in the First Fifty Years* (Random: New York, 1988); Herring, E. R., 'The decline of nuclear diplomacy', in Booth (note 6), chapter 4.
[48] Luard, E., *War in International Society* (I. B. Tauris: London, 1986); Mueller, J. P., *Retreat from Doomsday. The Obsolescence of Major War* (Basic Books: New York, 1989). See also the comments of such notable exponents of the classical tradition in strategy as Brodie, B., *War and Politics* (Collins:

have been internal rather than interstate, and between small rather than major powers. Large-scale interstate war is losing its utility. The 1990–91 Gulf crisis indicates that costs can sky-rocket even when a Third World regional power marches into a defenceless neighbour. The major powers in particular believe that war between them can no longer serve as an acceptable instrument of policy, and so their disputes have to be lived with or settled by alternative means. There obviously remain several dangerous possibilities in the Middle East and Southern Asia, but the likelihood that long-standing disputes will end in war is lower than ever before in modern history. Acceptance of the idea that significant regions of the world are in a post-Clausewitzian condition will have important spin-offs for the way we think about the future of nuclear weapons.

Rethinking the cold war. With the end of the cold war, the historical debate will become less of a loyalty test than previously. This will make for a more sophisticated understanding of the dynamics of the cold war, which in turn should point to revised 'lessons'.[49] It would not be surprising, in this re-evaluation, if the morality and legality of nuclear weapons did not come under scrutiny, given the enormous risks which were run (and which were institutionalized). Civilization survived (in a physical sense at least) but is there not a better way?

Building the future

Security regimes. Regimes can redefine international relationships, as they did in traditionally war-torn Western Europe after 1945. The heart of our problem is the need to achieve change without instability and violence. This requires the creation of institutions to manage conflict. 'Regime theory', borrowed from international law and economics, can be useful, and it attracted growing attention through the 1980s.[50] Whether a comprehensive security regime can be established between the major military powers remains to be seen, but recent developments are encouraging and should make even cautious supporters of the idea from a few years ago more optimistic.[51]

Rethinking security. Although the theory and practice of strategy has been dominated by a state-centric approach, the 1980s witnessed the growth of the belief that 'national security' is not enough. Modern military technology rules out 'national' defence; security now depends on co-operation with ostensible enemies. Meanwhile many problems affecting the security of individuals, states and the whole human community transcend national borders (the arms race, debt, pollution, poverty, oppression, crime and disease),[52] and serve to broaden

---

London, 1973), pp. 274–75; and Howard, M. 'War and social change', eds F. Cerutti and R. Ragionieri, *Rethinking European Security* (Taylor & Francis: New York, 1990), pp. 12–13.
[49] See, for example, Kaldor, M., *The Imaginary War* (Basil Blackwell: Oxford, 1990).
[50] See Krasner (note 41).
[51] George (note 45), pp. 13–14.
[52] Booth (note 6), *passim.*

the concept of security. It is being seen less in military and national terms: it is being conceived as a holistic and global phenomenon.[53]

Rethinking the notion of 'enemy'. In the course of time the simple cold war notion of a Manichean duality became undermined by more sophisticated analyses of the social function of 'enemies', ethnocentrism, threat perception, the dynamics of perception and misperception in an anarchical system, and more detached histories of international conflict.[54] The spread of such ideas is steadily casting the drama of international politics into a tragedy rather than a morality play. From this perspective, there is an emphasis on common predicaments rather than confrontation; this should lead to an exploration of security co-operation rather than the search for unilateral military advantage.

Improving the prospects for arms restraint. Whereas it is unlikely that there are any new theoretical ideas to be found in disarmament or arms control, arms reduction remains a central issue in international security. Controlling arms—formally and informally—cannot be ignored by those who wish to ease the mistrust that exists between states. Several trends are greatly improving the prospects for success.[55] In addition to improved superpower relations, the crisis in the Gulf will probably lead to the reconsideration of arms trade policies. But the problem is not just a matter of reducing arms; it is also a question of how the reductions will take place. This is where the relatively recent theory of non-offensive defence can come into its own; it is a concept around which stable reductions can take place.

Conflict resolution and peaceful change. One of the themes which has emerged from the 'new political thinking' of the second half of the 1980s has been the idea that security policy is not ultimately a military issue; it should have political accommodation as a persistent aim. Gorbachev, in particular, has stressed that political means are more important than military–technical factors in improving the security of the Soviet state. One dimension of this has been the renewed attention given to the United Nations in several regional conflicts, most significantly in the Security Council's resolutions passed in the aftermath of Iraq's invasion of Kuwait. The creation of a 'non-violent conflict culture' requires the development of ideas for conflict resolution and peaceful change.[56]

Conceptualizing alternative security systems. The existing international system provides a high degree of security for some, and could for more,[57] but there remain enormous problems. There can be no doubt that world politics are undergoing profound change. Increasingly the focus of political action is not

---

[53] Buzan, B., *People, States and Fear*, 2nd edn (Wheatsheaf Books: Brighton, 1991).

[54] See, *inter alia*, Booth, K., *Strategy and Ethnocentrism* (Croom Helm: London, 1979); Finlay, D. et al., *Enemies in Politics* (Rand McNally: Chicago, Ill., 1967); Jervis (note 13); Weston, B. H. (ed)., *Toward Nuclear Disarmament: A Search for Alternatives* (Westview Press: Boulder, Colo., 1984), chapter 6 'Rethinking "The enemy"'.

[55] Sharp, J. M. O., 'Disarmament and arms control: a new beginning?', in Booth (note 6).

[56] Note the overlooked chapters in E. H. Carr's classic exposition of political Realism: *The 20 Years' Crisis 1919–1939* (Macmillan: London, 1966); 2nd edn, chs 13 and 14.

national political systems, but international authorities. The important decisions that shape the security of states and people, their economic welfare, human rights, social justice and environmental protection are increasingly taken and shaped by international bodies. Politics are becoming globalized.[58] In these circumstances it is vital that security thinking be forward-looking, since the past is only prologue. Ideas for promoting alternative conceptions of security—including defence strategies, political arrangements and new conceptions of politics—are at a premium.[59]

A new research agenda: what next?

The research agenda just proposed offers considerable scope for those who have decided or will decide that nuclear weapons should have a decreasing role in world politics. If current trends continue in the various areas proposed, the intellectual context within which policy decisions are made will be significantly different from the recent past, at least in the 'Northern' world. Compared with the cold war years, when relations between the major powers of the day were seen through a missile tube, there will be a different outcome if: (*a*) the conclusion is reached that the cold war was a tragic knot tightened by the nuclear arms race; (*b*) nuclear diplomacy becomes seen as ineffective and is delegitimized; (*c*) the idea of the 'enemy' (who is 'us' and who is 'them'?) becomes blurred in an emerging global community; (*d*) major war becomes inconceivable; and (*e*) progress is made in thinking through security regimes, conflict resolution techniques and other largely non-military dimensions of security. A world in which the policy-makers in the most powerful countries share such attitudes will be one in which there will be downward pressure on nuclear arms, the promotion of non-provocative military postures, and a search to institutionalize common security. In short, it will be a world moving increasingly towards an anti-nuclear non-violent conflict culture.

Those who try to bring about major changes in international politics too quickly can easily become discouraged. One of the advantages of the process-utopian approach discussed earlier is the understanding that progress will take time and that set-backs can be expected in a contrary world. But because movement towards an anti-nuclear non-violent conflict culture must be incremental and across a broad front, many different people and organizations can be involved; it is not the monopoly of governments. The process-utopian strategy should be social, cultural and educational, as well as diplomatic and strategic. Progress will not be made unless people believe it is possible, and so there must be consciousness-raising, as well as changes in policies.

Process-utopian strategies might include crisis prevention centres to control the dangers of inadvertent war, but they also should involve at the personal level cultural and educational efforts to reduce stereotyping. Common security

[57] See Buzan (note 25).
[58] Luard, E., *The Globalization of Politics* (Macmillan: London, 1990).
[59] Weston (note 54), chs 10–12, offers a selection of relevant readings.

requires a more cosmopolitan perspective, in which the dichotomy between 'us' and 'them' is broken down as a result of the appreciation that the 'enemy' is us as well as them. The people and governments of smaller countries can play an important role in this task. How far these processes develop partly depends on the world we think we see developing, and partly on what we want to develop.

There is a crucial relationship in strategy between the 'images' of the players and the 'reality' of what happens. This is one reason why the open-ended present is so crucial; the scope for research and action is now wide. Little initial effort in the field of nuclear abolition can be expected to come from governments. As in the 1980s, all of the interesting thinking about security will likely begin outside the official framework. Indeed, the 1980s were a testimony to the potential significance of non-state actors in determining national and international agendas; it is enough merely to note the significance of Solidarity, peace movements, 'civil society' in Eastern Europe and environmental pressure groups. Non-state actors were crucial in bringing about a strategic cultural revolution in East–West relations, and it is not impossible that this might also be the case, at some point, with nuclear disarmament. For this to happen benevolent processes must become mutually reinforcing and impose a systematic bias in world politics towards an anti-nuclear non-violent conflict culture. For some time at least we will be living in one of those periods in world politics when significant progress can be made in a short time. East–West relations have ameliorated and there is a big margin of safety which could be exploited to push back the war system and improve security with radically fewer nuclear weapons. But moments do not become eras without momentum.

XI. Conclusion: 'Obtain the possible: demand the impossible'[60]

There are no quick fixes in this transcendent matter of cosmic life or death. No earthly prices are likely within the next decade or so to agree to give up nuclear weapons on the basis of a grand treaty, even if it were to contain excellent verification schemes, a comprehensive legal regime, a strengthened UN or progressive ideas about peaceful settlement. Despite such caution it is nevertheless desirable that people think constructively about such possibilities, since there may come a day when their time will come and the international community will need a ready-mixed body of concrete thought. But at present a grand treaty cannot simply be dropped into the existing international situation and be expected to conjure up a situation of 'security without nuclear weapons'. A Sudden Disarmament Initiative would be almost as misconceived as an impenetrable peace shield as was Reagan's Strategic Defense Initiative. Both ignore political dynamics.

The gradualist approach to radical arms reduction has the advantage of flexibility about timing and method. The disadvantage is that it is prolonged,

[60] This is the title of chapter 19 of Lifton and Falk (note 7).

supporters are impatient and want results, and delay gives the opportunity for matters to get worse. But there seems to be no feasible alternative to gradualism at present. However, if the idea of gradualism is understood positively, then momentum can be built up, and what is considered feasible can expand. If it is accepted that the process-utopian approach discussed earlier is the only practical one, then it would not be sensible for anti-nuclear opinion to adopt an overly managerial approach to the problem of nuclear weapons. This would be counter-productive and wasteful of energy. It would be easy to become bogged down in trying to overly manage the future when the project may require 25–50 years to achieve. Because the events, the new actors, the concerns and the new ideas of that future period cannot be foreseen, it is better to keep open-minded about end-point structures. Nevertheless, the stress on process and gradualism does not rule out the need for intermediate milestones and structures. To do so would be politically naïve. Practical politics requires that targets be identified and pursued in order to mobilize support, while structures are necessary to carry the processes forward. But anti-nuclear opinion should avoid trying to overmanage the future; instead, a process-dominated approach should be favoured. If we look after the benevolent processes, the structures should look after themselves.

Although the project of which this chapter forms a part was not conceived as an exercise in prescription, it is never easy to keep knowledge and interest, and fact and value apart. As Robert Cox has put it, theory is always for someone and for something.[61] Traditional strategic theory (which includes the idea of minimum nuclear deterrence) serves the traditional realist view of the world. The latter's answer to the question 'whose security are we talking about?' is simple and well established: it is the security of the nation-state (and from this perspective nuclear weapons are often seen as the ultimate guarantors of sovereignty). But there are other answers to the question. For those who want to adopt a more holistic view of security—one for the world community at the highest level and the individual person at the lowest—the security referent is humankind, and for this the global elimination of nuclear weapons is a rational strategic goal. Even if abolition is very far off, and even if its achievement cannot be guaranteed, there are still good reasons for acting as if a world community does exist, and for pursuing the objective of nuclear elimination. Clearly, the traditional explanations of and prescription for international politics cannot satisfactorily deal with the whole basket of global problems and human needs which now confront mankind.

Despite the ending of the cold war, it appears highly unlikely that the major powers could create such a framework of international security such that nuclear weapons could be abolished by Gorbachev's 1986 target of the year 2000. Indeed, most strategic analysts would still concur with the Harvard Nuclear Study Group and describe such a goal within *any* time-scale as a

---

[61] See Hoffman, M., 'Critical theory and the inter-paradigm debate', *Journal of International Studies*, vol. 16, no. 2 (summer 1987), p. 237.

'fictional utopia'. We agree that there are enormous difficulties confronting the achievement of global nuclear elimination: why therefore should we 'demand the impossible'? The reasons are various. If zero is *not* kept as a goal, then: (*a*) nuclear proliferation is legitimized; (*b*) a catastrophe of cosmic significance is risked; (*c*) technological determinism and strategic theory may encourage a reversal of trends towards denuclearization; (*d*) the taboo against nuclear use is weakened; (*e*) a standard against which to measure our efforts in arms control is lost; (*f*) the security dilemma as a result of the inherent characteristics of nuclear weapons is fuelled; and (*g*) the degradation of our culture continues.

While there are many morbid symptoms present in the contemporary international situation, there are also glimpses of more benevolent possibilities, in which the framework of the politically feasible could expand. At that future point, the presently huge step involved in moving from minimum to zero nuclear weapons might not seem such a big step or huge risk. But one thing is clear: if policy-makers and analysts cannot be persuaded to imagine that a nuclear weapons free world is ever likely to be possible or desirable, then it will never happen. The first task remains to legitimize the issue on national and international agendas. Because we do not yet know how to get rid of the last few hundred warheads, it was argued earlier that this is not a sufficient reason for not going in that direction. As the numbers of warheads reduce we will be participating in a learning process. It would be surprising if the character of interstate relations did not change alongside a radical reduction in weaponry. There would be different institutions, norms and procedures. It would become a somewhat different world in the course of a gradual but radical denuclearization process; it would, in short, become an anti-nuclear non-violent conflict culture. In such circumstances the complete abolition of nuclear weapons would become feasible.

This chapter has dealt with a range of complex and contentious issues. It would be useful to summarize the main arguments:

1. One should never say 'never' about the evolution of human society, and in particular it is too soon in history to conclude that the international system is immutably a war system. To use Kenneth Boulding's aphorism: 'We are as we are because we got that way'. There is scope to change the strategic culture of world politics. The structure in structural nuclearism is in the mind. In order to achieve a different, more benevolent world politics, it is necessary to believe that it is possible, and then to mobilize politics to try to achieve it. Brodie was in part correct when he said that the rigidity is in the situation. The marriage of nuclear weapons and a world of sovereign states does create a powerful 'structure'. But Brodie ignored the extent to which the rigidity is in our thinking, and the close interrelationship between 'situation' and 'thinking'. While we should not minimize the strength of the obstacles to denuclearization, neither should we ignore the sociological reality that the rigidity in the situation is in part because of the rigidity in our thinking.

2. It is too soon in history to decide that the abolition of nuclear weapons is not feasible (that it is a 'fictional utopia'). Political feasibility has to be assessed dynamically, in a context of learning and relearning, and not statically as a result of a fixed belief about the essential unchangeability of 'human nature' and 'international politics'. Major changes are necessary in the way states relate to each other, but they are not impossible; there are some hopeful trends in the way international relations are presently evolving. If nuclear weapons did not now exist, would states be rushing to reinvent them?

3. The most promising approach to thinking about nuclear abolition is through process utopias rather than grand treaties. The organizing principle should be the creation of an anti-nuclear non-violent conflict culture. Progress in this direction is feasible at present, and could within 10 to 20 years create a strategic culture in which nuclear weapons are marginalized and ritualistic. By the creation of new institutions, norms and procedures a significant transformation could take place in the definition of and attitudes towards what is politically desirable in the nuclear weapon field. Nuclear weapons cannot be disinvented, but they can be destroyed and nuclear strategies unlearned.

4. The governments of the existing nuclear powers and near-nuclear powers for the most part cannot be expected to initiate action pushing towards global nuclear elimination. Consequently there is abundant scope for research, education and action in the area of security with fewer (and ultimately zero) nuclear weapons. Issue areas range from rethinking history to security regimes, and from arms limitation schemes to ideas about conflict resolution. The 1980s showed the important role non-state actors can play in determining the international agenda.

5. The complete abolition of nuclear weapons will not be easy to achieve and, if it ever is, it will not come soon. But this does not mean that abolition should be disregarded as a goal of policy. There is an analogy with the Ten Commandments and similar principles in non-Christian cultures. Even if the members of international society do not yet know how to secure the global elimination of nuclear weapons, or even whether they can, it is important to accept it as a goal—to act as though it can be done and that we can discover how to do it. To do otherwise not only commits us to a future in which nuclear weapons may be used at some point, but it also reinforces the realist belief that there is no stronger basis for the coexistence between peoples than genocidal fear. It reinforces, through the presence of horrifying levels of destructive power, dyads of 'us' and 'them'. Over a prolonged period such pessimistic and minimalist thinking seems—even by realist thinking—bound to prove a recipe for disaster. Pursuing the goal of global nuclear elimination is therefore crucial even if, in practice, it does not now appear achievable.

3. Towards non-nuclear security: costs, benefits, requisites

Erwin Häckel

I. Introduction: the economic perspective on nuclear weapons

Economic considerations have played an elusive role in the debate about nuclear weapons. Pro-nuclear as well as anti-nuclear arguments are often couched in economic terms. From one perspective, nuclear arms are a good bargain to obtain national and international security by some particularly cost-effective deterrent. From another perspective, they are a waste of money on a scheme for global disaster. Both arguments are usually not carried to great lengths. They tend to be cut short by other than economic reasons: political, strategic, technical or moral reasons weighing for or against nuclear weapons. This may reflect the view that an enormous issue such as the nuclear question should not be judged primarily on economic grounds. It may also reflect the fact that not very much is known about the economics of nuclear weapons, and what is known appears to be fragmentary and inconsistent. Finally, it may reflect the elusive nature of the nuclear question itself which is not defined precisely enough to be accountable in any given currency.

All this may be true. It would indeed be frivolous to weigh the pros and cons of nuclear armaments purely or mainly in economic terms. It would be preposterous to gloss over the dearth of sufficient data on nuclear economics. It would be folly to deny the presence of muddled thinking about nuclear problems of all sorts. An issue which gives rise to high-strung emotions and irreconcilable policy prescriptions is unlikely to be settled by an assessment of material costs and benefits.

Still, to take the economic viewpoint is necessary as well as inevitable. Economics is basically an exercise in the evaluation of alternative decisions, measured in terms of comparative advantages or disadvantages flowing from the use and allocation of resources. In this sense, the evolution of strategic concepts in the nuclear age owes much to economists and economic thinking.[1] Arguments about nuclear risks and risk-taking are based on economic reasoning. Even the debate about nuclear ethics is often predicated on economic

---

[1] See, for example, the seminal works of Schelling, T., *The Strategy of Conflict* (Harvard University Press: Cambridge, Mass., 1960); Brodie, B., *Strategy in the Missile Age* (The RAND Corporation: Santa Monica, Calif., 1959); Richardson, L. F., *Arms and Insecurity* (Quadrangle Press: Chicago, Ill., 1960); Boulding, K. E., *Conflict and Defense* (Harper & Row: New York, 1962); Kahn, H., *Thinking About the Unthinkable* (Horizon Press: New York, 1961); Snyder, G. H., *Deterrence and Defense* (Princeton University Press: Princeton, N.J., 1961); Martin, L. W. (ed.), *Strategic Thought in the Nuclear Age* (Johns Hopkins University Press: Baltimore, Md., 1979).

assumptions.[2] Economic considerations, even though in an unsystematic and subdued fashion, are more pertinent and pervasive in pro- and anti-nuclear thought than is usually acknowledged.

Attitudes about nuclear weapons are mostly shaped by the belief or disbelief in nuclear deterrence. If deterrence works to prevent war, the costs of nuclear armaments are fully justified, whatever their amount. If deterrence fails, the costs of failure may be such that they cannot ever be justified. Of course, since the wager has never been put to the test, the price of nuclear security remains a matter of probabilistic risk assessment or, more properly, pragmatic judgement. If the argument stops here, no further discussion about the merits of nuclear weapons is possible.

This chapter seeks to open up a new approach by addressing a few questions, the answers to which may at first hand appear to be foreclosed. Why do some countries possess nuclear weapons while others don't? What can be learned from the case for nuclear weapons which some countries have made and others shunned? What is known about the real cost of nuclear armaments? What is the utility of nuclear weapons? How does it impinge on the prospects for nuclear proliferation? What are then the requisites for nuclear disarmament and the prospects for a transition to non-nuclear security?

II. The case for nuclear weapons

Nuclear weapons, like all kinds of weaponry, are a military means to a political end. They are likely to be sought, obtained and retained by any country which has reached the decision that nuclear weapons will contribute to its national security more effectively than alternative military means it can afford. This is first and foremost an economic decision, although reasons other than economic ones may figure more prominently in it.

It can be illustrative to examine the historical record. Studies of nuclear decision-making have often dealt with the question why some countries have chosen to 'go nuclear', but it may be more illuminating to ask why so many countries have not. Until now, only a few countries have made a decision in favour of nuclear weapons. Most of the world's governments never considered nuclear weapons seriously as a national option. But the reasons could be quite varied for different classes of countries.

For the vast majority of Third World countries, the major restraint at all times must have been economic. While the costs of nuclear armament were nowhere precisely established they could be assumed to be simply out of reach for an underdeveloped economy. It was well known that the acquisition of nuclear weapons had required a major national effort even from those select and power-

---

[2] Major contributions to this theme include Bennett, J. C. (ed.), *Nuclear Weapons and the Conflict of Conscience* (Scribner: New York, 1962); Walzer, M., *Just and Unjust Wars: A Moral Argument with Historical Illustrations* (Allen Lane: London, 1978); Nye, J. S., *Nuclear Ethics* (The Free Press: New York, 1986); Nerlich, U. and Rendtorff, T. (eds), *Nukleare Abschreckung: Politische und ethische Interpretationen einer neuen Realität* (Nomos: Baden-Baden, 1989).

ful countries which managed one after another to join the nuclear club. Therefore, rare was the instance where a maverick leader from a poor developing country, such as Idi Amin of Uganda, dared to make himself a laughing stock for fantasizing about 'going nuclear'. More seriously taken was a Third World leader like Libya's Muammar Qadhafi in his ambition to purchase nuclear weapons from abroad; but as it turned out, a rich petroleum cash flow alone was insufficient for a developing country to acquire nuclear status if it lacked foreign partners willing to co-operate.

If economics was a major restraint for developing countries, the option for or against nuclear weapons was in principle open for advanced industrial countries. This appeared indeed to be the situation during the early years of the 'atomic age'. But again, there were different cases. Large industrial economies such as Germany and Japan (and to a lesser extent, Italy) were generally believed to be fully capable of developing nuclear weapons for themselves after a period of post-war reconstruction. Political objections, however, were forbidding. One major purpose of international non-proliferation policies, consummated in the Non-Proliferation Treaty (NPT) of 1968, was therefore to bar these countries from acquiring nuclear weapons; as a corollary, they were given security assurances under the nuclear umbrella extended by the United States. For the former Axis Powers lacking a sovereign choice of their own, this was the best possible bargain to obtain.

There was another class of industrial countries that were faced with a real choice in the post-war period: well-off though relatively small-sized economies with an advanced technological base but limited national resources. Governments in this group, which included allied or neutral nations such as Canada, Belgium, Sweden, Switzerland and Norway (some of whom had in fact played an auxiliary role in the development of the first atomic bomb), were for some time in a position to consider nuclear weapons as a serious and legitimate national option. It should be noted that the question which loomed largest in their deliberations was whether they could afford to shoulder the unknown economic burden of a nuclear weapon programme. In the end they all came out against it, but in some cases the decision was not reached before the early 1960s.[3] By that time it had become obvious that small nations in a region dominated by two nuclear superpowers could no longer hope to reap sizeable security benefits from nuclear forces of their own.

An additional incentive to forego nuclear weapons stemmed from the rising interest in civilian nuclear power use. President Dwight Eisenhower's 'Atoms

---

[3] For a survey of early nuclear policies in minor industrial nations see Beaton, L. and Maddox, J., *The Spread of Nuclear Weapons* (Chatto & Windus: London, 1962); Birnbaum, K. E., 'Sweden's nuclear policy', *International Journal*, vol. 20, no. 3 (summer 1965), pp. 279–311; Steiner, A., *Canada: The Decision to Forego the Bomb* (Pan Heuristics: Los Angeles, Calif., 1977); Winkler, T., *Kernenergie und Außenpolitik: Die internationalen Bemühungen um eine Nichtweiterverbreitung von Kernwaffen und die friedliche Nutzung der Kernenergie in der Schweiz* (Berlin Verlag: Berlin, 1981), pp. 150–69; Dunn, L. A., *Controlling the Bomb: Nuclear Proliferation in the 1980s* (Yale University Press: New Haven, Conn., 1982), pp. 11–14; Potter, W. C., *Nuclear Power and Nonproliferation: An Interdisciplinary Perspective* (Oelgeschlaeger, Gunn & Hain: Cambridge, Mass., 1982), pp. 145–72.

for Peace' programme, launched in 1953, had established an international quid pro quo in which the pledge of peaceful use was rewarded with the promise of US nuclear aid and collaboration. In a similar vein a bargain was struck in 1968 when the NPT guaranteed to member states without nuclear weapons the unfettered use of nuclear technology for peaceful purposes—an assurance which was valued highest by industrial states such as Germany, Japan and Switzerland. As the evolving international non-proliferation regime removed nuclear industries from military uses, it became increasingly costly for an increasing number of states to consider a reversal to a nuclear weapon option at the expense of industrial investments and international collaboration.

While the separation of nuclear capabilities from military purposes has raised the price of proliferation for many countries, the lack of such a separation remains typical for a group of approximately a dozen nations. They are those countries which have individually established their nuclear weapon capability—either by actually 'going nuclear' or by asserting with credibility that they could if they wished. The group comprises the recognized nuclear powers (the United States, the Soviet Union, Britain, France and China) as well as the 'threshold states' with unsafeguarded nuclear facilities (India, Pakistan, Israel, South Africa, Brazil, Argentina, and possibly a few others such as Iraq and North Korea). While the threshold states have wrapped themselves in ambiguity, the five nuclear powers are the only ones to have openly paid the price for a full-fledged nuclear weapon force.

It is worth noting that none of these states has ever deemed it necessary or appropriate to present the case for nuclear weapons in economic terms. The nuclear road was taken under the cover of official secrecy and, it seems, almost regardless of the costs involved. Each of the nuclear powers pursued the development of a primary nuclear capability in the style of a heroic national endeavour, culminating in the demonstration of a successful test explosion.[4] Only afterwards were some attempts allowed to calculate what had been spent on the accomplishment. And it was only after the decision had been made to transform one's demonstrated capability into a militarily useful nuclear force that nuclear costs entered into national defence expenditure. Even then, the true costs remained shrouded in secrecy, camouflage and uncertainty.

Economic arguments have been used from time to time to justify the further development and deployment of nuclear weapons. Thus, the Joint Chiefs of

[4] For the United States, see Groves, L., *Now It Can Be Told: The Story of the Manhattan Project* (Harper & Row: New York, 1962); Hewlett, R. H. and Anderson, O. E., *The New World, 1939–1946: History of the United States Atomic Energy Commission, vol. 1* (University of California Press: Berkeley, Calif., 1962); for the Soviet Union, see Holloway, D., *The Soviet Union and the Arms Race*, 2nd edn (Yale University Press: New Haven, Conn., 1984); Heinemann-Grüder, A., *Die sowjetische Atombombe*, Arbeitspapiere der Berghof-Stiftung für Konfliktforschung, no. 40 (Berghof-Stiftung für Konfliktforschung: Berlin, 1990); Cochran, T. B., Arkin, W. M., Norris, R. S. and Sands, J. J., *Nuclear Weapons Databook, vol. 4: Soviet Nuclear Weapons* (Harper & Row: New York, 1989), pp. 2–6; for Britain, see Gowing, M., *Independence and Deterrence: Britain and Atomic Energy, 1945–1952* (St. Martin's Press: New York, 1974); for France, see Kelley, G. A., 'The political background of the French A-bomb', *Orbis*, vol. 4, no. 3 (autumn 1960), pp. 284–307; Mendl, W., *Deterrence and Persuasion: French Nuclear Armament in the Context of National Policy, 1945–1969* (Praeger: New York, 1970); for China, see Lewis, J. W. and Xue, L., *China Builds the Bomb* (Stanford University Press: Stanford, Calif., 1988).

Staff in 1953 urged an accelerated production of thermonuclear devices as being 'the cheapest method to obtain high-yield weapons and more destructive capability' for the United States.[5] This was in line with the Eisenhower Administration's policy to seek a more effectively deterrent military posture with a reduced national defence budget. The 'New Look', as presented by Secretary of State John Foster Dulles in 1954, promised to supply 'more basic security at less cost'.[6] It was based on the threat of 'massive retaliation' with nuclear weapons and at the same time on the deployment of large numbers of nuclear weapons with US ground forces. This, according to Dulles, was 'the modern way of getting maximum protection at bearable costs'.[7]

Advertisement of nuclear deterrence as a cost-cutting scheme during the 1950s was as short-lived as the doctrine of massive retaliation. But it helped to establish nuclear weapons as a central component of US military preparations. The nuclear aspect dominated strategic calculations to such an extent that the economics of lengthy conventional wars could be discounted for the United States on the ground that nuclear weapons had made 'destructive power . . . so cheap that wars can be won or economies destroyed before there is time for mobilization'.[8]

Economic considerations also played a prominent part in the decision of the British Government in the early 1950s to put an increased emphasis on nuclear deterrence in national defence planning and in NATO's strategic doctrine.[9] Later on, it was again in Britain—alone among the nuclear powers—where considerations of the economic burden of nuclear weapons led to severe cuts in nuclear modernization programmes and, indeed, to serious thoughts about abandoning the national nuclear force altogether.[10] In the end, however, nuclear arms in Britain were there to stay.

Economic arguments about the merits of nuclear weapons have not played a visible role for the other nuclear powers. In France, economic considerations were never allowed to cast doubts on the viability of the national nuclear force; at dispute was only the size and speed of its expansion. In the Soviet Union and China, if ever there was a debate about nuclear armaments in economic terms, it did not come to the surface.[11] While the overall burden of military spending is

[5] Hewlett, R. G. and Holl, J. M., *Atoms for Peace and War, 1953–1961: Eisenhower and the Atomic Energy Commission, History of the United States Atomic Energy Commission, vol. 3* (University of California Press: Berkeley, Calif., 1989), p. 166.

[6] Dulles, J. F., quoted in Peter, T., *Abschrecken und Überleben im Nuklearzeitalter: Präsident Eisenhowers Sicherheitspolitik des 'New Look'* (Verlag Rüegger: Grüsch, 1990), p. 137.

[7] Dulles, quoted in Peter (note 6), p. 147.

[8] Hitch, C. J. and McKean, R., *The Economics of Defense in the Nuclear Age* (Harvard University Press: Cambridge, Mass., 1960), p. 15.

[9] Rosecrance, R., 'British incentives to become a nuclear power', ed. R. Rosecrance, *The Dispersion of Nuclear Weapons* (Columbia University Press: New York, 1964), pp. 48–65; Pierre, A. J., *Nuclear Politics: The British Experience with an Independent Strategic Force, 1939–1970* (Oxford University Press: London, 1972), pp. 76–94; see also Peter (note 6), pp. 158–62.

[10] Smart, I., *Future Conditional: The Prospect for Anglo-French Nuclear Co-operation*, Adelphi Papers, no. 78 (International Institute of Strategic Studies: London, 1971), pp. 17–22; Freedman, L., 'Britain: the first ex-nuclear power?', *International Security*, vol. 6, no. 2 (autumn 1981), pp. 80–104.

[11] It was reported, however, that Nikita Khrushchev admitted in a conversation with Charles de Gaulle in 1960 that the Soviet Government had been quite unhappy after the first successful test explosions to

now being discussed vigorously in the Soviet Union, no suggestion has been made to do away with Soviet nuclear weapons for economic reasons.

The fact that all nuclear powers have retained and expanded their nuclear arsenals over the decades proves that the nuclear burden was felt to be an acceptable one. None of the nuclear powers has found nuclear weapons costly enough to outweigh the benefits (military, political or whatever) which were believed to accrue from them. This lesson is not likely to be lost on other nations which have until now refrained from 'going nuclear'.

III. The costs of nuclear weapons

What are the real costs of nuclear weapons? Reliable data are notoriously absent. The most obvious measure would be government expenditures on nuclear armaments. Imperfect as this measure may be (about which, more later), the sad fact is that government expenditures on nuclear armaments are not readily at hand. Budgetary figures or statistical accounts are often not available. If available they may conceal more than they reveal—not because they would be deliberately distorted (this happens, too) but because the criteria from which they are derived remain unknown or uncertain. Any attempt at precise quantification in this field is likely to be futile and misleading.

Nevertheless, an outline can be sketched with reasonable confidence. Missing data can be extrapolated from comparison; fragmentary evidence can be complemented by historical experience; doubtful assumptions can be validated by informed judgement. Official figures on nuclear weapon expenditure appear to be fairly reliable in the case of the three Western powers: consistently detailed for the United States, brief and schematic for France, curt and somewhat erratic for Britain. No official figures on nuclear weapon expenditure are available for the Soviet Union and China. Again, no figures are available for a country such as Israel which is widely believed to possess a nuclear arsenal of some size.

Table 3.1 presents an overview of national expenditures on strategic nuclear forces since 1970. Data are compiled from a variety of sources and spread over a period of two decades to discount for short-term fluctuations. No attempt has been made to cite absolute amounts in national currencies or US dollars. Given the perennial riddle of the size and content of the Soviet and Chinese defence budgets,[12] in addition to uncertain and unsteady exchange rates, it will be more useful to look for relative proportions in the respective national defence efforts. Figures for the Soviet Union and China represent best-guess estimates with a considerable margin of error.

learn about the actual costs of building up a veritable nuclear force; see Goldschmidt, B., *Le Complexe atomique: Histoire politique de l'énergie nucléaire* (Fayard: Paris, 1980), p. 155.

[12] See, for example, Jacobsen, C. G. (ed.), SIPRI, *The Soviet Defence Enigma: Estimating Costs and Burden* (Oxford University Press: Oxford, 1987); Steiner, J. E. and Holzman, F. D., 'CIA estimates of Soviet military spending', *International Security*, vol. 14, no. 4 (spring 1990), pp. 185–98; Rogov, S., 'The end of the cold war and Soviet military spending', *Disarmament*, vol. 13, no. 3 (1990), pp. 9–23.

Table 3.1. Estimated average annual expenditure on strategic nuclear forces, 1970–90

	Share of defence procurement (%)	Share of total defence expenditure (%)
USA	14	11
USSR	18–25	15–18
Britain	12	7
France	32	21
China	20–25	12–15

Sources: International Institute of Strategic Studies, *The Military Balance*, various issues; Stockholm International Peace Research Institute, *SIPRI Yearbook: World Armaments and Disarmament*, various issues; US Department of Defense, *Soviet Military Power*, various issues; Cockle, P., 'Analysing Soviet defence spending: the debate in retrospective', *Survival*, vol. 20, no. 5 (Sep./Oct. 1978), p. 215, table 3; Berkowitz, B. D., 'Technological progress, strategic weapons and American nuclear policy', *Orbis*, vol. 29, no. 2 (summer 1985), p. 248, figure 2; Heisbourg, F., 'The British and French nuclear forces', *Survival*, vol. 31, no. 4 (July/Aug. 1989), pp. 309–10; Williams, C., 'Strategic spending choices', *International Security*, vol. 13, no. 4 (spring 1989), p. 27; Hansen, L., Murdoch, J. C. and Sandler, T., 'On distinguishing the behaviour of nuclear and non-nuclear allies in NATO', *Defence Economics*, vol. 1, no. 1 (Jan. 1990), p. 53, table A.1; Valmy, M., 'Frankreichs Wehrbudget: Weiterhin Vorrang für die Kernwaffen', *Europäische Wehrkunde*, vol. 39, no. 4 (Apr. 1990), pp. 225–28.

The best that can be said with regard to the reliability of these figures is that they approximate what has been widely used and accepted unchallenged for a lengthy period of time. Usage alone, of course, is no proof of validity. If, however, estimates for financial outlays are compared with personnel figures, given in table 3.2, a similar pattern can be observed which lends credence to those estimates. Again, personnel figures are subject to a variety of methodological caveats. But the important point is not whether these figures are really exact. Together with estimated expenditure they reflect relative magnitudes which appear to be functionally sound, coherent and plausible.

In considering tables 3.1 and 3.2 it should be noted that they refer to 'strategic' nuclear forces only. The meaning of 'strategic', in the slightly non-sensical way of official parlance, has come to denote long-range nuclear forces. Not included are sub-strategic (i.e., tactical, theatre, battlefield, short- and medium-range) nuclear forces, for which comparable figures are not available. The sub-strategic component is quite sizable in the US and Soviet forces but rather marginal in the forces of the lesser nuclear powers.

What emerges from tables 3.1 and 3.2 is, first of all, the fact that with all nuclear powers the nuclear component (even allowing for additional sub-strategic units) consumes only a minor fraction of total financial and manpower resources devoted to national defence. This is not a new insight but still a surprising one in view of the overpowering stature which the nuclear powers derive from their nuclear status. Seen in this way, nuclear weapons reflect a uniquely cost-effective allocation of military resources.

Table 3.2. Military personnel in strategic nuclear forces, 1989

	Number[a]	Share of total armed forces (%)
USA	. .	. .
USSR	410 500	9.6
Britain	2 100	0.6
France	18 700	4.0
China	90 000	3.0

[a] Practices of manpower utilization differ widely in national armed forces. The Soviet Union is well known for inefficient manpower management ('over-staffing'). In Britain, major functions in the nuclear strategic force are carried out by civilian personnel. No equivalent figures are available for the USA. However, the US Department of Defense had certified 76 588 persons 'with access to nuclear weapons' in 1989. This figure, which obviously includes personnel in sub-strategic nuclear missions, would amount to 3.6% of US armed forces.

Sources: International Institute of Strategic Studies, *The Military Balance, 1989–1990* (Brassey's: Oxford, 1989), pp. 16, 33, 59, 78, 146; 'Nuclear notebook', *Bulletin of the Atomic Scientists*, vol. 46, no. 7 (Sep. 1990), p. 48.

Nuclear weapons are a capital-intensive kind of military hardware, as is reflected by their prominent position in procurement programmes. But a closer look reveals that the lion's share of nuclear procurement budgets goes into auxiliary and peripheral systems such as aircraft, ships, missiles, communications and other support structures. Nuclear weapons in the strict sense, that is the atomic fission and thermonuclear fusion devices themselves (bombs, missile and torpedo warheads, artillery shells, mines and other explosive charges) require only a small proportion of the total expenditure on nuclear forces.

The US Department of Energy, which is responsible for the development and production of nuclear explosives, estimated in 1982 that the nuclear warheads account for 10 to 20 per cent of a nuclear weapon system's cost.[13] In the United States, an amount of approximately $89 billion has been spent on the design, testing and manufacture of nuclear warheads between 1943 and 1985, whereas the cumulative expenditure on nuclear delivery vehicles came to some $700 billion for the same period.[14] The price differential between a nuclear warhead and its delivery system can be staggering in some cases. For example, US nuclear warheads come at an average price of $4.2 million while the price of a B-2 bomber is set at $1.1 billion apiece.[15]

[13] Cochran, T. B., Arkin, W. M. and Hoenig, M. M., *Nuclear Weapons Databook, vol. 1: U.S. Nuclear Forces and Capabilities* (Ballinger: Cambridge, Mass., 1984), p. 15.

[14] Cochran, T. B., Arkin, W. M., Norris, R. S. and Hoenig, M. M., *Nuclear Weapons Databook, vol. 2: U.S. Nuclear Warhead Production* (Ballinger: Cambridge, Mass., 1987), p. 2. Figures are in current currency; if converted into 1986 dollars they would be 230 billion and 1850 billion, respectively.

[15] 'Nuclear notebook', *Bulletin of the Atomic Scientists*, vol. 45, no. 3 (Mar. 1989), p. 51, and vol. 46, no. 4 (May 1990), p. 57.

Table 3.3. US Department of Energy: atomic energy defence activities and expenditures, 1990

Programme activities	Expenditure (US $m.)
Weapons activities[a]	4 541
Verification and control technology	171
Materials production	2 287
Waste transportation and site management	1 684
Nuclear safeguards and security	88
Security investigations	40
Naval reactor development	644
New production reactors	304
Total	**9 761**

[a] 'This program provides for the research, development, engineering, testing and production of all U.S. nuclear weapons; maintenance of these weapons for their stockpile life, and retirement and disposal of nuclear weapons from the stockpile. . . . This program also provides for the certification of safety, reliability and performance of new weapon systems and surveillance of the existing stockpile. . . . In addition, this program provides for facility construction, maintenance and restoration for the weapons research and development, testing and production activities'.

Source: Office of Management and Budget, *Budget of the United States Government: Fiscal Year 1991* (Government Printing Office: Washington, DC, 1990), p. A-661.

From 1949 to 1990, annual outlays on nuclear warheads and related activities averaged 3.3 per cent of US national defence expenditure.[16] Research and development for 'military uses of atomic energy' averaged 7.7 per cent of defence-related R & D expenditure by the US Government during the same period.[17] In 1990, atomic energy defence activities in the United States amounted to 3.2 per cent of the total authorized national defence budget of $301.6 billion.[18] Table 3.3, which gives a breakdown of individual budget items, suggests that the bulk of this amount was devoted to the manufacture of nuclear warheads, that is nuclear weapons in the strict sense.[19]

Detailed figures of this kind have not been released for the other nuclear powers. But it can be assumed that the cost structure of nuclear forces elsewhere is not totally different from the experience of the United States. In all countries with a full-fledged nuclear force, then, a major difficulty in identifying the real cost of nuclear weapons lies in their definition: what is 'nuclear', and what is a 'weapon'? Strictly defined, nuclear weapons are responsible only for a tiny part of national defence expenditure. Broadly defined, they weigh heavily on the size and composition of defence budgets. This is so because

[16] *Nuclear Weapons Databook, vol. 2* (note 14), p. 4, table 1.1; U.S. Bureau of the Census, *Historical Statistics of the United States: Colonial Times to 1970,* Part 2, series Y-473 (Government Printing Office: Washington, DC, 1972); Office of Management and Budget, *Budget of the United States Government, Fiscal Year 1991* (Government Printing Office: Washington, DC, 1990), Historical tables, pp. A 292–95, tables 3.1 and 3.3. Annual amounts have ranged from a peak of 4.7% in 1960 to a low of 1.6% in 1968.

[17] *Budget of the United States Government* (note 16), Historical tables, pp. A 315–16, table 10.2. Annual amounts have ranged from a peak of 13.4% in 1957 to a low of 4.4% in 1975.

[18] *Budget of the United States Government* (note 16), p. 153.

[19] It should be noted that at least one of the items in table 3.3, naval reactor development, is not necessarily related to nuclear weapons.

large numbers of (relatively cheap) nuclear warheads make military sense only with large numbers of (relatively expensive) delivery systems. Delivery systems, however, are often dual-capable, and it is impossible to ascertain where their 'nuclear' function ends and their 'conventional' function begins. Even the most meticulous budget accounts cannot, therefore, indicate the precise cost of nuclear weapons.

The economic burden which a country carries for its nuclear force is not identical with governmental expenditures. Real costs may differ from visible costs in a variety of ways. Prices for military goods are notoriously delusive; all the more so in a secretive business such as nuclear armaments; and still more, of course, in command economies of the Soviet and Chinese type where market prices have been unknown for decades. Budgetary expenditure does not include external costs such as environmental damage resulting from nuclear weapon tests, discounted costs such as fissile material production for military purposes in dual-purpose facilities (a common practice in all nuclear weapon states), hidden or potential costs such as nuclear accidents,[20] deferred costs such as individual compensation claims,[21] or follow-up costs such as delayed waste disposal and nuclear facility clean-up.[22]

On the other hand, national expenses can be saved if a country shares certain items of its nuclear force with other countries. All nuclear powers have in some ways profited from such an arrangement. Britain, France and Israel have been aided by the United States in their nuclear programmes for many years.[23] China profited from Soviet aid at least in the initial stage of its nuclear development.[24] Both the Soviet Union and the United States saved the costs of those nuclear delivery vehicles (aircraft, artillery, missiles) which their respective allies furnished to carry Soviet or US nuclear warheads.

All these factors tend to blur the real costs of national nuclear forces. But they will not affect dramatically the basic structure of costs. The conclusion to be drawn from the experience of nuclear powers is that while the core cost of a nuclear arsenal may appear rather small (although still a lot of money in absolute terms), it is inevitably bound up with the expense of a fully developed nuclear force which few countries can afford. Put differently, this means that only a country which is willing and able to support a large military force can afford nuclear weapons. Earlier expectations, as quoted above for the

[20] Shaun, G. and Edwards, A., 'The hidden costs of deterrence: nuclear weapons accidents 1950–1988', *Bulletin of Peace Proposals*, vol. 20, no. 1 (Mar. 1989), pp. 3–26.

[21] In Oct. 1990, President Bush signed a federal law granting damage compensation of up to US $50 000 dollars for US citizens who suffered from atmospheric weapon tests in Nevada between 1945 and 1963. See *Frankfurter Allgemeine Zeitung*, 17 Oct. 1990.

[22] According to estimates by the US Energy Department and General Accounting Office, the cleaning up of 17 badly contaminated nuclear weapons production sites in the United States could cost over US $150 billion—many times what had previously been set aside for this purpose. See 'Nuclear notebook', *Bulletin of the Atomic Scientists*, vol. 45, no. 3 (Mar. 1989), p. 51.

[23] Ullmann, R. H., 'The covert French connection', *Foreign Policy*, no. 75 (summer 1989), pp. 3–33; Smith, G. G. and Cobban, H., 'A blind eye to nuclear proliferation', *Foreign Affairs*, vol. 68, no. 3 (summer 1989), pp. 53–70; 'Nuclear notebook', *Bulletin of the Atomic Scientists*, vol. 46, no. 5 (June 1990), p. 47.

[24] Lewis and Xue (note 4), pp. 105–7.

Eisenhower Administration, to the effect that nuclear security can be had on the cheap, have not come true.

IV. The utility of nuclear weapons

Costs are not the only measure to judge a weapon's merits in economic terms; they have to be set against the benefits derived from it. What are nuclear weapons good for? Their utility is by no means obvious. In fact, it has been at dispute ever since the outset of the 'atomic age'.

One of the earliest observers was Paul Nitze (later to become an influential policy adviser to several US Presidents) who visited Japan in the fall of 1945 as a member of the US Strategic Bombing Survey to conduct '. . . a careful study of the effects of the atomic bombs dropped on Hiroshima and Nagasaki. At that time newspapers in the United States were filled with speculation, some of it proclaiming the atomic bomb to be of limitless power—the ultimate weapon. The survey's task was to measure as precisely as possible. . . the bomb's true capabilities as well as its limitations'.[25]

Noting that the devastations at Hiroshima and Nagasaki, appalling as they were, had been actually less severe than the effects of a single fire-bomb raid against Tokyo earlier in 1945, Nitze concluded: 'The significance of the atomic bomb was that it compressed the explosive power of many conventional bombs into one and thus enormously enhanced the effectiveness of a single bomber. With each plane carrying ten tons of high explosives and incendiaries, the attacking force required to equal the effects of a single atomic weapon would have been 210 B-29s at Hiroshima and 120 B-29s at Nagasaki'.[26]

What Nitze observed then with the shrewd eye of the Wall Street banker still holds true today. Nuclear weapons are attractive to military planners not primarily on account of their destructive power but because they promise to enhance the efficient use of military resources for destructive purposes. There is a pay-off between nuclear weapons and their delivery systems. What counts, however, is not the (cheap) nuclear explosive but the (expensive) system carrying it to its target. It is the delivery vehicle to which a nuclear weapon adds the decisive upgrade, not the other way around. The warhead itself, unless it can be delivered by mail, is almost useless without an adequate means of transportation. (At the same time, however, the means of transportation is not at all useless without nuclear weapons.)

The relationship between nuclear weapons and their delivery systems has unfolded over the years in a peculiar way. At first, nuclear weapons tended to become ever more big and powerful, requiring large bomber aircraft to carry them over long distances. Then, as warheads became increasingly smaller in

---

[25] Nitze, P. H., *From Hiroshima to Glasnost: At the Center of Decision: A Memoir* (Grove Weidenfeld: New York, 1989), p. 42.

[26] Nitze (note 25), p. 43. It should be added, however, that the Strategic Bombing Survey underestimated the actual number of casualties at Hiroshima in 1945 as the delayed effects of radiation were then not fully known.

size, lighter in weight and cheaper to manufacture, there was a growing demand for a variety of delivery systems to perform variable nuclear missions. As a result, all branches of US and Soviet armed forces were increasingly nuclearized during the 1950s and 1960s. By the early 1970s, the US nuclear arsenal had reached its peak in terms of megatonnage, number of warheads and number of delivery systems; in the Soviet Union, this stage was reached by the 1980s.[27] Thereafter, both superpowers have gradually reduced the role of nuclear weapons, notably in tactical missions. Some military functions, such as air defence and field artillery, have become progressively denuclearized. It should be noted that this incipient retreat from nuclear weapons came about mostly by unilateral military decisions rather than through negotiated arms control agreements.

There is a limit to the utility of nuclear weapons, and it has become more visible in recent years. The limit is reached where nuclear weapons contribute no longer to the efficient use of military resources—a point which is not fixed once and for all but may be changing at any time. Again, what counts most is the impact of nuclear weapons on the economy of delivery systems.

Several factors have contributed to the reassessment of nuclear weapons from time to time. Technological advances made warheads more versatile but also more demanding on the capability, range and performance of delivery systems. Some systems were specially designed for and dedicated to the delivery of nuclear explosives: this applies mainly to 'strategic' systems. Others are nuclear-capable but can also deliver conventional munitions: this applies mainly to 'tactical' systems. However, a clear distinction cannot be made between these categories since many strategic systems may also be used in tactical missions. Indicative of designations (rather than capabilities) is the fact that presently 61 per cent of nuclear warheads in the US stockpile are set aside for strategic uses and 39 per cent for tactical uses; in the Soviet Union the respective figures are estimated to be 53 per cent strategic (offence and defence) and 47 per cent tactical.[28]

Doubts about the utility of nuclear weapons have been raised mainly in regard of their tactical role with dual-capable delivery systems. Tactical nuclear weapons are found to be a burden for the military rather than an asset, difficult to control, cumbersome to manage and protect, obstructing the conventional capability and flexibility of battlefield action and, above all, causing collateral damage in unpredictable ways. Battlefield nuclear weapons are frightening and possibly demoralizing in combat for friend and foe alike. Many critics who

---

[27] See *Nuclear Weapons Databook, vol. 1* (note 13), p. 14, figure 1.3; *Nuclear Weapons Databook, vol. 2* (note 14), p. 17, figure 1.4; *Discriminate Deterrence: Report of the Commission On Integrated Long-Term Strategy* (Government Printing Office: Washington, DC, Jan. 1988), p. 39 [Iklé, F. C. and Wohlstetter, A., chairmen]; *Nuclear Weapons Databook, vol. 4* (note 4), pp. 22–28; 'Nuclear notebook', *Bulletin of the Atomic Scientists*, vol. 45, no. 9 (Nov. 1989); p. 53, and vol. 46, no. 6 (July/Aug. 1990), p. 49.

[28] 'Nuclear notebook', *Bulletin of the Atomic Scientists*, vol. 46, no. 5 (June 1990), p. 48; and vol. 46, no. 6 (July/Aug. 1990), p. 49.

accept nuclear weapons in principle have long argued that their tactical variety could and should be abandoned altogether.[29]

Unwanted side-effects are one factor limiting the utility of nuclear weapons. Nuclear weapons are feared by many military commanders for their operational repercussions as much as they are disliked by many politicians for their controversial legitimacy. A weapon whose use would imply an uncertain balance of gains and losses is not a very useful weapon.

Another factor limiting the utility of nuclear weapons is the dramatic advance in the performance of certain delivery systems. Some of them, notably cruise missiles, have attained the ability to hit targets over long distances with such precision that nuclear warheads are no longer needed to destroy hardened military targets. Conventional high-yield explosives will do the job. At present this unprecedented capability is realized only for theatre warfare; in a few years it may be accomplished for intercontinental warfare as well.[30] Nuclear weapons are then no longer the most efficient means of destruction for all strategic missions.

Although a retreat from nuclear weapons in war-fighting scenarios has been going on for some time it must not be expected to lead to the complete abandonment of nuclear arms in a foreseeable future. Sceptics who regard nuclear weapons as unfit for most military tasks still agree that they may retain the limited but extremely important role of deterring war between nuclear powers. Even those critics who, like former US Secretary of Defense McNamara, insist that 'nuclear weapons serve no military purpose whatsoever. They are totally useless',[31] hasten to add: '. . . except only to deter one's opponent from using them'.[32] In fact, this may have been their main function for decades.[33]

Recent official statements have emphasized the limited role of nuclear weapons. The Joint Chiefs of Staff now assign to US nuclear forces the task 'to deter nuclear aggression and help to deter other forms of aggression against the United States, its allies, and its interests . . . and as a hedge against emerging nuclear-capable regional powers'.[34] Allied heads of state and government now seek to adopt 'a new NATO strategy making nuclear forces truly weapons of

---

[29] See, for example, York, H. F., 'Beginning nuclear disarmament at the bottom', *Survival*, vol. 25, no. 5 (Sep./Oct. 1983), pp. 227–31; Kaufmann, W. W., *The 1986 Defense Budget* (Brookings Institution: Washington, DC, 1985), pp. 23–26; Quester, G., 'Maritime issues in avoiding nuclear war', *Armed Forces and Society*, vol. 13, no. 2 (1987), pp. 189–214.

[30] See *Discriminate Deterrence* (note 27), pp. 8 and 36; Brement, M., 'Reaching out to Moscow', *Foreign Policy*, no. 50 (autumn 1990), pp. 56–77; Odom, W. E., 'The Soviet military in transition', *Problems of Communism*, vol. 39, no. 3 (May/June 1990), pp. 56–57.

[31] McNamara, R. S., 'The military role of nuclear weapons: perceptions and misperceptions', *Foreign Affairs*, vol. 62, no. 1 (autumn 1983), p. 79.

[32] McNamara (note 31), p. 79.

[33] See Bundy, McG., *Danger and Survival: Choices About the Bomb in its First Fifty Years* (Random House: New York, 1988).

[34] US Joint Chiefs of Staff, *1990 Joint Military Assessment* (Government Printing Office: Washington, DC, 1990), pp. IV–1 and 2.

last resort'.[35] These are more modest objectives for nuclear arms than have been pronounced for many years.

However, if fact is distinguished from doctrine and rhetoric it appears that the limited utility of nuclear weapons has been acknowledged all along. It was during the heyday of 'massive retaliation' that one of its authors cautioned: 'Our planning does not subscribe to the thinking that the ability to deliver massive atomic retaliation is, by itself, adequate to meet all our security needs. It is not correct to say we are relying exclusively on one weapon, or one Service, or that we are anticipating one kind of war. I believe that this nation could be a prisoner of its own military posture if it had no capability other than to deliver a massive atomic attack'.[36]

And it was John Foster Dulles, the avowed herald of 'massive retaliation', who argued: 'We cannot however assume that the deterrent of nuclear power will resolve all our problems. One certain thing which history proves is that it is impossible to forecast certainly the character of future war. We dare not put all our eggs in one basket. There must be diversity of capability and must be flexibility'.[37]

Accordingly, neither the United States nor any other nuclear power has ever devoted more than a minor share of its military resources to nuclear armaments. All of them have engaged themselves during the past decades in a variety of military actions (except against each other) in which they found their nuclear weapons to be unusable, even in defeat. Viet Nam and Afghanistan are the most obvious cases. None of these engagements, however, involved the essence of national security for the nuclear powers. Meanwhile, the doctrine of 'mutual assured destruction', as it evolved since the 1960s, maintained the price of war between the superpowers at a level where the actual use of nuclear weapons could no longer serve as an instrument of gainful policy between them.[38]

What may be learned from this experience is that nuclear weapons are not a substitute for conventional arms. They cannot, therefore, relieve a country with military ambitions from the large expenditure associated with conventional armaments. Nuclear weapons can play a role for actual war-fighting only if and where truly vital interests of nuclear powers are at stake. Political developments may reduce the demand for deterrent capability among nuclear powers. Technological developments may further reduce the comparative advantages of nuclear over conventional arms. Nevertheless, as long as nations find it opportune to threaten other nations with large-scale destruction, nuclear weapons will retain a residual utility.

[35] 'London declaration on a transformed North Atlantic Alliance', 6 July 1990, *Survival*, vol. 32, no. 5 (Sep./Oct. 1990), p. 471.
[36] Admiral Radford in a speech to the Economic Club in New York, 9 Mar. 1954, quoted in Peter (note 6), p. 152.
[37] Secretary of State Dulles in a speech to the North Atlantic Council, Aug. 1956, quoted in Peter (note 6), p. 276.
[38] The Soviet Union, although it never accepted officially the nuclear doctrines of the United States, has for several decades practiced a nuclear posture that was in effect akin to western doctrinal assumptions; see van Oudenaren, J., *Deterrence, War-fighting and Soviet Military Doctrine*, Adelphi Papers no. 210 (International Institute of Strategic Studies: London, 1986).

V. Nuclear proliferation

Would-be nuclear powers, if they try to emulate previous nuclear powers, may find the utility of nuclear weapons to be even more limited in the future than in the past. They can hardly expect to catch up with established nuclear powers who have enjoyed a lead-time of several decades to build up their nuclear arsenals. And they may come to realize that developments in non-nuclear technologies (conventional, chemical or biological) offer them new means of destruction that are possibly as lethal and fearful as nuclear weapons but at the same time easier to handle and less inhibiting in their use for war-fighting purposes.[39]

All this may serve as a disincentive for nuclear proliferation. However, the balance for proliferation-prone countries is not unequivocal. Late-comers in an arms race are not necessarily at a disadvantage. They can copy or improve earlier patterns of nuclear weapon construction laid out by previous nuclear powers, thereby avoiding or cutting short many circuitous or erroneous routes of technological development which their forerunners may have tried and failed at great expense.[40] They can draw on scientific expertise, technical skills and basic knowledge about nuclear weapon design which are much more widespread, more easily available and less costly to acquire than ever before. They can now procure the full range of components for nuclear weapons on an increasingly globalized and competitive international market either openly, clandestinely or illegally. They can go for advanced warhead designs (such as tritium-boosted fission) which make more efficient use of scarce fissile material in nuclear explosives. By computer simulation they may be able to develop nuclear warheads with a reasonable degree of operational reliability even without actual test explosions. In short, they can now avail themselves of a large number of cost-saving schemes on the road to nuclear weapons.[41]

Attempts to derive the costs of nuclear proliferation for a country from the experience of the Manhattan Project of World War II, the first nuclear programme in history, would be entirely misleading. In the early 1940s, billions of US dollars (by today's standards) were required for an experimental nuclear detonation. Since then, the degression of costs for developing a nuclear explosive device has been such that, according to one author, 'economic cost will

[39] Rose, S., 'The coming explosion of silent weapons', *Naval War College Review*, vol. 42, no. 3 (summer 1989), pp. 6–29; Welch, T. J., 'Technology change and security', *The Washington Quarterly*, vol. 13, no. 2 (spring 1990), pp. 111–20; Thränert, O., 'Biologische Kampfstoffe: Die Gefahren der Gentechnologie und der Weiterverbreitung in der Dritten Welt', *Österreichische Militärische Zeitschrift*, vol. 28, no. 5 (Sep./Oct. 1990), pp. 403–7.

[40] The Chinese profited most obviously from a careful analysis and evaluation of alternative nuclear weapons routes that had been explored previously by other countries; see Lewis and Xue (note 4), pp. 104–108.

[41] Fakley, D., 'New technologies and nuclear proliferation', v. Baeckmann, A. and Fakley, D., *New Technology, the NPT and the IAEA Safeguards System*, Occasional Paper no. 4 (Programme for the Promotion of Nuclear Nonproliferation: Southampton, UK, 1989), pp. 1–6.

deter almost no nation from attempting to develop nuclear weapons'.[42] However, this statement has to be qualified in two important respects in order to be realistic.

First, it is not the financial expense alone which serves as an economic barrier against potential proliferators. The amount of a few hundred million US dollars that may be necessary, according to various estimates,[43] to build a nuclear bomb could be spent quite easily by the governments of many countries if they wished. What many governments, even financially solvent ones, do not possess is access to the broad range of national resources required for a nuclear programme: raw materials, infrastructure, production facilities and—above all—qualified manpower such as scientists, engineers, technicians, skilled workers, planners and administrators. The lack of qualified manpower is, of course, a universal characteristic of developing countries and the most difficult to overcome. Deficiency in overall economic development is therefore the major obstacle to a nation's indigenous nuclear capability.[44]

A few developing countries may be able to get over this obstacle by the sheer size of their human resources. Not accidentally, China and India, the two most populous nations in the world, were the first and only developing countries up to now to construct nuclear explosives by their own effort.[45] But for the bulk of developing countries a nuclear weapon programme will remain out of their reach as long as they remain developing countries.

The second economic barrier to nuclear proliferation relates to the military utility of nuclear weapons. As has been argued above, a nuclear force in order to make military sense requires a large array of delivery vehicles and other support systems, the costs of which far exceed those of the nuclear warheads. Any government considering nuclear armaments will have to consider at the same time the size of these associated expenses. Moreover, given the fact that nuclear weapons are unfit for many military tasks, it must in addition provide for a conventional force commensurate to its nuclear ambition at a cost which will again go far beyond the cost of the nuclear force. The total military burden for a nuclear weapon programme then requires an economic effort which only a nation aspiring to great power status may sustain. Not many countries in the world are willing and able to pay such a price.

It follows that nuclear proliferation is not a problem that might involve any number of countries. Economic restraints will continue to dissuade most countries from going nuclear. Perhaps the number of potential proliferators will in the future not rise significantly above the rather limited group of 'threshold

[42] Graham, T. W., 'The economics of producing nuclear weapons in nth countries', eds D. L. Brito, M. D. Intrilligator and A. E. Wick, *Strategies for Managing Nuclear Proliferation: Economic and Political Issues* (Lexington Books: Lexington, Mass., 1983), p. 23.

[43] Graham (note 42), p. 12, table 2.1.

[44] In a perverse way this has been acknowledged by certain Third World leaders who called for nuclear weapons as evidence of their nations' economic advancement.

[45] Construction of the first Chinese nuclear bomb between 1957 and 1964 is said to have required a task force of '300 000 staff and workers on the "nuclear industrial front". Of these 300 000, about 60 000 to 70 000 were engineering and technical personnel and over 1000 were senior scientific research personnel'. See Lewis and Xue (note 4), pp. 272–73.

countries' that have been eyed with suspicion for a good many years. But there is no reason for complacency. For it is precisely these countries where the factors restraining others can actually work as an incentive for proliferation.

A country like Pakistan may serve as an illustration. Underdeveloped and destitute, it is populous enough to provide a sufficient reservoir of skilled manpower for a nuclear programme, large and cohesive enough to provide the necessary infrastructure, and strategically insecure and politically ambitious enough to warrant the search for a nuclear deterrent capability. Its nuclear industrial outfit may be inefficient and decrepit but it is good enough to provide continuous training for specialized personnel and effective enough for the production of modest amounts of fissile nuclear material. The country has a large and powerful military establishment with a long tradition of commanding a major share of the nation's resources. There is an indigenous arms industry of some international reputation. Last but not least, the armed forces are equipped with a wide range of modern weaponry, including high-performance aircraft that could serve as nuclear delivery vehicles.

For a country such as Pakistan, the decision to go for nuclear weapons involves not much of an additional burden. Where various building blocks are already in place, putting them together for a new design can be quite economical as well as effective. The buildup of a small nuclear arsenal may in this case represent an optimal choice towards the synergetic utilization of available resources for national security purposes.

It is an ironical reflection on the pitfalls of non-proliferation policy that two essential elements in this composite design result from previous efforts to halt the spread of nuclear weapons. In Pakistan as in similar countries, the foundation of nuclear industrial capabilities was laid originally by helping hands from abroad as part of the 'Atoms for Peace' programme providing nuclear aid in exchange for pledges to its use for non-military purposes. Later on, lavish supplies of advanced military equipment were sold or donated to the country in order to satisfy its security needs without recourse to nuclear weapons. It remained for the recipient government finally to fit the disjointed elements together for a purpose of its own.

Non-proliferation policy has long overlooked the composite nature of advanced military capabilities where hardware and software, dual- or multiple-use items, peripheral technology (such as missiles, electronics and spacecraft), industrial management and innovative skills make up a pool of resources that can be combined and recombined for variable purposes. International control and denial of 'sensitive' nuclear technology worked fairly well to prevent or slow down the spread of nuclear weapons as long as potential proliferators were dependent on technology holders not only for nuclear but for other supplies as well. To the extent that this dependency is reduced through autonomous development or collusion among new suppliers, the nuclear option becomes more widely accessible, feasible and affordable.[46]

Under such circumstances, the traditional tenets of non-proliferation policy require some reappraisal and fresh thinking. A strict policy of denial, even if expanded to cover beside nuclear technology also missiles, computers and what not, would be difficult to sustain and still not stem the tide. In fact, it could be counter-productive by encouraging independent national break-out efforts. Nuclear power, now used for electricity generation in 27 countries, is likely to be spreading to some but not many more countries. Under international safeguards, it represents a significant economic incentive not to misuse it for military purposes. With inadequate or incomplete safeguards, it may entail an equally significant economic incentive to do just that. The concept of promoting international co-operation for nuclear energy development under safeguards will therefore continue to be a valuable non-proliferation tool. To be true, it does contribute to the spread of basic nuclear weapon capabilities. The point is, however, that it helps to keep these capabilities demilitarized.

The 1968 Non-Proliferation Treaty, which combines an economic entitlement with a military disclaimer in the field of nuclear technology, remains an indispensable framework for the time being.[47] But it cannot guarantee non-proliferation; it will not hold forever on its own; it needs to be bolstered and supplemented by additional policy instruments. If the number of states holding nuclear weapons is unlikely to decrease and even likely to increase, though perhaps slowly and marginally, the security of all will depend on the reconciliation of two opposite requirements: living with nuclear weapons while getting rid of them.

VI. Nuclear disarmament

Discussions about nuclear disarmament are often based on the erroneous assumption that what is at stake is simply the abolition of nuclear warheads by the five nuclear powers. If that were so, the price tag for nuclear disarmament would be easy to fix. It would cost little and save little. In reality, things are more complicated, and the issue of nuclear disarmament needs to be defined more thoroughly before the economic dimension can be assessed. Along this way, the abolition of nuclear arms shall first be dealt with as if it were an imminent policy option, leaving the question of practicality aside for later consideration.

The group of countries with a nuclearized security policy comprises more than the recognized nuclear weapon states. It includes all non-nuclear weapon

[46] For various aspects of this process see Potter, W. C. (ed.), *International Nuclear Trade and Nonproliferation: The Challenge of the Emerging Suppliers* (Lexington Books: Lexington, Mass., 1990); Mahnken, T. G. and Hoyt, T. D., 'The spread of missile technology to the Third World', *Comparative Strategy*, vol. 9, no. 3 (July 1990), pp. 245–63; Rosh, R. M., 'Third World arms production and the evolving interstate system', *Journal of Conflict Resolution*, vol. 34, no. 1 (Mar. 1990), pp. 57–73.

[47] Thompson, G., 'NPT review: Treaty a useful relic', *Bulletin of the Atomic Scientists*, vol. 46, no. 6 (July/Aug. 1990), pp. 32–33.

states that are allied in a mutual défence agreement, bilateral or multilateral, with the United States and the Soviet Union. While these states have renounced the possession of nuclear weapons as parties to the NPT they are, tacitly or explicitly, covered by the nuclear umbrella of one of the superpowers. Add to this the nuclear threshold states outside the NPT who have reserved the right to take recourse to nuclear weapons at their convenience, and the number of states with some sort of nuclearized national security policy stands at thirty.[48]

This group of nuclear and quasi-nuclear states makes up less than one-fifth of the international community of states. But it accounts for two-thirds of the world's population, three-fourths of world economic output and more than four fifths of world military expenditure.[49] It happens also to be largely identical with the group of countries possessing nuclear power plants and having, in principle, the capacity to manufacture nuclear weapons.[50]

Relations among this core group of states have been shaped and permeated by the nuclear factor for many years. Nuclear deterrence among just a handful of nuclear powers has served as a disciplining force among a much larger group of nations. Outside the nuclear or quasi-nuclear group, nuclear weapons have not prevented frequent war fighting, although they have probably contributed to the stability of the international system at large. Abolition of nuclear weapons would remove a fundamental pillar from the international hierarchy of states. Without an effective substitute in place, such abolition would be neither possible nor desirable to achieve.[51]

Costs and benefits of nuclear disarmament have to be judged by the same terms as nuclear armaments. What this means becomes clearer when one considers the technical side of nuclear armaments. Nuclear forces, as has been explained above, entail an elaborate array of equipment and capabilities in which the nuclear component, strictly defined, is a small though vital item in the full panoply of delivery systems and support structures, some of which are nuclear-specialized while others are dual-capable. For disarmament, then, it is inconceivable to do away with nuclear warheads only and leave the remainder of nuclear forces untouched. As a matter of fact, arms control and disarmament efforts have concentrated on the limitation, reduction or abolition of nuclear

---

[48] The formal dissolution of the Warsaw Pact in 1991 may have reduced this number by a handful of states, but the evolving transformation of the Soviet Union into a commonwealth of more or less independent states may again increase it by as many.

[49] Data according to standard reference works such as *World Bank Atlas 1990* (The World Bank: Washington, DC, 1989); SIPRI, *SIPRI Yearbook 1990: World Armaments and Disarmament* (Oxford University Press: Oxford, 1990); International Institute of Strategic Studies, *The Military Balance 1990–1991* (Brassey's: Oxford, 1990).

[50] For a recent survey of worldwide nuclear power capacities see 'International Data File', *IAEA News Features*, no. 8 (Sep. 1990), p. 1.

[51] For an elaboration of this argument see Häckel, E., 'Zukunftsaufgaben der internationalen Nuklearpolitik: Nichtverbreitung und Abrüstung von Kernwaffen in langfristiger Perspektive', eds C. Eisenbart and D. v. Ehrenstein, *Nichtverbreitung von Kernwaffen: Krise eines Konzepts* (FEST: Heidelberg, 1990), pp. 90–119. See also Waltz, K. N., 'Nuclear Myths and Political Realities', *American Political Science Review*, vol. 84, no. 3 (Sep. 1990), pp. 731–46.

delivery systems, leaving the grounded warheads out of consideration.[52] In the long run and in more ambitious disarmament schemes, nuclear warheads will of course have to be dealt with, too. But it makes sense to start with a step by step process which seeks first to immobilize nuclear weapons, thereby gradually reducing their war-fighting utility to the basic essentials of deterrence. As a side effect, often overlooked even among arms control experts, such a process can result in a significant limitation or reduction of conventional military capabilities bound up in dual-capable hardware.

Nuclear disarmament, in order to contribute to more international stability rather than less, has to satisfy several requirements at the same time. It must strike a balance between the interests of nuclear, quasi-nuclear and non-nuclear nations; between deterrent and war-fighting capabilities; and between nuclear and conventional weaponry; between the build-down of military means and the buildup of political instruments for international conflict resolution. Nuclear disarmament must take place in conjunction with non-nuclear disarmament, and it will not take place unless it is embedded in a co-operative security arrangement between the world's leading states. This is obviously a political rather than a military requisite. Disarmament results from peaceful accommodation among nations, not the other way around.

Seen in this way, nuclear disarmament is but one aspect of a far-reaching programme of international conciliation. There is a message here which contains good news and bad news. The good news is that the abolition of nuclear weapons, when it comes about, may entail enormous savings in military expenditure. The amount of savings is impossible to figure; it boggles the mind. Precisely because nuclear weapons make up only a small part of total armaments clustered around them, theirs is a multiplying effect. If nuclear arms are reduced and abolished, the volume of delivery systems, supporting structures, dual-purpose equipment and conventional weapons that must go with them is many times as large. Any amount saved by the disarmament of nuclear warheads may involve a manifold amount saved by associated arms reductions.

Naturally, there are also costs involved in disarmament, and they are not negligible. The dismantling and disposal of weapons (including nuclear warhead material such as plutonium, high-enriched uranium and tritium) and of weapon production or maintenance facilities, the safeguarding and verification of disarmament treaty compliance, the conversion of military plant and personnel to civilian purposes all require expenses that may run as high as the original costs of armament—witness the as-yet-untold billions of dollar expenditure incurred by US–Soviet agreements on chemical and nuclear (INF) disarmament in the late 1980s. But they are only a temporary burden, most of

---

[52] This has been the case with the SALT I and II, ABM, INF and START agreements. In the INF case, the first treaty between the superpowers to abolish completely a class of nuclear delivery systems (ground-based ballistic and cruise missiles in the 500–5000 kilometer range), it is significant to recall that the two parties insisted on having a non-nuclear third party, the Federal Republic of Germany, also abolish its equivalent missiles (Pershing 1A) *without* nuclear warheads.

which would have fallen on the national budgets anyway (even without disarmament agreements) at a later stage.

Possible savings from nuclear disarmament accrue not to the nuclear powers alone. Abolition of nuclear-capable delivery systems in allied countries without nuclear weapons of their own must be added to the account. Furthermore, if disarmament by the nuclear powers is agreed by mutual consent not to work to their disadvantage in relation to non-nuclear powers, it follows that the latter have an obligation to make an equivalent disarmament contribution from their conventional weapon stocks. Under these circumstances, the abolition of nuclear warheads by nuclear weapon powers is bound to have a multiple ripple effect of disarmament throughout the international system. Relatively modest savings in the core area of nuclear armed forces may in the end add up to a huge 'peace dividend' of capital and productive capacity, released from the military budgets to the benefit of the entire world economy.

There, then, is the good news. The bad news is that the 'peace dividend' is a dividend flowing from peace and from nothing else. Everybody loves peace, but how is that happy state to be brought about? Surely not by nuclear disarmament. Political preconditions for the abolition of nuclear arms are so demanding that they may appear to be wholly impossible to fulfil. If nations first have to agree among themselves about their mutual security interests, how can nuclear disarmament ever arrive? Once they have agreed, what additional security gains can be derived from nuclear disarmament? Is nuclear deterrence indispensable so long and just as long as nuclear disarmament is held to be unachievable?

Put in the stark terms of all-or-nothing, the quest for nuclear disarmament may indeed be a moot question. However, the way that might lead to non-nuclear security is not a leap but a process. The process allows for intermediate stages, gradual adjustments and partial accomplishments between dependence on nuclear weapons and their abolition. If abolition is regarded as unfeasible without global peace, nuclear weapons are here to stay. And yet, arms control and disarmament can go a long way towards non-nuclear security. The role of nuclear weapons can be diminished to such an extent as to become more and more irrelevant.

There are several possible ways to this end. Nuclear weapons may be removed from an increasing number of military uses. They may be excluded from an increasing number of states, territories, regions, geographical locations, functional deployments or designations. Possession, use or control of nuclear weapons may be legally circumscribed, restrained, limited or prohibited. Each of these methods has already been employed at various times and in different places. They contribute not to the total abolition of nuclear weapons everywhere but to their gradual containment or displacement in a variety of conflict situations. To the extent that such methods are increasingly employed, nuclear weapons will be more and more restricted in their application. At the same time, areas of non-nuclear security become more expansive. Nuclearized security systems are in this process not completely discarded or fully dismantled. But they can be incrementally reduced, replaced or superseded by alternative security arrangements. What is important, then, is not the very existence of nuclear weapons but their ascribed security relevance.

Recent developments in Europe illustrate this point. With the cold war officially declared over in 1990, nuclear weapons are still present throughout Europe. But they have lost their central relevance for security. European security now rests largely on a process of political accommodation among formerly hostile governments. In the process, a continuous move towards disarmament, both nuclear *and* conventional, has set in. While it will not lead to the complete denuclearization of Europe, the role of nuclear weapons is likely to recede further as European security becomes less dependent on military means of coercion and deterrence.

Nuclear disarmament must be understood not as the cause but as a corollary to the development of peaceful relations among states. Here the economic balance again comes to the fore. When the competitive performance of national economies becomes more important than military might as a measure of international status and influence, nations with a heavy military burden are likely to find themselves at a growing disadvantage compared to nations without. In such a situation, the economic imperative may act as a powerful motivation for disarmament. The Soviet Union today presents the obvious case of a military superpower whose national security is threatened by economic decline more than by anything else. There, a decreased emphasis on military security will most likely entail a reduced reliance on its nuclear component. But again, whatever benefits may result from disarmament, the nuclear component alone can make only a modest contribution.

If there is an economic incentive for disarmament there is at the same time a built-in factor retarding nuclear disarmament. Any nation's economic performance is today predicated on the basic stability of its international environment. Nuclear deterrence among the great powers, regardless of all its questionable aspects, contributes to the stabilization of the world system probably more than any other kind of military posture. The benefit of this becomes more evident at the margin. Once the role of nuclear weapons has been reduced to the bare minimum of deterrence (whatever that may be), any further reduction could imply the loss of the most powerful safeguard of international discipline. As long as nations are set on the prevention of war by military means, nuclear deterrence is likely to remain the most efficient underpinning of order and collaboration among sovereign states. The cost of nuclear weapons, in this way, can be seen as an insurance premium for international economic security. But, of course, this is a kind of insurance policy without reinsurance.

VII. Conclusion

An economic analysis of nuclear weapon policy can refine our understanding of security in several ways. It provides objective criteria to measure material requirements, inputs and outlays connected with the calculus of nuclear armaments. Assumptions about nuclear forces which are often based on scant knowledge and putative reasoning can be put to the test of empirical evidence. More important, however, than the necessarily imperfect precision of quantitative measurements is the contribution of economic rationality to a demystified conception of nuclear security. To define nuclear security in terms of costs, benefits and requisites distributed unevenly among unequals highlights the political nature of nuclear choices in a game of power where anticipated gains are derived from the control over competitive rules and resources.[53]

The economics of nuclear weapons are as intricate and inconclusive as the logic of nuclear security. Considerations of costs and benefits abound in nuclear thinking, but the balance remains unsettled. The case for nuclear weapons as a mainstay of national security has been made in the affirmative by a few countries only, but their persistent adherence to nuclear armaments shows that the economic burden was found to be tolerable. An analysis of military expenditures of the nuclear powers confirms that the costs of nuclear weapons, while difficult to establish in precise terms and certainly large in absolute amounts, do not weigh heavily in national defence budgets. All nuclear powers have devoted only a minor share of their military expenditure to nuclear armaments, and within this share nuclear weapons in the strict sense again constitute only a minor portion as compared to delivery systems and support structures. The military effort of all nuclear powers has always remained largely a non-nuclear one. The utility of their nuclear weapons was controversial from the outset; it is seen increasingly as being limited to the deterrence of rival nuclear powers. Nuclear weapons are therefore not a substitute for conventional military capabilities. A nuclear weapon state with great power ambitions will always have to carry the additional burden of more expensive non-nuclear armaments.

The experience of nuclear weapon states has an ambivalent bearing on the prospects for nuclear proliferation. With a basic nuclear weapon capability becoming increasingly attainable and affordable for a growing number of countries, there seems to be an imminent danger of nuclearized arms races spreading throughout the world. On the other hand, the limited utility of nuclear weapons, the increasing possibility to substitute them and the continuing necessity to complement them with non-nuclear armaments all tend to work against runaway proliferation. More likely is the acquisition of nuclear weapons by a relatively small number of threshold states with the capacity to make efficient use of the composite nature of a full-fledged nuclear force.

---

[53] For a classic interpretation of the distributive concept of power see Lasswell, H., *Politics: Who gets What, When, How* (McGraw-Hill: New York, 1936).

Nuclear disarmament, then, is a process which entails more than the abolition of nuclear weapons. Its potential for financial savings and economic gains may be enormous. However, it can succeed only within a comprehensive security arrangement encompassing nuclear and non-nuclear arms reductions in nuclear and non-nuclear states together. Even then, a residual capacity for nuclear deterrence may continue to be more cost-effective as a contribution to international stability than any other military means.

Within the international system of states, there is more to the distributive effect of nuclear weapons than meets the eye at first sight. Nuclear powers obviously bear most of the cost of nuclear armaments, but not all of it. Non-nuclear weapon states share some of the total cost and bear a considerable part of the total risk of nuclear armaments. At the same time, the nuclear powers reap most of the benefits of nuclear deterrence, but not alone for themselves. To the extent that nuclear deterrence helps stabilize relations among the great powers, non-nuclear states also gain from the collective advantage of international order and accommodation.

All things taken together, the attempt to assess nuclear armaments in terms of costs and benefits comes full circle to return to the basics of international politics. Disagreement about nuclear weapons is not really about nuclear weapons. It is about what makes for peace, order and security in a world of nation-states. If power, unequal status and a modicum of intimidation among states are accepted as inevitable ingredients of international stability, the persistence of nuclear weapons is the price to pay. To the extent only that these conditions will be overcome can security without nuclear weapons be attained.

4. Legal issues concerning the feasibility of nuclear weapon elimination

Julie Dahlitz

I. The relevance of international law

Nuclear weapons are the most deadly, the most accurate and the most versatile weapons, representing the most potent threat of force and the most feared projection of power. Control over the horizontal and vertical spread of these weapons represents the highest achievement of arms control. The elimination of all nuclear weapons would be the most significant stage along a continuum of the arms control process, which includes prohibitions on the manufacture, testing and deployment of these weapons.

Arms control is not possible without international law. Provided our civilization is not destroyed in the meantime, total elimination of nuclear weapons will only be feasible when a highly developed international legal system exists; when other weapons also will be under strict control; when there will be confidence that agreements regarding such control will be observed; when matters relating to observance, including the interpretation of treaties and verification, can be conducted in a co-operative framework with efficiency; and when international disputes can be settled by non-military means. International law will also be needed in a perfected form in order to create an international climate of amity that would reinforce the political will to reduce the number of nuclear weapons, eventually to zero.

In theory, the elimination of all nuclear weapons could be achieved without the input of international law *if* the following conditions were to apply—if everyone, without exception, who is capable of influencing the outcome were committed to the total abolition of nuclear weapons and if that was to remain the position into the future. However, as the experts in the strategic and political fields do not foresee an automatic transformation of that type but, on the contrary, anticipate a gradual inching toward the prohibition of all nuclear weapons, in the face of opposition and the constant possibility of cheating—at least during the earlier phases of the reduction process[1]—international law represents the only known method for the co-ordination of nuclear weapon elimination.[2]

[1] Reluctance to halt and reverse the vertical nuclear arms race is amply demonstrated by current stocks. See SIPRI, *SIPRI Yearbook 1991: World Armaments and Disarmament* (Oxford University Press: Oxford, 1991), chapters 1 and 2; International Institute for Strategic Studies, *The Military Balance 1990–1991* (Brassey's: Oxford, 1990), pp. 216–24.

[2] Flowerree, C. C., 'On tending arms control agreements', *Washington Quarterly*, vol. 13, no. 1 (winter 1990), pp. 199–214.

International law, in this context, comprises the words that express a series of prohibitions which, acting together, will result in first reducing and later eliminating nuclear weapons. It is also the law which lays down the methods by which the prohibitions are put in place and later applied. Those prohibitions include matters such as non-manufacture, curbs on testing and deployment, directives for dismantling and destruction of weapons and weapons facilities, supervision of non-diversion of radioactive substances, and restrictions on delivery vehicles, as well as guidance and triggering mechanisms. Only international law can prescribe who is bound by those limitations—namely which states and successors of states, supra-national organizations, natural and legal persons within states and stateless persons. It is via international law that arrangements have to be made to monitor the performance of the agreed acts and prohibitions, decisions reached as to how disputes are to be settled, and by what means the agreements may be altered as the need for changing them may arises from time to time.

All of these agreements and procedures have to be arrived at in a manner that is universally accepted to be authoritative, such as at a plenipotentiary conference, and thus have to be presented in a form regarded as binding, preferably in a treaty duly signed and ratified. There also has to be the expectation that the treaties will survive and that they will continue to be interpreted and applied as originally contemplated or in harmony with some other, continuously acceptable formula. The above indispensable functions of international law in connection with the elimination of nuclear weapons would also presuppose the existence of an overall system of law in which these functions have a meaning. For instance, it is necessary to have a common understanding as to what is a state, what is a 'binding' agreement among them, how the citizens of states may communicate efficiently in the confident knowledge that they are addressing the appropriate representative of other states, and so forth.

Currently, it has become fashionable to regard 'verification' as the most important aspect of arms reduction. The fundamental question is, however, what it is that is to be verified—that is precisely what agreement, among whom and with what consequences? Appraising verification in isolation is like asserting that the most important thing to sustain life is to breathe, without reference to the nature of the gas that is to be breathed.

The everyday unobtrusiveness of international law tends to obscure its pervasive presence, and it is only in conditions of special stress that the inevitable reliance upon it becomes apparent. Attempts to limit weapons create such stress situations. The total elimination of nuclear weapons and every step of the process leading up to that condition would test the quality and adaptability of international law. Furthermore, the transformation of international law in a manner that could facilitate the achievement of a nuclear weapon-free world could not come about automatically or as a natural and effortless evolution. It could only occur as the result of concerted, systematic endeavour. The quality and dimensions of that task will become more evident after consideration of the precise role of international law in the arms control and disarmament process.

II. The role of international law

Public international law is the system used for designating the rights and duties of states in relation to each other and for overseeing the manner in which those rights are exercised and those duties observed. The system manifests itself in international law—as in all law—by one of two 'modes' of exerting influence, to be referred to as 'Mode A' and 'Mode B' in this chapter.[3]

Mode A is the expression of norms, namely the standards of conduct to be followed, in the form of laws. The notion that law 'establishes' norms is medieaval shorthand. Norms are agreed upon by decision makers and are *presented in the form of laws,* which acquire their authority from those who made them and those who accept them. In international law, the norms can be embodied in the form of treaties, several other types of explicit undertakings, tacit agreements, and implied rights and duties.

Mode B is the exertion of influence by use of a *legal methodology* regarding the creation of norms and the ways of applying them. This includes the manner in which a state may signal its commitment to be bound or the wish to be absolved from a duty to other states, as well as procedures to encourage other states to observe their commitments. The methodology involves: treaty-making procedures; the creation of customary rules; the invention of various other types of commitment, such as resolutions; unilateral statements; and politically binding commitments. Also included in this mode of influence are: the methods of adjudication; arbitration; rules regarding implementation; and measures to ensure observance of the norms.

On the basis of the foregoing summary it can be seen that international law is a socially created tool for achieving certain desired purposes. The tool cannot achieve anything in itself, including the abolition of nuclear weapons. It is equally evident that, if it is sought to abolish nuclear weapons, it is the legal tool that has to be utilized in both modes. At present, international law is not sufficiently developed to sustain the implementation of such an intent. Hence, the further development of international law would be an indispensable concomitant of a process that would eliminate all nuclear weapons and ensure the effectiveness of non-nuclear weapon security.

In order to be effective, the law would have to make a suitable impact in three areas, which will be referred to as the 'legal impact points' in this chapter. Improvements at each of the impact points are needed, as follows:

---

[3] Modes A and B are usually referred to merely as 'norms' and 'legal method', respectively, but the presentation used in this chapter seeks to give greater emphasis for the benefit of non-lawyers. For further reading see Morris, J. H. C., *The Conflict of Laws*, 3rd. edn (Stevens and Sons: London, 1984); Dixon, M., *Textbook on International Law* (Blackstone Press Ltd: London, 1990).

1. Treaty law would have to be improved so as to facilitate the elimination of existing nuclear weapons, the prohibition of their replacement and prevention of the development of comparable new weapons.

2. A universal international regime is needed within the framework of which the prohibition of nuclear weapons and all other weapons of mass destruction could be accomplished effectively.

3. Mechanisms containing elements of compulsion for the peaceful settlement of international disputes, including those involving the supreme security interests of states, have to be created so as to obviate the need for the threat or use of strategic force.

III. The measurement of legal feasibility

A comparison of the current state of international law as it relates to nuclear weapons (in its two modes, at the three main impact points), together with an estimation of what would be required so as to transform it into a suitable tool for the total elimination of nuclear weapons, will indicate the extent of the changes required. On that basis, the feasibility of those changes—leading to the objective of a secure world without nuclear weapons—might be assessed. In this assessment, 'international security' will be taken into account, both from the viewpoint of the state and of the individual. With regard to the state, international security is understood to mean territorial integrity and political independence. With regard to the individual, it consists of all the things essential for well-being, in the absence of any danger that they will be taken or destroyed—excepting unpreventable natural processes. With respect to both the state view and the individual view, it is recognized that there are various degrees of security.

While international law in itself cannot provide either type of security, it is instrumental in the creation of both state and individual security. For example, in the absence of the United Nations and its agencies,[4] all established pursuant to treaties, we would be much less secure in both respects. Nevertheless, the impossibility of achieving a desired result by exclusively legal means is also easily illustrated. From the strictly legal point of view, the prohibition of all nuclear weapons could take the form of a simple prohibition, such as the prohibition to station nuclear weapons in outer space, as provided by the 1967 Outer Space Treaty, or the prohibition of nuclear weapons in the Antarctic, as provided by the 1959 Antarctic Treaty. Alternatively, it could be a very detailed treaty concerning the manner in which the prohibition is to take effect, adverting to procedures for destruction, non-development, exchange of data, verification, settlement of disputes, compliance measures, and so on, in the manner of the 1987 INF Treaty. Taking a formalistic approach, it is true that either approach would be immediately feasible. If we further postulate that the states of the world would be prepared to conclude such a treaty, the question

[4] *The United Nations at Forty: A Foundation to Build on* (United Nations: New York, 1985).

becomes whether they could rely on its observance on the basis of its legal status alone. At present, the unequivocal answer is in the negative. That is not because international law lacks authority. Here it is noteworthy that, since the end of World War II, no state has withdrawn from an arms control treaty of any kind—not even on permissible grounds—following ratification or accession. International law has authority, but not absolute, unconditional authority.

The authority of the law, including international law, is the outcome of the interaction of many factors, as this chapter amplifies in connection with the relationship between law and force. It follows that the legal innovations could not be implemented on their own in the absence of other necessary factors, so as to precede nuclear disarmament. Nor, as noted above, is it possible to achieve nuclear disarmament in the absence of an adequate legal base, to be followed by legal adjustments. Thus, the process has to be *an integrated sequence*. The sequential progression towards nuclear disarmament will also have to contain other types of international development, including further economic co-operation, heightened cultural interchange and, most importantly, an evolution in global psychology and self-perception. There has to be simultaneous progress in all those areas. For example, international law can provide mechanisms for the settlement of international disputes. It cannot overcome entrenched aggressiveness, which can only be quelled by countervailing threats. However, aggressiveness as a motivating force can be overcome by societal norms of behaviour and the channelling of aggressive impulses into socially useful outlets for the performance of dangerous and exacting tasks.

In view of the foregoing, when assessing the feasibility of a nuclear weapon-free world, it is not useful to think in terms of time-frames but rather in terms of 'sequential order' of advancement. The sequences could occur quite rapidly, precipitated by catastrophic events, or their timely anticipation in society, and by the input of exceptional individuals. In planning for the part to be played by international law, it is essential to recognize the limits of what law can accomplish. This will provide the pre-conditions for the most rapid progress possible of arms control and disarmament-related law, avoiding detours that have to be abandoned. For instance, the overly ambitious role assigned to the International Court of Justice (ICJ)[5] has been a major hindrance to the development of international law relating to international security.

Those who assert that nuclear weapons having been invented, a nuclear weapon-free world will never be possible, are victims of the little boy/grandfather misconception: 'When grandfather was a little boy like me, he must have looked very strange with his white beard'. The boy's fallacy is easy to perceive, yet in discourse about the feasibility of eliminating all nuclear weapons, a similar error is mostly tolerated. In essence, it amounts to failure to confront the proposition that the world in which nuclear weapons can be totally eliminated without jeopardizing international security will be a substantially

[5] Damrosch, L. F. (ed.), *The International Court of Justice at the Crossroads* (Transnational Publishers: Dobbs Ferry, N.Y., 1987).

different world than the one we know today. Not only will there be different international law and a different international security 'regime'—there will also be a new international security 'climate'.

Unlike the process of human growth and ageing, the changes needed to accommodate a nuclear weapon-free world can be accelerated at will, provided they are undertaken in a concurrent and integrated manner. This chapter is concerned with the legal aspects of the necessary changes, on the understanding that those changes can only occur in tandem with other changes. The further development of international law will be presented by an overview of the present state of the law, followed by what could be the 'first wave' of legal input in an integrated movement forward and then the 'last wave' of input. No doubt, there could be intermediate moves forward but the first and last will be sufficient to provide a general perspective. While it is useful to contemplate what the last wave might look like, it is the first wave of input that is most important—partly because it is essential in order to carry the process forward and partly because it would greatly add to international security even in the short term.[6]

By tailoring international law so as to make minimum nuclear deterrence on a co-operative basis possible,[7] the law will be moving to a stage where it can accommodate a nuclear weapon-free world. The requirements for that ultimate situation will be a natural progression along the path that can accomplish massive arms cuts, together with a freeze on circumvention. Furthermore, only as the path of nuclear weapon reductions and prohibitions is pursued will the next steps to be taken become clear. This applies to both legal modes at each of the three impact points.

Certainly from a legal aspect, there is no disharmony between the end objective and every step that leads to it. The notion that partial limitations on nuclear weapons could be inimical to ultimate denuclearization stems for the misconception that nuclear weapons could be 'legitimized'. There are two reasons why this could not occur. First, as noted above, there are limits to the authority of international law—it cannot go counter to the overall consensus of states. If states wished to divest themselves of something as horrible and dangerous as nuclear weapons, then even the most explicit treaty purporting to legitimize them into endless posterity would be overturned in some way. Secondly, treaties only bind the parties to them and, in addition, those treaties can be amended or abandoned by consent.

Admittedly, there is a theoretical argument that a treaty limiting nuclear weapons could become customary international law,[8] creating a universal regime entrenching the provisions of that treaty. This is an aspect of the theory of international law that is entirely unsuited to the arms control and disarmament process. Incidentally, the theory of the continuous creation of customary

[6] Iklé, F. C., 'Behind the diplomacy, it's still a nuclear standoff', *International Herald Tribune*, 28 June 1990, p. 6. Iklé was Undersecretary of Defense during the Reagan Administration.

[7] Dahlitz, J., *Co-operative Deterrence: A Bridging Strategy* (International Peace Research Institute, Oslo: Oslo, 1989).

international law is probably unsuited to other areas of public international law as well. In practice, this theory causes less problems than might be feared and is, for example, virtually never referred to in the context of commercial treaties. It is reassuring to note that no state has ever maintained that partial limitations on the development, testing and deployment of nuclear weapons should be interpreted so as to prohibit their further reduction and limitation.[9] Hence, the claim of inadvertent 'legitimation' of nuclear weapons is not a realistic concern but a deliberately misleading disorientation, intended to inhibit feasible measures to reduce and, eventually, to eliminate nuclear weapons.

IV. The relationship between law and force

As we have noted, the authority of the law stems from many factors. Foremost among them is that it constitutes a clear and accessible statement of relevant norms; that it is the pronouncement of a person or body perceived to be one that should be obeyed—usually having the means to punish transgression; that it conforms to the prevailing standards of justice; and buttresses established relationships and procedures.

International law is said to derive its ultimate authority from 'custom'.[10] If one is prepared to examine this notion more closely, some original motivations can be surmised. For instance, it has been established by custom to conclude and to observe peace treaties. While not explicitly stated, the expectation was, however, that the treaties would only be observed for some years or decades at most. Peace treaties, as well as the procedures for interpreting and applying them, were tolerant of loopholes and other imperfections, affording opportunities to abandon them when convenient. This suited states bent on territorial conquest which, nevertheless, wanted periods of respite for recovery and consolidation. Ian Brownlie puts the situation succinctly when he writes that, 'Treaties of peace are *presumably* not open to unilateral denunciation'.[11] These lackadaisical methods for ensuring international security are no longer suitable. In order to bring international law into line with the requirements of nuclear weapon elimination, it would be desirable not only to conclude new treaties but also to reformulate the theoretical structure of the law so as to conform with its contemporary functions.

It is still the prevailing belief that, in international relations, the law has no teeth because there is no effective enforcement agency, the United Nations having played only a modest part in peacekeeping and treaty enforcement. Yet, as the lethality of weapons increases, the underlying motivation to observe *a*

[8] Brownlie, I., *Principles of Public International Law*, 4th edn (Clarendon Press: Oxford, 1990), pp. 4–15.

[9] It is partly out of a concern about 'legitimation' that the following objective is often included in the preamble of arms control treaties: 'general and complete disarmament under strict international control'.

[10] Chiu, H., 'Chinese view on the sources of international law', *Harvard International Law Journal*, vol. 28, no. 2 (spring 1987), pp. 289–307; Contra: Tunkin, G. I., *Theory of International Law* (Harvard University Press: Cambridge, Mass., 1974).

[11] Brownlie (note 8), p. 617 [emphasis added].

system of law that can lessen or remove that threat grows proportionately. Hence, without the introduction of any new system of punitive sanctions for breach or abandonment of security-related treaties, their authority has greatly increased. The same would still apply in the absence of nuclear weapons, if the alternative would carry the danger of their resurgence.

There is likely to be a growing recognition that the system of arms control legality—that is to say, the operation of Mode B in the limitation and elimination of weapons—needs to be restructured for the attainment of the desired effectiveness of envisaged arms control measures. It is the actual or latent threat of 'nuclear-armed chaos' which acts as the sanction and which will give the treaties (under Mode A of exerting legal influence) greatly enhanced authority. So far, international law has developed in an environment of opposing imminent threats. This has been most relevant in the shaping of the law regarding security based on mutually agreed restraint. How legal theory and method could be modified so as to fully respond to the sanction of an overall latent threat, without the immediate threat of opposing forces, is a matter for conjecture.

Before this question can be usefully confronted in any detail, it should be asked whether the law is adequate in the present condition of the alignment of forces, being the genocidal threat of weapons of mass destruction controlled by politically competing governments that are, nevertheless, fearful of unintended consequences of their actions. What we find is that, although states increasingly wish to make truly binding and reliable arms control commitments, international law as it relates to international security has not kept pace with those desires for accommodation.

The changes in international law postulated in the following comparisons could only occur as the result of very deliberate effort. A commitment to take the envisaged disarmament steps would entail one kind of determination. Perhaps even more difficult would be the undertaking to alter the theory and practice of international law,[12] not only in an accustomed, leisurely mode, like codifying customary law, but with a view to restructuring the law fundamentally. That will run counter to the training in which all lawyers are steeped. It will be necessary to overcome the mystique of the law, without diminishing the respect accorded to it, partly on that account. When undertaking the following steps it will be essential to retain the majesty of the law, however, not so much in reverence of its great past but more in recognition of its pivotal role for the future.

V. The current situation

An assessment of the legal feasibility of the elimination of all nuclear weapons, if it is to be more than idle guesswork, can best be achieved by an appraisal of

[12] Schachter, O., 'Towards a theory of international obligation', *The Effectiveness of International Decisions*, Proceedings of the Conference of the American Society of International Law (Oceana: Dobbs Ferry, N.Y., 1971).

the current situation compared with the remaining steps to be taken and bearing in mind the intermediary processes involved. Regarding Mode A, in relation to agreed norms operating at the first impact point—dealing with treaty law to eliminate nuclear weapons—there has been a substantial development of the law since the weapons became technically available. Nevertheless, even cumulatively, the treaty provisions fall far short of a global abolition of nuclear weapons.[13] Yet, from a legal standpoint, these norms could be easily extended so as to encompass far wider prohibitions. For example, nuclear tests are forbidden in all environments, except underground. That exception could be removed. Furthermore, the stationing of nuclear weapons is prohibited anywhere in outer space and in several nuclear weapon-free zones, including the whole of Antarctica. Stationing could be prohibited anywhere beyond state borders. The overwhelming majority of states have undertaken not to create or acquire nuclear weapons. Further creation or acquisition could be prohibited for all states.

In their present form, the above-mentioned treaty provisions have all been honoured to a remarkable degree of compliance—even by states not parties to the treaties. The worst hiatus in compliance issues has been the failure of the nuclear weapon states (NWS) to reverse the nuclear arms race, as inferentially undertaken under the terms of the 1963 Partial Test Ban Treaty (PTBT) and the 1968 Non-Proliferation Treaty (NPT). However, these undertakings were formulated in a vague and non-specific manner, so it is difficult to pin-point which state is the culprit and exactly when the breaches occurred. The most specific wording is to be found in Article VI of the PTBT: 'Each of the Parties to the Treaty undertakes to pursue negotiations in good faith on effective measures relating to cessation of the nuclear arms race at an early date and to nuclear disarmament, and on a treaty on general and complete disarmament under strict and effective international control'.[14] It can be validly argued that, on the one hand, negotiations have continued 'relating' to the cessation of the arms race as required and, on the other hand, that *no* state is ready to negotiate a treaty on general and complete disarmament.

Currently, the following substantive treaty provisions to curb nuclear weapons operate among the parties to those agreements (see tables 4.1 and 4.2).

Regarding multilateral treaties, namely treaties made among three or more parties, the earliest treaty mentioned—the Statute of the International Atomic Energy Agency (IAEA)—contains the attributes most suitable to serve as a blueprint for future agreements for the drastic reduction and the eventual elimination of nuclear weapons. This statute is a treaty only marginally concerned with nuclear weapons curtailment—it prohibits the diversion of nuclear materials and equipment supplied under the auspices of the Agency. However,

---

[13] Ipsen, K., 'A nuclear-weapon-free world: legal problems', Paper presented at the 40th Pugwash Conference on Science and World Affairs, Egham, UK, 15–20 Sep. 1990, p. 15.

[14] Reprinted in Goldblat, J., SIPRI, *Arms Control Agreements: A Critical Survey* (Taylor & Francis: London, 1982), p. 173.

Table 4.1. Multilateral treaties relevant to nuclear weapons

Treaty	Entered into force
Statute of the International Atomic Energy Agency (IAEA)	29 July 1957
Antarctic Treaty	23 June 1961
Treaty banning nuclear weapon tests in the atmosphere, in outer space and under water (Partial Test Ban Treaty)	10 Oct. 1963
Treaty on principles governing the activities of states in the exploration and use of outer space, including the moon, and other celestial bodies (Outer Space Treaty)	10 Oct. 1967
Treaty for the prohibition of nuclear weapons in Latin America (Treaty of Tlatelolco)	22 Apr. 1968
Treaty on the non-proliferation of nuclear weapons (NPT)	5 Mar. 1970
Treaty on the prohibition of the emplacement of nuclear weapons and other weapons of mass destruction on the sea-bed and the ocean floor and in the sub-soil thereof (Sea-Bed Treaty)	18 May 1972
Convention on the physical protection of nuclear material (Nuclear Material Convention)	8 Feb. 1987
Convention on the prohibition of military or any other hostile use of environmental modification techniques (ENMOD Convention)	5 Oct. 1978

Sources: Compiled by author from original sources.

the efficiency of the legal machinery provisions of this treaty have turned it into a suitable instrument for giving effect to the NPT with its far wider impact.

Regarding bilateral treaties, the 1987 Treaty between the USA and the USSR on the elimination of their intermediate-range and shorter-range missiles (the INF Treaty)[15] contains legal machinery features suitable for emulation in the further limitation and elimination of nuclear weapons held by the two super-powers. For instance, the INF Treaty serves as an invaluable precedent at the current negotiations for a strategic arms reduction (START) treaty, and may also serve as a prototype for reduction and elimination treaties among the other NWS.

Whereas the INF and START treaty texts and regulations made under them will contain many detailed duties and prohibitions to be adhered to by the parties—all of them prone to lead to disputes—these are bound to be relatively minor disputes amenable to rapid solution. Such an approach is to be preferred to broad generalization, more easily agreed upon but predictably leading to future major uncertainties.[16]

Extensive headway has also been made regarding the second impact point under Mode A, namely the establishment of an international regime that would facilitate the elimination of all nuclear weapons. The cornerstone of that regime

[15] The INF Treaty includes: (*a*) Treaty articles; (*b*) Memorandum of Understanding regarding the establishment of the data base for the Treaty; (*c*) Protocol on procedures governing the elimination of the missile systems subject to the Treaty; and (*d*) Protocol regarding inspections relating to the Treaty. The text of the 1987 INF Treaty, including protocols, is reprinted in SIPRI, *SIPRI Yearbook 1988: World Armaments and Disarmament* (Oxford University Press: Oxford, 1988), pp. 395–489.

[16] For example, 'broad' and 'narrow' interpretations of the 1972 ABM Treaty.

Table 4.2. Bilateral (US–Soviet) treaties relevant to nuclear weapons

Treaty	Entered into force
USA–USSR Memorandum of understanding regarding the establishment of a Standing Consultative Commission (SCC Agreement)	21 Dec. 1972
Interim Agreement on certain measures with respect to the limitation of strategic offensive arms (SALT I)	3 Oct. 1972[a]
Treaty on the limitation of Anti-Ballistic Missile systems (ABM Treaty)	3 Oct. 1972
Treaty on the Limitation of underground nuclear weapon tests (TTBT)	not in force[b]
Treaty on underground nuclear explosions for peaceful purposes (PNET)	not in force[c]
USA–USSR Treaty on the Limitation of Strategic Offensive Arms (with Protocol, Memorandum of Understanding, and Joint Statement) (SALT II Treaty)	not in force[d]
Memorandum of Understanding on the USA–USSR Direct Communications Link ('Hot Line' Expansion Agreement)	17 July 1984
Agreement on the establishment of Nuclear Risk Reduction Centres (Risk Reduction Centres Agreement)	15 Sep. 1987
Treaty between the USA and the USSR on the elimination of their intermediate-range and shorter-range missiles (INF Treaty)	1 June 1988
START RV (Re-entry) vehicle inspection agreement	29 Jan. 1990[e]
US–Soviet Joint Statement on the Missile Technology Control Regime (MTCR)[f]	4 June 1990[g]
Strategic Arms Reduction Talks (START) Treaty	under negotiation[h]
Defence and Space Treaty (DST)	under negotiation[h]

[a] Currently expired.

[b] The TTBT was signed on 3 July 1974. In October 1990 the US Senate recommended ratification of the treaty. The USSR is also reportedly ready to ratify the treaty.

[c] The PNET was signed on 28 May 1976. In October 1990 the US Senate recommended ratification of the treaty. The USSR is also reportedly ready to ratify the treaty.

[d] Although not in force, the SALT II Treaty is still partially observed..

[e] Date of signature.

[f] See US Arms Control and Disarmament Agency, *Joint Statement on Non-Proliferation*, Official text (US ACDA: Washington, DC, 4 June 1990); and Navias, M., *Ballistic missile proliferation in the Third World*, Adelphi Papers no. 252 (Brassey's for International Institute of Strategic Studies: London, summer 1990), pp. 47–61.

[g] Date the US–Soviet Joint Statement was confirmed.

[h] As of 1990, the Strategic Arms Reduction Treaty (START) and a Defence and Space Treaty (DST) are still under negotiation and there are considerable differences between the positions adopted by the two sides. See US Arms Control and Disarmament Agency, *Nuclear and Space Talks: US and Soviet Proposals*, Issues Brief (US ACDA: Washington, DC, 3 July 1990).

Sources: Compiled by author from original sources.

is the United Nations, whose potential is habitually underestimated as a result of its relatively modest achievements during the period of the cold war. Nevertheless, the legal basis and structure of that organization, founded under the treaty known as the United Nations Charter, is suitable for executing the most demanding arms control measures, including fact-finding, adjudication and compliance measures, as well as enforcing the will of the great majority against a few states that may attempt to hold the rest of the world to ransom.

The United Nations is a superb vehicle of international law that has been driven by novices in survival skills. There are good prospects that a new generation, sharing a global outlook, could utilize the basic structure of the organization—with the addition of new committees and greatly extended functions of the Security Council[17]—so as to gradually and in an uneventful manner, arrive at an international regime not far removed from world government in matters of international security. This, in fact, was the intention of many who inspired the founding of the organization. The failures of the United Nations during its first half-century of operation bears out the contention, advanced above, that international law and the structures founded upon it can only be applied effectively in an appropriate international climate. For present purposes, broadly speaking, the legal machinery of the United Nations is sound.

Other bodies that play a fundamental role in the endeavour to create a regime outlawing nuclear weapons, are the permanent bodies created by arms control treaties. In the multilateral sphere, the most notable of these are the International Atomic Energy Agency (IAEA) and the Agency for the Prohibition of Nuclear Weapons in Latin America (OPANAL). In the bilateral sphere, the Standing Consultative Commission established by the SALT I/ ABM Treaties of 1972,[18] has many features for continued bilateral and also, eventually, multilateral applications which could make a profound impact on more co-operative treaty interpretation, application and continuous review.

With the exception of numerous low-key peacekeeping activities, the organization of military constraint under the auspices of the United Nations has been a fiasco, exemplified by the dormant condition of the Military Staff Committee (MSC). Yet, comparable experience in military co-operation among diverse states has occurred within the framework of NATO and the WTO (Warsaw Treaty Organization), although not on a universal basis. Nevertheless, the extensive experience gained of legal mechanisms for concerted military organization, notwithstanding sovereign diversity, could be readily utilized in a comparable body with universal membership—or several bodies linked in a common endeavour with suitable organizational connections. A precursor of such development may happen fairly soon in a new nexus between NATO and WTO leaderships in Europe. Thus, much of the legal machinery for organizing military co-operation that would facilitate extensive nuclear disarmament is already in place, albeit in a non-integrated form.

The third impact point, whereby international law is crucial for creating an international milieu in which the elimination of nuclear weapons would be possible, concerns the perfection of a smoothly functioning system for the settlement of international disputes, eliminating the need to use force for self-defence and the satisfaction of just demands. It is in this area of endeavour that the least

---

[17] For a summary of current functions of the UN Security Council, see UN Department of Public Information, *United Nations Security Council* (UNDPI, United Nations: New York, 1989).

[18] The SALT I agreements consist of the Interim Agreement of Strategic Offensive Arms and the Anti-Ballistic Missile (ABM) Treaty.

has been achieved since World War II, yet with some notable exceptions where efforts were crowned with considerable success.

Outstanding progress in the settlement of international disputes was achieved in the decolonization process,[19] which occurred with remarkably little bloodshed in contrast with other comparable changes. A large area of the globe was transformed into new sovereign states from the vast colonies that had been subjugated by force. Those mediation methods could be utilized to solve many of the territorial disputes of the present and the future, reassuring peoples that their fates will not be determined by their ability to exert or to threaten the use of force, including nuclear blackmail.

The other major success in creating international harmony has been with regard to trade and commerce among nations, laying down universal minimum standards of conduct, acceptable procedures for the settlement of commercial disputes, as well as creating an environment of interdependence and mutual benefit as the result of a massive increase in the exchange of manufactured goods and primary produce. Greatly improved settlement of international trade disputes and the pioneering work of the United Nations Commission on International Trade Law (UNCITRAL),[20] give a foretaste of what is legally achievable even in an environment of competing interests. Another recent milestone was the conclusion of the Vienna Convention on the Law of Treaties, resulting from a creative codification of customary international law in the field, undertaken by the International Law Commission.

Despite sincere devotion and endeavour by many, the International Court of Justice has not succeeded in making an adequate contribution to the settlement of international disputes. Especially with respect to matters relating to international security, dispensation of justice by the Court has failed to reassure states that they can abandon force and the threat of force as an instrument of national policy. The lack of success of the Court is demonstrated by the dearth of that category of cases referred to it.[21] One is drawn to the conclusion that the jurisdiction of the Court in those matters may even be an obstacle to progress because it is likely that, in its absence, more fruitful initiatives may have been taken to resolve disputes involving the supreme security interests of states. The unsatisfactory performance of the Court is often attributed to the very diverse backgrounds of its judges, the virtual absence of enforcement machinery, and the reluctance of states to surrender their sovereign options. Yet, while the above-mentioned obstacles no doubt exert an adverse influence, the chief difficulty may be the nature of the law to be dispensed.

This brings us to the exertion of influence by the use of legal methodology for the creation and application of international norms for arms control, which we have designated Mode B of the operation of international law. Here we must

[19] UN Special Committee on Decolonization, *Annual Report to the General Assembly*, UN documents A/AC.109.

[20] UNCITRAL, *Legal Guide on Drawing Up International Contracts for the Construction of Industrial Works* (United Nations: New York, 1988).

[21] Singh, N., *The Role and Record of the International Court of Justice* (Martinus Nijhoff: Dordrecht, 1989), p. 229.

distinguish between legal practice, which enjoys wide consensus and cohesion, as distinct from the theory behind the practice which is in considerable disarray. There is profound resistance to reappraising the basic tenets of the theory of international law, for fear that to do so might undermine the existing fragile consensus which is so valuable, despite its questionable foundations.

The theories on which modern international law is based were developed by European scholars from Roman times and have remained virtually unchanged during the past century.[22] Certainly no reappraisal has been made to accommodate the formidable changes of the post-World War II period, namely, the crucial period of development of the international law of arms control and disarmament. The studious avoidance of theoretical issues, no doubt instinctively by some people and deliberately by others, was in order to retain cohesion in practice and to bypass all avoidable grounds for dissension. This is a very sound approach provided theoretical issues do not interfere with the efficient exercise of legal practice in such matters as the negotiation, interpretation, application, verification, observance, adjudication and enforcement of arms control treaties.

Increasingly, the inconvenient fact is gaining recognition that the failure to pay attention to the theoretical aspects of public international law has interfered with the progress of arms control law and that it is an inhibiting factor in the conclusion of urgent treaties such as a chemical weapons convention[23] and a treaty to curtail conventional forces in Europe,[24] as well as a comprehensive test ban (CTB)[25] and a universal NPT.[26]

In general terms, the problem is that states fear to bind themselves to treaties relating to their vital security interests so long as they retain grave misgivings as to how those treaties might be applied over time. Needless to say, there are other reasons as well why states are reluctant to enter into treaties limiting their right to manufacture and deploy weapons, but the unsatisfactory legal aspects add to their concerns and sometimes also *serve to conceal the less plausible reasons for their reluctance.* The kind of phrase one hears among negotiators is, 'We are not ready yet to set this in concrete'.

Before it can be resolved by what method international law might be changed, one has to confront the problem as to what is the ultimate authority of international law. The sources of law enumerated in the Statute of the International Court of Justice, which the Court is to apply, follow closely in the

[22] D'Amato, A. A., Falk, R. A. and Weston, B. H., *International Law and World Order* (West Publishing Co.: St Paul, Minn., 1980).

[23] *Chemical Weapons*, Report of the Conference on Disarmament to the General Assembly of the United Nations, UN document CD/1039, 30 Aug. 1990, pp. 56–301.

[24] US Arms Control and Disarmament Agency, *CFE Negotiation on Conventional Armed Forces in Europe* (US ACDA, Office of Public Affairs: Washington, DC, 31 Aug. 1990). For summary of the CFE agreement 'in principle', see 'Farewell to many arms', *International Herald Tribune*, 6–7 Oct. 1990, p. 6.

[25] A proposed comprehensive test ban treaty would prohibit nuclear explosions underground in addition to existing prohibition in the other environments.

[26] If there were any consistency in the law regarding the creation of international custom, the NPT, with its 142 states parties, together with adherence to its terms by most additional states, would by now have created customary law applicable to all states. See International Court of Justice, *Nuclear Tests (Australia v France)*, ICJ Reports, 1974, p. 253.

footsteps of the sources of law applied by its predecessor established by the League of Nations—the Permanent Court of International Justice. Those sources are again identified in the Statute of the International Court of Justice as follows:

Article 38. 1. The Court, whose function is to decide in accordance with international law such disputes as are submitted to it, shall apply: (*a*) international conventions, whether general or particular, establishing rules expressly recognized by the contesting States; (*b*) international custom, as evidence of a general practice accepted as law; (*c*) the general principles of law recognized by civilized nations; (*d*) subject to the provisions of Article 59, judicial decisions and the teachings of the most highly qualified publicists of the various nations, as subsidiary means for the determination of rules of law.[27]

This statement of the law to be applied has two major flaws. First, it is not clear what the four clauses mean. For example, having mentioned treaties in the first position, does this mean that treaty law is paramount? The great majority of legal writing, with the exception of some noted Socialist and Third-World lawyers, asserts that international custom is the ultimate basis on which international law rests,[28] including the duty to observe treaties. The second problem is that, in so far as it can be established what the four clauses mean, it is evident that their contents are so imprecise as to make it impossible to foretell, with any confidence, what the outcome of an adjudication process might be. This general uncertainty also affects disputes concerning nuclear weapon reductions.

Disputes regarding the interpretation of nuclear weapon limitation agreements have never been referred to the International Court of Justice, nor are they likely to be in the future. Presumably, the law that applies with respect to the observance of those treaties is subject to the same legal rules applied by the Court in other types of cases. It follows that any uncertainties, for instance in the method of interpreting treaty provisions, hamper the ability of parties to arms control treaties to establish, among themselves, what their respective rights and duties are, thus aiding those who may wish to hide behind spurious technicalities.

The notion of international customary law is used in several contexts. The least precision and least agreement concerns the methods whereby new customary rules might arise.[29] On the other hand, there is substantial certainty and unanimity about certain structures on the international legal landscape, such as the notion of the sovereign state, sovereign equality, the need to observe treaties freely entered into, rules regarding state succession, diplomatic recognition, some of the more basic rules as to evidence, and so forth. While some of these tenets of custom have already been codified—and others may greatly

[27] The Statute of the ICJ is part of the UN Charter. For the full text of the Statute, see, for example, International Court of Justice, *I.C.J. Acts and Documents No. 4* (ICJ: The Hague, Netherlands, 1978), pp. 60–89.
[28] Rosenne, S., *Developments in the Law of Treaties* (Cambridge University Press: Cambridge, 1989), pp. 359–60.
[29] Starke, J. G., *Introduction to International Law*, 3rd edn (Butterworths: London, 1989), p. 41.

benefit from being set down in treaty form—most of the building blocks for a cogent theory are already in place.

Some of the immediately troublesome issues concern: (*a*) the cumbersome methods for concluding, amending or replacing arms control and other security-related treaties; (*b*) confusion as to what is 'binding'; and (*c*) the various degrees of commitment.[30] For example, how binding are expired treaties which the parties claim they will observe in principle; and what is the status of unilateral statements, 'politically binding' commitments and so on? Mediation and arbitration procedures, designed to assist willing arms control treaty partners to resolve differences, are notoriously underdeveloped, although there are satisfactory opportunities for registering complaints in case of apparent transgressions.

In sum, the current situation as to legal methodology pertaining to the reduction and elimination of nuclear weapons is deficient—even for present-day needs—but not so flawed as to constitute an insurmountable obstacle for rapid future development.[31] Perhaps the greatest defect in this aspect of legal method is the approach whereby academic lawyers ask in each case: 'What is the law?'. The appropriate questions to be asked, bearing in mind modern-day possibilities to change the theory and practice of international law with the aid of contemporary means of communication and organization, are: 'What should the law be?' and 'How could the law be changed in order to best serve the international community'?

VI. First wave legal contribution

While the first wave would not go far towards eliminating all nuclear weapons, it would entail substantial reductions. A high degree of international co-operation would be required to verify these agreements, for instance that of an international network for seismic monitoring. International institutions would have to be created to oversee some aspects of those activities, perhaps modelled on existing institutions like the IAEA and OPANAL. Deployment restrictions would be onerous and would, incidentally, help greatly to reduce any risk of unplanned use of the weapons. As the momentum of these changes gathered pace, it can be anticipated that states would be increasingly willing to undertake more and more restrictions which could leave the major part of the globe a virtual nuclear weapon-free zone. In order to conclude such far reaching agreements, substantially more streamlined methods will have to be found for negotiation of the treaties and for establishing the complicated institutional structures required to underpin them.

The above substantive requirements would not be met unless states could feel secure that the treaties to which they commit themselves will be subject to legal rules guaranteeing that no party can take unfair advantage of another, even after

---

[30] Sanders, D., *Lawmaking and Co-operation in International Politics* (Macmillan: London, 1986), chapters 3 and 4.

[31] Singh, N. and McWhinney, E., *Nuclear Weapons and Contemporary International Law*, 2nd rev. edn (Martinus Nijhoff: Dordrecht, 1989).

passage of time. Furthermore, it may not be possible to introduce new legal rules without international consensus regarding the foundations of international law, on the basis of which the necessary alterations could be made. As noted earlier, the political will to move in this direction must be influenced by other changes in the international political climate, such as we are witnessing over the past twelve months, whereby confrontation is giving way to co-operation at many levels. The legal improvements in both modes and at the three impact points would create further confidence, interacting with the other trends so as to give additional momentum to the wave of changes.

The new treaty provisions would probably extend to the following areas, whether as separate treaties or additions and amendments of existing treaties.

The nearest next step, which is overdue, would be the prohibition of all nuclear tests. Prohibitions on flight-testing of delivery vehicles and the manufacture of fissile materials are also on the near-term agenda. A start could be made on the destruction of all phased-out nuclear warheads and dismantled weapons, with conversion of fissile material for peaceful uses or safe storage. Reduction and later prohibition of battlefield and tactical nuclear weapons could be achieved with less difficulty than a chemical weapons convention and would be especially important, both for increasing the nuclear threshold and in order to persuade currently non-nuclear-weapon states to forego the option of acquiring such weapons. These treaty provisions should go hand in hand with substantial reductions in and elimination of other nuclear weapon categories, together with severe restrictions on weapon deployment, especially transport at sea and in the air. Perhaps within the first group of restrictions, or at a somewhat later stage, the stationing of land-based nuclear weapons beyond the borders of the nuclear weapon states could be prohibited.

The priorities enumerated here are not relevant to the issues of law considered in this chapter, except in so far as they indicate the type of substantive agreements that would have to be put into legal form.[32] It is evident, that even for this extent of denuclearization, a large body of treaty law would have to be concluded with all that such an undertaking would entail. The process might be assisted, for example, by establishing a United Nations Drafting Bureau for the rapid preparation of the first texts of arms control treaties that have been agreed in principle. Preparing the first texts in such a setting would have the advantage that it would not bind any party even by inference, and could therefore be prepared at substantial speed without risk of loss of face in case that major amendments had to be made to the draft. This is presented merely as an example of the type of legal technical fix that could be devised so as to strengthen the amalgam which in strategic shorthand constitutes 'political will'.

---

[32] See the other chapters in this book. For other recent lists of priorities, see Herby, P., *NPT Review Ends Without Agreement* (Quaker UN Office: Geneva, Sep. 1990), p. 5; Slocombe, W. B., 'Strategic stability in a restructured world', *Survival*, vol. 32, no. 4 (July/Aug. 1990), pp. 309–12. This would be a modest curtailment of forces, '[B]ut it is much less than what the US now plans . . .'; see Slocombe, p. 312.

Years of superpower confrontation have concealed the potential offered by the UN Security Council in the process of nuclear arms control and disarmament.[33] The Security Council already has full powers to establish an Arms Control and Disarmament Oversight Committee, perhaps together with a Fact Finding Bureau. Such a body, which might at first only perform *ad hoc* functions, could develop into a major institution as a type of appellate body for disputes that prove to be irreconcilable in the dispute-settling bodies established under the various nuclear weapon reduction treaties. The fact finding aspect of the work could eventually extend to operating an International Satellite Monitoring Agency, together with regular surveillance on land and at sea. However, these latter developments are more likely to occur at a later stage than what is envisaged here as the first wave of denuclearization.

It is evident that the legal contribution required if such functions were to be undertaken by the Security Council, would be very far-reaching indeed—even at the stage of *ad hoc* operations. Organizationally, the statute that constitutes the Charter of the United Nations, already presents a firm foundation for the new edifice. Nevertheless, the tasks envisaged would entail practical inroads on sovereignty with respect to matters concerning security interests, so as to greatly surpass anything known hitherto.

Before states could be persuaded to invest this degree of trust in the quasi-legal functions of the Security Council, much would need to be done to diminish attitudes of interstate rivalry, friction and hostility. One rather simple but influential step toward those ends might be to establish a United Nations State Borders Registry Office. Utilizing information provided by states, the Borders Registry Office could compile an authoritative record of all state boundaries, noting disputed territories wherever they may exist. A further body to be established for that purpose, could give consideration to the competing claims regarding the disputed territories—perhaps in a manner analogous to that used for the decolonization process. The removal of all ambiguity with respect to borders, upheld by international force if necessary, would go a long way to subdue warlike tendencies.

Even within the first wave of legal input, a reallocation of the functions now performed by the International Court of Justice would have to be undertaken. In fact, the Court does not 'function' with respect to international security-related issues. Yet, due to the fiction that the Court can deal with such matters, no serious effort is made to find alternative methods, apart from free-ranging negotiations. It is evident that not even the arbitration and mediation facilities offered by the Court are suitable for resolving either nuclear weapon-related disputes or the other types of disputes that develop into overwhelming antagonisms leading to war and the threat of war.

Much has been written already about reform of the Court but it appears that what is really required is the replacement of the Court or at least a total overhaul regarding the above-mentioned functions which the Court now purports to

[33] *Charter of the United Nations*, 24 Oct. 1945, chapters 5–8.

perform. Unwillingness to assume this task is symptomatic of the extreme tardiness with which all problems of International Law and organization are treated, especially when they relate in any way to the supreme security interests of states. While the reasons for such reluctance are understandable, they are inimical to the abolition of nuclear weapons and hamper even the immediate next stage of nuclear weapon reductions.

What we have at present is a mediaeval style Court, dispensing international law that is mediaeval in its main features and hardly changed for centuries. Even its rules and mode of operation are anachronistic, with the opinions formulated in a rambling style better suited to concealing rather than revealing the genuine reasons for the decisions handed down. The requirement for nuclear weapon control and elimination, together with all its related legal edifice, is the dispensation of razor-sharp findings presented with the precision and logical consistency of a top-flight scientific report. In order to make such a development in the dispensation of international law feasible, it would be necessary to make the law itself much more specific than it is today. Treaty language used for the limitation of nuclear weapons has already undergone a fundamental change, reaching its point of greatest refinement in the INF Treaty.

However, it is not only the treaty that has to be precise and specific but also the manner in which it is to be interpreted both as to its meaning[34] and evolution over time—its duration, for instance, if verbally renewed; membership, as in cases when states amalgamate or partition; how it will fare under altered technical circumstances: and methods that can be invoked to ensure its timely amendment or replacement. These problems are not as acute regarding bilateral treaties as they are in relation to multilateral treaties, because extra-treaty accommodation on a one-to-one basis diminishes the importance of legalistic concerns. By contrast, when faced with a multilateral treaty to which many of the parties have made lengthy, often incoherent reservations—a treaty that does not include all states to which the treaty, on account of its subject matter, ought to apply; and with some of the parties far more influential than others; in circumstances when other treaties also have a bearing on the issues—it is here that the amendment or beneficial replacement of the treaty is well nigh impossible.

If in such a situation a disputed interpretation were to come before the International Court of Justice, as presently constituted, the outcome would be quite unpredictable,[35] and whatever it would be—no matter how conscientiously prepared—the inference could not be dispelled that it was prompted by considerations other than legal ones. Yet, *what is most needed, is not so much a Court which makes decisions—but decisions which are so self-evident that they do not require a Court to declare them.*

---

[34] Sinclair, I., *The Vienna Convention on the Law of Treaties*, 2nd edn (Manchester University Press: Manchester, 1984).

[35] *Vienna Convention on the Law of Treaties* (1969) (entered into force Jan. 1980), articles 31 and 32; Brownlie (note 8), pp. 626–32.

It would therefore be most important for the legal input in the first wave of developments towards a nuclear weapon-free world, to make innovations that would ensure that the consequences of arms control treaty commitments would be more predictable over the long term than they are today. This requires, among other things, that there should be more sophisticated rules than at present for the amendment of the treaties and also that states should have confidence that what they had agreed to will not be distorted on the basis of antiquated rules invented to serve conditions at a time when deliberate, bureaucratically orchestrated amendments among a large number of states was not a practical possibility.

Further, in order to enhance certainty and predictability, distinctions have to be made without any ambiguity between commitments that are legally binding, such as treaties duly signed and ratified, and other types of arms control undertakings. A contra-indication for so doing at present is that often the only type of commitment states are prepared to make—for instance regarding deployment of sea-launched cruise missiles—falls short of such a binding commitment. Hence, the choice is between a lesser commitment of uncertain validity or no commitment at all. Under these conditions, it is felt that anything that would detract from the status of the partial commitment would be imprudent.

A new wave of thinking attuned to making rapid progress in ridding the world of the danger of nuclear weapons might bring with it a fresh approach to this problem. For instance, one could envisage a clear demarcation between strictly binding commitments and rules, and another category of undertakings and procedures that merely identify a trend that is to be pursued. A similar concept already exists in international law, drawing a distinction between *lex lata* and *lex ferenda*, differentiating between existing law and emerging law. Where the problem lies is that there are no clear rules: neither as to identifying what exists and what is emerging, nor as to the status of emerging law.

Despite the relative consistency of the notion of sovereignty, many states have domestic impediments for the exercise of that sovereignty as it affects arms control, including the limitation of nuclear weapons. It is particularly troublesome in the case of federal states and very powerful states which have for centuries regarded themselves as standing above international law whenever it suited them to do so. This is not a hurdle that will be overcome in one leap but the time is opportune, within the first wave of reforms, to examine what the desirable changes might be. The basic principles in this regard should ensure that, for the purposes of International Law, each state is able to assume its responsibilities as a single entity, namely, that the treaty making process is not unduly delayed and that all responsibilities assumed are faithfully carried out.[36] Furthermore, no loopholes can be allowed as to who is bound, including all natural and corporate persons having any connection whatever with the obser-

---

[36] See Jacobs, F. G. (ed.), *The Effects of Treaties in Domestic Law*, Colloquium Papers (Sweet and Maxwell: London, 1987), especially regarding Belgium, Denmark, France, the Federal Republic of Germany, Italy, the Netherlands, the UK and the USA.

vance of the treaty and over whose relevant actions the state party in question has jurisdiction in whatever form.

VII. Last wave legal contribution

While it is not useful and may even be counter-productive to dwell too much on the final stages leading to a world free of nuclear weapons, the broad outlines of that situation are foreseeable. There is no insurmountable obstacle in law related issues that could obstruct such an outcome. Whether denuclearization could happen before a cataclysmic catastrophe occurs will depend on the speed with which legal and other relevant reforms are implemented in a suitably correlated manner. In view of the virtual stalemate in the START negotiations at the time of writing,[37] and so long as naked aggression can occur, as in the cases of the invasion of Grenada by the United States and of Kuwait by Iraq, it appears that the last wave of reforms that could culminate in total nuclear disarmament is not yet on the horizon.

The formal implementation of nuclear weapon elimination would consist of destroying all such weapons and the support systems of the weapons, together with all facilities for their production, testing and deployment. This could be undertaken pursuant to one or more treaties or by a *new* form of binding commitment, for example, that of binding United Nations resolutions, if agreed by a majority required for amendment of the UN Charter. At this time it is too soon to discuss whether binding resolutions of this type would be advantageous.

It is improbable that consensus could be achieved for prohibiting nuclear weapons until all other kinds of genocidal weapons were also prohibited from all environments in all modes of deployment. That could constitute a more difficult problem of treaty language construction than the prohibition of nuclear weapons alone. The formulation could be a simple prohibition, along the lines of prohibiting the stationing of 'weapons of mass destruction' in outer space by the Outer Space Treaty.[38] However, such indefinite prohibitions—in this case failing to define a weapon of mass destruction either at its deployed state or at various developmental stages—inhibit satisfactory application and consequently impair confidence.

In order to ensure compliance with treaties requiring the elimination of all nuclear weapons and all other weapons of mass destruction, it will also be necessary, by legal means, to establish an international authority to administer an inspection regime capable of verifying the prohibition, including challenge inspection of all facilities capable of creating such weapons. Further, as there would have to be great reliance on the treaties—or equivalent resolutions—creating the aforementioned nuclear weapon-free regime, these would have to

[37] Smith, R. J., 'US–Soviet arms talks stall', *International Herald Tribune*, 6 Aug. 1990, pp. 1 and 5.
[38] Article IV: 'States Parties to the Treaty undertake not to place in orbit around the earth any objects carrying nuclear weapons or any other kinds of weapons of mass destruction, install such weapons on celestial bodies, or station such weapons in outer space in any other manner'. Reprinted in Goldblat (note 14), p. 160.

be preceded by several administrative treaties, for example providing that all treaties relating to international security would be automatically incorporated into domestic law.

The political will to proceed along such lines is, in turn, not likely to arise until an adjudicating mechanism is in place for the settlement of major international disputes, with adequate enforcement procedures. As we have seen, the prerequisite for that is an overhaul of the theories and rules of international law, especially as they relate to the security interests of states, in a manner that will lay down with great clarity the respective rights and duties of states.

Cumulatively, the preconditions that have been enumerated for achieving a nuclear weapon-free world, could be construed to amount to an advocacy of something approaching world government—a concept that is at present considered to be entirely utopian or, at best, very far down the road. In that regard three matters should be borne in mind in order to escape an emotive response.

1. Only security issues are of concern here, while full autonomy in all other matters could remain unimpaired.

2. The form the consensus would assume is not yet evident. The gradualist approach toward concerted action might achieve forms of co-ordination that could be readily accepted by a new generation much better attuned than their elders to a global outlook.

3. We have already come a long way towards working collectively in our efforts to avoid genocidal war, in ways unimaginable a generation ago.

While the security aspects of global collective action are still not far advanced, the legal and organizational forms are being developed at the regional level, as in the organizations of NATO, WTO, OAU (Organization of African Unity), OAS (Organization of American States), Arab League, ASEAN (Association of South-East Asian Nations), and so on. Transforming regional forms of organizations to global scope would not require great adjustment from a legal standpoint: the more so because the United Nations provides a ready-made framework for the transition. Perhaps it is alien sounding terms like 'world government' which best illustrate that specific planning for a totally nuclear weapon-free world may be counter-productive until at least the first wave of changes has been completed.

Many avenues are provided by the United Nations system for the achievement of international security in the absence of weapons of mass destruction. A brief survey of the powers of the Security Council reveals vast, as yet unexploited possibilities *even without any amendment of the United Nations Charter*. The Security Council has a substantial *arms control and disarmament power*. Under Article 26, it can propose 'a system for the regulation of armaments' so as to reduce them to the minimum compatible with the maintenance of international peace and security. It is empowered under Article 44 to take advice from the MSC—composed of the chiefs of staff of its permanent members—on 'the regulation of armaments, and possible disarmament'. The

MSC may also, under Article 47, establish regional sub-committees for this purpose, among others. Pursuant to Article 24, the Security Council has 'primary responsibility' for the maintenance of international peace and security, and within that ambit, it wields almost unlimited *administrative powers*. While each of its fifteen members are allotted only one representative each, the parent body may, in conformity with Article 29, 'establish such subsidiary organs as it deems necessary for the performance of its functions'. Decisions so arrived at must be carried out by all members of the United Nations, as provided by Article 25, while Article 12 requires the General Assembly to refrain from interfering in matters under consideration by the Security Council.

The *quasi-legal powers* of the Security Council have also remained dormant. It is provided by Article 34 that the Security Council may 'investigate' any dispute or situation that might lead to 'friction' and, further to Article 36, may recommend appropriate methods of adjustment of the dispute. While there is a presumption under sub-paragraph three of that Article that 'as a general rule' any 'legal disputes' should be referred to the International Court of Justice, the Security Council has complete discretion in the matter. In conformity with Article 37, the Security Council also may, failing resolution of the dispute, itself 'recommend such terms of settlement as it may consider appropriate'. Taken together, these powers of the Security Council give ample scope for massive inputs at the three legal impact points where movement could occur to a stage at which nuclear disarmament would be possible.

The legal component of the new security edifice may eventually have less weight to support than one might anticipate from a contemporary perspective, once the weapons are thought to be redundant. This would occur if, before the final stage of nuclear disarmament is reached, some nuclear weapon arsenals of strictly circumscribed types, ranges and locations were to be retained until their presence was clearly thought to be unnecessary. The stage of redundancy has already been reached regarding intermediate-range nuclear weapons and is now developing in relation to tactical nuclear weapons in Europe.

An attempt to foretell what will be the legal aspects of total elimination of nuclear weapons is useful provided it is undertaken as an exercise in reorientation and not with any expectation of accurate prediction or detailed forward planning. The most significant conclusion to emerge is that partial nuclear arms limitation and control is the only path to a nuclear weapon-free world. *The chief obstacle to be overcome is the insufficient rate of reaching arms control agreements*. That problem has more to do with the unsatisfactory condition of the applicable legal rules than with any assertion that could be sustained regarding legitimation of possession of nuclear weapons by the five permanent members of the Security Council.

5. Thinking about no nuclear forces: technical and strategic constraints on transitions and end-points

Paul C. White, Robert E. Pendley and Patrick J. Garrity[*]

I. Introduction

This chapter is intended to explore the effect that technological developments over the next several decades will have on the likelihood that nuclear weapons can be made an increasingly marginal factor in international relations, to the point where they might possibly be eliminated on a global basis.

In our view, there are two circumstances in which the complete elimination of nuclear weapons from national arsenals could be contemplated. The first is political and structural: a fundamental alteration of the character of the international system such that nuclear weapons are viewed as either completely irrelevant or actually harmful by all parties capable of possessing them. Because we take a 'techno-centric' rather than a 'policy' perspective on the subject at hand, this chapter does not attempt to define the exact character of such an international system. We assume, however, that the evolution of technologies might make significant contributions towards a process of denuclearization or, in some circumstances, could place inhibitions on that process. We provide an evaluation of future technology accordingly.

The second case in which the elimination of nuclear weapons might be contemplated is technology-driven: one can imagine technologies that would completely prevent the use of nuclear weapons—a perfect defence of some sort—and thereby render the possession of these weapons irrelevant. One can also posit technologies that would theoretically permit absolute verification that nuclear weapons did not exist, and that would ensure that nuclear weapons could not be re-manufactured without this fact becoming known in time for other parties to respond. Finally, it is possible to conceive of technologies that would in some way transcend nuclear weapons. Of course, whether any such technologies would actually permit the elimination of nuclear weapons would depend heavily on other factors, such as the absolute number of nuclear weapons in existence, and whether all parties could possess those technologies.

Based on this analytical framework, we have arrived at two basic conclusions. First, the evolution of technology over the next several decades may well

[*] This work was partially supported by the United States Department of Energy, under Contract W-7405-ENG-36; however, the views expressed are those of the authors, and are not necessarily those of Los Alamos National Laboratory or the United States Department of Energy.

play a role in defining a change in the character of the international system, and this change may well lead to a substantial marginalization of nuclear weapons. We are frankly sceptical whether such a change will be sufficient to permit the complete elimination of nuclear weapons on political grounds, but that judgement is better left to other authors. Second, we foresee no technical breakthroughs of the kinds described above that would make nuclear weapons completely transparent or irrelevant. This possibility can never be discounted entirely, but it should not be used, prematurely, to provide the substantive rationale for any future policy directed towards the elimination of nuclear weapons. We therefore focus our attention on the impact that less dramatic changes in technology will have on the propensity of states to maintain or acquire nuclear stockpiles.

Further, in contemplating, or perhaps even anticipating, a world without nuclear weapons, crucial links *between* technological and political developments in the international system must not be ignored. The post-war system of deterrence that emerged between the two major political blocs was in large part enabled by the existence of two new technologies: nuclear explosives, carrying tremendous energy in relatively little mass; and accurate long-range delivery vehicles, especially ballistic missiles, capable of projecting nuclear weapons over and beyond conventional lines of military defence, thereby threatening immediate and massive attacks against any nation (including the superpower homelands) if war were to occur. New concepts such as mutual vulnerability, stability and first-strike attack entered the vocabulary of international security and reinforced the organization of the political–military confrontation around two centres of power with the necessary technological capabilities to sustain this system.

As the Soviet bloc disassembles itself, and as new centres of national and international power arise, technological developments will help determine to some extent the next phase of evolution in the international system. For example, the acquisition of high-technology systems such as ballistic missiles and precision-guided missiles by a wide variety of states—not just those with great national wealth and a well-established scientific and industrial base—can substantially alter the geopolitical situation facing even very large powers such as the United States. These large powers will likely perceive the need to provide protection against such weapons not only for their own territories, but also for a substantial portion of the world (as we have observed in Operation Desert Storm). This suggests the need for a greater degree of multilateral co-operation, especially when the economic burden of providing such defences are considered as well. Similar arguments can be made for the impacts of the spread of chemical and biological weapon technologies.

Today when there are proposals for drawing down numbers of nuclear weapons significantly, there must be a corresponding reformulation of the definition of security or an evolution in the basic structure of international security. In particular, with regard to nuclear weapons and nuclear deterrence, these changes would almost by definition have to include the military doctrines and the operational practices of all nuclear weapon states, and take account of the most significant new and emerging technologies as well.

This chapter is organized in three sections. The first briefly examines the historical relationship between politics, technology and the propensity for war in international relations. The second section focuses on the new ways in which technology may be a factor in shaping the nature of any future international system, as well as the military and security environment within which the roles and numbers of nuclear weapons must be examined. In the final section, we examine in some detail specific factors that may become important if nuclear weapons are to be reduced or eliminated.

II. Technology, security strategy and the international system

The development of military or civilian technologies does not seem to have been the principal cause of war in the modern international system. War has resulted from the clashes of independent nation-states, each desirous of maintaining its independence and improving its relative power and status. In the absence of any authoritative supranational entity that could impose peace and allocate power and status among members of the international community— and in the absence of any international consensus about a common definition of security—resort to war has been the final court of appeal.[1]

This said, it is clear that technological developments have not been unrelated to the propensity of nation-states to engage in war. In a general sense, one can make the case that the evolution of technology since the Middle Ages has been instrumental in supporting the emergence and continuation of the nation-state as the dominant form in international politics.[2] More specifically, technology has been a pervasive element in the economic development of nations, and such development has in turn been a dominant factor in defining political and military power. For example, we have seen national power and status measured in terms of the level of industrialization, the extent and quality of transportation systems, the ability to acquire and convert natural resources into marketable commodities, the general rate of improvement in the quality of life of populations, and so on.

Almost invariably, the pursuit of this economic status has stimulated countries to develop the military capability to preserve, defend and enhance the

[1] This is the theme, among others, of Morgenthau, H. J., *Politics Among Nations: The Struggle for Power and Peace*, 5th edn (Knopf: New York, 1973); and Waltz, K. N., *Theory of International Politics* (Addison-Wesley Publishing Co.: Reading, Mass., 1979). This is not to claim that co-operation is impossible among nation-states, or that some fundamentally different type of international system is unimaginable. See, for example, Keohane, R. O., *After Hegemony: Cooperation and Discord in the World Political Economy* (Princeton University Press: Princeton, N.J., 1984). Nor should one ignore the importance of the character of particular regimes in determining the causes of particular wars.

[2] For a discussion of the historical relationship between technology, economics and politics, see McNeill, W. H., *The Pursuit of Power: Technology, Armed Force, and Society Since A.D. 1000* (University of Chicago Press: Chicago, 1982); and Mokyr, J., *Technological Creativity and Economic Progress* (Oxford University Press: New York, 1990).

assets that underpin their economies. In turn, the necessary military capacity has emerged directly from economic strength and resources, together with the technological know-how necessary to convert them into maximum qualitative and quantitative advantage. This intimate, mutually reinforcing relationship between technology and the resulting economic, military and political power has often enhanced the relative differences between 'have' and 'have-not' countries, and between rising and declining powers, sometimes leading to disputes, conflicts and wars.[3] Thus, while technology can offer the means for general improvement of economic vigour and the quality of life, its unequal availability, and the uneven means to exploit it can lead to an exaggeration of the differences and tensions that often lead to the use of military force.

International tensions can also occur when weapons, weapon systems and other military products of technology are more widely available, and more widely sought after, than the broader industrial and scientific infrastructure that supports fundamental economic strength and political stability. That such products are almost universally available is a natural consequence of the political and economic self-interest of producing nations. That these products are acquired and used by so many is a consequence of political ambition, religious zeal, geographic circumstance, strategic vulnerability, national pride, and a host of other real and imagined pressures. Technology and its general availability are not primary or direct stimuli for the conflicts that have historically resulted from such pressures. But the acquisition of advanced military technology by relatively backward nations has held out the prospect that resort to war can allow these states an edge over other states, including those that otherwise have stronger economies and political systems. Iraq's sustained accumulation of advanced military technologies throughout the 1980s—including ballistic missiles, advanced armour, artillery and aircraft, and the beginnings of a biological and nuclear weapon capability—is a prime example, and it contributed greatly to the eventual armed confrontation in 1991 with the US-led coalition.

The sudden introduction of the technology of nuclear weapons into the international system in 1945 did not change these historical generalizations about the relationship between politics and technology. The fear of national or global devastation engendered by these weapons did not produce an international decision to put an end to the sovereignty and autonomy of nation-states, as some thought necessary in order to save humankind.[4] By the same token, nuclear technology did not precipitate the emergence of a bipolar international system dominated by two hostile powers of continental size. Such a system

[3] See the different views on this subject by Gilpin, R., *War and Change in World Politics* (Cambridge University Press: Cambridge, 1981); and Kennedy, P., *The Rise and Fall of the Great Powers* (Random House: New York, 1988).

[4] Mandelbaum, M., *The Nuclear Question: The United States and Nuclear Weapons, 1946–1976* (Cambridge University Press: Cambridge, 1979), pp. 1–8. See also Jervis, R., *The Meaning of the Nuclear Revolution: Statecraft and the Prospect of Armageddon* (Cornell University Press: Ithaca, N.Y., 1989). The first important treatment of the impact of nuclear weapons on political and military affairs was, of course, Brodie, B., *et al.*, *The Absolute Weapon* (Harcourt, Brace: New York, 1946).

would have emerged in any case.[5] International power and status continue to flow from such factors as a nation's relative conventional military capabilities, economic production capacities and creative potential, and not just nuclear weapons. France and the United Kingdom owed their post-war status, albeit second-tier, to historical factors, economic recovery and alliance relation-ships; only later did they add nuclear weapon capabilities to reinforce (or to preserve) their status (or to re-establish their former status). Germany and Japan owe much of their current status to economic strength, and their military alliances with the United States, rather than to indigenous nuclear capabilities.

But nuclear weapons did play a critical role in defining the peculiar character of the post-war military and political competition, as they created a new source of uncertainty (and opportunity) for national strategies, and presented funda-mental challenges to the means of defining and creating international security 'systems'. To a large extent, especially in the early years of the so-called cold war, nuclear weapons were 'conventionalized'—that is, they were considered by the United States and the Soviet Union as instruments that could provide political and military utility, much as previous technologies (e.g., those repres-ented by the tank and the airplane) had done. The search to develop and exploit nuclear technologies for positive advantage, whether in peacetime or wartime, continued until recently.

But alongside this traditional view, the United States and the Soviet Union (especially the former) developed concepts and theories of nuclear deterrence— concepts that presumed to offer an alternative to large-scale warfare between the major international powers as a means of resolving international disputes.[6] The concept of nuclear deterrence did not suppose that the uneven development of national economies and technological capacity would cease, or that the diffusion of military technology could be halted (although efforts have been made to halt or slow nuclear proliferation). Nevertheless, the deterrence con-cept did hold out the prospect that these long-standing pressures for conflict in the international system could be dampened politically, given the general fear of nuclear war.[7]

[5] See Waltz (note 2), pp. 180–81. John Lewis Gaddis argues, however, that the existence of nuclear weapons may have perpetuated bipolarity longer than would otherwise have been the case. Gaddis, J. L., 'Nuclear weapons, the end of the cold war, and the future of the international system: a speculative essay', eds S. A. Maaranen and P. J. Garrity, *The Future of Nuclear Weapons* (Plenum: New York, forthcoming).

[6] For a review of this concept of deterrence, see Freedman, L., *The Evolution of Nuclear Strategy* (St. Martin's Press: New York, 1981); Gray, C. S., *Strategic Studies and American Policy: The American Experience* (University of Kentucky Press: Lexington, Mass., 1982); and Trachtenberg, M., 'Strategic thought in America, 1952–1966', *Political Science Quarterly*, vol. 104, no. 2 (1989), pp. 301–34. For a discussion of the differences between the Soviet and US views of the concepts associated with nuclear weapons, see Legvold, R., 'Strategic "doctrine" and SALT: Soviet and American views', *Survival*, vol. 21, no. 1 (Jan./Feb. 1979), p. 8.

[7] Those who accept, as we do, the general proposition that nuclear weapon technology and concepts of nuclear deterrence on the whole tended to dampen pressures towards war, tend to focus on two principal factors. The first is what the Harvard Nuclear Study Group has called the 'crystal ball effect': 'Ironically, the enormous horror of nuclear weapon effects means that modern leaders have the equivalent of a crystal ball showing them the devastation at the end of a major war. This crystal ball effect helps to give the nuclear world at least some measure of stability. Statesmen in the atomic age can envision the destruction of a full-scale nuclear war and it makes them determined to avoid it'. See Carnesale, A., *et al.*, *Living with*

Of course, there is a substantial body of opinion that holds that deterrence, based as it is on implicit or explicit threats to use nuclear weapons, is inherently destabilizing (i.e., it makes nations more rather than less prone to war).[8] But in point of fact, we have recently witnessed an extraordinary degree of international change, including the apparent strategic capitulation of one of the dominant powers, without war serving either as a catalyst or ratifier of the breakup of the old international order. There does not seem to be any historical precedent for this degree of peaceful change. Again, the significance of nuclear weapons in keeping the cold war from becoming hot, and in precipitating and guaranteeing the peaceful end of the cold war, is controversial. But in our judgement, a strong *prima facie* case can be made that deterrence based on nuclear weapon technology, while not solely responsible, was one major factor in preventing major-power catastrophe during a long, dangerous period.[9]

Nuclear Weapons (Harvard University Press: Cambridge, Mass., 1983), p. 44. The Study Group noted, however, that the crystal ball effect 'does not make war impossible. . . . For in the nuclear age, the crystal ball can still be shattered by accident, by negligence, by irrational blindness, or by miscalculation'. The second factor concerns the fact that nuclear weapons strengthens defending states against aggressors. As Stephen Van Evera has argued: 'conquest is far harder than before, because international conflicts shift from tests of will and capability to purer tests of will—to be won by the side willing to run greater risks and pay greater costs. This strengthens defenders, because they nearly always value their freedom more than aggressors value new conquests; hence they will have more resolve than aggressors, hence their threats are more credible, hence they are bound to prevail in a confrontation'. See Van Evera, S., 'Primed for peace: Europe after the cold war', *International Security*, vol. 15, no. 3 (winter 1990/91), p. 13. Whether this generalization is true everywhere and always is debatable, but the general tendency, at least in the post-1945 East–West context, would seem to be generally correct.

   [8] See, for example, the chapter by Ken Booth and Nicholas Wheeler in this volume. The most popular expression of this perspective over the past decade has been Schell, J., *The Fate of the Earth* (Knopf: New York, 1982). But this perspective is not limited to the so-called peace and anti-nuclear movements; it has also been embraced by a portion of the security studies community. See, for example, MccGwire, M., 'Dilemmas and delusions of deterrence', *World Policy Journal*, vol. 1, no. 4 (summer 1984), pp. 745–67; and Brement, M., 'Reaching out to Moscow', *Foreign Policy*, no. 80 (autumn 1990), pp. 65–66.

   [9] The *prima facie* case for the positive role of nuclear weapons in permitting peaceful international change rests on the assumption that the possession of nuclear weapons offered an important means of reassurance to the leaders of the major powers in Europe. This reassurance dampened pressures that in previous eras might have led to war. For example, both superpowers have been able to accept tactical setbacks in their geopolitical competition because nuclear weapons offered the ultimate guarantee of their vital interests, and especially their national sovereignty. Such setbacks might previously have created domestic and international political pressures for a much more aggressive international posture. This is not to say that the USA and the USSR failed to respond assertively to geopolitical losses—witness the US reaction to perceived Soviet advances in the late 1970s—but only to observe that such responses did not, and were not intended to, lead to war. Nuclear weapons have also reassured the superpowers that they stood a good chance of deterring war even if their opponent should become profoundly pessimistic about its domestic or international prospects (as long as that opponent's leadership remained rational). This situation allowed both the USA and the USSR to continue to pursue their conflicting geopolitical and ideological objectives, albeit in cautious fashion, in the expectation that international politics could be changed in favourable ways while still avoiding war. The entire history of the post-World War II period would have been much different, and probably more prone to conflict among the major powers, if either side had believed that its opponent was likely to resort to war rather than accept gradual political and economic defeat. In addition to the traditional argument that nuclear weapons played a major role in preventing a highly militarized East–West competition from breaking into open war, a good case can also be made that nuclear weapons have recently been instrumental in permitting a significant demilitarization of major power relations. In the past, war has been the catalyst (or ratifier) of international change, particularly between major powers that had fundamentally different notions about how international relations should be ordered. Or, to put it differently, war has been the means by which major powers measured their relative capabilities and by which an international hierarchy could be accordingly established. See Gilpin (note 4), especially pp. 9–49. We now are apparently witnessing an unprecedented

But now, in a day characterized by a crumbling of the Eastern bloc, a reduction of the perceived threat to Western Europe, and the economic resurgence of Japan and Western Europe, how relevant to security will be the technologies that undergirded the strategy (deterrence) that arguably prevented major conflict? This is not a purely academic question. Public discussion today seems to reflect a growing opinion that nuclear weapons are already, somehow, less relevant than they have been in the past, if not irrelevant entirely.[10]

There is no simple answer to the question of whether we should seek to maintain national policies, and to promote an international system, based to some degree on the concept of deterrence and the technology of nuclear weapons. For one thing, there is no certainty about the structure of the future international system. And as of yet there is no commonly accepted replacement for a strategy of nuclear deterrence. But if we attempt to eliminate the technology that supported the old order and permitted its eventual transformation, what do we desire as an international security system to replace it? A rejection of reliance on military concepts of security in favour of political solutions? In Europe, East and West, the creation of a 'common European house'? What role will the old factors of ethnic and nationalistic differences play? Even if feasible to conceive of a 'common house' in Europe, what will happen elsewhere, especially as we are now witnessing the rapid world-wide proliferation of advanced military technologies, such as in Iraq?

One possible replacement for nuclear deterrence would be to place significantly greater emphasis on economic development and competition. But more and more economic competition is equivalent to competition in state-of-the-art

---

exception to this rule: a major power is evidently prepared to abandon its ambitious international objectives, and to accept a basic weakening of its international position, rather than resort to war. And it can do so without facing attack by other powers seeking to take advantage of its manifest weakness. As a matter of policy, that nation is seeking to demilitarize its relations with other major powers, and in doing so is apparently willing to abandon or greatly modify some of its most basic concepts of national security—including the pursuit of effective military superiority. There is no simple reason why this remarkable development has taken place. The Soviet decision to allow the disintegration of its East European empire, and to accept a united Germany in NATO, was predicated on the Soviet leadership's recognition that its post-war political–strategic objectives in Europe could not be achieved with forward-deployed, offensively oriented military forces—at least, not in the presence of a disintegrating Soviet economy. The Soviets were particularly concerned that they could no longer afford to hold up their end in a new round of military–technical competition with the West. But these actions also represented an implicit recognition by Moscow that the continued existence of the Soviet state, and the opportunity for that state to regenerate itself, would not thereby be placed at risk by external threats. The possession of sizeable nuclear deterrent force may have helped the Soviet leadership to accept what is in fact a strategic defeat, and not just a series of tactical setbacks. In the words of Josef Joffe: 'Being broke made Soviet surrender advisable; nuclear weapons made it palatable; and the collapse of Leninist ideology made it inevitable'. See Joffe, J., 'What just happened: a lite history', *New Republic*, 13 Aug. 1990, p. 20. To be sure, we lack the contemporary documentation or any first-hand confirmation that the possession of nuclear weapons did indeed offer this kind of reassurance to the Soviet leadership. It is possible that this line of argument only represents an *ex post facto* rationale generated by the new civilian national security elites around Gorbachev. This question is an important one to pose, if *glasnost* lasts, to Soviet civilian and military officials who were in decision-making positions at the time.

[10] For example, William Hyland has written that 'the possession of nuclear weapons, even in stupendous quantities, has become less critical to Western security. It cannot be translated into any particular measure of power or influence except in relation to the other superpower'. See Hyland, W., 'Setting global priorities', *Foreign Policy*, no. 73 (winter 1988/89), p. 26.

technologies that frequently find military applications (e.g., computers, materials, electronics and optics).

In any event, with respect to a new international system, there must be some definition of a security concept sufficient to reassure all existing major and minor nuclear powers, and a number of would-be nuclear powers, before 'elimination' of nuclear weapons is conceivable. The concept must take into account, or somehow control, the advances in military and civilian technology that might impact on the reassurance of stability in a changed politico-techno-logical world. This concept must deal simultaneously with old and new issues such as Soviet requirements for security from threat of attack; a politically independent Eastern Europe; a united Germany with a dominant economic role in an integrating European Community; the future role of Japan, and East Asian fears of Japanese economic, political and military hegemony; and regional conflicts, including those in the Middle East, South Asia and Southern Africa.

The following sections of this chapter first examine general technical considerations in the transition to any new international system, and then focus on reduced levels of nuclear forces. With respect to the question of levels of nuclear forces *per se*, specific attention will have to be given to issues of stability and potential danger at several transition points: from large to moderate numbers; from moderate to small or very small numbers; from very small to extremely small nuclear forces; and finally from micro numbers to zero nuclear forces.

III. Technical issues in the development of a new security system

The above discussion illustrates the inherent problems in attempting to define a future international regime that provides for collective security while enabling reduced or even zero reliance on nuclear weapons. Given these difficulties, it is useful to explore some of the ways in which technical issues serve to control, influence or otherwise bear on the evolution of the international system, irrespective of particular end-points. In this section, we focus on more general ways in which technology will be a factor in shaping the nature of any future international system, and will more broadly guide the military and security environment within which the roles and numbers of nuclear weapons must be examined.[11]

The preceding section examined tendencies in the past for technological developments to increase the prospect of conflict in the international system. It would be inappropriate, however, to presume that the widespread availability of

---

[11] A number of these issues are explored in two reports of a conference held at Los Alamos National Laboratory in Sep. 1989: Pilat, J. F. and White, P. C., 'Technology and strategy in a changing world', *Washington Quarterly*, vol. 13, no. 2 (spring 1990), pp. 79–91; and Pilat, J. F. and White, P. C., *Conventional Forces and Arms Control: Technology and Strategy in a Changing World*, CNSS Occasional Paper no. 24 (Center for National Security Studies, Los Alamos National Laboratory, June 1990).

technology is always destabilizing to the international system, or that it necessarily serves to inhibit reduced reliance on nuclear weapons. Many technologies
are in fact inherently neutral in this regard, and it is their mode of employment
or the motives of their user that results in either a threat to, or a reinforcement
of stability.

It would be fruitless to attempt a complete list of technologies exhibiting this
dual nature. A few examples are illustrative, however. Biotechnology offers the
means to improve the quality and lower the costs of health care, to increase
agricultural productivity by enhancing crop yields and resistance to pests, and
even to counter the deleterious effects of certain kinds of pollution. For
instance, standard agricultural cross-breeding techniques have been used to
develop disease-resistant hybrids of staple crops, and genetic engineering is
now being used for the mass production of human vaccines. No one would
argue that such tools of technology do not promote the general welfare. On the
other hand, the very same scientific understanding and corresponding genetic
engineering tools can be used to develop resistant organisms for biological
weapons of mass destruction. The means of production for the latter can be, and
apparently have been, disguised as perfectly legitimate facilities for the former.
Almost the same observations apply to chemical science and engineering.

Computational science is another two-edge sword, usable either to increase
human productivity or to design the instruments of war. There is some tendency
to lump together all computer-related technologies; however, it is useful to
distinguish key sub-elements in this broad field. Many of the recent advances
that have begun to revolutionize some aspects of life in the developed countries
have derived from the miniaturization of key hardware components. Smaller,
faster microprocessors, linked together in ever smaller packages have brought
personal computers into homes and offices; integrated process controllers into
factory machinery; put fire-control computers into tanks and aircraft; and
dramatically increased the speed and capacity of the supercomputers that
simulate complex processes involved in, for example, weather forecasting,
aircraft design and oil recovery. Computers have become almost pervasive in
the educational, scientific and industrial life of the West. They are used to
educate, inform, communicate, analyse and design. A modern factory uses
these instruments to design the product, design and control the tools, analyse
market conditions and strategies, communicate with suppliers and buyers, and
record and report the net profit from sales. However, computers are also
important in the development and use of military instruments, being employed
to design modern artillery tubes and shells, as well as nuclear weapons, and to
manage the modern battlefield.[12]

Another good example is that of space satellites, which can be used for military or civilian uses based on their abilities to provide such functions as
communications, photographic and electronic imaging and navigation. The

[12] See, for example, White, P. C., 'The future of nuclear weapons technology', Los Alamos National
Laboratory Unclassified Report, LA-UR-3255 (1989).

proliferation of space-launch and space-satellite technologies is not *per se* a good or bad phenomenon. Sensor technology and communications capability together serve to amplify this point further. Quite apart from a whole range of purely civilian applications, the military uses of such technology can be ambiguous in themselves. To an ever increasing extent, countries have access to suites of earth- and space-based sensors capable of imaging and tracking in the infrared, optical and radio bands. Images produced by the French SPOT satellite are commercially available and have a resolution of 10 metres or so; the Soviet Union is actually selling even better quality imagery that was presumably originally generated for military/intelligence purposes. With growing access to commercial launch services, it is likely that space-based imaging will become even more broadly available. Similarly, more and more countries are likely to field their own communications satellites and to incorporate the associated capabilities into their military planning. Remote sensor data can be transmitted either to central processing facilities for fusion, interpretation and analysis before relay to forward-based units, or directly to active weapon systems for real-time integration and application. The weapon systems of the future will also have on-board capability to make active and passive use of the full range of the electromagnetic spectrum, deriving targeting information from infrared, radio and optical emissions. In these ways, individual weapon platforms can be linked into a broad, robust sensor network supplying real-time target and threat data and analysis from a wide area under virtually all conditions.

These applications are not unique, however. Precisely the same sensor suites, with precisely the same characteristics, including linkage and analysis capabilities, can be deployed to promote political and military transparency. Early and accurate warning of military or any other threatening activity can permit time for appropriate response, including political moves that might avoid conflict. These technologies can reduce tendencies to misinterpret intentions and thus promote confidence in the efficacy of non-military responses. They can also be used explicitly to support co-operative and confidence-building measures (CBMs). In a related application, sensor technologies will certainly play a prominent role in the verification of arms control agreements, including ones now under negotiation and others sure to follow. On the other hand, however, the very transparency that appears to promote confidence and stability can be used to exploit weakness in times of political tension. In effect, one nation's CBM is another's source of military intelligence.

These points are merely illustrative. In general, there is a broad range of advanced technologies that will become much more capable than at present, and that will become far more widely available than is now the case—but that will nevertheless remain ambiguous as to their ultimate impact on international stability. This ambiguity will haunt attempts to discount nuclear weapons as a hedge against other forms of military threat and strategic surprise.

The growing capability of conventional (non-nuclear) military weapon systems deserves further attention. Emerging concepts for directed-energy weapons represent one family of such weapons likely to play a role in the future. One class of such weapons involves the conversion of a portion of the energy from a random source of chemical (or nuclear) reactions into a form that is then focused over long distances, avoiding the normal loss of effectiveness with distance to the target. This group includes high-energy lasers and particle beams. The other class exploits the possibility of extreme down-scaling of component size and weight so that a miniaturized, 'smart' bullet can carry its own propellant and guide itself to a remote target. This category includes the so-called 'brilliant pebbles', as well as a family of weapons whose potential applications range from anti-ballistic missile roles, to anti-tank and other battle-field missions. To focus only on directed-energy weapons would be to think too narrowly, however. Advances in other non-nuclear weapons will also be important, and will derive from steady progress in electronics, computer science, materials science, chemistry and the ability more efficiently to translate abstract understanding into specific applications by means of more accurate and detailed numerical modelling. This progress will result in the development of high-energy explosives, including fuel-air explosives and improvements in the accuracy of delivery.[13]

The net effect of this evolution will be such that the military effectiveness (as opposed to the sheer destructiveness) of non-nuclear weapons will approach, and in some cases already has approximated, that of nuclear weapons. A full analysis will likely not emerge for several years, but the record of the Persian Gulf war gives ample testimony to the military effectiveness of precision guided munitions. In the meantime, a simple example illustrates this point: 4500 World War II B-17s would have had to drop a total of 9000 bombs (each 2000 lbs or about 900 kg), or 95 Viet Nam-era F-105s would have had to drop a total of 190 bombs to achieve the same probability of damage as one F-117 Stealth fighter carrying one 2000-lb smart bomb.[14] What is more, much of this potential for increased effectiveness will in the future likely require less investment in an elaborate production infrastructure than has so far proved to be necessary for nuclear weapons. Furthermore, investments in these capabil-ities are not meeting with the sort of international political condemnation that has generally greeted attempts to acquire nuclear weapons. It is also unlikely that the military use of such technologies will be as inhibited by international opinion as has been the case with nuclear weapons. In a reversal of the historical experience of the nuclear superpowers, it may be that advanced con-ventional weaponry may prove to be the more cost-effective investment for many states, in both economic and political terms.

[13] The evolution of military technology is discussed in Crow, S. and Bajusz, W., 'The future of military technology', unpublished paper, Los Alamos National Laboratory, Center for National Security Studies (July 1989); and Blechman, B. M., *Alternative Strategic Environments, 1994–2004*, P-1785 (Institute for Defense Analyses, Alexandria, Va., Jan. 1985).

[14] Dugan, M., 'The air war', *U.S. News and World Report*, 11 Feb. 1991, p. 29.

There are additional reasons that suggest a growing rather than a diminishing trend in the proliferation of high-technology, non-nuclear weapons. As alluded to above, the necessary technologies often derive directly from the knowledge and industry necessary for general economic development. For example, super-strong, super-light composite materials developed to reduce energy consumption and save money find their way into light, mobile armour. Fourth-generation computers and programming for industrial process control begin to offer greatly enhanced military command and communication possibilities. And ever more competitive markets and continuing pressures for growth and expansion provide strong incentives for the development of export markets. In this environment, it has been difficult for the international system to develop any satisfactory regime to restrain such proliferation, and unilateral and multi-lateral attempts to promote voluntary self-restraint have proved less than satisfactory. The result has been a world-wide proliferation of advanced non-nuclear weapon capabilities that includes ballistic missile and submarine propulsion technologies, and that threatens the current and future stability of international relations.[15]

The issue of nuclear proliferation also demands some attention in any treatment of the general role of technology in the future evolution of the international system. To an ever-increasing extent, conflict may draw its participants from a growing family of countries with nascent nuclear weapon capability. The continuing diffusion of technology related to the design and production of nuclear weapons, and to the production of the necessary nuclear material, will exacerbate this issue. This trend will be especially problematic for a set of developing nations that possess growing economic resources and that are engaged in political and military competition with rival states. On the one hand, attempts to limit this trend face many of the same conflicts with economic and political self-interest that are presented in the case of non-nuclear technological proliferation. On the other hand, because of the radiation emitted by all nuclear materials, technology offers a number of options for strengthening the verification regime of the 1968 Non-Proliferation Treaty in the future. These and other proliferation-related issues are dealt with more fully in the chapter on this subject by George Quester in this volume.

Attention was drawn earlier to the potential for significant improvements in the effectiveness of directed-energy weapons, possibly leading to capabilities competitive with nuclear weapons. There is an additional dimension to this issue. If research on defences against ballistic missile attack continues to be productive, there may also occur a 'sea change' in the issue of offence/defence balance in the strategic or the tactical arena. Such a change would certainly heighten the potential importance of other kinds of military technologies, but it would also raise fundamental questions about the nature of the future international security regime. Would a defence-dominant outcome be relevant only for

---

[15] See, for example, Navias, M., *Ballistic Missile Proliferation in the Third World*, Adelphi Paper no. 252 (International Institute for Strategic Studies: London, 1990).

the nuclear powers, or would there be collateral implications for the strategic security of other states? Would the emergence of effective and robust defences stimulate an 'arms race' for new offensive capability, or would it complete the marginalization of nuclear weapons? If nuclear weapons were to become less relevant, would there emerge a new class of conventional strategic threats designed to circumvent a defensive umbrella?

Perhaps more fundamental is the question of whether all nations would have equal access to offensive and defensive technologies. Given the likely continuation of significant differences in national levels of technological sophistication and rates of development, it is probable that the future international system would be substantially non-uniform with respect to the balance between offence and defence. Such an imbalance would in turn raise serious questions about the stability of such an international security regime.

The above discussion has offered a number of observations about ways in which technology will be a direct or indirect driver in the evolution of the international system. Technology will be important in influencing the character of that system, but it will be social, economic and political factors that will play the dominant role in determining how and if these questions and issues will be resolved. Indeed, it will be these non-technical factors that ultimately determine who will be the major actors, what will be the relative roles for commercial as opposed to military technologies in establishing national power and influence, what means will be available and effective for ensuring stability and enabling conflict resolution, and even whether nations will still be the fundamental units for defining instabilities and conflict.

IV. Technical issues associated with any path towards zero nuclear weapons

In addition to the general questions concerning the links between technological capabilities, technological changes and access to competitive technologies inherent in the above discussion, there are specific technical considerations that play central roles in defining several key stages in any path towards the elimination of nuclear weapons. But again, these 'technical' issues are not restricted to very narrow (and not very interesting) physical problems of monitoring weapon removal and destruction, management of nuclear materials, and other such mechanical procedures. Rather, these 'technical' issues are both political and technological, reflecting the interactive processes of reshaping or even redefining international security concepts as nuclear deterrence, developing adequate verification, physical security, and politically reassuring devices such as confidence-building measures.

The first stages of any path towards no nuclear weapons must involve very large and significant nuclear force reductions primarily by the United States and the Soviet Union, since they have by far the largest nuclear stockpiles. Several of the key technical questions emerge from examining the process by which these bilateral force reductions will be carried out. But later stages would have to include the forces of the other currently recognized nuclear powers (China, France and the United Kingdom), perhaps leading to the point at which force reductions by the USA and the Soviet Union result in a world with five nations with roughly equivalent nuclear stockpiles, at least as measured by numbers of weapons. This threshold will raise further questions of political, strategic and technological import.

Critical questions again arise when we contemplate the possible transition to force levels far below those of today, for in that case the nuclear capabilities of several additional nations come into play, whether or not they have eventuated in an actual weapon production capability. In order to examine the main technical issues associated with these various transitions, we inspect the issues raised at five indicative stages, including the ultimate ('zero') threshold.

The transition to smaller but still very large superpower arsenals

In terms of numbers, this is approximately the level that would be achieved by the START negotiations—on the order of 10 000 strategic nuclear weapons each for the United States and the Soviet Union, with the forces of other nuclear powers left untouched.

As we have now seen from the past few years of the START negotiation process, perhaps the key element in allowing this first step in reducing nuclear arsenals has been a general reduction in superpower tensions, accompanied by a gradual de-emphasis of nuclear weapon issues in Soviet and US national security policies and in their relations with one another. (Strategic deterrence is still supported by substantial commitments to strategic nuclear systems, however.) Reductions to and maintenance of these force levels are to be accomplished through the mediation of traditional, bilateral arms control, with heavy focus by both sides on the stability of the resulting deterrent relationship. There is no direct intent to achieve a fundamental restructuring of the international security system through these reductions.

Cuts in the superpower nuclear arsenals have also been enabled by the massive political and economic changes occurring inside the Soviet Union; indeed the collapses, political shifts and challenges to the existing order within and without the USSR have recently become so intense that some observers, including Paul Nitze, have concluded that the START reductions have already been rendered out of date by events, and that we should move immediately to a new round of further cuts in nuclear weaponry. But others participating in the treaty process, noticeably Richard Burt, the US negotiator, urge caution in the face of an unpredictable political and economic future for the Soviet Union.[16]

From a technical and operational point of view, these changes in forces have been accompanied by an emphasis on stability from both the retaliatory force

[16] Nitze, P. H., 'Leapfrog into START II', *New York Times*, 25 Oct. 1990, p. 27; Burt, R., 'Is START obsolete?', *Washington Post*, 13 Nov. 1990, p. A23.

and crisis management points of view, on the safety of systems from accidents or from accidental use, and on other risk-reduction factors such as security from unauthorized use by terrorists or others. Any significant changes leading to new capabilities or greatly increased effectiveness of systems on either side have been relatively limited. This has been true for both new warhead designs and new weapon platforms. In addition, from a military and strategic point of view, there has been increased discussion of a de-emphasis of counter-nuclear force attack and targeting options, while possibly turning towards an ability to attack general purpose forces with long-range nuclear weapons.[17]

Verification of nuclear reductions will be important, particularly at first when actual destruction of launchers, missiles and even warheads may be required, and will tend to follow lines now developing at the conclusion of the START agreement: that is, some amount of on-site inspection and observation, but with both sides placing their primary reliance for confidence in verification on national technical means of verification. At the levels of nuclear forces that would remain after START, however, the extant technologies of verification are neither a significant barrier to nor a stimulus towards reductions.

The verification of what is occurring in the realm of conventional arms in Europe may (at least in the short run) actually be more important than nuclear weapon monitoring *per se*. The Soviet Union has during 1990 moved very substantial amounts of conventional military equipment out of Germany and Eastern Europe, back to storage points beyond the Urals, outside the agreed monitoring boundaries of the Conventional Armed Forces in Europe (CFE) Treaty for on-site or overflight verification. Other personnel and equipment have been reassigned duty as 'naval marines', which effectively removes them from CFE reductions, as naval forces are not significantly constrained by the CFE draft agreement. These withdrawals, including those which result in dis-mantlement and/or destruction of equipment, together with other Soviet and Warsaw Pact reductions in force to reach CFE ceilings, will undoubtedly have a dominant role to play in determining how soon further nuclear reductions are subject to negotiation.

We feel that a certain period of time spent at START levels will permit the parties to decide whether further reductions are indicated. For example, the unification of Germany is now a fact, and how the Soviet Union responds to this geopolitical revolution may determine at least in part whether and how fast the next steps in nuclear reductions may be taken. Equally important is the course of events inside the Soviet Union and in Eastern Europe. It seems apparent that this period of time will not be driven so much by technical factors as by economic, political, ethnic and other social issues internal to the powers in Europe.

[17] Sloss, L., *Reexamining Nuclear Policy in a Changing World*, CNSS Report no. 11 (Center for National Security Studies, Los Alamos National Laboratory, Los Alamos, N. Mex., Dec. 1990).

The transition to moderate numbers

This stage would involve the reduction of Soviet and US nuclear forces to about 3000 weapons.

A number of US analysts contend that reductions of superpower arsenals from START levels to one-half this level or somewhat less (4000–5000) will not alter the global deterrent relationship in any fundamental way.[18] This is not to say that such cuts do not pose immense difficulties for the United States and the Soviet Union, because their respective abilities to carry out the myriad of missions assigned to nuclear systems will become increasingly problematic. But the situation at 5000 weapons would still remain fundamentally characterized by two dominant nuclear powers that possess substantially more nuclear capability and flexibility than other powers.

The transition down to a level of 3000 or fewer nuclear weapons, while not apparently a gigantic change (only about a factor of three) from large arsenals, is in fact a highly significant move.[19] At these levels, the United States (and presumably the Soviet Union) would begin to reach major technical limits, both with respect to flexibility and target coverage. Although the most important nuclear deterrent relationship would remain that between the two largest nuclear powers, their capacity to carry out business in usual ways would no longer exist.

A level of 3000 weapons also begins to represent a shift from the world of a bipolar superpower nuclear confrontation with ancillary nuclear powers, towards a world of about five approximately equivalent nuclear powers. Such developing trends in the international system will have large technological and political consequences. The nuclear forces of China, France and the United Kingdom, to this point largely unaffected by the nuclear reductions of the United States and the Soviet Union, must now begin to be considered on an equal footing with the others. The basic strategies which underlie the acquisition of these third-country forces must be carefully understood, as well as their types and deployments, if a revised notion of nuclear stability is to be sustained in this situation.[20]

---

[18] Sloss (note 18). See also Zhihai, Z., 'The future of nuclear weapons: a Chinese perspective', in Maaranen and Garrity (note 6). In their prominent 1988 study of nuclear weapon reductions, Michael May and his colleagues concluded that a force of some 3000 US strategic weapons might be sufficient for the purposes of deterrence. A close reading of their study reveals, however, that a somewhat higher number is probably justified given all of the associated uncertainties. May, M. M., Bing, G. F. and Steinbruner, J. D., 'Strategic arsenals after START: the implications of deep cuts', *International Security*, vol. 13, no. 1 (summer 1988).

[19] For the purposes of this simple analysis, we do not distinguish between 'strategic' and 'tactical' nuclear weapons at this level, but instead focus on a representative number of total weapons.

[20] On the future of the European nuclear forces, see Heisbourg, F., 'The British and French nuclear forces', *Survival*, vol. 31, no. 4 (July/Aug. 1989); and Boyer, Y., 'The British and French nuclear deterrents in an era of uncertainties', in Maaranen and Garrity (note 6). On the Chinese nuclear weapon programme, see Lin, C.-P., 'From panda to dragon: China's nuclear strategy', *The National Interest*, no. 15 (spring 1989); and Lin, C.-P., *China's Nuclear Weapons Strategy: Tradition Within Evolution* (Lexington Books: Cambridge, Mass., 1988).

In terms of technical–operational issues, the possible uses of nuclear capabilities and technologies for war termination and escalation control on a global level must be questioned, as the capabilities shrink compared to the number of things they are asked to accomplish. There would also be questions raised about the ability of the United States and the Soviet Union to account for nuclear use by one of these second-tier nuclear states without opening themselves to significant threats by one or a combination of the remaining nuclear powers.

Technologies and policies to ensure against the further proliferation of nuclear weapon materials, facilities and technical capabilities begin to be of much greater interest and importance than they have been up to this time. And, in this system, the diffusion of new conventional military technological capabilities begins to take on greater significance as well. As a technical requirement for maintaining the stability of deterrence, the nuclear powers may find it necessary to take measures to deny the advantages of technology breakthroughs to potential adversaries. Paradoxically, within the nuclear weapon research and development (R&D) realm this may entail requirements to maintain the intellectual capabilities of scientists and engineers, the R&D technology base and facilities, and adequate force structure hedges against surprise (e.g., technical threats to the survivability of remaining forces).

Questions of what constitutes the nature of 'stability' in this system come to the fore. What are the political, organizational and technical arrangements for dealing with crises? What roles should the second-tier nuclear powers begin to play in crisis stability? Is the potential emergence of another nuclear power, especially in tinderbox areas like the Middle East, a crisis in and of itself? And technologically, limited deployments of anti-ballistic missile defences may come to appear stabilizing, at least against the accidental use of nuclear weapons, or their use by parties with limited capabilities.

Further steps to assure stability in relations via technical means become of greater and greater utility. As numbers decrease, but are still substantial, the safety of individual weapon systems, and indeed of individual weapons, becomes of increasing importance to maintaining retaliatory capabilities. The nuclear powers may want to investigate the possible sharing of safety and control principles and technologies such as permissive action links (PALs), and even design principles such as one-point safety approaches and technologies, and other safety and security concepts. Modern nuclear design techniques, including new materials, insensitive high explosives and modern electronics, permit a very high degree of intrinsic safety to be included in nuclear weapon systems, minimizing the likelihood that accidents could ever produce nuclear yield or even scatter hazardous materials into the environment. In similar fashion, PALs using miniaturized electronics and sensors, together with other control techniques, can be incorporated into nuclear systems, minimizing the possibility that the weapon could be launched or detonated without authorization.[21]

The transition to small nuclear forces

Reductions to about 1000 weapons would be a key step in the evolution of the international system and the role of nuclear weapons in that system. The five current nuclear powers would have essentially equivalent nuclear forces, with the US and Soviet forces existing with considerably reduced levels of weapons and capabilities. The concept of deterrence would require extensive redefinition to fit this situation.

All nuclear powers would face severe constraints on numbers of weapons, nuclear operations concepts and nuclear security strategies. With five powers of roughly equal capability, but with no one of them capable of covering all the targets of value in all other nuclear nations, the policy situation becomes quite complex. Any consideration of a nuclear 'war-fighting' strategy—whether a policy of massive or even selective retaliation—could potentially leave a nation adopting such a policy essentially exposed to the nuclear threats of third parties. This situation would probably mark an inflection point in international politics between the great powers, as non-nuclear capabilities, technological creativity and economic prowess begin to hold sway over nuclear weapons as utilitarian tools of exercising power. The definition of which nations were still 'great powers' at this juncture would be more and more dependent on how non-nuclear, and especially commercial (or dual-use) technologies, had advanced in the more dynamic countries.

Would continued possession of nuclear weapons at these levels contribute more to stability or instability? Because this level of nuclear forces represents an inflection point, the answer to this question depends on the status of non-nuclear forces and technologies, how nuclear forces are structured and managed, how defences against strategic and tactical offensive weapons have evolved, and other trade-off factors. The evolution of defensive technologies at this point could be particularly critical in determining the military stability of nuclear relationships. And to the extent they can be developed to the point of providing extremely high levels of protection of residual nuclear forces against successful attack by either nuclear or conventional means, they might contribute to a very stable relationship between the nuclear-armed powers.

A major technical requirement, if there is to be any possibility of stability while deterrent forces are in the transition to these sizes and relationships, is that strategies for nuclear forces must increasingly shift towards a 'defensive deterrence' stance and posture. Technically, this means that capabilities for counterforce targeting and other so-called 'war-fighting' measures must steadily be de-emphasized (or, to put it another way, the survivability of residual nuclear forces must be steadily increased). Another technical requirement is

[21] See, for example, White (note 13).

that changes in nuclear forces during draw-downs from large to moderate force sizes should further emphasize issues of safety and security of existing forces.

Technical emphasis for any further nuclear weapon system development would be placed primarily on safety, survivability, command and control. This would require further changes in weapon platforms, and probably in many weapons themselves. This in itself would undoubtedly engender a ferocious debate about the need for further 'modernization' of nuclear systems in a world of apparently few systems. In such an atmosphere, it might be productive to consider a sharing between the nuclear powers of the actual techniques for the safety and command and control of warheads and delivery systems.

At some point in the reduction of the number of nuclear forces, the emerging complementarity of nuclear and conventional forces must be faced. In this system, the impacts of the proliferation of advanced conventional weapons and technologies could be very dramatic. The emergence of not just smart but even brilliant conventional weapon systems is even now imminent, with further improvements in precision-guided munitions, standoff missiles such as the Exocet and the cruise missile, and others; not to mention advances in materials and other factors that influence the armour–anti-armour equation, steady advances in stealthy aircraft, the increasing leverage provided by space-based C^3I systems, and the gruesome potential for use of chemical weapons.

With such technological concepts not just emergent but in many cases with us now, if nuclear forces are reduced without substantial, parallel reductions in conventional forces, there may be a nuclear–conventional cross-over point at which conventional capabilities become independently attractive as a strategic first-strike force during crises. The difference is that the inhibitions about the actual use of conventional forces have in the past been far less constraining that those against actual nuclear use. If agreements to balance off countervailing conventional forces, or to obviate their necessity through other (presumably political) means, have not been accomplished, this can become a period of great instability, with an increased chance of conventional conflict *and* probably an increased chance of escalation to nuclear conflict.[22]

Politically, the inference from these discussions is clear. There can be no question of a move to very low or zero forces without technical reassurance that 'offensive' conventional and nuclear forces have been largely if not completely neutralized through a combination of weapons and doctrinal changes. This means in turn that verification will be very important, at least at first, thus requiring new and higher levels of intrusiveness in inspections, and the destruction of warheads themselves as well as weapon carriers. Verification could become less important over time, however, if the political climate improves substantially.

---

[22] The historical record with respect to conventional deterrence is discussed in Mearsheimer, J. J., *Conventional Deterrence* (Cornell University Press: Ithaca, N.Y., 1983).

Very small arsenals

The most fundamental requirement for a transition to about 100 weapons is enormous political and military transparency in the international system, and enormous levels of international trust as an inherent part of a new international security order. Nations would demand and require great confidence levels and very early warning of any dangers to the stability of this system, whether technological or political.

Strategically, these remaining nuclear arsenals would serve as a sort of 'existential nuclear hedge' against unknowns and unpredictable events, for example, substantial technical advances and/or breakthroughs in non-nuclear weapons or defence technologies; terrorists or other 'wild card' international actors who might want to generate a clandestine capability for mass destruction, through nuclear, chemical or other means; or cheating by some players who intended to use small numbers of nuclear weapons for purposes of coercion or blackmail.

Presumably, any attempt to 'escape' or 'break out' from the system by reverting to large-scale conventional alternatives would be barred by conventional arms control agreements; at such very low levels of nuclear weapons, confidence in and verification of such agreements would have to be very substantial.

The problem of nuclear proliferation, in the form of an unexpected nuclear power on this scene, would be much more destabilizing than at present. The announcement of the possession of even tens of or just a few weapons by a new nuclear party could be expected to cause severe doubts about its motives. Another fundamental requirement for the achievement and maintenance of this global system would therefore seem to be a much different international approach to the problem of nuclear proliferation, involving development of joint mechanisms for enforcing desired limitations on nuclear technologies.

There is another interesting analytical inflexion point possible as the number of global nuclear systems goes down to a very low level. At some time in the process of reducing numbers of nuclear weapons, it is possible that a level is reached at which the belief in their deterrent value vanishes, primarily because their capabilities are reduced below the minimum level for causing sufficient uncertainty in the mind of an antagonist. But they are not yet at zero levels. There may be a fairly distinct cross-over point between nuclear deterrence and nuclear punishment, where there was not sufficient punishment potential to deter major conflict, but there was enough total destructive power to create major damage. In this case, if conventional forces are dramatically reduced and are increasingly restructured into 'defensive defence' or 'non-provocative' postures and deployments, there may be situations in which the use of a few nuclear weapons could be decisive, even to the point of restoring offensive capability. If nuclear weapons appear to be the only effective military alternative, they may be hard not to use.

Some R&D on nuclear phenomena, and some elements of the technical weapon infrastructure, would necessarily have to remain in place for reasons of assuring confidence in and the safety of the existing small stockpiles, and to permit a slow buildup of greater nuclear capability should there occur very undesirable shifts or reversals in key international variables.

Detailed nuclear verification may not be practical or even feasible, in the sense of today's requirements, but specific technical verification measures may be less important than the verification of intent, assisted by an open political system, free access to and good communications between nuclear and non-nuclear states, and so on. Any rigid verification regime might be so intrusive as to threaten economic competitiveness, because other technologies than those traditionally associated with nuclear weapons would have to be monitored very closely.

Approaching zero nuclear weapons

This is the final step, the final end-point posited in this project. It raises a number of very difficult considerations and requirements.

The transition to the previous level of nuclear arms ('small nuclear arsenals') may be the last clearly definable and feasible step available for some time. This may seem an unreasonable analytic position to adopt, but we argue that we do not yet have a clear idea of what it means for the world to have 'no' or 'zero nuclear weapons'.

What does it mean to 'eliminate' nuclear weapons? When calling for extremely reduced levels, or elimination of nuclear weapons, it is usually the actual warheads deployed in stockpiles and arsenals of weapons that are referred to. If the intent is to 'totally eliminate' nuclear weapons, is it sufficient to disassemble all currently existing warheads? But small secret stockpiles are easy to hide and hard to find. An immediate additional question is what happens to all the fission and fusion fuels from existing weapons. Fissionable metals alone would yield on the order of thousands of metric tonnes of material. Does 'elimination' of nuclear weapons require the physical destruction of all these materials?

What about the facilities that physically produce weapons? Do we require the destruction of all production reactors, which in some cases may be used for other purposes, including electric power for civilian use? Does this include enrichment and separation plants, which again in many cases can be intricately tied to non-weapon fuel cycles? Should all facilities capable of handling nuclear materials, even if their function is not weapon-related, be abandoned? In some cases (such as dedicated warhead fabrication facilities) it may be feasible to consider decommissioning plants, but in others (such as enrichment facilities) it may not always be possible to destroy the plant without also destroying part of a domestic energy supply system. Minimal nuclear weapon production capacity could easily be hidden in a world filled with other advanced technologies, for instance, laser isotope separation plants.

Do we eliminate nuclear physics R&D, nuclear knowledge or even nuclear scientists? It is not feasible to control knowledge of nuclear physics. The scientific knowledge base is at this point extremely widespread and well documented, easily available to and retrievable by anyone with a will to accumulate it. Similarly, most of the basic technologies involved have proliferated as well. Previous attempts at 'technological denial' as a means of controlling access to a militarily useful technology have not always turned out well. The experience of trying to deny nuclear technologies to the world as a means of stopping (as opposed to slowing or controlling) nuclear weapon proliferation is perhaps compelling in its relative degree of failure. Without political assurances of stable security, science will be exploited for military use. And knowledge of nuclear weapon technology will persist indefinitely.

More importantly, there are key technical questions about the fundamental nature of the international security system at this point. Questions of the acceptability of the international security system become paramount; several crucial issues are involved, at least.

What is the prevailing nature of the resulting system? How is power distributed? Are nations, or other groups, left to deal with threats to their interests and survival on their own, or are there joint mechanisms for managing threats and conflicts? What other means of reassuring stability of relations are available? What are the technical means available to hedge against technological surprise of an unwanted nature? At a nominal zero nuclear level, there would be no hedge left against military applications of other technologies that might upset the balance of relations in this situations.

What is the relationship to other arms control and limitation agreements; in particular, what is assumed to happen to conventional military forces? At a nominal level of zero nuclear weapons, we must realize and cope with the fact that their deterrent effect against the threat of large-scale conventional violence has also disappeared.

What is the relationship to defences, including defences against strategic (nuclear and non-nuclear) attack? What has occurred in other advanced technological developments that could deeply affect the future relationships between nations? How have assurances of stability been extended to new, important areas of operation, especially uses of outer space?

In addition to these issues which are primarily strategic and political in nature, there is an additional technical requirement at this level of armament to provide extraordinary protection against nuclear deceit and cheating. One of the first such contingencies that demands attention is that of the hidden arsenal, retained secretly and outside a global reduction to micro or zero forces.

At global micro (or nominal zero) nuclear force levels, the sudden introduction of hundreds or even tens of previously unannounced nuclear weapons would be enormously destabilizing, especially since the prime motivation for concealment would always be suspected to be an attempt at hegemonic power of some kind. The effects would probably be most acute in places of regional disputes where massive conventional forces were not available to counter such a move, or where there were massive conventional asymmetries. The effects on other powers with former nuclear forces could only be to call seriously into question their continued commitment to a world with zero nuclear weapons.

And finally, even assuming that all the technical criteria were met for a complete, global 'elimination' of nuclear weapons, there must be similar protection against the retention of a clandestine capability for reintroducing nuclear stockpiles. Such a capability for nuclear force reconstitution would be viewed by many as just as dangerous as the actual possession of weapons. It would have a strongly negative effect on a presumed trend towards zero nuclear weapons. And it could severely alter perceptions of the safety, security and stability of the international security system, and challenge its very basis.

V. Conclusion

We must again stress the critical point that was made at the beginning of this chapter: technology will not be the decisive factor that determines whether it will ultimately be possible to marginalize, or eventually eliminate, nuclear weapons. To be sure, advances in science and technology made nuclear weapons feasible, but those weapons were first developed, and are still in existence, because of political decisions taken in the context of an anarchic international system. This said, developments in technology will inevitably affect the character of future domestic and international politics, thus making nuclear marginalization/elimination seem either more or less attractive.

At the broadest level, we foresee no alteration in the fact that economic development—driven in large part by increasingly rapid technological change—will continue to be uneven and hence will be a source of international tension as long as the nation-state remains the basic unit of account.[23] The nature of this rapid technological change is important, because it points towards the development of important classes of technologies that are inherently dual-capable (i.e., supporting both civilian and military applications). In the future, military power will be increasingly defined as much by the ability of major states to utilize 'soft' dual-use technologies (e.g., sensors and advanced computational capability) as by the deployment of 'hard' technologies (e.g., tanks and aircraft). These soft technologies are difficult to control and measure, and yet are inherent in the continued development of modern economies (as well as military force structure). It is not inconceivable that a revisionist power could develop over time a substantial offensive capability without massive increases

---

[23] Many economists believe that we are now moving towards a regionalized world economy (Asia, North America and Europe) within an overall multilateral framework.

in the size of its conventional force structure, especially if other powers lagged in their ability to master and utilize these new technologies.[24]

On the whole, we therefore would judge that these technologies will have a net negative effect on the prospect of nuclear elimination, even though there may well be a substantial marginalization of nuclear weapons due to a range of political factors.[25] Nations will be inclined to retain nuclear weapons as a hedge against the uncertainties created by the necessarily widespread development of dual-use technologies. This is not to say that radical reductions in (or the elimination of) nuclear weapons are necessarily impossible on these technical grounds, but rather that they would require substantial changes in the character of international relations—to the point where the development of dual-use technologies is no longer regarded as a serious, if potential, threat.

It should be emphasized, however, that some aspects of dual-use technologies could support radical nuclear reductions or elimination, assuming a favourable evolution in international politics. These technologies are those associated with communications and information. At one level, the communications revolution will arguably support the development of open, democratic political systems, which are arguably much less prone to go to war (at least with each other) than are authoritarian or totalitarian political systems.[26] More to the point for our purposes, the increased political transparency that is implied by the information revolution may ease the technical requirements for dedicated verification capabilities that might otherwise be required to permit radical nuclear reductions. It is probably feasible to verify nuclear stockpiles in the 10 000- and 3000-weapon ranges with existing or projected technologies. To verify much lower levels in a truly closed society might well be technically too stressing.

At the more narrow military level, there seems to be considerable reason to believe that technology will support a substantial move away from nuclear weapons, if not necessarily to zero. It would be incorrect to say that advanced conventional weapons can now rival the military effectiveness of nuclear weapons—that is, an ability to destroy targets—across the board. Nevertheless, the so-called nuclear revolution in military affairs—which was based on nuclear weapons, ballistic missiles and computer-enhanced accuracy—has

---

[24] This is particularly important because Japan and Germany, which are major powers that have been hitherto relatively restrained in their development of military forces, are at the forefront of the development of many dual-use technologies.

[25] These political trends towards the marginalization of nuclear weapons are discussed in Garrity, P. J., 'The future of nuclear weapons: final study report', CNSS Report no. 6 (Center for National Security Studies, Los Alamos National Laboratory, Los Alamos, N.Mex., Feb. 1990).

[26] This is, of course, a contentious point that has been advanced most systematically by Michael Doyle in three articles: Doyle, M., 'Liberalism and world politics', American Political Science Review, vol. 80 (Dec. 1986); Doyle, M., 'Kant, liberal legacies, and foreign affairs', Philosophy and Public Affairs, vol. 12 (summer 1983); and Doyle, M., 'Kant, liberal legacies, and foreign affairs, part 2', Philosophy and Public Affairs, vol. 12 (autumn 1983). The communications revolution arguably will support the expansion of democratic political systems because (a) it will become increasingly difficult for dictatorial regimes to deny their citizens outside information and internal communications; and (b) dictatorial regimes will come under growing pressure to liberalize in order to participate fully in the communications/information revolution, without which they will not be competitive in the international economic system.

reached the point of diminishing marginal returns, if it has not played itself out completely.[27] The next technological imperative would seem to be that driven by the 'information revolution', wherein it will become relatively easier to 'see' mobile or concealed military targets on land, in the air and space, and at sea. If targets can be located with fewer false detections, and if the information can be distributed effectively and rapidly, the conventional battlefield will become more transparent and potentially more lethal than it is at present—especially if information systems are married to such rapidly developing areas of military technology as improved conventional munitions and directed-energy weapons.[28] These information systems seem to promise (or threaten) a revolution of the conventional battlefield and it is in this realm, not that of nuclear weapons, that military planners and technologists are likely to focus their attention over the next several decades. This technological trend will reinforce the growing political reluctance of national leaders, at least in Western nations, to contemplate the use of nuclear weapons on the battlefield. As the circumstances in which nuclear weapon use would be contemplated decline, one must assume that the numbers and types of these weapons would likewise decline.

Still we must be careful not to take this argument too far. Not all states have the financial or technological capacity to build armed forces around these revolutionary conventional technologies. For them, nuclear weapons may actually become more attractive, in that they can serve to equalize or offset the superior non-nuclear military systems of countries such as the USA. There are already indications that the Soviet military may be thinking about nuclear weapons in this way, at least until the economy of the USSR (or a successor state) can fully support the development of high-technology conventional weapons. Also, states such as Iraq, witnessing the course and outcome of the Persian Gulf War, could conclude that it is better to concentrate on acquiring weapons of mass destruction (including nuclear weapons) than to try to match the great powers across the full spectrum of advanced conventional systems.

In short, although it is possible to identify a number of technical trends that point to the marginalization of nuclear weapons, these trends are by no means unambiguous, and they do not point towards the complete elimination of nuclear weapons in the foreseeable future. There would seem to be a certain 'stickiness'—inherent limits on how far and how fast any denuclearization can proceed. This is not to make a hard and fast judgement about the long-term probability of reaching zero nuclear weapons, but rather to place technical factors in their proper context.

---

[27] This conclusion has apparently been reached by Soviet military forecasters. See Trulock, N., Hines, K. L., and Kerr, A. D., *Soviet Military Thought in Transition: Implications for the Long-Term Military Competition*, PSR Report no. 1831 (Pacific-Sierra Research Corporation: Arlington, Va., May 1988); and Odom, W. E., 'Soviet force posture: dilemmas and directions', *Problems of Communism* (July/Aug. 1985), pp. 1–14.

[28] This point is made, among other places, in *Discriminate Deterrence: Report of the Commission on Integrated Long-Term Strategy* (Committee on Integrated Long-Term Strategy: Washington, DC, Jan. 1988), p. 8.

6. Verification of nuclear weapon elimination

Patricia M. Lewis

I. Introduction

Verification of arms control treaties has been a central and positive feature of negotiations and agreements over the past few years. This is primarily because there is now acceptance by states in both East and West about the need for on-site inspections and other intrusive techniques in order to effectively monitor arms control and reduction treaties. There has however also been a growing realization of the cost of verifying treaties.[1] The bilateral Treaty between the USA and the USSR on the elimination of their intermediate-range and shorter-range missiles (the INF Treaty) of 1987, the multilateral Stockholm Document of 1986 and the difficulties encountered in funding the International Atomic Energy Agency (IAEA) to safeguard the 1968 Non-Proliferation Treaty (NPT) have brought home the harsh realities of paying for treaty verification in terms of both hard cash and valuable resources (such as personnel and organizational structures), and in terms of the degree of intrusion into daily affairs of state and military planning. As a result there has been a tempering of the hard-line view that verification should be able to detect the smallest infringement and that on-site inspections should be allowed 'any time, anywhere'.[2] Instead, there is a return to the idea of 'reasonable sufficiency' in verification. An effective verification regime is now defined as one which would, in the first place, deter violations and would be able to identify important infringements of a treaty.[3] Such an attitude to verification is one which will build confidence over time by building up trust between the states in an atmosphere of co-operation—a vital process if the elimination of nuclear weapons is ever to occur.

In order to consider verifying the elimination of nuclear weapons, we have to make certain assumptions.

---

[1] For example the US fiscal year (FY) 1991 verification budget was raised by Congress from $150 million to $170 million. The US OSIA (On-Site Inspection Agency) budget for 1990 was $40 million and is expected to climb by as much as $200–300 million per year because of new treaties. The IAEA safeguards budget is $54.2 million, although it is based on a zero/negative growth.

[2] 'Any time, anywhere' became the catch-phrase for the attitude contained within the US approach to CWC (Chemical Weapons Convention) inspections. The attitude was first embodied in Article 10 of the US draft of the CWC. See Conference on Disarmament document CD/500, 18 Apr. 1984.

[3] Effective verification is now defined by the US Administration as being designed to: (*a*) deter violations by increasing the likelihood of detection and making cheating difficult; (*b*) permit timely detection of violations so as to allow formulation of appropriate responses; and (*c*) ensure confidence in the agreement. See *Ronald F. Lehman, II, Director of the US Arms Control and Disarmament Agency, Testimony to the US Senate Foreign Relations Committee* (17 July 1990). For a detailed definition of verification, see *Study on the Role of the United Nations in the Field of Verification*, United Nations General Assembly, A/45/372 (28 Aug. 1990), p. 20.

First, we shall assume that the process (the 'process utopia') will be gradual, occurring over a period of years, either by agreement or by unilateral steps. Second, we shall also assume that it is the *global* elimination of nuclear weapons that is the issue. In other words, while a main focus will be on the known nuclear weapon states (NWS) reducing their nuclear arsenals, the undeclared NWS should also be brought to eliminate their stockpiles and the non-nuclear weapon states (NNWS) should remain as such.

The process will probably not proceed at a steady pace. Nor should it be assumed that the steps to disarmament will necessarily be sequential. There will probably be periods of large-scale activity in reductions of stockpiles and initiations of other measures such as fissile material cut-offs or nuclear testing limitations followed by resting periods during which there is very little movement or even some building up of nuclear missiles to agreed ceilings. Nor should it be assumed that negotiated agreements will form the main part of the elimination process.[4] Arms control from the national treasury—limitations of a state's weapon programme imposed by shrinking defence budgets—could become one of the main instruments of disarmament. Such unilateral measures are not completely unverifiable. They can be checked either by the fact that the weapon systems which have been independently reduced are already covered by an existing treaty with its own verification regime or by voluntary invitations to other states to check the reductions for themselves. This is discussed in more depth (see below).

As with the 1987 INF Treaty, the total absence of a class of weapons is far easier to verify than are the numbers of limited missiles. In the case of limits, all missile infrastructure (production, testing, maintenance, storage, training and deployment) remains intact. A missile found by overhead imagery means no more than that: it would be almost impossible to know whether or not it was a legally allowed missile. If, however, the treaty prohibited all nuclear weapons, the total infrastructure would no longer exist, which in itself is relatively easy to verify and any missile seen after the period of destruction would be an immediately obvious violation. Consequently, the argument that it is easier to verify the absence of nuclear weapons than low limits on them is strongly made in this chapter.

II. Building on foundations

To establish a gradual process which can be verified cost effectively, the treaties which are currently in existence and functioning could be built upon. In order to include as many countries as possible, the current multilateral treaties such as the 1968 NPT and the 1963 Partial Test Ban Treaty (PTBT) should be prime candidates. For example, the NPT could have a stricter safeguards

---

[4] Indeed, Kenneth Adelman, a former Director of the US ACDA, is advocating 'arms control without agreements' as a series of informal, unilateral and reciprocal steps so as to take advantage of the 'quasi-inevitable process' of force reductions due to financial constraints. See Adelman, K. L., *The Great Universal Embrace: Arms Summitry—A Skeptic's Account* (Simon & Schuster: New York, 1989).

regime than it has now, such as that proposed, with a majority following, at the 1990 NPT Review Conference in Geneva (but because there was no final document, the hard-fought agreement was not binding) and be applicable to all installations in the party states, not just to declared sites.

The extension of bilateral treaties into multilateral treaties is also a possibility for involving clandestine and threshold NWS. However, it is important that this process should not put any existing treaties at risk; and, therefore, building on these treaties may not involve direct alterations to these treaties, rather a building on the treaties to form new and separate agreements or new protocols. Of course, later treaties may make earlier treaties redundant, and the verification for treaties which directly follow on from previous agreements can be incorporated with the previous verification regime.

Treaties are not the only way to achieve progress: unilateral moves (which could be reciprocated) such as the removal of short-range nuclear artillery from Europe could be the quickest and most effective way to achieve reductions. These moves could be checked on a voluntary invitation basis, if the exact nature of the changes is declared in detail. For example, prior to the 1990 Conventional Armed Forces in Europe (CFE) Treaty, the USSR started withdrawing troops from Eastern Europe and the USA also began similar action in Western Europe. Neither of these moves was verified but President Gorbachev invited the West to send observers in order to witness the withdrawals,[5] and the Western media were in full attendance for the first phase of Soviet tank divisions being pulled out of eastern Germany. The issue of verifying unilateral measures is discussed below.

Given that we have no choice but to start from where we are now, it seems likely that elimination of the nuclear weapons already in existence will continue as a result of a process of negotiated treaties and national or alliance decisions on defence needs. The next treaty to deal with nuclear weapons is the Strategic Arms Reduction Treaty (START). Commonly referred to as START I, it is assumed that the START process will not stop with one agreement but that further cuts will be negotiated and embodied in the form of START II, START III and so on (which are also known as 'deep cuts' depending on the extent of the proposal). START I is a US–Soviet bilateral treaty and will be verified on that bilateral basis. Follow-on START negotiations will probably have to include, at the insistence of the Soviet Union, British and French strategic nuclear weapons. The inclusion of Chinese nuclear forces will also at some point have to be brought into the picture.

Either in conjunction with or following on from these agreements there could be another serious push for a comprehensive nuclear test ban (CTB). A CTB would not completely stop the nuclear arms race and certainly would not in itself bring about arms reductions; it would stop the development of new nuclear weapon designs and would help to halt the spread of nuclear weapons to NNWS. After the failure to reach a consensus final document at the 1990

[5] *The Times*, 18 July 1987.

NPT Review Conference, which was due entirely to the issue of a CTB treaty (CTBT) (non-aligned states, particularly Mexico, blocked attempts to achieve consensus because they felt that the NWS have not fulfilled their obligations under Article VI of the NPT and that they should have by now negotiated a CTBT), the future of the NPT is seriously in doubt. In 1995, along with the final Review Conference, there will be a conference to decide for how long the NPT should be extended. If serious progress towards a CTBT is not made by the NWS by that time, then a number of states may well block any significant extension of the NPT, thereby putting in jeopardy the few inhibitions to the spread of nuclear weapons that currently exist. If the curbing of nuclear weapon proliferation is to continue, then serious advances towards a CTBT must be made before 1995.

Current positions on the value of a CTB are far apart. Of the five NWS, only the Soviet Union makes positive statements about a CTB. France shows no interest in any limitations on nuclear testing, stating that it will not endorse a test ban unless it is part of a process for reducing nuclear weapons.[6] The current position of the USA and the UK is that because nuclear weapons are required for defence there can be no ban on testing—a CTB is therefore considered a 'long-term goal'.[7] China holds to a softer line and has often indicated that it would be willing to join a CTBT. In 1990 China stated that it would consider a CTB if the USA and the USSR reduce their nuclear weapons by 50 per cent.[8] The NNWS are also divided on the issue of a CTB, depending on which alliance they are in. The neutral and non-aligned states are pro-CTB and the East European states vote a pro-CTB line in the UN General Assembly, while Western NNWS tend to abstain in UN voting on the issue. Verification is a contentious issue in any consideration of a CTB and is discussed below.

In conjunction with reductions in nuclear missiles there will also have to be reductions in conventional forces (including naval forces) and the elimination of chemical weapons. Significant progress is being made in these areas. The negotiations of conventional force reductions and of confidence- and security-building measures (CSBMs) in Europe look set to continue.[9] The verification provisions for these agreements will be far-reaching and intrusive on a scale not previously known. Likewise for the Chemical Weapons Convention (CWC), if the negotiations ever produce a treaty, the verification provisions will involve

---

[6] Institute for Defense and Disarmament Studies, *Arms Control Reporter* (IDDS: Brookline, Mass.), June 1982 and Aug. 1987.

[7] See IDDS (note 6), 1990, sheet 608.A.2.

[8] See IDDS (note 6).

[9] See three articles in the *RUSI Journal*, vol. 135, no. 3 (autumn 1990): Hopkinson, G. W., 'CFE: A dead end?', pp. 31–34; Lewis, P., 'Verification and the Vienna Negotiations', pp. 35–39; and Borawski, J., 'The Vienna Negotiations on Confidence Building and Security Measures', pp. 40–44.

on-site inspections at industrial and commercial facilities as well as at military installations, and the inspections will be almost global in scope.[10]

III. Verification of missile and warhead reductions

The world has already seen the beginning of missile reductions thanks to the 1987 INF Treaty. This Treaty has a highly intrusive verification regime which has, over the past 3 years, built confidence and trust in the Treaty and has in itself promoted good relations between the USA and USSR. The INF Treaty eliminates a whole class of ground-launched nuclear missiles over a period of 3 years and verification continues for a further 10 years. Initially, it was assumed that the Treaty would allow for provision of 100 INF missiles on each side, and the verification measures which were envisaged were even more stringent. In 1987 General Secretary Gorbachev agreed to relinquish all INF weapons, and consequently, because the INF infrastructure would eventually be shut down, the verification measures were not as strict. This is a good illustration of the differences between verification requirements of a treaty banning a whole class of weapons and of a treaty limiting the number of weapons in a class.

In the first place, the data exchanged between two sides were checked by a series of baseline on-site inspections. Thereafter, the withdrawal and destruction of the missiles were witnessed by inspectors from both sides and bases which had all of their assigned missiles removed were closed-out under observation. Warheads were not affected by the INF Treaty and they are assumed to have returned to the national stockpiles for re-use in some form. Active bases are visited by inspectors to check the deployed numbers of deployed missiles at short notice. From mid-1988 to mid-1991, 20 such inspections are allowed per annum per party; for the following 5 years, 15 challenge inspections are allowed; and for the final 3 years of the Treaty, 10 per annum will be the maximum. Concerning verification of INF missile production, the USA is monitoring the SS-25 production facility at Votkinsk and the USSR is monitoring the Hercules production plant at Magna, Utah. The Votkinsk facility is certainly suffering from an abundance of technical equipment. To monitor that SS-25 production is not hiding the production of banned SS-20s, the USA has installed a portal perimeter monitoring system[11] that consists of 25–30 personnel, an infra-red profiler, an X-ray cargo scanner,[12] and a room full of computers to drive, monitor and analyse the system.

The INF Treaty pays significant attention to the role of national technical means (NTM). In particular, Article XII contains a provision for a co-operative

[10] See the SIPRI Chemical and Biological Warfare Studies series for detailed approaches to CWC verification (volumes in the series are published by SIPRI/Taylor & Francis, 1985; and SIPRI/Oxford University Press, 1986–present).

[11] The portal perimeter monitoring system was developed at Sandia National Laboratory in the USA, primarily for use in monitoring strategic arms.

[12] The installation of the X-ray cargo scanner has been fraught with difficulties. See IDDS (note 6), sheets 403.B.713, Nov. 1988; 403.B.727, Jan. 1989; 403.B.743, Feb. 1990; and 403.B.745, Mar. 1990; and *Trust and Verify*, no. 8 (Verification Technology Information Centre: London, Mar. 1990).

measure which grants the right to request open displays of road-mobile ground-launched ballistic missiles at operating bases. No later than 6 hours after such a request is received, roofs of all launch structures are slid open, and missiles and launchers are moved into the open for a period of 12 hours. Each side is allowed 6 such requests per annum. Article XII also contains an interesting reference to strategic arms reductions, linking the INF Treaty to a START treaty. The open display provision will be in effect until a treaty reducing and limiting strategic arms enters into force, but in any event for no more than 3 years after the INF Treaty became effective. In other words if a START agreement which contains a similar provision for co-operative NTM is not under way by mid-1991, then this opportunity will be lost.

There have been a few problems[13] with the INF Treaty but the verification regime, particularly the close collaboration between the USA and USSR which has been needed to operate it, has enabled these problems to be sorted out in an amicable fashion without threatening the Treaty.

Assuming that a START agreement is negotiated, what will its verification regime look like? The main way in which the START treaty will differ from the INF Treaty is that for START, not only would a considerable number of missiles and warheads be allowed to remain on each side (well over 50 per cent of current stockpiles) but also the whole infrastructure, such as the operating bases, factories and storage sites, would still be operational. The INF Treaty, on the other hand, benefited from the fact that at the end of the 3-year reduction/elimination phase there should be no INF missile at all, anywhere, and none of the INF bases will be operating—the infrastructure for INF will not exist. Therefore, after the 3-year destruction period, if one INF missile is seen, it is a clear violation. As a result of this 'zero option', verification of the INF Treaty was made a good deal easier than if 100 missiles on each side, as had been proposed earlier in the negotiations, had been accepted. The principle of verifying the total absence of treaty items being easier than verifying numerical limits is an important one. In particular, it is important when considering verifying the total absence of nuclear weapons as opposed to verifying numerical limits, and it is a point to which this chapter will return.

The START I agreement (and follow-on agreements) will call for monitoring the end results of a treaty which will limit the number of missiles on bombers and launchers, and on the number of warheads on individual missiles. Excess missiles will be destroyed but, as with INF, warheads will return to the national stockpiles for re-use. There will be a need for intrusive on-site inspections using equipment such as nuclear radiation detectors (to ascertain how many warheads are on a multiple-warhead missile or to discriminate between nuclear-

[13] For example, in 1990 Czechoslovakia reported that SS-23 missiles had been deployed there since just before the signing of the INF Treaty yet never declared (the same turned out to be also true for the GDR and Bulgaria) and certainly never spotted by US intelligence satellites. See *Trust and Verify*, no. 9 (Verification Technology Information Centre: London, Apr. 1990); and *Trust and Verify*, no. 13 (Verification Technology Information Centre: London, Aug./Sep. 1990). This caused grave concern, particularly given the fuss that the USSR made over the German Pershing 1As before the signing of the Treaty.

and conventionally tipped dual-capable missiles), and tags and tag-readers in order to identify legal missiles and to check the safe passage of equipment scheduled for destruction. There will be a need for production monitoring and this may well include procedures such as those currently in effect at the monitoring facility at Votkinsk. NTM, in particular remote sensing by satellite, will continue to play a pivotal role in monitoring strategic arms. If an 'Open Skies' agreement[14] is negotiated, then aerial overflights will also aid in monitoring the treaty. It will also allow other states *not party to the treaty* and not equipped with high resolution imaging satellites to monitor developments of the US and Soviet strategic forces.

Following on from START, the process of reductions starts to become interesting. It is proposed that deeper cuts in strategic forces will follow. What these will be is not clear. Deep cuts could mean anything from going down another 30 per cent or so on each side or down to a thousand missiles (perhaps with single warheads) on each side along with reductions in the strategic arsenals of Britain and France.

Going down to these levels may mean including the destruction of some or all of the affected warheads. As numbers decrease, verification becomes increasingly important—small infringements take on a new significance as they become a larger percentage of the whole. On the other hand, deep cuts in strategic forces will be following on the heels of the START treaty and, it is hoped, the verification of START will have built up confidence in the ability of the USA and the USSR to ascertain the strategic forces of each other. So even though verification will have to become more and more reliable, this may be achieved more easily due to experience from other treaties.

The inclusion of Britain and France, and possibly even China, is highly likely at this stage of deep cuts. Certainly the UK will be affected in any case by the limitations imposed on US missile development and deployment because so much of its own planning is dependent on US technical progress. Their inclusion will complicate the negotiations greatly. Not only because the weapon systems of the three lesser nuclear powers differ widely in their capabilities and operational roles from each other, and from the USSR and US strategic forces (which makes it difficult to bargain), but also they bring with them very different attitudes.

The British and French attitude towards intrusive verification is likely to be reasonably positive once a decision is made to go into negotiations. Both states are party to the Stockholm Document and as such are open to inspections by Warsaw Treaty Organization inspectors. Both states have participated in the inspection procedures as hosts and inspectors. For example, France conducted an inspection in the USSR in August 1989 for the first time and the USSR inspected a French exercise in September 1989, whereas UK inspectors carried

---

[14] The original 'Open Skies' proposal was made by US President Eisenhower in 1955 and it was revamped by President Bush in 1989. It is a proposal to establish an agreement to permit flights by aircraft for the purpose of inspections over the territories of the states party to the agreement. For a full chronology, see IDDS, *Arms Control Reporter*, section 409, 1990.

out their first inspection (in the GDR) in September 1988. Both states are participating the the CFE process and in the CSBM talks in Vienna. The negotiations and agreements involve very intrusive inspections; and although both the British and French opposed inspections of production facilities, they have generally been constructive in the negotiations on verification procedures.

The problem of involving China is an unknown quantity. It is not known how likely it is that China would enter into an agreement to reduce its nuclear arsenals, let alone how it would view intrusive on-site inspections. This could be a major problem: if China is not brought on board it seems unlikely that the USSR, or the other NWS would contemplate going down to very low levels of nuclear weapons or eventually down to zero. If China were to agree to nuclear reductions then it may be that they would agree to intrusive verification. The Chinese comments at the Conference on Disarmament in Geneva are certainly in favour of verification for a CWC[15] which will have the most intrusive on-site inspection regime of all the current or proposed treaties. Work should start as soon as possible in order to prepare China for the possibility of being included in talks and for intrusive verification of their strategic arsenals.

IV. Verification of very low levels of nuclear missiles

Before we get to zero, there could be a period of very low levels of nuclear weapons which belong to a number of states (USA, USSR, UK, France, China and others). At this point all those weapons will have to be declared if verification can be effective for a global reduction. The problem is that these low levels (perhaps as low as 0–500 weapons per nuclear weapon state) are very vulnerable to small increases because a small clandestine store of extra nuclear weapons possessed by one of the countries would drastically alter the balance. Now it could be that this would be irrelevant strategically—if the numbers of nuclear missiles already held are more than sufficient to destroy the enemy— but politically it would be very important. Imagine that a nation which has agreed to have the same number as another nation has an extra 50 weapons hidden away on land or sea platforms. If the numbers agreed to were high (a few thousand) then an extra 50 would not be very significant. If however, the numbers agreed to were 50 each, then a hidden 50 would double the force of the cheating nation with respect to the complying nation. As a result, verification of these low levels must be extremely stringent and costly. This could be achieved the 'traditional' way of monitoring production plants, maintenance facilities, ports, ships, deployment sites and so on using NTM, on-site inspections (OSI), portal perimeter monitoring and so on. The verification scheme

[15] The Chinese Foreign Minister Qian Qichen stated in the Conference on Disarmament, Geneva, 1990 that, '[The] Chinese position . . . is in favour of an effective, reasonable and feasible verification regime under the convention, including challenge inspections. In the meantime, we maintain that challenge inspection should not go beyond the purposes, objectives and scope of the convention and that any abuse should be strictly guarded against' See *PEACE*, no. 18 (June 1990), published by the Chinese Peoples' Association for Peace and Disarmament.

would then be the same as for START I and START II and so on but even more rigorous, involving more countries, at which point the question would be asked: Why are we spending so much money on and putting so much effort into monitoring the whereabouts of so few missiles? It could be that the point of stringent verification and its attendant costs would by then be so well understood by the public and legislators that the question would be quickly answered by 'we need to spend this money on verification for our security'. It should not be forgotten that similar answers have worked in the past when the public and politicians have been debating very expensive new weapon systems.

Another way to solve the verification problem at low levels would be to close down all but one or two nuclear weapon deployment areas in each country, which could be safeguarded. In this situation no nuclear weapons could ever be taken out of their designated deployment sites (these sites could be quite large for mobile missiles). If inspectors or satellites or aerial overflights ever spotted a nuclear missile out of area, that would be an obvious violation. The problem with this approach is that unless they were highly mobile, which could defeat the verification objective anyway, the weapons would be very vulnerable to attack. There is a technical fix to the problem and that's the use of tags which can store data from the Global Positioning System which can then be read at a later date, thus not giving real-time information, and the positions checked to ensure that they had not been out of their allowed areas. Any untagged missile would be an immediately obvious violation.

Crucial to all these verification schemes are tags. The function of uniquely identifying a missile or warhead as an allowed and legal missile is called tagging. There are many ways to tag weapons (the principles are explained in the appendix and some examples are given) but the most important aspect of tagging is that the whole inventory problem is much simplified and is reduced almost to a 'zero option'. It means that only tagged weapons are allowed and any untagged weapon or wrongly tagged weapon found is in contravention with the treaty. Inspectors then only have to check tags on weapons and check that all weapons have valid tags.

Yet another idea, which could provide a route to zero nuclear weapons at a later date, would be to close down nuclear weapon facilities in all countries and allow the nuclear nations to keep mobile nuclear missiles and warheads in a 'bank'[16] in order to protect against 'breakout' (a state clandestinely developing a cachet of nuclear weapons and then announcing the threat). The missiles and warheads would be deposited in the bank by the owning states and kept under safeguards. The bank could exist in several places. At any point in the future a nation could remove its missiles and warheads (no gain due to investment interest!) but that action would be open and made known to the world. The

[16] There have been a number of similar proposals over the years but this one should not be confused with the numerous proposals to make the United Nations the custodian of nuclear weapons and of the means of delivery, in short to turn the United Nations into a nuclear force. For a recent illustration of such proposals see Rotblat, J., 'Time to think again about general and complete disarmament', eds J. Hassard, T. Kibble and P. Lewis, *Ways Out of the Arms Race* (World Scientific: London, 1989), p. 198.

bank would not have any operational control over the weapons; it would exist in the same way as a safe deposit, guarding the weapons only. From the verification point of view, this is very much the easiest option for such low small numbers of missiles. There would be no legally allowed missiles anywhere else. If any nuclear weapon facility or any nuclear missiles were ever to be spotted by remote-sensing satellites then that would be immediate grounds for suspicion and for a challenge inspection. The 'banked' weapons under safeguards would also act as an insurance for their owners in case a clandestine force were ever to be discovered or used for blackmail in the future. Any potential nuclear blackmailer would be quite aware that other states have fast access to the bank and so threat in order to gain leverage could be quite useless, particularly if all the other nuclear nations acted in concert against the threat. For this reason it is unlikely that any of the states keeping missiles in the bank would feel the need to develop a clandestine stockpile. If any of those states ever wished to play nuclear blackmail they could more easily withdraw their weapons from the bank than build a secret force with all the attendant risks of being caught. A near NWS could also decide to develop nuclear missiles for deposit it the bank as an insurance policy against any of its regional adversaries developing a clandestine force.

There are problems with such an approach: In which countries would such a bank be situated? Would the host countries be in a position to prevent the removal of the weapons by their owners in a time of crisis? How could a hostile force be prevented from attacking the bank? How vulnerable to attack would missiles be in transit once removed? How strong would be the protection from terrorists?

Despite these problems, such a solution could play a role as an intermediate step in going to zero. It seems to be a natural progression to the Schell[17] proposal of deterrence by the knowledge of re-manufacturing processes (as outlined by Booth and Wheeler in chapter 2). The significant difference between the two ideas is the speed at which a nuclear capability could be achieved if ever needed. In the proposal of Schell, nuclear rearmament in the face of a nuclear blackmailer could take of the order of months. In the case of the nuclear weapons 'bank', nuclear rearmament would be of the order of days. Thus, the requirement to be able to deter nuclear blackmail could be better served by a bank than purely the possession of re-manufacturing knowledge (which would also exist in the bank situation).

V. Going to zero

The difficulty of verifying such low levels, with all the inherent dangers, contrasts strongly with the ease of verifying zero levels.

From the verification point of view, it is highly preferable to go to zero than to have a few hundred nuclear weapons scattered around the world which

[17] Schell, J., *The Abolition* (Picador: London, 1984).

require continual monitoring and vast areas where missiles could be deployed or stored, perhaps legally or illegally, which require monitoring. A great deal of effort, expense and resources would have to go into monitoring a small number of missiles. On the other hand, if at some point from the situation of a few thousand nuclear weapons (strategic, tactical, land, air and naval), the reductions went straight to zero nuclear weapons, this difficult situation becomes much easier, and cheaper, to verify.

As with the INF Treaty, but this time for *all* nuclear missiles and warheads, the infrastructure for the missiles and warheads would be dismantled. There would be no more production of nuclear missiles, no more testing of warheads or nuclear tipped ballistic missiles. Weapon-grade plutonium and highly enriched uranium would no longer be needed and any missile seen or warhead observed would be an immediate sign of a violation. Verification would be carried out by remote-sensing aircraft and by remote-sensing satellites. The right to challenge on-site inspections would have to exist for all areas within the states party to the treaty. In order to achieve this, for many countries verification procedures would be have to be institutionalized into some sort of international inspectorate for the agreements.

By this time, all countries would have to be involved in the process so that nuclear weapons should not exist anywhere. For this, attention has to be paid to horizontal proliferation and verification.

VI. Nuclear non-proliferation and verification

Since 1968 when the Non-Proliferation Treaty was negotiated, the nuclear weapon states must have felt very satisfied that they have, to a large extent, inhibited the spread of nuclear weapon materials and technologies to other states while being able to develop new designs of nuclear warheads themselves. The implementation of the NPT relies heavily on the IAEA and its safeguards programme. The IAEA has provision to safeguard nuclear materials in civil reactors (achieved by bilateral agreements between the states party to the Treaty and the IAEA). The inspections are comprised of routine, *ad hoc* and special inspections. These allow for routine monitoring, random spot checks and challenge inspections respectively. The notice required for *ad hoc* and routine inspections is at least 24 hours while for special inspections no notice is laid down other than 'as promptly as possible after the Agency and State have consulted'. The Department of Safeguards of the IAEA has about 180 safeguards inspectors plus an additional 15 inspection assistants.[18] Special inspections have not as yet been carried out but there are moves afoot to do so in the near future.[19]

---

[18] Turrentine, A. R., 'Lessons of the IAEA safeguards experience for on-site inspection in future arms control regimes', eds L. A. Dunn and A. E. Gordon, *Arms Control Verification and the New Role of On-Site Inspection* (Lexington Books: Lexington, Mass., 1990), p. 46.

[19] At the NPT Review Conference 1990 (CD Geneva), agreed language for the Final Document (which failed on the issue of nuclear testing) stated: 'The Conference therefore urges the Agency not to hesitate to

The IAEA safeguards are based on several different legal regimes (set out in IAEA Information Circulars—INFCIRC/66/Rev.2 and INFCIRC/153) and special arrangements which vary from state to state.[20] Currently, the IAEA administers three kinds of safeguards: (a) full-scope safeguards on all the nuclear plants in 43 NNWS which have signed the NPT and also have significant nuclear activities; (b) one-off safeguards agreements on single plants or batches of nuclear material in states which have not signed the NPT (these are a consequence of nuclear trade and apply to 11 states including six near-NWS); (c) voluntary-offer safeguards on the civil nuclear plants in the five NWS.[21]

While the IAEA safeguards are very extensive and have formed the most intrusive verification package for decades, there are defects in the regimes which would need to be rectified if we were to head to a world without nuclear weapons. For example, the IAEA has no right to obtain information about new nuclear facilities at an early stage in their development. In fact, under IAEA safeguards, an entire reprocessing or enrichment plant could be supplied to an NPT country without any notification to the IAEA.[22] There are other initiatives which have a profound influence on the success of safeguards. One of these is export controls or the 'trigger list'. In July 1974, a committee of the main nuclear technology suppliers agreed a list of of the materials (other than source and special fissionable materials), equipment and components that would require the application of safeguards. In a follow-on in 1977, the Nuclear Suppliers Group or the London Club[23] agreed Guidelines for Nuclear Transfers (INFCIRC/254) which included items already on the trigger list and other technologies along with steps for the implementation of restrictions on supplying nuclear-related technologies and substances.[24]

For the effective verification of nuclear non-proliferation in an era of low levels of nuclear weapons and eventually in a time of zero nuclear weapons, the IAEA, or whatever body is charged with the task of monitoring the potential spread of nuclear weapons and related technologies, will have to be given much greater powers than exist now. Full-scope safeguards and special inspections will need to be implemented as soon as possible so that the maximum amount of information that can exist on states' current activities is known well in advance of the end of the process. Some follow-on agreement to the NPT may

take full advantage of its rights, including the use of special inspections as outlined in paragraphs 73 and 77 of INFCIRC/153. The Conference notes that as yet no experience exists of such special inspections and would welcome a study by the Agency of the possible scope, application and procedures of such inspections, including their implications for the information requirements and policy of the Agency'.

[20] Safeguards documents circulated in this form include the safeguards systems, safeguards agreements and the contents of the *Trigger List* and the *London Suppliers Guidelines*. See Fischer, D. and Szasz, P., SIPRI, *Safeguarding the Atom: A Critical Appraisal*, ed. J. Goldblat (Taylor & Francis: London, 1985), p. xvi.

[21] The Nuclear Non-Proliferation Treaty, the Geneva Review Conference and the United Kingdom— An Information Pack, European Proliferation Information Centre, London, Aug. 1990.

[22] Fischer and Szasz (note 20), p. 80.

[23] Belgium, Canada, Czechoslovakia, France, GDR, FRG, Italy, Japan, Netherlands, Poland, Sweden, Switzerland, UK, USA and USSR.

[24] Fischer and Szasz (note 20), pp. 101–3.

well have to be negotiated so that the distinction between nuclear and non-nuclear weapon states no longer exists in law for the purposes of safeguards.

VII. Proliferation and nuclear testing

States which are considered to possess an undeclared small arsenal of nuclear weapons and states which are on the verge of obtaining nuclear weapons are of particular interest in any discussion of verifying the non-proliferation of nuclear weapons.

The near-NWS have not carried out nuclear tests (with the possible exceptions of South Africa and Israel). Certainly none has ever carried out an overt, declared nuclear test. If one of these nations were to do so, then such action would undoubtedly spur a nuclear arms race in the region of that state. Such a nuclear arms race would be very difficult to contain and is likely to be highly unstable. It is for this reason that a global, verifiable comprehensive test ban takes on a new urgency. There are a number of ways to approach a test ban. It is possible to approach it gradually, as is now the case. The problem is that this gradual approach could be too gradual and achieve nothing. Another way is to agree on a phased approach in a way that limits the numbers and yields of tests step by step over a defined period. Another is to just cease testing completely from a set date. From the verification standpoint, the total cessation of tests is by far the easiest to monitor. Total absence of tests would mean total absence of the infrastructure and facilities for testing.

To verify a comprehensive test ban a number of methods would have to be employed. By far the most important of these is a global network of seismic stations which could monitor and locate seismic activity around the world. The network needs to be able to discriminate between earthquakes and explosions and it needs to be able to monitor down to a specified threshold of a yield of explosion. This threshold could be anywhere between say a 0.3 to 5 kt yield. Recent calculations have shown that a network monitoring down to 400 tonnes (which could be muffled) is feasible and would cover most concerns about sub-kilotonne developments. There could be a high false alarm rate in that there would be a high number of seismic events between 400 and 1000 tonnes the vast majority of which would be easily discountable as nuclear tests. Some of the events could be more ambiguous and for this reason it is necessary to include other verification methods. These include remote sensing by satellite, aerial overflights, on-site inspections and radioactive material monitoring. Taking all of these technologies and methodologies in concert, a CTBT is verifiable to the extent that a state considering cheating would run a high risk of being caught at some point, either in the preparations, by seismic detection or by extensive on-site inspections.

There is considerable evidence that NNWS, including those in the developing world, would be prepared to accept seismic stations and on-site inspections on their territories. The positions of France and China are not clear. Neither is party to the 1963 PTBT although both observe it. However the Partial Test Ban

Treaty, which prohibits tests above ground, is somewhat easier to verify than a CTB and has been adequately verified using NTM since it came into force. If France and China[25] were to sign a CTB then they would have agreed to a stringent verification regime; if, however, one or neither of them were to sign, then their nuclear tests would be monitored seismically and by imaging satellites (as they are now).

VIII. Verification of warhead destruction

To date there has been no inclusion of a provision to eliminate warheads in missile reduction treaties. The warheads subject to the INF Treaty have returned to national stockpiles and the same will happen for warheads of missiles eliminated by the START agreement. In future, however, there will be pressure to destroy warheads along with missiles, particularly when deep cuts are being negotiated.

How will warhead reduction be verified? The main difficulty with checking destruction of a warhead is the secrecy involved over warhead design. A method has to be found which allows inspectors to be certain that the warheads no longer exist as such while at the same time not allowing the inspectors to gain any sensitive information on warhead design. This can be achieved in a simple way by a series of steps.[26]

1. The warheads are brought to a central warhead dismantling facility under safeguards. The tagged locks which sealed the warheads at the point where they were removed from their deployment sites, are checked and the warheads are removed. The type of nuclear material in the warhead is detected and recorded.

2. The warheads are then taken to a room, which can be inspected before and after but not during the removal of sensitive material such as guidance systems and design features from the warhead, and placed in a sealed container.

3. All of the parts are then shown to the inspectors and checked against the record taken in step 1. Crushable parts are crushed, fissile and fusile material is put under safeguards or returned under safeguards to the warhead owners. The inspectors witness the removal of all the parts and can go back into the middle section where dismantling actually occurred to check that there was no possible way in which the materials could have been substituted.

---

[25] China was 'positively considering participation in the experiment of international seismological data exchange, so as to accumulate experience for the future establishment of an effective international verification mechanism for a comprehensive nuclear test ban'. Foreign Minister Qian Quichen, quoted in *PEACE*, no. 18 (June 1990), published by the Chinese Peoples' Association for Peace and Disarmament.

[26] For more details of such procedures, see Taylor, T. B., 'Warhead dismantlement and fissile-material disposal', eds F. von Hippel and R. Sagdeev, *Reversing the Arms Race: How to Achieve and Verify Deep Reductions in the Nuclear Arsenals* (Gordon and Breach: New York, 1990), pp. 91–115.

IX. Organization of verification

The organization of verification measures will depend entirely on the structure of the treaties and on parties to the treaties—this is a direct result of verification being treaty-specific.[27] Current nuclear arms control treaties and negotiations are bilateral and the verification procedures are also bilateral. If nuclear arms reductions are going to include the other NWS then the treaties are going to be verified by all of those parties. If this includes Britain, France and China then there are going to be five countries involved in verifying each other. Clearly, because of NATO, the UK, France and the USA will not be verifying each other and, hence, not carrying out on-site inspections on each other's territories. China and the USSR will definitely want to inspect each other, the USA, France and the UK will want to inspect the USSR and China, and the USSR and China will also want to inspect, France, the UK and the USA. This brings about an odd situation in a multilateral treaty of the five NWS. It means that although such a treaty will be multilateral three of the states will be acting essentially as one group. This would allow a larger number of pooled inspections and greater resources for monitoring and analysis for the group of three. Such a situation would probably not be acceptable to the USSR and China unless all British, US and French weapons were given a common ceiling as though they were one state—which, in turn, would not be acceptable to them! There is a way out of the dilemma and that is for each state to act individually in the multilateral talks and treaty, and to set-up, collectively, an agency to monitor the implementation of the treaty. The agency, acting in a similar fashion to the IAEA, could act for the five states and report to them with data collected from inspections and other monitoring measures. States could still use their own NTM for monitoring compliance and they would come to their own decisions on compliance, therefore retaining their sovereignty.

Such a model for verification could provide an incentive to other states to participate in the disarmament process. As the numbers of nuclear weapons decrease to very low levels, other near-nuclear or nuclear-but-keeping-quiet-about-it states could be helped into the process by the existence of a successful monitoring agency. As the monitoring agency is seen to work for the five, confidence in the process could grow. Much would, of course, depend on the political climate, but over a period of several years, it is possible to see the practical inclusion of the nuclear threshold states. It would be impossible however if the five NWS are not seen to be drastically reducing their arsenals.

If the process of nuclear arms reductions can continue to include states such as India, Israel and South Africa, then it would also be possible to imagine the inclusion of Iraq, Pakistan, Libya and so on. If they could see that the reductions and eventual absence of nuclear missiles are verifiable and that they can participate in the verification procedures through a monitoring agency, then it is easier (although at the time of writing still very difficult) to see how they might

[27] *Study on the Role of the United Nations in the Field of Verification*, United Nations General Assembly, A/45/372 (28 Aug. 1990), p. 32.

be involved. In reality, it would not be feasible to think of including one Middle Eastern country without including all Middle Eastern states and it would not be feasible to include India in the process without Pakistan (China by this time already being involved). Eventually the process could lead to all of the major states being involved in reductions or declarations of non-possession of nuclear weapons. The process would have to be seen as leading to a world without nuclear weapons and a world that was verifiably so. For this reason alone it is clear that steps towards multilateralizing the nuclear reductions process, and hence the verification process, should happen as soon as possible in order to fire the imaginations of those who may one day be involved.

The point at which it is decided between all the states involved (and that, for obvious reasons, would have to be all the states with a technical capability of making nuclear weapons) to go to a situation of zero nuclear weapons has to be the point when the states have enough confidence in the working of the international monitoring organization (and in the IAEA which would still be safeguarding nuclear materials and by then with full-scope safeguards)[28] to be sure that a world without nuclear weapons could be properly verified.

X. Verification of unilateral measures

The progress of arms reductions will not only be one of negotiations and treaties. As we have seen over the past few years, arms reductions are also brought about very quickly by budget constraints coupled with positive changes in the international atmosphere. Indeed, levels of armaments are increased unilaterally for similar reasons—negative trends in international relations coupled with enough money in the national coffers to allow increases in the defence budget. The catch is that while none in their right mind would wish to discourage such a process of independent disarmament, we are heavily dependent on the word of the state making the unilateral reductions that they are doing so. Many such steps can be adequately monitored by satellites (such as withdrawals of conventional forces, cuts in ICBMs and so on) or other technical means (for example, the 1985–88 Soviet unilateral moratorium was monitored by both satellites and by seismic detectors) but many cannot (such as the non-production of biological weapons). In any case, few states possess the capabilities to monitor treaties solely by NTM. Unilateral steps can often be part of or a precursor of or related to negotiated agreements (for example the Czechoslovak moratorium on tank production and the USSR withdrawal of troops from Eastern Europe were both preliminary steps towards the CFE treaty) in which case they can be monitored as part of the monitoring procedures for the agreement.

---

[28] Full-scope safeguards were agreed in principle at the 1990 NPT Review Conference in Geneva. Unfortunately, because a final consensus document was not reached (over the issue of lack of progress towards a nuclear test ban) the agreement does not have the weight it would otherwise have. However it is clear that the IAEA will start to prepare for a full-scope safeguard regime based on the agreement reached between the NPT states.

Another approach, which has many pitfalls but is better than no monitoring at all, is to declare unilateral reductions or to declare levels of stocks and allow other states to carry out *ad hoc* inspections as a token of good faith. A good example of this approach was the proposal from the USSR in mid-1988 that NATO states would be supplied with details of the strength and weaponry in Eastern Europe and then allowed to carry out inspections before the CFE Treaty came into force. Unfortunately this gesture was never put to the test because the US response was that such a proposal was old and diversionary.[29] There could be several reasons for this negative reaction. One reason could be the nature of the inspections. In 1987, representatives from states participating in the CWC negotiations in Geneva visited the Soviet chemical weapons research station at Shikhany.[30] Although the visit was successful in that the USSR was encouraged further in openness, there were several problems arising from the visit such as the absence of any modern chemical munitions on display.[31] Later the UK was invited by the USSR to visit the Shikhany facilities as part of an exchange of visits between the experts from Shikhany and from the UK Chemical Defence Establishment at Porton Down. The UK visit was treated in a similar way to an on-site inspection and included an overflight of the area and visits to requested buildings.[32] However, one incident marred the visit and brought into stark relief the type of problems which can occur on invited visits (and on bona fide on-site inspections for that matter). The UK delegates requested that they be allowed to visit a complex which was linked by road to the Shikhany site and showed a satellite photograph (taken by the French commercial satellite SPOT) clearly depicting the complex and linkage.[33] Their request was refused and the outcome has been used by Her Majesty's Government as a example of why it is not particularly wise to visit facilities by invitation, rather than as part of an inspection to verify compliance with a treaty, ever since.

Obviously, in these circumstances there is no form of redress; the USSR was not demonstrating compliance with a treaty nor was it demonstrating compliance with its own figures. On the positive side, the 1985–87 Soviet unilateral moratorium on nuclear testing was monitored and subsequently verified to have been adhered to, however. It was not reciprocated by the USA, as had been the hope of the USSR, but it did show that it was possible to monitor such a moratorium at a distance. With in-country networks[34] and other non-seismic techniques (such as remote sensing satellites, aircraft, on-site inspections and

---

[29] *The Times*, 18 July 1988.

[30] See IDDS (note 6), sheets 704.B.244, Oct. 1987.

[31] See IDDS (note 6), sheet 704.B.325, Dec. 1988.

[32] See IDDS (note 6), sheet 704.B.295, June/July 1988.

[33] *Statement on the Defence Estimates 1989*, vol. 1, Cm 675-I (Her Majesty's Stationery Office: London, 1989).

[34] The joint US–Soviet (unofficial) seismic verification project, set up in 1987 by the Natural Resources Defence Council in Washington D.C. and the Soviet Academy of Sciences, installed several seismic stations in the USSR and monitored the latter part of the unilateral moratorium in-country.

radiation monitoring), the long-term unilateral absence of nuclear tests in the USSR would be verifiable to a very high degree.[35]

It is not impossible to imagine that a declaration of, say, equipment levels could be deposited with other states or with the United Nations and provision for verification measures could be an integral part of the declaration. For example, imagine that the USSR decides, for economic reasons, to reduce the size of its post-START Treaty nuclear arsenal by 75 per cent (strategic and non-strategic). It could make that declaration to the world press and deposit details of the numbers, sites and destruction plans with the USA, the UK, France and China. The four nations would, as always, be able to monitor the reductions and deployments by NTM but the USSR could also include the rights of short-notice inspection to deployment sites, production facilities and storage depots. It could also notify the dates, times and places of destruction and invite inspectors from the other four NWS to witness the elimination of the missiles. The inclusion of the other NWS in the monitoring process could also encourage their participation in future negotiations. The point of this approach is that, in making the declaration and in inviting inspections, the state making unilateral cuts would be held to account by the states enabled to monitor the declaration. In this way, a unilateral measure takes some of the status of an international agreement. Of course, it could be that the verification provisions contained in the unilateral declaration are not sufficient for the task. In this case, the inspecting states could make the point strongly to the declaring state and hope that international opinion persuades it to become more open. Otherwise, the states would probably accept that, although far from perfect, a small amount of intrusive verification provision is better than none at all and carry out the inspections as invited.

XI. Verification as security

In asking the question, 'could we have security without nuclear weapons?', it is important that we think about what security is and if it can ever exist. A concept of security based on being able to blow civilization to bits is not a concept which has its roots in a long-term stable security. In going from a world with tens of thousands of nuclear weapons to a world with none, what could form the basis of that security? Jonathan Schell in *The Abolition*[36] suggests that the knowledge of how to rebuild nuclear weapons coupled with the limitation of conventional forces and with anti-nuclear defences could form a stable and secure world. He pays little attention to verification except to rightly say that it cannot be perfect. Schell thus justifies the deployment of anti-nuclear defences because at low numbers the successful cheater has a great disadvantage if defences are not in place.

---

[35] *Scientific and Technical Aspects of Verifying a Comprehensive Test Ban* (The Verification Technology Information Centre: London, Apr. 1990).

[36] Note 17.

Another approach is to see the role of verification as one which can provide security in itself. While not suggesting that verification alone can provide all the required security and that defences could be entirely done away with, it is possible to see that in a world of reduced military hardware where there exists more openness and transparency, in which states were in possession of a nearly complete set of information about other nations capabilities, training procedures and production potential, that the degree of security would be far higher than it is today. Not only the possession of this information is required, however, but the act of going to inspect facilities to check compliance with agreements and declarations ensures that states are open to foreign military experts and that they run a very high risk of getting caught if they should decide to build nuclear weapons. Such a situation is different from that of intelligence gathering. Verification occurs because of the treaties or declarations that are being verified. The act of checking compliance with the agreements not only provides information but also provides interaction between military personnel of previously hostile countries and opportunities to assess capabilities and intents with a much greater degree of confidence, and increases trust between states as they move to a situation in which they cannot annihilate each other.

Looking at verification from this point of view, the confidence-building aspects could eventually be its single and most important role. If the high defence spending states, in moving from a position of large numbers of nuclear weapons to a position of zero nuclear weapons, could spend a small fraction of their defence budgets on verification requirements, then we could move from a position of the threat of nuclear war as security to one of verification as security.

In addition, investment in verification in order to form part of the overall security structure would ease the transition for the military allowing verification duties to be a significant part of a military career. Already this is the case for many young officers and soldiers. The US On-Site Inspection Agency (OSIA) is providing a career step for personnel who have language ability. Trained inspectors can move in and out of the verification cadre as their careers dictate. Because of the CFE Treaty, the NATO and former WTO states now also have teams of trained inspectors, mostly from the military forces, who see that the future is more secure for them if they are skilled in verification techniques rather than if they stick with the traditional training.

XII. The costs of verification

It is impossible to truly say what the future costs of verification are going to be. What we can do is look at costs which exist now for verification tasks and look at some of the predictions which have been made for the near future. The most useful thing to do would be to compare the costs of implementing treaties with the costs of not doing so and see if there are significant savings.

Generally, hitherto the investment in verification has not been particularly large, with the exception of high resolution observation satellites and signals intelligence (of the USA and the USSR, which are used also for military information, such as target acquisition and missile guidance systems. Take, for example, the IAEA's role of verifying compliance with safeguards for the Non-Proliferation Treaty. The IAEA carries out on-site inspections at nuclear facilities all over the world and yet it has been on a zero-growth budget for several years. Its 1989/90 budget for safeguards is a mere $54.2 million out of a total budget of $162.8 million for the entire agency. In contrast, the US OSIA, which carries out the inspections for the INF Treaty and will be carrying out inspections for other treaties in the future, has a operations budget of $40 million. This budget is predicted to climb to some $200–300 million per year when the OSIA is assigned the responsibility for other treaties. In addition, the US Government issued a $24 million contract to Hughes Electronics in Detroit, Michigan, USA, to undertake technical work monitoring the output at the USSR Final Assembly Plant in Votkinsk. The German Centre for Verification Tasks which will have some 400 staff has an estimated annual budget for personnel and operations of some $20 million.[37]

In September 1990, the US Congressional Budget Office published a report on the costs of verification and compliance for forthcoming arms treaties.[38] The study looked at five pending agreements: START, CFE, TTBT, PNET and a CWC, and considered the full scope of treaty implementation, that is, verification reductions and force restructuring. It estimated on-time costs and annual costs for the USA only. Its conclusions were that the total one-time costs for all the five treaties will be between $0.6 and $3.0 billion (over a period of 5 to 10 years after the treaties enter into force) and annual costs will be between $190 and $660 million. The range of costs reflect uncertainties in the amount of equipment to be destroyed, numbers of inspections and amount of restructuring of forces required. When considering the savings from the treaties, the study found that the largest savings will come from the CFE and START treaties. These agreements were estimated to bring savings to the USA of at least $9 billion per annum, whereas the other three treaties were estimated to bring savings of some $0.2 billion per annum between them. Apart from the CWC, as a result of each of these treaties, the infrastructure for the weapon systems and testing activities will still remain. Consequently, the costs will not be reduced substantially.

From this we learn that if a treaty banning, say, all nuclear tests or all strategic nuclear weapons were agreed, then the infrastructure for nuclear weapon testing or for strategic weapons would disappear. Fewer inspections would be carried out; there would be fewer places to monitor by satellite; and, therefore,

[37] *Trust and Verify*, no. 14 (Verification Technology Information Centre: London, Oct. 1990).
[38] Congressional Budget Office, Congress of the United States, *US Costs of Verification and Compliance Under Pending Arms Treaties* (Congresssional Buget Office: Washington, DC, Sep. 1990).

much larger savings would be made.[39] However, at very low levels, because the extent of verification provisions would have to be so large, there could well come a point in the process of the reductions to zero when the verification procedures were more expensive than the costs of maintaining the weapon systems themselves. At that point, there would be an incentive for economic reasons to go to zero so that the costly infrastructure could be disbanded leaving only the costs of compliance.

XIII. Conclusion

Going to a world which is considered secure without nuclear weapons, if possible at all, will be far from easy. Central to the sense of security during the process of reductions and at the point at which the decision is made to destroy the last remaining nuclear weapons is verification. Vital to the continuance of certainty that the world is going to remain nuclear weapon-free is verification. So it is verification, its technologies, its methodologies and its complexities that we should be investing in now.

At the levels of nuclear weapons that will exist post-START and post-whatever short-range nuclear forces (SNF) measures are agreed, that is still at the level of tens of thousands of nuclear weapons, perhaps it can be thought that verification measures do not have to be as stringent as at a time when the levels of nuclear weapons are very low (a few hundred). A word of caution is in order here. While it is true that a few extra weapons not noticed in ten thousand are not particularly significant, if those few nuclear weapons remain undetected throughout the whole process of reductions then, when there are very few left, they will attain a new significance. It is now, post-INF and post-START, when we are building the foundations of a verification system for the future. So it is important that we get it right.

Because of the significance that a few clandestine weapons can acquire when the levels are very low, it might be better to go from a time of some thousands of nuclear weapons to the point of zero. This is because when zero nuclear weapons exist there will be not be any nuclear weapon production, nor will there be nuclear weapon deployments, storage or maintenance. With low limits on nuclear weapons, however, all of the infrastructure will continue to exist and it would be much easier to hide a few weapons in the system. When a 'significant violation' could mean as few as, say, 10 nuclear missiles, then a verification regime would have to be extraordinarily tight. However, if the system had the advantage that there were supposed to be no nuclear weapons anywhere, and all nuclear weapon facilities were dis-established and dis-

---

[39] Lall, B. G. and Brandes, P. D., *Banning Nuclear Tests: Verification, Compliance, Savings* (Council on Economic Priorities: New York, 1987). The discrepancy in costs and savings is illustrated in this comparison between a low-threshold test ban (in which the infrastructure would still remain) and a comprehensive test ban (in which the nuclear testing establishment would no longer exist). The study by Lall and Brandes showed that there would not be great savings from a threshold test ban but the savings from a CTBT would be very significant.

mantled, then the verification procedures would be much easier and with a far greater degree of confidence. It cannot be stated strongly enough that verification of absence is much easier, less costly and more reliable than verification of limits.

However, at any level of numbers of nuclear weapons, verification is always possible. The degree of certainty in compliance will depend on the verification effort. This really amounts to saying that for a high degree of certainty in verification when the levels of nuclear weapons are very low, a larger amount of money, effort and resources would have to be invested in verification.

Several factors can work together. In addition to the reduction in numbers of nuclear weapons, if the safeguards procedures for monitoring nuclear non-proliferation were made more stringent and a strongly verified comprehensive test ban were in force, then it would be harder and harder for a state to success-fully cheat by producing a clandestine force of nuclear weapons.

A process involving well verified reductions in the nuclear arsenals of the USA, the USSR, the UK, France and China, coupled with unilateral reductions which are incorporated into existing inspection regimes or allow *ad hoc* inspections to check declarations, needs to be augmented with the eradication of the nuclear arsenals of other states such as Israel and South Africa. This can be achieved through a process of increased powers for the IAEA safeguards programme, a global comprehensive test ban and a multilateralization of the arms reduction process (plus heavy doses of corridor diplomacy).

The verification regimes for going to zero would consist of the following. For deep reductions in the number of missiles and warheads, an extended INF/START regime would be required. This would be comprised of a system of checking that missiles were being destroyed along with warheads, carried out by on-site inspections and the use of tags, a system of checking that warhead/missile production had stopped and a series of spot-checks on deployment sites, maintenance and storage facilities. Satellites and aerial inspections (under the 'Open Skies' treaty) would play a role in gathering information and providing triggers for on-site inspections.

In conjunction with missile and warhead reductions, the non-proliferation regime needs to be strengthened by carrying out inspections of suspected sites and of military facilities. More states need to be brought into the NPT, particu-larly India, Pakistan and Israel. Export controls need to be tightened especially in such technologically advanced countries as Germany and Japan. A CTB would enhance the NPT significantly, both by making it politically easier and by acting as a strong inhibitor to the development of new nuclear weapon programmes. A CTBT would be verified by global networks of seismic stations and radioactive debris detectors, aerial inspections, satellites and on-site inspections.

A situation of no nuclear weapons anywhere in the world would require a comprehensive verification programme, using the verification for non-proliferation, a CTBT, as well as for missile reductions. It would probably be easier to allow these verification regimes to carry on as they are (not all states may be party to the same treaties) so that they continue to be treaty specific. It is possible to imagine that, if all states signed up to all the treaties, then the verification regimes could be merged and handled by a single agency.

The organization of verification regimes needs to evolve with the changing times. As nuclear reductions become more and more multilateral, more and more states will be involved with the verification regimes that exist. At some point, treaties which have involved a few countries may become treaties which have over a hundred parties. It would be plainly ridiculous to have each state party to a large multilateral treaty inspect all the other states parties. The institution of an agency for the verification of a specific treaty would have to be considered in order to relieve the verification burden. Because each treaty will have a different set of parties and because verification of a treaty is specific to that treaty, each multilateral treaty (such as the NPT, CTBT, CWC and a global nuclear reduction treaty etc) will have its own agency for monitoring compliance. It is hard to to see how this could be otherwise: if a single agency were to be set up, the different parties to each treaty would be concerned that states not party to the treaty were receiving information to which they had no right. In addition, the specialist tasks involved in verifying the very different treaties would make it very difficult for a single agency to properly manage the huge tasks involved.[40] One exception is the use of satellites. In every arms reduction treaty, satellites have a major role to play and their use cuts across the divide of the different treaties and verification regimes. For this reason it may be possible to consider establishing an international satellite monitoring agency[41] or some regional satellite monitoring agencies[42] to provide information to states which do not possess their own satellites for verification.

In summary, verification would be vital to the security of a nuclear weapon-free world. It would play its part in deterring a state from clandestinely producing nuclear weapons and holding other states to ransom (albeit for a matter of weeks if the capabilities to re-manufacture are in a state of readiness). In order for verification to do its job well, we should be investing heavily in research into future technologies and methods now. It is now, in the period of the first reductions, that we can build confidence in our knowledge that nuclear weapons are being eliminated and it is that confidence which we need to build on for the future.

[40] Compare, for example, the tasks involved in verifying a CTBT with those of a nuclear arms reduction treaty—for the former, seismic detectors, magnetic detectors and radioactive debris detectors are needed; for the former, tagging technologies, radiation detectors and portal perimeter monitoring would be required. The UN Document, *Study on the Role of the United Nations in the Field of Verification* (note 3), considered the proposal of a single verification agency under UN auspices and could reach no definitive judgement on the issue. The Group of Experts did suggest that such an organization could possibly come into existence as an 'umbrella' organization resulting from the co-ordination of two or more future verification systems (see p. 87 of the UN study).

[41] *The Implications of Establishing an International Satellite Monitoring Agency*, UN document A/AC.206/14 (United Nations: New York, 1983).

[42] Jasani, B. and Sakata, T. (eds), SIPRI, *Satellites for Arms Control and Crisis Monitoring* (Oxford University Press, 1987), part III, pp. 117–57.

Appendix 6A. Tagging for verification

Tags are used in everyday life for internal accounting purposes. They are more commonly known as vehicle registration numbers, engine serial numbers, bar codes in supermarkets and so on. Pieces of hardware limited by a treaty may possess identification for internal accounting purposes. The difficulty with using the same method of accounting for verification as for internal accounting is that there is no guarantee that the identification numbers are genuine. It may be possible to have one set of, for example, registration numbers, for the inspectors and a completely different set for the internal accounts. In this way, it could be possible to keep substantially more numbers than allowed, by moving registration numbers around. During experimental inspections in the 1960s under the CLOUD GAP programme, the US military showed that it was possible to fool inspectors by duplicating[1] US Army equipment numbers.

One of the major advantages of tags is that they simplify the problems of violations and verification of limits on numbers. In a sense tags allow verification of treaty limited items (TLI) to be as simple as the zero–zero option in the 1987 INF Treaty: any untagged TLI observed is a clear treaty violation as any INF missile after the reduction period is a treaty violation.

Tags also simplify the sampling procedures for inspections. The problem of data collection is then the simple one of data verification, that is, TLI are checked on an inventory check-list. This allows sampling procedures to be more accurate than if the inspectors were counting the number of TLI seen at the site, particularly if the numbers observed do not match up with the numbers notified.

Tags, locks and seals are three different concepts. A seal is a device which seals the item of interest in a such a way that to open or enter the item the seal has to be broken. A broken seal is then an indication that the item has been tampered with. A lock is a device similar to a seal except that it can be opened with a key. If the key is not available then the lock would have to broken like a seal. A lock for arms control purposes should have a facility to monitor and record all openings so that any illegal entry would be noted. A tag is a device which identifies an item. The identification can be unique or it can identify as one of a batch. A tag has to be in some way attached to the item by a lock or by a seal. Locks and seals can also be tags if they can be used as identification.

In order to be effective, tags have to be: (*a*) copy resistant, tamper resistant, and tamper indicating; (*b*) no more observable than the item itself; (*c*) display no more information than is needed for verification purposes; and (*d*) not interfere with the tagged item's function.

[1] Lewis, P. M., 'Verification Experiments in the 1960s: from CLOUD GAP to Exercise "FIRST LOOK"', eds R. Kokoski and S. Koulik, SIPRI, *Verification of Conventional Arms Control in Europe: Technological Constraints and Opportunities* (Westview Press: Boulder, Colo., 1990), p. 264.

Tags fall into two main categories:

1. Those which provide their own identification—i.e., they are electronic tags and provide digital information. These are usually called 'active' tags.
2. Those which require comparison with a record for their identification. These are based on the techniques of pattern recognition. They are usually called 'passive' tags. Until recently, passive tags have had the most attention from researchers developing tags for arms control.

Passive tags all rely on pattern recognition. A sophisticated method for recognizing patterns is the measurement of the degree of correlation between the two patterns. In the perfect world, two *identical* patterns should be correlated 100 per cent and two non-identical patterns should be correlated 0 per cent. In reality, of course, it is seldom so easy. Two photographs of the same pattern will not, in general, produce 100 per cent correlation. The reasons are purely statistical. Any measurement has a measurement error associated with it. Error can arise from a slight alteration in the positioning of the recorder, in the light, in the temperature or in the vibrations affecting both the item of interest and the measuring equipment. Errors due to fluctuations in the measuring equipment will always be present. Consequently the auto correlations (the patterns *are* the same) are considered good if they are over 70 per cent. The cross correlation (the patterns are *not* the same) should still centre around 0 per cent; the correlation can be negative, which means that the patterns are opposite to each other.

If the auto and cross correlations do overlap and the tag, when read, falls into this 'grey' area, it will not be clear whether or not the tag is valid. Tags with correlation functions which fall into this category are not particularly useful for arms control.

How would tags be used? One method would be for each side to be given the required numbers of tags to attach to their own TLI themselves and then to return the inventory list giving the ID number assigned to each TLI. Another would be for inspectors of opposing sides to attach the tags during the baseline inspections (if the baseline inspections are a 100 per cent sample). Tags are very useful for highly mobile systems (such as mobile ICBMs or SLCMs) which are supposed to be assigned to a certain area—the discovery of tagged missiles out of area would be direct evidence of contravention.

7. Nuclear weapon elimination: fissile material and warheads

Frank von Hippel

I. Introduction

This chapter outlines the technical basis for advancing nuclear arms control to a point at which the production of fissile material for nuclear weapons is halted, warheads are verifiably dismantled and separated fissile material is placed under international safeguards.

Although the process of nuclear arms control has resulted in limitations on the number of nuclear warheads permitted to be deployed on certain classes of missiles and aircraft, the problem of limiting the *total* number of nuclear warheads (deployed and non-deployed) has not been addressed. This may reflect the fact that until recently nuclear arms control was limited to agreements that could be verified by 'national technical means', especially reconnaissance satellites. Because nuclear warheads are small and movable, they can be easily hidden from such verification means. Now that intrusive on-site inspections are rapidly becoming the norm, agreements controlling warheads and the fissile material that they contain are no longer beyond reach.

The 1987 Treaty between the USA and the USSR on the elimination of intermediate-range and shorter-range missiles (the INF Treaty) eliminates all Soviet and US land-based ballistic and cruise missiles with ranges between 500 and 5500 km and the associated launchers. However, the nuclear warheads carried by these missiles were exempted from elimination. These warheads or the fissile material (material that can support a fission chain reaction) that they contain may be recycled into warheads for other uncontrolled nuclear weapon delivery systems. Indeed, the warheads of the US Pershing II missile that has been eliminated according to the terms of the INF Treaty are being converted into nuclear bombs for fighter-bomber aircraft.[1]

The Strategic Arms Reduction (START) Treaty is expected to limit the USA and the USSR to 4900 deployed strategic ballistic missile warheads and 6000 total *counted* and deployed strategic nuclear warheads on each side. Although several thousand strategic nuclear warheads will not be counted,[2] the agreement

---

[1] Norris, R. S. and Arkin, W. M., 'Beating swords into swords', *Bulletin of the Atomic Scientists*, vol. 46, no. 9 (Nov. 1990), pp. 14–16.

[2] According to the 'counting rules' agreed to at the 1986 Reykjavik summit meeting, bombers not carrying ALCMs will be counted in the START treaty as carrying only one nuclear warhead—although many of these aircraft can actually carry 16 or more. At a February 1990 meeting in Moscow between Soviet Foreign Minister Eduard Shevardnadze and US Secretary of State James Baker, it was agreed that Soviet and US bombers carrying ALCMs would be counted as carrying 6 and 10 warheads respectively,

is nevertheless likely to result in a reduction by a few thousand in the number of deployed strategic nuclear warheads on each side.[3] As in the case of the INF Treaty, both sides are free to recycle the warheads or the fissile material that they contain into other weapon systems.

Limiting and reducing nuclear weapons with controls on dedicated nuclear weapon delivery vehicles alone would be inadequate for verifying a nuclear weapon-free world, since nuclear weapons can be delivered by virtually any vehicle, including fighter-bombers and even civilian transports. It is therefore necessary to extend nuclear arms control to include direct controls on nuclear warheads and the fissile material from which they can be produced.

With regard to the verifiability of such controls, at least two areas of concern should be kept in mind, however:

1. Although the detection of *large-scale* clandestine production of weapon-grade fissile material (i.e., enough for thousands of warheads) should be technically possible, the clandestine production of enough fissile material to make tens or even hundreds of warheads could probably be hidden in the background 'noise' of activities associated with civilian nuclear power. Therefore, a necessary if not sufficient condition for the complete elimination of nuclear weapons may be the elimination of nuclear power.

2. Even if it became possible to assure that no weapon-useable fissile material was being produced, there would still be great uncertainty in accounting for all of the weapon-grade fissile material produced in the past 45 years. In 1977, the US Government made public that it could account for the weapon-grade uranium that it had produced only to within an accuracy of several thousand kilogrammes—the equivalent of many hundreds of warheads.[4] The uncertainty of any outside authority concerning past production of weapon-grade fissile material would likely be considerably greater than that of the producing agency.

Thus, from a technical point of view, it may be impossible ever to prove that we have achieved a nuclear weapon-free world. However, it may not be necessary to have such proof in order for countries to be able to act as if nuclear weapons no longer existed (see below).

II. A production cut-off of nuclear weapon fissile material

Every nuclear weapon contains a few kilogrammes of fissile material. The core of the Hiroshima bomb contained 60 kg of uranium containing approximately 90 per cent uranium-235 ('weapon-grade' uranium). The core of the Nagasaki

---

although it was agreed that the aircraft could be equipped to carry up to twice as many. At the June 1990 Washington summit meeting, it was agreed to limit the number of nuclear-armed long-range SLCMs (sea-launched cruise missiles) to 880 on each side—but outside the START totals.

[3] With the exception of land-mobile missiles, such as the Soviet Union's single-warhead truck-carried SS-25 and rail-mobile SS-24 ICBMs, START will apparently not limit non-deployed nuclear weapons.

[4] US Energy Research and Development Administration (ERDA), *ERDA Issues Report on Inventory Differences for Strategic Nuclear Materials*, press release 77-130 (ERDA: Washington, DC, 1977). ERDA is now the US Department of Energy.

bomb contained 6 kg of plutonium.[5] The USA has produced about 500 000 kg of weapon-grade uranium and 90 000 kg of plutonium for nuclear weapons[6]— an average of 15–25 kg of weapon-grade uranium and 3–4 kg of plutonium for each of the 20 000–30 000 nuclear warheads in the US nuclear arsenal. According to the statement of a Soviet official[7] and an independent estimate,[8] the USSR has produced about as much plutonium for weapons as the USA. As yet, no information is available concerning the amount of highly-enriched uranium produced for weapons by the USSR but this number is probably also comparable to that produced by the USA.

Because fissile material is required to produce nuclear weapons and because the production of weapon-grade fissile material requires unique facilities, efforts to control the spread of nuclear weapons have focused on the control of these materials and of their production. About 140 non-nuclear-weapon states (NNWS) have signed the 1968 Non-Proliferation Treaty (NPT), which commits them to put all of their nuclear facilities that contain or could produce significant amounts of fissile material under the safeguards administered by the International Atomic Energy Agency (IAEA).

It would be natural, therefore, as part of an agreement to end the production by *all* nations of fissile material for weapons, to extend IAEA safeguards to cover by stages the nuclear facilities and fissile materials of the nuclear weapon states (NWS) and the NNWS that have not yet joined the NPT.

Plutonium

Plutonium is produced by neutron absorption in uranium-238 in nuclear reactors.[9] In NNWS that are signatories to the NPT, all 'reprocessing' facilities at which plutonium is separated chemically from irradiated uranium are subject to safeguards, as is the plutonium thereafter. In addition, because of the possible existence of small-scale clandestine reprocessing plants,[10] safeguards are extended to the entire nuclear reactor fuel cycle, starting with the delivery to the first plant in the fuel cycle of uranium oxide after it has been separated from

[5] Cochran, T., Arkin, W. M. and Hoenig, M. M. (eds), *US Nuclear Forces and Capabilities* (Ballinger: New York, 1984), p. 32.

[6] von Hippel, F., Albright, D. H. and Levi, B. G., *Quantities of Fissile Materials in US and Soviet Nuclear Weapons Arsenals*, Report no. 168 (Center for Energy and Environmental Studies, Princeton University: Princeton, N.J., 1986), p. 4; Cochran, T. B., Arkin, W. M., Norris, R. S. and Hoenig, M. M., *US Nuclear Warhead Production* (Ballinger: New York, 1987), pp. 75 and 191.

[7] Interview with Evgeniy I. Mikerin, Head, Main Department of Manufacturing and Technology, USSR State Committee for the Utilization of Atomic Energy, 7 July 1989.

[8] See von Hippel, Albright and Levi (note 6), p. 4.

[9] Uranium-233 is another artificial fissile material that can be produced, like plutonium, as a result of neutron absorption by a naturally occurring 'fertile' isotope in a nuclear reactor. (In the case of plutonium, the fertile isotope is uranium-238. In the case of uranium-233, it is thorium-232.) Uranium-233 has not been used in significant quantities for weapons. However, because the same processes are involved in the production and recovery of uranium-233 as for plutonium, the same safeguard arrangements would prevent its diversion to weapon use.

[10] US Comptroller General, *Quick and Secret Construction of Plutonium Reprocessing Plants: A Way to Nuclear Weapons Proliferation?*, Report no. EMD-78-104 (US General Accounting Office: Washington, DC, 1978).

ore. In NPT NNWS, this brings the coverage of IAEA safeguards to all but the lowest-power research reactors[11] and to spent fuel storage sites as well as to any locations where kilogramme quantities of separated plutonium are stored for non-weapon use.

Given a universal cut-off on the production of plutonium for nuclear weapons, such safeguards would have to be extended to cover nuclear reactors, their fuel cycles and any separated plutonium in all countries.

Reprocessing is a controversial subject for those concerned about the effectiveness of safeguards because separated weapon-useable plutonium is present in solution and powder form at reprocessing plants, and diversions of one per cent or so could be hidden in measurement errors. Although one per cent is a small amount, the expected annual combined rate of separation of plutonium at the two large civilian reprocessing plants currently under construction in France and Britain is about 20 000 kg.[12] Smaller reprocessing plants are already in operation in these countries and in the USSR and Japan. One per cent of 20 000 kg is 200 kg—enough to produce about 20 warheads.

Of course, a diversion of this magnitude would not be easy at a reprocessing plant subject to a well-designed safeguard system. For example, division of the throughput of the plant into small batches would require the diversion of a large quantity of plutonium to be accomplished in many small diversions. Also, in order to remove the plutonium from the plant, the diverter would have to bypass portal sensors able, in principle, to detect the radiation from sub-kilogramme quantities of plutonium.[13] Nevertheless, the unavoidable measurement uncertainties will make it impossible to prove that no plutonium has been diverted.

It has sometimes been argued that the plutonium separated from spent power reactor fuel cannot be used to make nuclear weapons, because it ordinarily contains far larger percentages of plutonium-240 and other higher plutonium

[11] A nuclear reactor fissions about one gram of 'heavy metal' (uranium or plutonium) per megawatt (MW)-day of fission energy released. Each fission releases an average of two to three neutrons. One of these neutrons must fission another atom if the chain reaction is to continue at a constant rate. The remaining neutrons are available to convert a fertile isotope such as uranium-238 into a fissile isotope such as plutonium-239. A nuclear reactor can therefore produce up to about one gram of fissile material per MW-day. A typical power reactor releases on the order of 3000 megawatt-days of fission energy and produces a net of about one kilogram of plutonium per day. Research reactors usually have much lower powers—typically about one thermal MW(t). India obtained the plutonium for its 1974 test of a nuclear explosive from the fuel of a rather powerful 40 MW(t) unsafeguarded research reactor, and Israel is believed to have obtained the plutonium for its nuclear arsenal from a similar 40–150 MW(t) unsafeguarded reactor. See, for example, Spector, L. S., *Nuclear Ambitions* (Westview Press: Boulder, Colo., 1990), pp. 87 and 172.

[12] The design numbers are about 4000 kg and 15 000 kg of plutonium recovered per year for the British and French reprocessing plants respectively. A typical modern 1 million kilowatt (3 million kilowatt thermal) electric power reactor discharges about 250 kg of plutonium in its spent fuel each year. Therefore, between them, France and Britain plan to reprocess the equivalent of the fuel from about 75 1-gigawatt (GW) reactors. For comparison, in 1990, the world total nuclear power capacity was about 300 GW; see Albright D. and Feiveson, H. A., 'Plutonium recycling and the problem of nuclear proliferation', *Annual Reviews of Energy, 1988*, vol. 13 (Annual Reviews Inc.: Palo Alto, Calif., 1988), p. 239.

[13] See, for example, Albright, D., 'Portal monitoring for detecting fissile materials and chemical explosives', eds F. von Hippel and R. Sagdeev, *Reversing the Arms Race: How to Achieve and Verify Deep Reductions in the Nuclear Arsenals* (Gordon and Breach: New York, 1990), p. 239.

isotopes than standard weapon-grade plutonium. However, nuclear-weapon designers have repeatedly asserted that, while high percentages of the heavier plutonium isotopes are undesirable, nuclear weapons can be made from 'reactor-grade' plutonium—even by terrorists.[14]

Since reprocessing is not economical at current or foreseeable prices of natural uranium and enrichment (and does not simplify the disposal of the spent fuel produced by modern power reactors), it is possible to hope that current plans for large-scale reprocessing will be cancelled and most power-reactor plutonium will be kept relatively inaccessible in highly-radioactive spent reactor fuel stored in safeguarded repositories. Current commitments to the reprocessing of spent reactor fuel is in part a result of incorrect projections during the 1960s and early 1970s of an enormous expansion of world nuclear power capacity by the year 2000 and a resulting depletion of high-grade uranium ore deposits. Plutonium breeder reactors would convert the ^{238}U that makes up 99.3 per cent of natural uranium into chain-reacting plutonium, thereby multiplying by one hundred times the energy resource represented by the 0.7 per cent of ^{235}U in natural uranium. Reprocessing would be required to recover plutonium for recycling in both breeder and ordinary 'burner' reactors.[15]

In the absence of reprocessing, tagging and item counting can in principle keep track of the plutonium in the spent fuel to arbitrary accuracy—just as a bank can keep track of money to arbitrary accuracy. In practice, the task is much more difficult in the case of the spent fuel, because its intense radioactivity requires that the integrity and identity of individual spent fuel assemblies be checked by remote means. Therefore, the spent fuel storage facility has to be well designed and the inspectors require adequate time and instrumentation to do their jobs properly. Once the measurements have been taken on a batch of fuel, however, the fuel can be placed in a sealed container so that subsequent inspections will only have to ensure that the integrity of the container and seal has not been violated.

Weapon-grade uranium

In the case of weapon-grade uranium, the facilities of concern are uranium-enrichment plants. Until the 1970s, the world's uranium-enrichment plants were huge, expensive and confined to the NWS. During the past decade, however, uranium-enrichment technologies have been developed that can be

[14] See, for example, Carson Mark, J., Taylor, T. B., Eyster, E., Maraman, W. and Wechsler, J., 'Can terrorists build nuclear weapons', eds P. Leventhal and Y. Alexander, *Preventing Nuclear Terrorism* (Lexington Books: Lexington, Mass., 1987), pp. 55–65.

[15] Japan and the Federal Republic of Germany provided most of the actual initial funding for the construction of large-scale commercial reprocessing plants in France and Britain because their anti-nuclear movements demanded a solution to the problem of disposing of spent nuclear fuel. (Britain and France had developed expertise in reprocessing as a result of their nuclear weapon production programmes.) The 'solution' of sending the spent fuel to Britain and France is only a temporary one, however, since the reprocessing contracts stipulate that the high-level radioactive waste resulting from reprocessing must ultimately be returned to the country of origin.

deployed on a small scale and uranium-enrichment technology has become at least as important a potential route to nuclear weapons as reprocessing technology has been.

The problems of safeguarding uranium-enrichment plants would be very similar to those of safeguarding nuclear-fuel reprocessing plants if their primary product were highly-enriched uranium. Fortunately, however, most uranium is enriched only up to the level of a few per cent ^{235}U for use in the fuel of nuclear power reactors. Therefore, if it can be verified that an enrichment plant is producing only low-enriched uranium, the diversion risk at that facility becomes much less serious. Arrangements have been established at the centrifuge enrichment plants operated by the European consortium, URENCO (Uranium Enrichment Company), to allow the IAEA to verify that highly enriched uranium is not being produced.[16]

However, a small percentage of non-weapon uranium-enrichment demand *is* for uranium enriched to what is essentially weapon-grade (above 90 per cent ^{235}U). In the USA, the largest non-weapon demand for weapon-grade uranium is for naval propulsion reactor fuel (about 5000 kg per year in 1983–85)[17] with the remaining demand being for research and prototype reactors (about 1000 kg per year).

If there is still to be naval nuclear propulsion in a nuclear weapon-free world, it would be desirable to convert the propulsion reactors to use low-enriched uranium fuel. Enrichment to at least 20 per cent in ^{235}U is required for even a very cumbersome nuclear explosive.[18] Soviet[19] and French[20] officials have both stated that their naval nuclear reactors are fueled with uranium enriched to less than 10 per cent in ^{235}U. However, converting US reactors to low-enriched uranium might not be compatible with the US Navy's desire to avoid the necessity of refueling its naval reactors during their lifetimes.

Because of concerns about the possible theft of highly-enriched uranium fuel from poorly safeguarded research reactors, the USA during the Carter Administration launched the Reduced Enrichment for Research and Test Reactor Program (RERTR). This programme has successfully developed low-enriched fuels to replace high-enriched fuels in most research reactors with minimal performance penalties.[21]

---

[16] Hexapartite Safeguards Project, 'Safeguards approach for gas centrifuge type enrichment plants', *Nuclear Materials Management* (winter 1983), p. 30.

[17] Cochran, Arkin and Hoenig (note 5), p. 71.

[18] Taylor, T. B., 'Nuclear safeguards', *Annual Reviews of Nuclear Science*, vol. 25 (1975), p. 407.

[19] Interview with Evgeniy I. Mikerin (note 7).

[20] Miller, M., 'Nuclear-powered attack submarines and the proliferation of nuclear weapons', Paper presented at the Conference on Latin American Nuclear Co-operation: New Prospects and Challenges, Montevideo, Uruguay, 11–13 Oct. 1989. The proceedings of this conference will be published in Leventhal, P. and Leventhal, S. (eds), *Averting a Latin American Nuclear Arms Race: New Prospects and Challenges* (MacMillan: London, forthcoming).

[21] Travelli, A., 'Changing over to low-enriched fuels', *Nuclear Engineering International*, vol. 34, no. 419 (June 1989), pp. 72–74. Unfortunately, because of opposition within the US DOE, it appears that the RERTR programme has not received funding in the FY 1991 budget to develop substitute low-enriched fuel for the DOE's own high-powered research and isotope-production reactors and those of

There is no way to add an extra layer of protection against the possibility of clandestine uranium-enrichment activities being conducted except to extend safeguards to stockpiles of natural uranium and to the uranium mills at which natural uranium oxide is produced. To date, the IAEA has not attempted to extend its safeguards to cover natural uranium oxide—probably because there are many uranium mills and they are inherently difficult to safeguard. However, the possibilities of safeguarding uranium mills should be studied as part of the larger programme of research that should be undertaken if nuclear weapon-free world is to be established.

The concern about clandestine enrichment facilities focuses primarily on nozzle, centrifuge and laser-enrichment technologies. Because thousands of stages of enrichment are required at for the original gaseous-diffusion uranium-enrichment technology developed by the USA, until recently, all the known gaseous-diffusion facilities were very large and easily identifiable.[22]

Nozzle, centrifuge and laser-enrichment technologies require far fewer enrichment stages and far less energy per unit output than gaseous diffusion. South Africa has built a nozzle-enrichment plant and Pakistan a centrifuge-enrichment plant. Each of these plants is believed to have produced enough highly-enriched uranium for anywhere between a few to tens of nuclear warheads.[23] In each case, the facilities were identified by the intelligence services of other nations, but this task was made easier by the fact that neither country has large-scale overt nuclear activities that could be used to mask the clandestine activities. Brazil also has an active research and development programme in centrifuge enrichment.[24] None of these countries has signed the NPT.

Beyond a certain scale, it would be difficult to conceal clandestine enrichment activities even in an advanced industrial state with a large civilian nuclear power programme. Enough people would be aware of the nature of the activity that the information would 'leak' out. Also, the large demand for natural uranium (about 200 kg to produce one kg of weapon-grade uranium) would potentially provide a unique indication of large-scale clandestine uranium enrichment. However, the diversions required to mount an enrichment programme large enough to produce only a few weapons might well be concealed. This is one reason why the large-scale use of nuclear power—even without reprocessing or production of highly-enriched uranium—might simply be incompatible with a nuclear weapon-free world.

---

other countries for which the USA provides fuel. There are relatively few of these high-powered reactors but they account for most of the demand for highly-enriched uranium from research reactors.

[22] In Nov. 1983, on the eve of the inauguration of President Alfonsín, the Argentine military revealed that it had clandestinely built a small gaseous diffusion plant in the Andes. In late 1988, the facility began to produce 20 per cent-enriched uranium but, as of early 1990, there was no evidence that the plant had produced more highly enriched material; see Spector (note 11), p. 229.

[23] Spector (note 11), pp. 282, 299.

[24] Spector (note 11), p. 250–51.

III. Nuclear warhead dismantlement

If it could be assured that the production of fissile material for nuclear weapons had been halted, then the arsenals could in principle be reduced to zero by the process of dismantling the warheads that they contain and placing the recovered fissile materials under safeguards. This warhead dismantlement process could be part of a more comprehensive nuclear arms reduction agreement which would start by eliminating destabilizing weapon systems such as heavily MIRVed ICBMs and tactical nuclear weapon systems deployed in areas of confrontation and on ships.[25]

There would be nothing new involved in the task of dismantling warheads. Obsolete warheads are being dismantled continually to recover the fissile material that they contain for the manufacture of replacement warheads. The average US nuclear warhead is operational for only about 20 years. Therefore, if the dismantlement process continued unabated while the replacement process was halted, the US nuclear arsenal would be eliminated in approximately 20 years.

If the dismantlement took place under a nuclear-warhead agreement, however, it would have to be verified.

Verification arrangements for nuclear-warhead dismantlement have been sketched out by former US nuclear warhead designer, Theodore Taylor, for the case of a bilateral US–Soviet nuclear warhead reduction agreement.[26]

According to Taylor's scheme, in order to assure that sensitive design secrets would be protected, each country would dismantle its own warheads in the privacy of its own facility. The other country would be allowed to establish portal-perimeter controls around the facility so that it could verify that the agreed warheads had been taken into the facility for dismantlement and that the fissile material that they contained was placed under safeguards when it was removed. Between dismantlement campaigns, the inspectors would be allowed to examine the inside of the facility and verify that it contained no intact warheads or fissile material. The dismantlement facility could be an existing warhead dismantlement facility if its location and design were amenable to the necessary portal-perimeter controls.

The most challenging part of the arrangement would be to verify, without revealing classified information, that the objects brought into the dismantlement facility were indeed intact warheads of the agreed types. This problem was the subject of a study done under the auspices of the US Arms Control and

---

[25] Such a reduction scheme for strategic nuclear weapons is described in Feiveson, H. A. and von Hippel, F., 'Beyond START: how to make much deeper cuts', *International Security*, vol. 15, no. 1 (summer 1990), p. 154. The case for eliminating tactical nuclear weapons at sea is made by Fieldhouse, R., 'Naval nuclear arms control' in *Security at Sea: Naval Forces and Arms Control*, ed. R. Fieldhouse (Oxford University Press: Oxford, 1990), p. 158.

[26] Taylor, T. B., 'Verified elimination of nuclear warheads', *Science and Global Security*, vol. 1, no. 1–2 (autumn, 1989), p. 1.

Disarmament Agency (ACDA) in 1967 which was only recently declassified.[27] In the appropriation authorization bill for the US Department of Energy (DOE) for fiscal year (FY) 1991, the US Congress has mandated a new study and has requested that the President establish a joint US–Soviet working group on the same subject.[28] In the meantime, the Federation of American Scientists and the Committee of Soviet Scientists for Peace and Against the Nuclear Threat are co-operating on an unofficial study.

Highly-enriched uranium recovered from the dismantled warheads could be diluted with natural or depleted uranium to the low-enrichment level used in the fuel of nuclear power reactors. The amount of ^{235}U in US and Soviet nuclear weapons could fuel the world's reactors for several years and save tens of billions of dollars in costs for natural uranium and uranium isotope enrichment. This would pay back the costs of dismantling the nuclear warheads many times over.[29]

Since there is on average only about one-fifth as much plutonium as ^{235}U in US warheads, the energy content of the plutonium recovered from nuclear warheads would be correspondingly less. Furthermore, because of the occupational hazards involved, the costs of recycling the plutonium in nuclear power reactor fuel would be comparable to the savings of ^{235}U that would result.[30] This plutonium could therefore either be burned in special safeguarded reactors or disposed of with other radioactive waste.

IV. Accounting for already-produced fissile materials

Even if the cessation of production of unsafeguarded plutonium and enriched uranium, and the dismantlement of identified nuclear warheads could be verified, NWS and NNWS that had not previously placed their nuclear complexes under international safeguards would still have to account for and place under safeguards all fissile materials that had been previously been produced.

In accounting for this material, there would inevitably be uncertainties. As mentioned above, in the 1970s the US Government made public the fact that it could not account for the weapon-grade fissile materials that it has produced to an accuracy of better than several thousand kilogrammes—or enough for hundreds of nuclear warheads.

Even if a programme of 'nuclear archeology' were initiated immediately, it is unlikely that declarations of past production and disposition of weapon-grade fissile materials could be verified with uncertainties of less than about 10 per

[27] US Arms Control and Disarmament Agency, Demonstrated Destruction of Nuclear Weapons, Field Test FT-34 (Jan. 1969; largely declassified, 16 July 1990). A summary of this study may be found in von Hippel, F. 'The 1969 ACDA study on warhead dismantlement', Science and Global Security, vol. 2, no. 1 (autumn, 1990), pp. 103–8.

[28] 'Production of plutonium and highly enriched uranium for nuclear weapons and disposal of nuclear stockpiles', National Defense Authorization Act for Fiscal Year 1991, Section 3151 (US Government Printing Office: Washington, DC, 1990).

[29] See Taylor (note 26), p. 6.

[30] See, for example, Albright and Feiveson (note 12).

cent. This would correspond to approximately 100 000 kg of fissile material worldwide—enough to make many thousands of nuclear weapons.[31] If the programme of nuclear archeology is delayed for more years, the verifiability of declarations of past production will continue to worsen with time, as relevant records are destroyed or lost and shut-down production facilities are dismantled, and as the cumulative use of fissile material by the civilian nuclear sector grows and adds to the uncertainties in the difference between materials produced and materials used.

Because of these huge uncertainties, it is unlikely that either the USA or the USSR would be willing to agree to eliminate all of its nuclear warheads within any period of time measured in less than decades. The uncertainties may even make it difficult to achieve an agreement on 90 per cent reductions to 'finite-deterrence' levels[32]—much less to much lower 'minimum-deterrence' levels— since a 10 per cent uncertainty in the original stockpiles would thereby be converted into a 100 per cent uncertainty in the residuals after 90-per cent reductions.

Logically, the objections to 90 per cent reductions can be overcome. It is not difficult to design a 2000 nuclear-warhead force that would be adequately survivable to mount a devastating retaliation after an attack by a force with more than twice as many warheads.[33] Indeed, the nuclear forces of France, Britain and China, all have considerable deterrent value, despite the fact that each has only about 2 per cent as many warheads as the USA or the USSR.

V. Conclusion

It would appear from the above that it is physically impossible to *prove* that a nuclear weapon-free world has been achieved.

This does not mean, however, that it would be easy to maintain a clandestine nuclear arsenal undetected for the period of several decades or longer, during which time the world might steadily reduce its acknowledged stockpiles toward zero. If there were any activities at all associated with the maintenance of the clandestine stockpile, they might inadvertently reveal its existence to either foreign intelligence services or to official and unofficial domestic watch-dog groups. Self-organized domestic groups dedicated to ensure that their governments were complying with an international agreement to eliminate all nuclear weapons could be particularly important in this connection.[34] Since conditions allowing such groups to operate effectively are likely to be present only in a

---

[31] von Hippel, F., 'Warhead and fissile-material declarations', eds. F. von Hippel and R. Sagdeev, *Reversing the Arms Race: How to Achieve and Verify Deep Reductions in the Nuclear Arsenals* (Gordon and Breach: New York, 1990), p. 61.

[32] Feiveson and von Hippel (note 25).

[33] See, for example, Feiveson and von Hippel (note 25).

[34] Since the return of civilian governments in Argentina and Brazil, physicists in both countries have organized groups to work for civilian oversight of their nations' nuclear programmes. See Albright, D. and Higinbotham, W., 'Working for non-proliferation controls in Argentina and Brazil', *F.A.S. Public Interest Report* (Federation of American Scientists: Washington, DC, Apr. 1990), p. 1.

democracy, a precondition to the achievement of a nuclear weapon-free world may be the achievement of democracy in all countries potentially capable of producing nuclear weapons.

Even in non-democratic organizations and countries, however, there is always the possibility of a 'leak'. Indeed, this possibility would now appear to be almost a certainty, given past experience and the likely widespread perception of moral duty in an avowedly nuclear weapon-free world. One need only recall that, although the USA is a democracy, its nuclear weapon programme was run during World War II by a military obsessed with secrecy and the US weapon-design laboratory at Los Alamos was isolated behind fences in a remote area of the country, much as Soviet weapon laboratories were in the following decades.[35] Nevertheless, Klaus Fuchs was still able to provide the Soviet Union with detailed technical descriptions of the US nuclear weapon development programme.[36] Similarly, in the early 1960s, when the USSR was still very much a closed society, Oleg Penkovskiy, a high-level military official, provided the USA with information from central Soviet Army files about the Soviet military complex.[37]

In any case, after all safeguards are in place and after all efforts at nuclear archeology have been completed, and the existing arsenals have been reduced to 'minimum-deterrence' levels and perhaps below, each NWS will have to decide whether or not to proceed all the way to zero and join the 'club' of NNWS. How each NWS chooses will depend upon how it answers two questions about 'deterrence':

1. Can the NWS relinquish nuclear weapons as a deterrent to nuclear attack from some other country that may have succeeded in keeping a clandestine nuclear arsenal or could quickly put one together? The risk might seem acceptable if there were a world security system in which no state could threaten another with nuclear weapons without knowing that many other powerful states would commit themselves fully to bringing the renegade under control—with quickly produced nuclear weapons if necessary.

2. Can the NWS give up nuclear weapons as a deterrent to some other threat to its 'vital interests'? Because such a vital interest may include the very existence of the nation (as in the case of Israel), it appears that some nations might, before they were willing to go to zero, require guarantees from a world security system far beyond assurance of solidarity against nuclear threats.

---

[35] For a description of the security arrangements surrounding the Soviet nuclear-weapon laboratories during the 1950s and 1960s, see Sakharov, A., *Memoirs* (Alfred A. Knopf: New York, 1990), chapter 7, pp. 106–20.

[36] Chadwell Williams, R., *Klaus Fuchs Atom Spy* (Harvard University Press: Cambridge, Mass., 1987).

[37] Penkovskiy, O., *The Penkovskiy Papers* (Doubleday and Co.: Garden City, N.Y., 1965).

8. The end of superpower nuclear arms control?

Lynn Eden[*]

Kahn had got it wrong. The most demanding intellectual challenge for strategists—the real 'unthinkable'—was (and remains) the contemplation of a world without nuclear weapons.

Ken Booth and Nicholas J. Wheeler, 1992[1]

Social science does not predict the future. At best, it generates expectations about future outcomes, assuming that certain causal conditions are present.

Jack Snyder, 1987[2]

I. Introduction

Could it be politically feasible to eliminate completely nuclear weapons in the Soviet Union and United States as part of a larger project of world-wide elimination of nuclear weapons?[3] To approach this large and difficult question, I address the following questions below. In undertaking an analysis of political feasibility, what conditions should we assume in the international environment and domestic environments of both countries? Who would be the crucial domestic actors who would have to initiate a proposal to eliminate nuclear weapons and whose approval would be necessary? On the basis of historical precedent and hypothesized conditions, can we broadly predict the possible or even probable responses of those crucial actors? Finally, given all these considerations, what overall assessment can we make of the political feasibility of eliminating nuclear weapons in the United States and Soviet Union?

In addressing these questions, several broad analytical assumptions are made. First, the political feasibility of eliminating nuclear weapons in the two nuclear superpowers will depend on complex interactions of both international and domestic factors. Second, for purposes of this analysis, it will be possible to make certain assumptions about the international environment and then to focus primarily, although not exclusively, on domestic factors. Third, historical

[*] I am grateful to the Center for International Security and Arms Control, Stanford University, for intellectual and other support. I would like to thank Marc Bennett, Coit Blacker, George Bunn, James Goldgeier, Regina Cowen Karp, Michael McFaul, Steven Miller, Scott Sagan, Paul Stockton and Kimberly Zisk for guidance and detailed comment. I also thank Charles Glaser, Barry O'Neill and Charles Tilly for brief stimulating comment.
    [1] See Booth, K. and N. J. Wheeler, 'Beyond nuclearism', chapter 2 in this volume.
    [2] Snyder, J., 'The Gorbachev revolution: a waning of Soviet expansionism?', *International Security*, vol. 12 (winter 1987/88), p. 131.
    [3] On political feasibility and the contours of a world-wide elimination of nuclear weapons, see Regina Cowen Karp, 'Introduction', chapter 1 in this volume.

precedent regarding state structure and process, particularly in connection with strategic nuclear arms control agreements, will be relevant in providing a basis for thinking about the future; indeed, eliminating nuclear weapons in the United States and Soviet Union can usefully be conceived of as the ultimate nuclear arms control agreement.

Because it is difficult to imagine the complete elimination of nuclear weapons, for illustrative purposes the outline of a proposal to which both the United States and Soviet Union could, in theory, commit themselves is presented first. On 15 January 1986, Mikhail Gorbachev made a three-stage proposal for the 'complete elimination of nuclear weapons throughout the world'.[4] The first stage called for a 50 per cent reduction of strategic nuclear weapons, each side retaining no more than 6000 warheads, along the lines originally envisaged for the START (Strategic Arms Reduction Talks) Treaty. Also included was a provision to completely eliminate Soviet and US intermediate-range missiles in Europe, and a provision to stop all nuclear testing and to get other states to join such a moratorium as soon as possible. Only the Soviet Union and United States were required to make commitments during the first stage, and that in order to set an example for the other nuclear powers.[5]

In the second stage, the other nuclear powers would join the process of nuclear disarmament. The Soviet Union and United States would eliminate remaining intermediate-range nuclear weapons and freeze tactical nuclear systems. Other nuclear powers would agree to freeze all nuclear weapons, and then all nuclear powers would eliminate tactical nuclear weapons. Accompanying measures would include prohibition of space-strike weapons, a ban on development of non-nuclear weapons with destructive effects close to those of nuclear weapons, and a ban on all nuclear weapon tests.

In the third stage, the elimination of all remaining nuclear weapons would be completed. These would include the remaining strategic weapons of the United

[4] For full text, see Institute for Defense and Disarmament Studies, *Arms Control Reporter* (IDDS: Brookline, Mass.), sheets 611.D53–D59, Feb. 1986. What follows are some of the main features of Gorbachev's proposal. In the proposal itself, the stages are bounded in time and overlap; the second and third stages would each begin before the previous one was fully completed. All three stages would be completed by the year 2000. By 1989 Gorbachev advocated minimum deterrence, a radical notion, but less radical than the 1986 proposal. On the Soviet debates on reasonable sufficiency and minimum deterrence, see 'Of reasonable sufficiency, precarious parity and international security', *New Times*, 13 July 1987, pp. 18–21; and Shenfield, S., 'Minimum nuclear deterrence: the debate among Soviet civilian analysts', Center for Foreign Policy Development, Brown University, Nov. 1989. I am grateful to Kimberly Zisk for drawing these sources to my attention.

[5] The first stage of Gorbachev's proposal contains the foundations of the then draft treaty on strategic nuclear weapons, START, and the Dec. 1987 agreement banning intermediate-range ground-based nuclear missiles in Europe (known as the Intermediate-range Nuclear Forces Treaty, or INF Treaty). Estimates vary on the number of weapons each side will retain under START, although it appears to be many more than 6000 warheads. See Bunn, M., 'SAC force proposal: 11 700 warheads under START?', *Arms Control Today*, vol. 20 (Feb. 1990), p. 31; *New York Times*, 20 May 1990, describes START as a 30% cut in strategic nuclear warheads. According to George Bunn, there were similar practical results from the Outline of a Treaty on General and Complete Disarmament drafted in the Kennedy Administration in 1962; the draft provided ideas used in the 'Hot Line' Agreement of 1963, the Outer Space Treaty of 1967 and the Non-Proliferation Treaty of 1968. The draft also proposed a cut-off of production of fissile materials. Bunn, G., Private communication with the author, 1 Apr. 1991.

States and the Soviet Union, and the strategic weapons of Great Britain, France, and China, as well as any nuclear weapons held by other states.

Extremely difficult security issues would have to be resolved to successfully complete the process of nuclear elimination. First, the United States and its NATO allies would have to be satisfied that the conventional military threat to Europe had been virtually eliminated. Since Gorbachev's announcement in late 1988 that the Soviets would undertake large unilateral force cuts, as well as the subsequent collapse of Soviet power in East Central Europe, this issue, remarkably enough, has been largely resolved. Second, as nuclear weapons became less prominent, chemical and biological weapons would take on new significance. A multilateral agreement to reduce or eliminate these weapons, and to verify and enforce that agreement, would have to be in place before the final elimination of nuclear weapons; the first steps towards such an agreement have also been taken. Third, multilateral schemes for exceptionally wide-ranging inspection, verification and enforcement of the elimination of nuclear weapons would have to be devised and approved. Fourth, assuming that intermediate- and short-range nuclear systems could be eliminated (a non-trivial assumption), assurances and plans would have to be worked out for the phased final elimination of strategic nuclear weapons. This could be accomplished two ways. First, all other powers besides the United States and Soviet Union would have to eliminate their remaining nuclear weapons and the potential to produce nuclear weapons on short notice. This is a highly problematic proposal which assumes that Great Britain, France and China, as well as undeclared nuclear powers, would all be willing to eliminate nuclear weapons. Second, the Soviet Union and United States could agree to give up nuclear superpower status before other states had completely eliminated their nuclear weapons, perhaps by reducing their nuclear weapons to numbers commensurate with other powers. This is also a problematic proposal.[6]

II. Conditions

The essential problem in thinking about the feasibility of eliminating nuclear weapons in the United States and Soviet Union is conceptualizing the relationship of change and stasis in the international and domestic environments. The anarchic world of sovereign states as of the summer of 1991 is composed of two nuclear superpowers, the United States and Soviet Union; three lesser but substantial nuclear powers, Great Britain, France, and China; four *de facto* nuclear weapon states, Israel, India, Pakistan and South Africa; and other states that have either taken important steps towards gaining nuclear arms in the past,

[6] Allen Lynch argues that 'nuclear weapons provide an irreducible element of security for the Soviet Union that they do not provide for the United States. Without nuclear weapons, the United States would retain all of the significant trappings of superpower status. This is not the case for the Soviet Union. . . . [T]he Soviet Union would be the last country to forego the possession of nuclear weapons'. See Lynch, A., 'The Soviet Union: nuclear weapons and their role in security policy', ed. R. Cowen Karp, SIPRI, *Security with Nuclear Weapons? Different Perspectives on National Security* (Oxford University Press: Oxford, 1991), pp. 100–23, at 122.

such as Argentina, Brazil, Taiwan, South Korea and Libya, or that have very recently pursued or are believed to be pursuing nuclear arms, such as Iraq, Iran and North Korea.[7] In this environment, in which severe regional conflict is rife and in which verification and enforcement of nuclear elimination would be highly problematic, it is difficult to imagine crucial actors in the Soviet Union and United States radically changing their definitions of security and deciding that the complete elimination of nuclear weapons is feasible.

Likewise, given current conceptions of security, entrenched bureaucratic interests and powerful political interests of crucial actors in states that have acquired, or may acquire, nuclear weapons, it is difficult to imagine bringing about the requisite climate of opinion and mechanisms of co-operation and enforcement in the international environment to make the elimination of nuclear weapons feasible.

This could lead us to conclude that radical change is not possible and to a very quick conclusion of a very brief chapter.

However, simply because something is difficult to imagine does not mean that we should not imagine it. If we conclude that change, including radical change, is possible—an assumption both justified theoretically and historically—then the question is *how* to analyse the interaction, or co-determination, of change in the internal environments of states and the external international environment.[8] If we assume that crucial changes could occur at both levels, where do we start our analysis? What conditions should we assume in each environment?

Conditions in the international environment

I propose to 'bracket' the international environment, that is, take certain conditions as a given for purposes of analysis,[9] and then focus on possible changes and resistance to change at the domestic level in both the United States and Soviet Union. But what conditions should we assume?

We have seen above that if we assume the anarchic international environment of sovereign states, it is very difficult to imagine radical change in conceptions

---

[7] See Spector, L. S. with Smith, J. R., *Nuclear Ambitions: The Spread of Nuclear Weapons, 1989–1990* (Westview Press: Boulder, Colo., 1990), chapter 1.

[8] Most broadly, this is the agent–structure problem (in which the agent is the state and structure the international environment) discussed by Wendt, A. E., 'The agent–structure problem in international relations theory', *International Organization*, vol. 31 (summer 1987), pp. 335–70. On conceptualizing the relationship between domestic politics and the international environment, see also Katzenstein, P. J., 'International relations and domestic structures: Foreign economic policies of advanced industrial states', *International Organization*, vol. 30 (winter 1976), pp. 1–43; Gourevitch, P., 'The second image reversed: the international sources of domestic politics', *International Organization*, vol. 32 (autumn 1978), pp. 881–911; Putnam, R. D., 'Diplomacy and domestic politics: the logic of two-level games', *International Organization*, vol. 42 (summer 1988), pp. 427–60; Snyder, J., 'International leverage on Soviet domestic change', *World Politics*, vol. 42 (Oct. 1989), pp. 1–30; and Art, R. J., 'The United States: nuclear weapons and grand strategy', ed. R. Cowen Karp, SIPRI, *Security with Nuclear Weapons? Different Perspectives on National Security* (Oxford University Press: Oxford, 1991), pp. 57–99.

[9] A more complex notion of 'bracketing' originates in the phenomenology of Edmund Husserl. The more simple use of the term above is that of Anthony Giddens. See Wendt (note 8), pp. 364–65.

of security and security policy at the domestic level. However, if we assume radical change in the international arena, such as world government or mechanisms which allow the absolute enforcement of nuclear abolition in the absence of world government, and then ask if elimination is feasible, we skew our answer the other way: we find ourselves in the situation of the hungry economist on the desert island who stares at the tuna fish can and saves himself by 'assuming a can opener'. If we assume sufficiently radical change in the international environment, domestic political feasibility begins to look far greater.[10] And, of course, we beg the question of how these international conditions came about.

For the purposes of this chapter, it seems most reasonable to assume the following:

1. We begin with conditions in the contemporary world.

2. In addition to changes resulting from war, radical transformations are possible in the international environment of today. These changes are already resulting from large-scale historical change, such as the economic failure of centralized communist systems, the resurgence of nationalism, and from intended and unintended consequences of deliberate strategies to change international relations such as Mikhail Gorbachev has undertaken. In addition, future catastrophic events could mobilize world opinion and action (for example, an environmental tragedy or an accidental nuclear launch and explosion). And future technological breakthroughs, not directly related to nuclear weapons, could provide conditions that would make the elimination of nuclear weapons more feasible (for example, the development of very cheap solar energy could eliminate incentives to build or maintain nuclear reactors for power generation and thus could, to some degree, simplify issues of international inspection).

3. A project to eliminate nuclear weapons would be step-by-step and would contribute to the transformation of the international environment. In Sidney Drell's words:

The removal of nuclear weapons must be tightly coupled to progress in reducing distrust, fear, intolerance, and in removing the image of the enemy between nations with adversarial relations. That is not to suggest that political and social progress must precede large reductions in our nuclear arsenals—or vice versa. Each can assist the other.[11]

---

[10] However, even were we to hypothesize the most favorable international relations for the elimination of nuclear weapons, they would be enabling conditions, but not necessarily sufficient. Peter Gourevitch argues that '[t]he international system, be it in economic or politico-military form, is underdetermining. . . . Some variance in response to external environment is possible. The explanation of choice among the possibilities therefore requires some examination of domestic politics'. See Gourevitch (note 8), p. 900. Similarly, Jack Snyder argues that 'the international setting interact[s] with preexisting domestic conditions in shaping outcomes'. See Snyder (note 8), pp. 3–4.

[11] Drell, S. D., 'Not so fast', *Bulletin of the Atomic Scientists*, vol. 45 (July/Aug. 1989), p. 28. For a pioneering and detailed statement emphasizing the step-by-step creation of plateaus of military, political, and technological stability on the route to abolition, see Forsberg, R., 'The freeze and beyond: confining

4. At many points in the process, a degree of uncertainty or ambiguity would remain about how to interpret the current state of the international environment and future trends, providing a basis for continuing domestic disagreement about policy.

Let me elaborate this last point. In politics, ambiguity cannot be fully acknowledged (if acknowledged at all) by actors; rather, events in the international environment are construed by factions and coalitions to gain (or not lose) political advantage. Generally, international conditions are mediated by domestic cultural understandings, institutions, and political actors and do not directly determine domestic political outcomes.[12] A loss of domestic credibility stems not from the sheer force of external events but from how those events are interpreted in the context of domestic politics. In democratic societies, a major loss of credibility can occur when broadly accepted interpretations of events do not jibe with previous predictions made by political claimants. For example, the bombing by Japan of Pearl Harbor discredited the claim of 'America Firsters' that the USA would not be drawn into international conflict and, therefore, need not get involved; the Tet Offensive discredited the claim of the Johnson Administration that the Vietnamese communists were already virtually beaten. Conversely, under dictators, major external shocks may not be sufficient to discredit official interpretations. For example, despite the extensive damage inflicted on Iraq and the catastrophic military defeat of Iraq's forces in Kuwait during the Gulf War, in the immediate aftermath, Saddam Hussein maintained his power and controlled the public interpretation of events. Both situations suggest that, with rare exceptions, the international environment does not directly determine domestic political outcomes but rather is refracted through the interpretative lenses of domestic political actors embedded in cultural and institutional contexts.

In sum, for purposes of this analysis, I do not assume that issues of sequencing the reduction and elimination of classes of weapons and issues of verification and enforcement have been magically solved, but I also do not assume that these issues have proved intractable. By not assuming clear disconfirmation of the feasibility of eliminating nuclear weapons, I treat the international environment as permissive and non-determinate.

Conditions in the domestic environment

Without ignoring the international environment, this chapter focuses on the political feasibility of eliminating nuclear weapons in the domestic contexts of

the military to defense as a route to disarmament', *World Policy Journal*, vol. 1 (winter 1984), pp. 285–318, at 287. See also Booth and Wheeler, 'Beyond nuclearism', in this volume.

[12] See note 10 above. Deliberate interventions by foreign actors can, in extreme situations, such as conquest or assassination, directly alter domestic institutions or the cast of important actors; less extreme situations, such as international economic effects or external actors providing monetary, information, or other resources to targeted domestic political actors, can certainly affect domestic politics, but such effects are mediated by domestic factors.

the United States and the Soviet Union. I make the following assumptions about domestic conditions:

1. There is great political stability in the United States and a highly fluid and unstable situation in the Soviet Union (indeed, a revolutionary situation).

2. The procedures for gaining domestic political approval to eliminate nuclear weapons would be similar to those for gaining approval for nuclear arms control agreements. This is so even though an agreement to eliminate nuclear weapons would be unprecedented. In the United States, underlying political processes and institutional actors would be the same as those involved in the domestic political negotiation of past arms control treaties. In the Soviet Union, political process is in flux, but some of the major institutional actors would probably be the same or similar to those involved in past arms control negotiations. In both cases, a 'complex balancing of internal constituencies and forces' will forge arms control policy.[13]

3. As with arms control, only more so, a proposal to eliminate nuclear weapons would cut across issues of overall conceptions of security, mission and strategy of the armed forces, force posture, and budget. Historically, arms control has been incremental and modernizing, allowing—in some cases, facilitating—significant growth in numbers and lethality of US and Soviet nuclear arsenals; since such nuclear bargains could not be struck under a scheme of elimination, bargaining for domestic political support could be much more difficult.[14] Arms control has engaged bureaucratic and political passions; proposals and agreements have been responded to by actors not simply on the basis of substance (if such a response were ever possible in politics) but on the basis of both enduring organizational interests and shorter-term political opportunities.[15] A proposal to eliminate nuclear weapons would likely lead to even more intense political contention.

4. Bargaining positions among major actors would to some degree change, due both to changing domestic conditions (for example, political reorganization in the Soviet Union; and, on a much lesser scale of change, the budget squeeze

[13] Blacker, C. D. and G. Duffy (eds), Stanford Arms Control Group, *International Arms Control: Issues and Agreements*, 2nd edn (Stanford University Press: Stanford, Calif., 1984), p. 34.

[14] START is a partial exception in that it calls for a decrease in numbers of warheads; more important, however, it does not prevent the acquisition of modernized weapon systems. On the growth of arsenals under SALT, see Miller, S. E., 'Politics over promise: domestic impediments to arms control', *International Security*, vol. 8, no. 4 (spring 1984), pp. 67–90, at 77: '[I]n the 1970s, the decade of SALT, there occurred an enormous buildup of strategic nuclear forces *on both sides*. Both the United States and the Soviet Union added thousands of nuclear weapons to their arsenals during this period; between 1971 and 1980 the American stockpile of deployed nuclear warheads doubled while the Soviet Union's tripled' [emphasis in original].

[15] Blacker and Duffy (note 13), pp. 34–35, write that '[a]rms control policy in the United States, and apparently in the Soviet Union, is immersed in a context of people and organizations all at odds with one another over the most effective means of promoting security, and, incidentally, all promoting their personal or institutional interests'. See also Miller (note 14), p. 82.

in the United States) and to changing international conditions which provides grist for domestic political mills.[16]

III. Crucial domestic actors and possible responses

Given that a process of gaining domestic approval to eliminate nuclear weapons can be understood as an arms control process, let us explore more specifically what that means. What is that process? Who are the crucial actors? What is the relative power of actors to enact or block arms control proposals? What range of possible and probable responses might we expect? What coalitions might be formed and what bargains struck?

This section begins with a broad comparison of the arms control process in the United States and Soviet Union. Each is then analysed in more detail. The past working of the arms control process is explored and persistent organizational interests and responses are delineated. A discussion follows on how changes already underway and changes conceivable in both the domestic and international environments could affect the responses of crucial actors in the domestic arena to the notion of eliminating nuclear weapons.

How can the arms control processes in the Soviet Union be broadly compared with those in the United States? The United States and Soviet Union have markedly different state structures and are markedly different in how larger societal interests are represented (or not) in political decisions. The state structure of the United States is one of 'checks and balances', that is, separation of executive, legislative and judicial powers, even a fragmentation or dispersion of power, and it is a state structure interpenetrated to a large degree by societal interests, not least of all in the electoral process.[17] The Soviet Union, by contrast, has had a state apparatus controlled by a single undemocratic party, highly insulated from society, under a principle of fusion, not dispersion, of power.[18]

From the perspective of analysing the arms control process, the single greatest difference between the two states is that the legislative arena is a crucial one in the United States: a decision to eliminate nuclear weapons could not be made and carried out solely by the president and the executive branch of the United States. By law, such a decision would have to be approved by Congress;

[16] On the changing nature of domestic US bargaining under the impact of the changing international and domestic environment, see the recent innovative work of Paul Stockton, 'The new congressional politics of arms control and force modernization', *International Security*, vol. 16 (autumn 1991).

[17] Krasner, S. D., 'United States commercial and monetary policy: unravelling the paradox of external strength and internal weakness', ed. P. J. Katzenstein, *Between Power and Plenty: Foreign Economic Policies of Advanced Industrial States* (University of Wisconsin Press: Madison, Wis., 1978), pp. 51–87, esp. 61–66.

[18] A useful comparative historical analysis of changing Soviet state structure is found in Teague, E. and Mann, D., 'Gorbachev's dual role', *Problems of Communism*, vol. 39 (Jan.–Feb. 1990), pp. 1–14. For a broad comparison of Soviet and US state/society relations , see Evangelista, M., *Innovation and the Arms Race: How the United States and the Soviet Union Develop New Military Technologies* (Cornell University Press: Ithaca, N.Y, 1988). For a vivid sense of the workings of the Soviet party–state structure during the period of the negotiation of the SALT treaties, see Gelman, H., *The Brezhnev Politburo and the Decline of Detente* (Cornell University Press: Ithaca, N.Y., 1984), esp. chs 2–3.

in addition, precedent gives Congress an informal role in shaping agreements before the formal legislative process begins—through anticipation in the executive branch of congressional reaction and through direct consultation with influential legislators. Thus, one cannot discuss the possible political feasibility of eliminating nuclear weapons without analysing congressional dynamics and the interrelationship of bargaining in the executive and congressional arenas.

Historically, in the Soviet Union, the formal ratification process involved legislative approval of a sort, but the operative arms control process was limited to a handful or so of very high level party and state officials (often the same individuals). Indeed, until 1989, legislative functions based on representation through popular election were non-existent; rather, through the *nomenklatura* system, the Communist Party strictly controlled the selection of candidates to a rubber-stamp legislature, the Supreme Soviet (as well as appointment to all important official posts).[19] In 1989, the Soviet Union began to develop nascent democratic legislative functions when the newly created and partially popularly elected Congress of People's Deputies then elected a reconstituted Supreme Soviet. It seems likely that the Supreme Soviet will play a role in the ratification of arms control agreements in the future.

With this crucial difference in mind, we can, with caution, sketch out certain historical similarities in the arms control processes in both states. First, in both the Soviet Union and United States, the active interest in, support of and active politicking on the part of the general secretary or president has been crucial in both the internal political negotiation and the international negotiation. Second, in both states, there has been an intense intra-executive bargaining process in formulating initial positions (and in gaining approval for any modification of positions). Third, in both states the military has been unquestionably subordinate to civilian authority (in the Soviet Union, civilian party authority). Within this context of formal subordination, the military in both states has had significant intra-executive bargaining power; in the United States, the military has had additional leverage gained by its ability to appeal to Congress. Fourth, in both states, the military has used its bargaining power to shape arms control agreements in ways that have protected counterforce modernization and protected the ability of each military to carry out its missions in the event of nuclear war. This has not been an uncontentious process. According to Henry Kissinger, who had occasion to observe behaviour on both sides: '[B]oth sides have to convince their military establishments of the benefits of [arms control] restraint, and that is not a thought that comes naturally to military people on either side'.[20] Were the military's conceptions of mission and the power of the

---

[19] Teague and Mann (note 18), pp. 2 and 4.

[20] Kissinger, H., 'News conference at Moscow, July 3', *US Department of State Bulletin*, no. 71 (29 July 1974), p. 210, quoted in Garthoff, R. L., *Detente and Confrontation: American–Soviet Relations from Nixon to Reagan* (Brookings Institution: Washington, D.C., 1985), p. 430. For a good brief discussion of the conflict between arms control as 'an effort to interfere with the defense policy process' and the interests of the military, see Miller (note 14), pp. 80–81; also see Miller, S. E., 'The limits of mutual restraint: arms control and the strategic balance', Ph.D. dissertation, Fletcher School of Law and Diplomacy, 1988, especially chapter 3, 'Arms control theory versus doctrinal reality'.

military to continue relatively unchanged into the future, it would be a significant block to the elimination of nuclear weapons.

It is worth noting that it has not been uncommon to treat the United States and Soviet Union as extremely different in terms of their policies regarding nuclear weapons. US policy is taken to be 'deterrence', based on strategic civilian ideas of mutual assured destruction, and Soviet policy has been said to be one of war-fighting and war-winning. Thus, according to Richard Pipes:

American and Soviet nuclear doctrines . . . are starkly at odds. The prevalent U.S. doctrine holds that an all-out war between countries in possession of sizable nuclear arsenals would be so destructive as to leave no winner. . . . Soviet doctrine, by contrast, emphatically asserts that while an all-out nuclear war would indeed prove extremely destructive to both parties, its outcome would not be mutual suicide: the country better prepared for it and in possession of a superior strategy could win and emerge a viable society.[21]

Pipes, however, fudges distinctions in both the United States and Soviet Union between civilian declaratory policy and operational military doctrine. Implicitly, Pipes compares US declaratory doctrine with Soviet military doctrine; this is an analytically unsound comparison of apples and oranges. A correct analysis would compare US civilian statements with Soviet civilian statements and would compare US operational strategy with its Soviet counterpart. When this is done, the differences between the two are greatly diminished.[22]

Let us look in more detail at the arms control process in the United States and Soviet Union, focusing on the process itself, delineating persistent organizational interests and responses, and speculating on how crucial actors might respond to the idea of eliminating nuclear weapons. Said otherwise, we will examine how organizational interests and bargaining relationships affect actors' positions on the necessity of maintaining, or the feasibility of eliminating, nuclear weapons. We will pay particular attention to the relationship of the political and military realms.

[21] Pipes, R., 'Why the Soviet Union thinks it could fight and win a nuclear war', *Commentary*, vol. 64 (July 1977), pp. 21–34, at 21.

[22] For brief balanced treatments, see Miller (note 20), chapter 3; and Sagan, S. D., *Moving Targets: Nuclear Strategy and National Security* (Princeton University Press: Princeton, N.J., 1989), chapter 2, 'Second-strike counterforce', pp. 46–97. On the roots of US operational doctrine, see Rosenberg, D. A., 'The origins of overkill: nuclear weapons and American strategy, 1945–1960', *International Security*, vol. 7 (spring 1983), pp. 3–71. For a very good discussion of Soviet thinking about nuclear war, see Holloway, D., *The Soviet Union and the Arms Race*, 2nd edn (Yale University Press: New Haven, Conn., 1983), chapter 3, 'Thinking about nuclear war'. For broad discussion of Pipes's arguments, see 'A Garthoff–Pipes debate on Soviet strategic doctrine', *Strategic Review*, vol. 10 (autumn 1982), pp. 36–63; and Snyder, J., 'Science and Sovietology: bridging the methods gap in Soviet foreign policy studies', *World Politics*, vol. 40 (Jan. 1988), pp. 169–83. For a more subtle reading than Pipes on Soviet military thinking on the possibility of victory in nuclear war, see also Herspring, D. R., *The Soviet High Command, 1967–1989: Personalities and Politics* (Princeton University Press: Princeton, N.J., 1990), pp. 129–30.

The United States

As noted above, domestic US arms control bargaining occurs in and between two interrelated arenas, the executive branch and Congress.[23] What are the bargaining dynamics in each arena and between them, and how can we extrapolate from arms control negotiations to prospects for the elimination of nuclear weapons?

The president

Historically, what role has the president played in achieving arms control agreements? What incentives has he had to engage in and complete arms control accords? And what incentives and disincentives might he or she have to eliminate nuclear weapons?

As with any major foreign policy initiative, no arms control agreement, and no proposal to eliminate nuclear weapons, can succeed without the active involvement of the president in all arenas: intra-executive, congressional and international.[24] The president must commit him- or herself to initiate the arms control process, must maintain a clear vision, remain sufficiently committed to it to steer the proposal through and override objections in the executive branch, know when to modify in the face of intransigence, and to gain required congressional support, must be prepared to provide substantial sweeteners for those whose support is essential, and be skilled in framing the issues and mobilizing public opinion. The skilled commitments of Presidents Kennedy and Nixon led, respectively, to the ratification of the Partial Test Ban Treaty in 1963 and the SALT I accords (comprising the Anti-Ballistic Missile Treaty and the Interim Agreement on the Limitation of Strategic Offensive Arms) in 1972. President Jimmy Carter was able to gain executive branch agreement to SALT II and to

[23] What about the influence of those involved in the research, development and production of weapons and other military equipment? Without denying strong vested interests and possible substantial influence, I take a state-centred approach on grounds of parsimony: influence from industry should be exerted largely through the state actors discussed here—the president, the military and congressional representatives. This section draws heavily on the syntheses of the US domestic arms control process by Miller (note 14) and Stockton (note 16). See also Miller, S. E., 'The viability of nuclear arms control: US domestic and bilateral factors', *Bulletin of Peace Proposals*, vol. 16, no. 3 (Sep. 1985), pp. 263–76. Miller refers to the negotiation primarily within the executive branch as the 'policy formulation phase'. He notes that 'this may be the most difficult part of arms control. President Carter has observed, for example, that SALT II required as much negotiation in the United States as it did with the Soviet Union'. Miller (note 14), p. 80, citing Jimmy Carter, *Keeping Faith: Memoirs of a President* (Bantam Books: Toronto, 1982), p. 218. George Bunn refers to these arenas as bargaining committees. He notes a third important bargaining committee for the US president: the allies who will be affected by the negotiations. See Bunn, G., *Arms Control by Committee: Managing Negotiations with the Soviets* (Stanford University Press: Stanford, Calif., forthcoming).

[24] A major conclusion of Bunn (note 23), chapter 11, is that 'direct participation by the president has been essential' at all stages of the bargaining process and in all arenas. Miller notes the importance of the president and says 'the strong and direct commitment of the President and his close associates in the White House seems to be a decisive element in determining whether and how much arms control can succeed'. See Miller (note 14), pp. 82–83, quotation at p. 89.

successfully negotiate the treaty with the Soviet Union, but he was unable to gain ratification by Congress.[25]

What historical incentives have presidents had to engage in arms control negotiations and to reach arms control agreements? Since the late 1950s or early 1960s, presidents have found it politically advantageous, both internationally and domestically, to appear to be serious about negotiating arms control agreements, and, since the conclusion of SALT I, there has been a strong domestic expectation that a successful president will make significant progress in negotiating further arms control agreements. Presidents appear to have an incentive to conclude a major agreement both for their enduring historical reputation and for shorter-term political benefits.[26] In addition, presidents have been strongly motivated by wanting to limit the nuclear arms of others and, in the case of anti-ballistic missile (ABM) systems, even of the United States. President Kennedy wanted a comprehensive test ban in large part to limit nuclear proliferation; President Johnson wanted to forestall a US ABM system by persuading the Soviet Union to begin negotiations on strategic arms (negotiations which eventually led to the SALT I accords); in concluding the SALT I agreements, President Nixon wanted to limit the Soviet strategic missile buildup, particularly of 'heavy' Soviet ICBMs.[27] Finally, presidents have found that ongoing arms control negotiations offer powerful leverage in gaining congressional approval of the administration's strategic modernization programmes. Ostensibly, arms control has been about limiting arms; in practice, the arms control process has greatly facilitated approval of new nuclear weapon programmes.

What incentives and disincentives might a president have to commit him- or herself to eliminate nuclear weapons, a radical departure from the generally incremental and modernizing arms control agreements we have had thus far? Given the contemporary world, one can easily imagine strong disincentives: there would be strong domestic political objection that US security would be jeopardized and that the United States should not prepare to give up nuclear superpower status. In addition, there could be a lack of enthusiasm from the predominant voice of the arms control community, political and academic,

[25] Good brief broad accounts are Miller (note 14), pp. 89–90; and Blacker and Duffy (note 13), pp. 40, 257. On Kennedy's role and skill, see Neidle, A., 'Nuclear test bans: history and future prospects', eds A. L. George, P. J. Farley and A. Dallin, *US–Soviet Security Cooperation: Achievements, Failures, Lessons* (Oxford University Press: New York, 1988), pp. 195–214, at 195; on Nixon's determination despite political and military opposition, see Kissinger, H., *White House Years* (Little, Brown and Co.: Boston, Mass., 1979), pp. 1232–33; on Carter's lack of involvement in mobilizing public support, see Flanagan, S. J., 'SALT II', eds A. Carnesale and R. N. Haass, *Superpower Arms Control: Setting the Record Straight* (Ballinger: Cambridge, Mass., 1987), pp. 105–38, at 117; also see Talbott, S., *Endgame, The Inside Story of SALT II* (Harper and Row: New York, 1979), chapter 3, 'The making of a debacle', pp. 38–67.

[26] Blacker and Duffy (note 13), p. 35.

[27] On Kennedy, see Seaborg, G. T., with the assistance of B. S. Loeb, *Kennedy, Khrushchev, and the Test Ban* (University of California Press: Berkeley, Calif., 1981); on Johnson, see Blacker and Duffy (note 13), p. 37, quoting Garthoff, R. L., 'Salt I: an evaluation', *World Politics*, vol. 31 (Oct. 1978), pp. 2–3; and on Nixon and Kissinger, see Kissinger (note 25), pp. 196–97, 537, 550, 815–1218. See also Hampson, F. O., 'SALT I: Interim Agreement and ABM Treaty', eds A. Carnesale and R. N. Haass (note 25), pp. 65–103, at 71.

which has argued that nuclear war is best deterred by a robust nuclear retaliatory capability—in other words, a world in which the United States and Soviet Union each have thousands of survivable nuclear weapons.[28]

However, given a not inconceivable change in international relations and political climate—for example, the conclusion of START II or III leading to minimum nuclear deterrent postures of a few thousand nuclear weapons; continued peaceful relations among the great powers; the successful creation of a pan-European political community; and perhaps a catastrophic nuclear weapons accident or nuclear use by a small nuclear power—it is not beyond the realm of imagination that, within a decade or two, a US president could find it very attractive, for political and substantive reasons, to participate in an international effort to eliminate nuclear weapons. (Certainly it should not be harder to imagine this than to imagine the president pushing the nuclear button, a perfectly mundane image in the scenario of credible deterrence.) And, as we have seen with President Reagan's Strategic Defense Initiative, a president can seriously and effectively commit to a policy that comes as a shock to the bureaucracy and does not meet with its initial approval.

In sum, the skilled support of the president would be crucial to the feasibility of a proposal to eliminate nuclear weapons. It would not, however, be sufficient. If we assume, for purposes of analysis, that this initial condition of presidential commitment had been met, what further conditions would have to be fulfilled for such a proposal to be feasible?

The military

The first task would be to frame a proposal that would be acceptable within the executive branch.[29] Let us focus on the most influential potential obstacle to arms control historically, the military. What do we know of the bargaining power of the military within the executive branch? What has it wanted from arms control agreements and what has it got? How is the bargaining relationship currently changing? And how might the bargaining process unfold in the face of a presidentially backed proposal to eliminate nuclear weapons?

---

[28] For a very careful argument about the advantages of robust retaliatory capabilities, see Glaser, C. L., *Analyzing Strategic Nuclear Policy* (Princeton University Press: Princeton, N.J., 1990), especially chapter 6, 'Why disarmament is probably more dangerous than MAD', pp. 166–203.

[29] Miller provides a nice statement of the range of actors and the broad dynamics of the intra-executive branch negotiation: 'The players in the internal game are many: the White House, which often has its own agenda of political, budgetary, and foreign policy concerns; the State Department, with its concern for the international political relationships involved; the Arms Control and Disarmament Agency, a weak player in its own game; the various divisions and subdivisions of the Defense Department, which often have the most directly at stake; and occasionally key individuals from Congress, for example, Senator Henry Jackson, who figured prominently in the early months of the Carter Administration. The goal of the game is to produce an arms control proposal or position that is essentially acceptable to all. The structure of the game is simple: each of the organizations involved will seek, within the limits of its influence and effectiveness in the bureaucratic politics of the situation, to preserve its own interests or, at the least, to avoid having them badly violated'. See Miller (note 14), p. 80. Bunn (note 23), chapter 11, depicts the players in the executive branch as fewer and very high level, as does Carter (note 23), p. 218.

Historically, every president from Kennedy through Bush has tried to gain support of the Joint Chiefs of Staff (JCS) in the formulation of policy in the executive branch, both because it would be extremely awkward to enter an international negotiation without their support and because, in Paul Stockton's words, '[N]o nuclear arms treaty has ever been ratified without the support of the Joint Chiefs of Staff'. According to Steven Miller, '[B]ecause military support for agreements is thought to be, and probably is, crucial to the *ratification* process, as well as because military programs are directly effected, the military voice is a powerful one in the *policy formulation process*'.[30]

The impact of the military has been twofold: it has been able to shape arms control proposals themselves (for example, by making sure that the agreements do not constrain modernization programmes); and it has been able to extract strong administration support for its modernization programmes before Congress. This pattern has held from the ratification of the Partial Test Ban Treaty in 1963 through the 1991 START Treaty.

In the negotiations that led to the Partial Test Ban Treaty, despite opposition from the Joint Chiefs of Staff, President Kennedy strongly backed a *comprehensive* test ban. He could not, however, hope to have a comprehensive treaty ratified if he could not satisfy the Chiefs on an adequate number of inspections or on technical issues of monitoring. The USSR was not forthcoming on these issues and when it changed its position from opposition to a limited test ban to support of it, Kennedy took the agreement that was there. Even so, Kennedy paid a high price for the Chiefs' support and for Senate acceptance: a four-point 'safeguard' programme that included an expanded programme of underground nuclear testing.[31] Regarding SALT I, Secretary of Defense Melvin Laird and the Chairman of the Joint Chiefs of Staff, Admiral Thomas Moorer, predicated their support for the agreement on congressional approval of an accelerated programme for the Trident submarine, the B-1 bomber and other strategic modernization programmes.[32] In SALT II, Secretary of Defense James Schlesinger advocated a large strategic modernization programme, including the MX missile, the Trident missile and submarine, and cruise missiles, partly on the basis of their contribution to US bargaining strength in SALT II. More baldly, General David Jones, Chairman of the Joint Chiefs of Staff during the Carter Administration, announced that he would have 'deep reservations' about supporting SALT II unless funding for the MX missile programme continued.[33]

---

[30] Stockton (note 16), citing Neidle (note 25), p. 200; see also Miller (note 14), p. 81 [emphasis in original].

[31] Seaborg (note 27), pp. 220–29; 277–79; Miller (note 14), p. 69; Blacker and Duffy (note 13), pp. 41, 133.

[32] Bresler, R. J. and Gray, R. C., 'The bargaining chip and SALT', *Political Science Quarterly*, vol. 92 (spring 1977), pp. 65–88, at 73, citing congressional testimony. See also Hampson (note 27), pp. 87–87; Smith, G., *Doubletalk: The Story of the First Strategic Arms Limitation Talks* (Garden City, N.Y.: Doubleday & Co., 1980), p. 30; Miller (note 14), pp. 69, 82.

[33] Garthoff (note 20), pp. 423, 444–45; Flanagan (note 25), p. 109; Stockton (note 16); Miller (note 14), p. 81.

The military continued this bargaining stance into the START negotiations. The Chiefs' desire for the deployment of the B-2 bomber shaped START counting rules, allowing for a great discount on weapons on penetrating bombers; and in the spring of 1990, General John T. Chain, Jr, then Commander-in-Chief of the Strategic Air Command, strongly conditioned his support for START on congressional funding of the B-2. Yet, Stockton argues that, first, in the context of a widely perceived decrease in the Soviet threat in the international environment and, second, in the context of a post-Reagan budget-constrained domestic environment, the bargaining position of the military has noticeably weakened; he claims congressional support for strategic modernization is so weak that a JCS threat to withhold support for START will not provide sufficient leverage to gain congressional funding for modernization programmes.[34]

This is a significant departure from the history of nuclear arms control to this point, and it has some obvious implications for understanding the role of the military in the face of a proposal to eliminate nuclear weapons. We saw demonstrated in the spring and summer of 1990 that what had appeared to be an enduring power of the military to gain approval of its modernization programmes was not so enduring after all. In a situation in which, in terms of military capability, the external threat has only begun to be reduced, the bargaining power of the Chiefs has already been significantly diminished.

But what about the other side of the arms control bargain? Could START be ratified without the support of the JCS? Would the president want to try to do so? On the one hand, if the Chiefs could still extract a price for support of START, and they very likely can, what would that price be? One can imagine, for example, that they, along with congressional allies, could demand guarantees protecting nuclear roles and missions that could seriously constrain future START agreements (much as the Jackson amendment to SALT I shaped SALT II) and could make it very difficult for a proposal to eliminate nuclear weapons to succeed in the US political environment.

On the other hand, the US military has been drastically demobilized before, and one can imagine that in the face of a very substantially reduced conventional threat to Europe and greatly increased international co-operation to reduce and eliminate nuclear weapons, over time the ground for resistance could be cut out from under the military.

In the face of a proposal to drastically cut or eliminate nuclear weapons, certain parts of the military would be far more affected than others. The service most adversely affected would be the one that has most benefited from nuclear weapons, the United States Air Force, particularly the Strategic Air Command and, to a lesser degree, the Tactical Air Command. Military leaders might adapt by looking for new missions while, at the same time, trying to protect core functions and capabilities by extracting assurances and budget guarantees.

---

[34] Morrocco, J. D., 'SAC chief indicates scaled back B-2 bomber procurement possible', *Aviation Week & Space Technology*, vol. 132 (12 Mar. 1990), p. 22; and Gordon, M. R., 'Chief of Air Command questions Bush plan to cut nuclear missiles', *New York Times*, 5 May 1990. See also Stockton (note 16).

How effective the resistance of the military would be to the elimination of nuclear weapons could depend on two things: the organizational resources of the military; and, closely related, the credibility of a proposal to eliminate nuclear weapons.[35] (The greater the resources of the military, the greater the ability of the military to cast doubt on the credibility of such a proposal.) The organizational ability of the military to resist the elimination of nuclear weapons could be greatly reduced, possibly at considerable political cost to the president, if presidential authority had already been brought to bear in redefining military missions (for example, redefining the nuclear mission to one of minimum deterrence), reorganizing those parts of the military most affected by redefined missions, and promoting new leadership within the military amenable to redefined missions and organization. The credibility of a proposal to eliminate nuclear weapons would depend on the continued public perception of reduced threat, public perception of a real possibility of international cooperation to eliminate nuclear weapons, the commitment of the president to eliminate nuclear weapons, and the skill of the president in selling that vision and in providing assurances to the public that the security of the United States would not be compromised.

The Congress

Any international negotiation to eliminate nuclear weapons would undoubtedly involve consultation with Congress. And, of course, the successful negotiation of an agreement to eliminate nuclear weapons, which would almost certainly be in the form of a treaty, would require congressional approval. What are the legal requirements for congressional approval? What are the congressional coalition-building processes regarding arms control? What is the bargaining power of the military vis-à-vis Congress? And what implications do the answers have for assessing the political feasibility of eliminating nuclear weapons?

The legal requirements for congressional approval of international agreements and treaties are stable features of the political landscape and will endure well into the future. However, following recent scholarship, this chapter argues that the coalition-building process and the bargaining power of the military vis-à-vis Congress has begun to shift in the decade of the 1990s. This chapter examines the pattern that has held until 1990, sketches the changes that appear to be underway since then and, finally, speculates about the implications of these changes for the political feasibility of eliminating nuclear weapons.

Legally, the president may make binding international agreements (by executive agreement) which need not be submitted to Congress for approval. However, in the area of arms limitation, in order to forestall such executive agreements without congressional approval, the Arms Control and Disarma-

---

[35] A third factor could be the ability of civilian authority to 'buy off' the military by providing new missions and budget. But this could be problematic in an environment of reduced threat and tighter budgets.

ment Act of 1961 requires that the president submit agreements to Congress. The act says: 'No action shall be taken under this or any other law that will obligate the United States to disarm or to reduce or limit the Armed Forces or armaments of the United States, except pursuant to the treaty-making power of the President under the Constitution or unless authorized by further affirmative legislation by the Congress'. In other words, any agreement to disarm or reduce or limit armaments must be submitted to Congress either in the form of a treaty which must be approved by a two-thirds vote in the Senate in order to be ratified (strictly speaking, the Senate consents to ratification), or in the form of an agreement which must be approved by a majority vote in both houses of Congress.[36]

This is the framework within which arms control agreements have come under the purview of Congress and under which an agreement to eliminate nuclear weapons would fall. However, issues of arms control are not decided in isolation from other issues, for at least two reasons. First, as discussed above, congressional and other debates on arms control agreements have not been isolated from larger arguments about the nature of the international environment and external threat, the proper strategy to insure the security of the United States, and the proper defence programme of the United States, particularly regarding the procurement of nuclear weapons.[37] These larger debates both reflect and shape the political discourse within which specific arms control proposals are decided, and they provide the argumentative materials from which senators and representatives craft their political positions.[38] Second, coalitional support in Congress is generally required to gain the requisite two-thirds or majority vote for a treaty or agreement, and this often involves a log-rolling process in which members of Congress trade support for each other's initiatives to gain the required votes on each. Historically, Congress has been split among those who put greatest priority on arms control agreements, those who put greatest priority on nuclear weapons modernization programmes and those who wanted both.[39] Thus, in Congress, arms control issues have tended to be linked to other issues, particularly strategic nuclear weapon procurement.

[36] Blacker and Duffy (note 13), p. 43; Bunn, G., 'Missile limitation: by treaty or otherwise?', *Columbia Law Review*, vol. 70 (Jan. 1970), pp. 1–47, at 10–12. The latter is an authoritative discussion of the legal aspects of executive–congressional relations in negotiating international agreements.

[37] On the debates over Soviet objectives, the requirements for deterrence, measuring the strategic nuclear balance, and verification of agreements, see the chapters in Eden, L. and Miller, S. E. (eds), *Nuclear Arguments: Understanding the Strategic Nuclear Arms and Arms Control Debates* (Cornell University Press: Ithaca, N.Y., 1989).

[38] Recent scholarship argues that, on defence and arms control and issues, the opinions and economic interests of geographical constituencies do not predict the voting of members of Congress, but that ideology, and to a lesser extent, party affiliation, do. See Wayman, F. W., 'Arms control and strategic arms voting in the US Senate: patterns of change, 1967–1983', *Journal of Conflict Resolution*, vol. 29 (June 1985), pp. 225–51; and Lindsay, J. M., 'Parochialism, policy, and constituency constraints: congressional voting on strategic weapons systems', *American Journal of Political Science*, vol. 34 (Nov. 1990), pp. 936–60; for his broader analytical and historical treatment, see Lindsay, J. M., *Congress and Nuclear Weapons* (Johns Hopkins University Press: Baltimore, Md., 1991).

[39] Stockton (note 16).

As shown above, the military has been able to gain administration backing for its nuclear modernization programmes in exchange for its support for arms control. Given the coalition-building requirements in Congress, two arguments have been used before Congress by administration and military officials that have proved particularly effective. First, they have argued that military modernization programmes were needed as 'chips' to be used for bargaining purposes in arms control negotiations.[40] Second, they have argued that arms control agreements made modernization programmes necessary to the security of the United States. In this log-rolling process, congressional approval of arms control agreements has proceeded in tandem with procurement of modernized nuclear forces. In this arrangement, arms controllers, force modernizers, and those who wanted both arms control and force modernization could be more or less satisfied.

Thus, historically, the arms control process has been predicated on the acquisition of new nuclear weapons: agreements to limit nuclear weapons could only be obtained by agreements to build more modern nuclear weapons. Were such a pattern to continue indefinitely, it would, by definition, be impossible to eliminate nuclear weapons.

However, according to recent work by Paul Stockton, this log-rolling pattern, which endured for almost three decades, is being broken in the decade of the 1990s for two interrelated reasons. First, the congressional perception of external threat from the Soviet Union has declined, undercutting arguments for expensive nuclear modernization programmes. Second, Congress has strong incentives to cut the defence budget because of the national budget squeeze. (Neither, by itself, is determinate. Arguments about the decrease in the Soviet threat have undoubtedly had more salience given Congress's desire to cut the defence budget. And Congress has indicated it is willing to spend money it does not have in the face of perceived international threat, as in the case of the Gulf War.) The result has been that, in 1990, Congress focused on cost, suffering from what is known colloquially as 'sticker shock', and ignored the military's arguments based on the Soviet threat. Further, Congress ignored threats that the military would oppose START without support for its modernization programmes[41] and refused to fund production of MX missiles and procurement of B-2 bombers. It seems that, in 1990, the old arms control–arms modernization coalition was not operative; rather, a new budget cutting–weapons killing coalition formed. For the first time, arguments and threats regarding arms control did not work to gain congressional approval for major weapons procurement programmes; clearly, the bargaining power of the military was weakened.

If weapon programmes can no longer be sold on the basis of later support for arms control, can arms control agreements be approved without new weapon programmes? It may be that without congressional support for weapons

---

[40] The next several paragraphs are largely drawn from Stockton (note 16). On bargaining chips, see also Bresler and Gray (note 32).

[41] See note 34.

modernization, it will not be possible to build the necessary coalition to approve arms control treaties. We will not really know what will happen until the START Treaty is brought before Congress. At that point, the military may be able to extract more from those strongly supporting arms control than they were able to in 1990. Crucial will be the perception of the international situation. If the Soviet Union appears benign in the international arena, the arms control–arms procurement link may very well be broken, setting a precedent for congressional approval of major arms control agreements without at the same time approving strategic nuclear modernization. This would make possible congressional approval of radical arms control agreements in the future, including, perhaps, the elimination of nuclear weapons. (A potential monkey wrench in the immediate future would be if the Soviet central government—commonly referred to as the 'centre'—were to become embroiled in large-scale violent repression within the republics. Although such action may be irrelevant to whether arms control treaties are in the interests of the United States or whether the Soviet Union could be expected to abide by such agreements, such action could sour the atmosphere so that arms control agreements would not be approved by Congress.)

In sum, if we imagine widespread acceptance in the United States that the Soviet threat had decreased, and that the threat from other nuclear, potential nuclear and conventional powers could be sufficiently controlled so as not to pose a threat to US national security, then, given changes in deal-making in Congress, continued commitment by the president and skilful neutralization or enlistment of the military, it seems that it could be possible to persuade Congress to embark on a course of action that could ultimately lead to the elimination of nuclear weapons.

The Soviet Union

Regarding the Soviet Union, a different kind of analysis is warranted from that done for the United States. First, since the mid-1980s, there have been dramatic changes in the party–state structure and in the political process; therefore, we cannot assume continuity in arms control policy or in the arms control process in the period before Gorbachev's advent to power in March 1985 and after. Second, since about mid-1990, we cannot even assume continuity of the state itself. Although it is commonplace to say that the Soviet Union is in economic and political crisis, the political crisis is of a particular sort, involving, in the words of Serge Schmemann, 'the fragmentation of the imperial center into an overlapping patchwork of competing powers'.[42] The Soviet Union is perhaps best understood as being in a revolutionary situation in which contending power holders are making competing and mutually exclusive claims to sovereign rule. Extending Trotsky's discussion of dual power in *History of the Russian Revolution*, Charles Tilly argues: '*Multiple sovereignty* is . . . the

[42] Schmemann, S., 'The Soviet slide', *New York Times*, 12 Apr. 1991.

identifying feature of revolutionary situations. A revolutionary situation begins when a government previously under the control of a single, sovereign polity becomes the object of effective, competing, mutually exclusive claims on the part of two or more distinct polities. It ends when a single sovereign polity regains control over the government'.[43]

Tilly clearly distinguishes between a revolutionary *situation*, which character-izes the situation of the Soviet Union since about mid-1990, and a revolutionary *outcome*, which in the case of the Soviet Union would involve the overthrow or dissolution of the central government as it has been historically constituted.[44]

As with the unexpected consequences of his policy towards Europe,[45] Gorbachev did not set out to foment revolution within the Soviet Union. Rather, we might say that he set out to remake the economy and the state, but that, with the onset of declarations of sovereignty in virtually every republic in 1990—we can single out the declaration of sovereignty by the Russian republic in June 1990 as critical—the state began to remake, or perhaps more accurately, unmake, itself.[46]

Given the dramatic changes that have already occurred and the even sharper discontinuities that could occur, an analysis of the history of the arms control process in the Soviet Union is not irrelevant to the future, but its relevance is problematic. If there are strong continuities between the present and the future, it is likely that policy will be largely shaped on the template of past procedures and organizations. If there are sharp breaks between the present and future, the result will be a more complicated borrowing from the past along with deliberate rejection of past precedent.

Since we do not know what the future holds, I will proceed in two ways. First, this chapter sketches out what we know historically of the arms control process in the Soviet Union and the relative bargaining power of the Soviet military. Next the chapter discusses the broad changes in Soviet politics since about January 1987 and how arms control policy under Gorbachev has changed. Second, this chapter discusses four kinds of possible futures for the Soviet Union and their implications for the complete elimination of nuclear weapons.

---

[43] Emphasis in original. See Tilly, C., *From Mobilization to Revolution* (Addison-Wesley Publishing Co.: Reading, Mass., 1978), p. 191. For our purposes, it is reasonable to understand polity to mean state power holders and those outside the government who accept governmental authority and are enfranchised by it.

[44] Tilly (note 43), p. 193, makes the general point.

[45] Blacker, C. D., 'The collapse of Soviet power in Europe', *Foreign Affairs*, vol. 70, Spec. issue 'America and the World 1990/91', pp. 88–102, at 88.

[46] A very good analysis of Gorbachev's efforts and the results through late 1987 is found in Colton, T. J., 'Gorbachev and the politics of system renewal', eds S. Bialer and M. Mandelbaum, *Gorbachev's Russia and American Foreign Policy* (Westview Press: Boulder, Colo., 1988), pp. 151–86; for an insight-ful diagnosis of the unfolding crisis in 1990, see Pipes, R., 'The Soviet Union adrift', *Foreign Affairs*, vol. 70, Spec. issue 'America and the World 1990/91', pp. 70–87.

Arms control process

For Western observers, far less is known about the arms control process in the Soviet Union than in the United States.[47] As mentioned above, although a formal ratification process exists, historically, it has not been important, but a rubber-stamp of decisions already made.[48] Rather, what has been crucial has been the decision-making process at the very top of the party, and relations between civilian party authority and the military.

Final authority regarding major defence decisions and arms control appears to have rested in the Politburo (the small decision-making body of the Central Committee of the Communist Party). In addition, scholars believe that the Politburo delegated to a joint Politburo–military leadership committee, the Defence Council, a more specialized role of oversight and decision on military issues. During the Brezhnev era, and especially after 1973, it appears that the Defence Council was chaired by the General Secretary in his role as Commander in Chief and included the Minister of Foreign Affairs, the Chairman of the KGB, the Politburo member who oversaw defence–industrial concerns, the Minister of Defence and the Chief of the General Staff.[49] After 1973, all but the Chief of the General Staff were members of the Politburo. According to Harry Gelman:

The extent to which Defense Council decisions have been subject to Politburo ratification remains quite obscure. Under Brezhnev, it is easily conceivable that some decisions of an ostensibly technical nature . . . may not have been presented to the Politburo at all. Many others surely were, particularly when they touched on broad questions of resource allocation or on foreign policy (as in the case of arms control negotiations). Even then, however, Politburo members who were not regularly briefed

---

[47] For a broad review of the literature on Soviet objectives in arms control, see Seay, D., 'What are the Soviets' objectives in their foreign, military, and arms control policies?', eds L. Eden and S. E. Miller (note 37), pp. 47–108. For an historical analysis of civil–military relations and security policy, see Parrott, B., 'Political change and civil–military relations', eds T. J. Colton and T. Gustafson, *Soldiers and the Soviet State: Civil–Military Relations from Brezhnev to Gorbachev* (Princeton University Press: Princeton, N.J., 1990), pp. 44–92. For an historical and forward-looking analysis of Soviet security and arms control policies, see Roberts, C., 'Limited adversaries, limited arms control: changing Soviet interests and prospects for enhanced security cooperation', ed. M. Mandelbaum, *The Other Side of the Table: The Soviet Approach to Arms Control* (Council on Foreign Relations Press: New York, N.Y., 1990), pp. 121–86. For a good brief statement of what is known regarding SALT, see Blacker, C. D., 'The Soviets and arms control: the SALT II negotiations, November 1972–March 1976', ed. M. Mandelbaum, *The Other Side of the Table: The Soviet Approach to Arms Control* (Council on Foreign Relations Press: New York, N.Y., 1990), pp. 41–87, at 69–75; This section draws heavily on this chapter.

[48] Formally, a treaty was first examined by the Council of Ministers. The Presidium of the Supreme Soviet then decided whether to ratify a treaty. On the instruction of the Presidium, the two chambers of the Supreme Soviet examined the treaty. The decision of the Presidium was then adopted by decree of the Supreme Soviet. On the basis of the decree on ratification, a ratification certificate was signed by the chair of the Presidium, and instruments of ratification were then exchanged. See IDDS (note 4), sheets 403.A.5–A.6, Jan. 1988.

[49] Rice, C., 'The Party, the military, and decision authority in the Soviet Union', *World Politics*, vol. 40 (Oct. 1987), 55–81, at 55, 66; and Gelman (note 18), p. 63.

on the technical background were probably at a great disadvantage in dealing with colleagues who customarily monitored such matters with the experts.[50]

Of course, the inclinations of the General Secretary and his power *vis-à-vis* his immediate party colleagues on the Politburo have been of the first importance. At the beginning of his tenure, before consolidating power as first among equals, in large part through controlling membership on crucial party committees, the power of the General Secretary could be quite limited. Upon consolidating control, however, the General Secretary's ability to shape policy (not to speak of his ability simply to remain in office for many years) went far beyond US presidential powers. Yet, because of the highly competitive collegiality of the Politburo, his authority was not unconstrained.[51]

An account by Raymond Garthoff provides a sense of the power relationships between the General Secretary and the two organizations he headed, the Politburo and Defence Council, as the SALT I agreement was being concluded:

In 1971 and 1972 key Politburo decision on SALT were often close, although after the Twenty-fourth Party Congress [in 1971] and Brezhnev's successful bid for a policy of detente toward the United States and his enhanced political power, much of the high-level SALT backup in Moscow apparently shifted to the Defense Council, already under his chairmanship. . . . During the negotiations the American delegation learned to expect that major new Soviet moves would be keyed to the usual weekly (Thursday) Politburo meetings. SALT issues required at least four Politburo meetings during the week of the 1972 summit conference.[52]

What more can we say about the role of the military in the Soviet arms control process?[53] What prerogative was accorded to the military, and what influence and bargaining power did it have? First, through its monopoly of expertise, the military appears to have wielded considerable influence in arms control matters. According to Condoleezza Rice:

---

[50] See Gelman (note 18), p. 64. Gelman's discussion of the Defence Council (note 18, pp. 63–70), is the clearest historical account I have seen. See also Jones, E., *Red Army and Society: A Sociology of the Soviet Military* (Allen & Unwin: Boston, Mass., 1985), chapter 1, pp. 1–30, for a good discussion of the dual party–state structure, including the Defence Council, in defence policy making. On defence decision-making, see also Meyer, S. M., 'Soviet national security decisionmaking: what do we know and what do we understand?', eds J. Valenta and W. Potter, *Soviet Decisionmaking for National Security* (Allen & Unwin: Boston, Mass., 1984), pp. 255–97; Meyer, S. M., 'Civilian and military influence in managing the arms race in the USSR', eds R. J. Art, V. Davis, S. P. Huntington, *Reorganizing America's Defense: Leadership in War and Peace* (Pergamon–Brassey's: Washington, DC, 1985), pp. 37–61.

[51] On Brezhnev's power as first among equals and constraints on it, see Blacker (note 47), pp. 70–71.

[52] Garthoff (note 20), p. 196.

[53] By the military, I refer to both the Ministry of Defence and the General Staff. A detailed analysis of the positions of the highest-level defence officials on, among other things, arms control and war-fighting, is Herspring (note 22). A very good recent review of the literature on Soviet civil–military relations is found in Colton, T. J., 'Perspectives on civil–military relations in the Soviet Union', eds T. J. Colton and T. Gustafson (note 47). The major arguments in the literature can be conveniently found in the opening chapters by R. Kolkowicz, W. E. Odom and T. J. Colton in *Civil–Military Relations in Communist Systems*, eds D. R. Herspring and I. Volgyes (Westview Press: Boulder, Colo., 1978).

Although the party leadership is the final authority in matters of defense, the absence of a coherent civilian staff institution that is competent to develop military strategy and force posture leaves political authorities heavily dependent on the professional military for information, expertise, and ultimately, policy options. . . . All available evidence suggests that the staff work for the Defense Council is carried out by the General Staff.[54]

More specifically, in the SALT process, initiatives were developed by the Ministry of Defence and the General Staff, reporting to the Defence Council. Civilian agencies, such as the Ministry of Foreign Affairs and also the Party's Central Committee staff, responded to US proposals rather than developed new Soviet positions.[55]

Second, there has been very high-level military participation in the arms control negotiations themselves. In SALT I, Generals Nikolay Ogarkov and Nikolay Alekseyev were particularly prominent. At a summit in the summer of 1974 when SALT II was at issue, very high-level Soviet military officers made direct presentations at the meeting, which was considered significant by the US delegation. At the Vladivostok summit meeting in late November of the same year, President Ford's national security adviser, Henry Kissinger, and Soviet Ambassador to the United States, Anatoliy Dobrynin, colluded to reduce the number of participants at the meeting in order to eliminate the two Soviet generals. According to Kissinger, 'The meeting started with two generals sitting behind Brezhnev—and whenever we started getting concrete they started slipping little pieces of paper to him or butting into the conversation one way or the other. So, at the first break, Dobrynin came to me and asked whether we couldn't confine the meeting to three people on each side—which got rid of the two generals'.

Under Gorbachev, Marshal Sergey Akhromeyev actively participated in US–Soviet summit meetings from Reykjavik on, even when his US military counterpart did not.[56]

Third, and perhaps most important, like their US counterparts, it appears that the Soviet military has had the internal bargaining power to ensure that arms control agreements did not constrain nuclear weapons modernization programmes.[57] The evidence is fragmentary, but provides some indication that military preferences were reflected in negotiating positions. Before breaking the moratorium on atmospheric nuclear testing in September 1961, Soviet negotiators indicated that they were under severe pressure from their military to test

[54] Rice (note 49), p. 55, 67. See also Herspring (note 22), p. 77.

[55] Garthoff (note 20), p. 186.

[56] Garthoff, R. L., 'The Soviet Military and SALT', eds J. Valenta and W. Potter (note 50), pp. 136–61; Rice (note 49), p. 75; Kissinger quoted in Garthoff (note 20), p. 430; Herspring (note 22), p. 121.

[57] For a succinct statement of the contours of Soviet force modernization, see Miller (note 14), p. 77. Regarding the broad internal power of the Soviet military, Snyder argues: 'In the Brezhnev era, in particular, the Soviet military was able to parlay . . . [a] lack of adequate strategic oversight and analytical competition into a huge military buildup, justified by specious arguments that civilian leaders were poorly equipped to contest'. See Snyder (note 8), p. 24. On Soviet military objectives in SALT, see Garthoff (note 56), pp. 141–42; on Soviet military concerns regarding SALT II, see Garthoff (note 20), p. 432.

the bombs that would be carried by strategic rockets. In perhaps the most important instance, in the SALT I negotiations, the USSR refused to accept the US definition of a 'heavy' missile as any missile larger than the largest existing 'light' ICBM because two of their new ICBMs under development would be larger than the 'light' missile they would replace, and hence, would be banned. According to Raymond Garthoff, 'the Soviets were quite straightforward in declining to accept the tight restriction proposed by the United States because of their requirements for allowed modernization.'[58] It may also be that the military was able to extract a generous share of the budget in return for co-operation with the arms control process.[59]

This is certainly not to argue that military power was unconstrained. The Politburo provided guidance and was the final authority on military decisions. And military preferences could be disregarded, as they were at the Vladivostok summit meeting when Soviet political leaders agreed to accept equal levels of strategic forces without counting US forward-based systems in Europe. Yet, military unhappiness with this concession may have been costly to Soviet political leaders and constrained them later. In 1977, as the United States considered bypassing the Vladivostok framework, a high-level Soviet official told the Director of the US Arms Control and Disarmament Agency, Paul Warnke, 'You shouldn't have disregarded the fact that Brezhnev had to spill political blood to get the Vladivostok accords'.[60] Still, all in all, it seems reasonable to argue that just as arms control agreements did not seriously constrain US nuclear modernization programmes, so too arms control agreements permitted 'the modernization of Soviet weapons systems to proceed largely on schedule'.[61]

Given the Soviet political and arms control process sketched above, one could not be remotely optimistic about the domestic political feasibility of embarking on a project to eliminate nuclear weapons. The pre-Gorbachev system was one in which party officials were insulated, cautious, conservative and aged; in which military officials played a strong role in formulating and negotiating arms control proposals; and in which both political and military officials were committed to substantial nuclear and other weapons modernization. There was no apparent incentive to reconceive the role of nuclear weapons, nor any obvious source of dynamism in this system.

Remaking the state

Under Gorbachev, this system ceased to exist. Gorbachev first put political reform on the domestic agenda in January 1987; by the spring of 1989 the first partially contested elections in Soviet history were held for the Congress of People's Deputies. At the same time, Gorbachev, already wearing dual hats as

[58] Blacker and Duffy (note 13), p. 129; Garthoff (note 20), p. 174. See also Garthoff, 'The Soviet Military and SALT', eds J. Valenta and W. Potter (note 50), pp. 150–51.

[59] See account of General Kulikov's testimony in Garthoff (note 56), p. 140; Blacker (note 47).

[60] Garthoff (note 20), pp. 464–65.

[61] Blacker (note 47), pp. 73–74.

general secretary and as president (a largely ceremonial post), increased his presidential powers as the old post was transformed into a new one with greater powers; the Congress of People's Deputies elected him to this new post in May 1989. This new presidential office took over some functions that had been previously reserved to the Communist Party's general secretary. Thus, Gorbachev had transferred some of his powers as general secretary to the presidency, and in so doing, had reduced party power and increased his own ability to manœuvre somewhat independently of the party.[62]

In the spring and summer of 1990, radical changes were made in the organization of state power. In March 1990, the Congress of People's Deputies abolished Article 6 of the Constitution, which had guaranteed the Communist Party's monopoly of power in the state, and it created a presidential system of government. Gorbachev was almost immediately sworn into this new office, a post, in the words of Elizabeth Teague, 'tailor-made by and for himself'. In this new system, the president was granted vast new powers, including the power to declare martial law and a state of emergency. In addition, two new consultative bodies were created, one of which, the Presidential Council (later disbanded), began to take on functions that had previously been under the purview of the Politburo and the Defence Council. Unlike the two older bodies, however, the Presidential Council did not operate under a principle of collective leadership but rather in a strictly advisory capacity to the president. At the time, there were rumours that Gorbachev might disassociate himself from the Communist Party, giving up his position as general secretary and moving his base of power to the office of the president. He did not, but he did staff the Presidential Council with a number of radical reformers to help him bypass party organizations and more effectively promote reform. By the end of the 28th Party Congress in July, the Politburo was reorganized into an insignificant centre of power. On the one hand, Gorbachev had stripped the Communist Party of its monopoly of power and had created strong alternative state institutions; on the other hand, the party still maintained significant power to block reform. By the end of the Party Congress, the party remained strongly dominated by conservatives, and Yeltsin and other reformers began to exit from the party.[63]

---

[62] In the autumn of 1988, Gorbachev had assumed the largely ceremonial position as chairman of the Presidium of the Supreme Soviet which entitled him to be treated as head of state; this office was often referred to in the West as president. In accordance with constitutional changes made at the end of 1988, the Supreme Soviet was transformed from an organization that simply ratified Party policy into a standing legislature elected by a newly created body, the Congress of People's Deputies. The office of chairman of the Presidium of the Supreme Soviet was replaced by a new position, chairman of the Supreme Soviet, and it was to this position which Gorbachev was elected in May. Both the new Supreme Soviet and the new presidency took over some functions that had been reserved to the Party. See Teague and Mann (note 18), esp. 1–5. On the period through late 1987, see Colton (note 46). On political changes leading to constitutional change, see Teague, E., 'Conference preparations run into trouble', *Radio Liberty Research Bulletin*, no. 19 (11 May 1988); Mann, D., 'Gorbachev's position consolidated', *Radio Liberty Research Bulletin*, no. 41 (12 Oct. 1988); Voronitsyn, S., 'Radical changes in the power structure in the offing?', *Radio Liberty Research Bulletin*, no. 44 (2 Nov. 1988); and Rahr, A., 'Gorbachev changes Party structure', *Radio Liberty Research Bulletin*, no. 49 (7 Dec. 1988).

[63] Teague, E., Radio Liberty, 'The powers of the Soviet presidency', *Report on the USSR*, no. 12 (23 Mar. 1990), pp. 4–7, quotation at 4; Teague, E., Radio Liberty, 'Gorbachev proposes dropping Communist Party monopoly', *Report on the USSR*, no. 6 (9 Feb. 1990), pp. 6–8; Rahr, A., Radio Liberty, 'From

In the year following the summer of 1990, Gorbachev zigzagged in his political tactics; he first moved sharply to the right in coalition with highly conservative elements and then, in the spring of 1991, moved to accommodate radical demands of the republics to share substantial power with the central government.

Although he had indicated a strong interest in implementing radical economic reform, in the fall of 1990, Gorbachev rejected a '500 day' economic reform plan drawn up at his request; by November, he appeared to have embarked on a rightward course of authoritarian crack-down. No doubt the most electrifying moments were the resignation of Eduard Shevardnadze as foreign minister on 20 December, in which he warned of looming dictatorship,[64] followed in mid-January by the lethal attacks by Soviet forces in Lithuania and Latvia. These were, however, only two of many indicators of a political crack-down. In mid-November, Gorbachev held a heated meeting with over 1000 military officers, many of them angry about the isolation of military garrisons in the republics, draft evasion, criticism of the military in the media and a decline in prestige. Gorbachev was not unconciliatory in this meeting, and a public hardening of position became evident 10 days later when Gorbachev asserted that attempts to break up the Soviet Union could result in bloodshed. Within days, Soviet Defence Minister Dmitriy T. Yazov denounced nationalist movements in the Soviet Union, particularly in the Baltic republics, and two days after that he announced on national television that the armed forces had been instructed to use force to counter what he contended were anti-military measures in the republics.[65] Further, one day before the resignation of Shevardnadze, an open letter to Gorbachev by over 50 prominent figures urged stronger measures to control internal conflict, specifically, 'instituting a state of emergency and presidential rule in zones of major conflict'. The signers included the Chief of the General Staff and the chief of Interior Ministry troops. (Minister of Defence Yazov did not sign the letter, but said he endorsed the sentiment in it.)[66] By the end of the year, Gorbachev had strengthened already vast presidential powers by gaining more direct control of the executive branch (and abolishing the Presidential Council).[67] In the new year, after Soviet forces had killed 15 indi-

Politburo to Presidential Council', *Report on the USSR*, no. 22 (1 June 1990), pp. 1–5; Teague, E., Radio Liberty, 'The Twenty-eighth Party Congress: an overview', *Report on the USSR*, no. 29 (20 July 1990), pp. 1–3.

[64] Keller, B., 'Shevardnadze stuns Kremlin by quitting Foreign Ministry and warning of "dictatorship"', *New York Times*, 21 Dec. 1990; for Shevardnadze's further explanation of his resignation given in an interview in the *Moscow News*, see Keller, B., 'Shevardnadze asserts possibility of a crackdown led him to quit', *New York Times*, 3 Jan. 1991. See also Crow, S., Radio Liberty, 'The resignation of Shevardnadze', *Report on the USSR*, no. 2 (11 Jan. 1991), pp. 6–8.

[65] Foye, S., Radio Liberty, 'Gorbachev, the army, and the union', *Report on the USSR*, no. 49 (7 Dec. 1990), pp. 1–3; Keller, B., 'Soviet military grows resentful at Gorbachev's policy of change', *New York Times*, 24 Dec. 1990; Keller, B., 'Soviet Army told to use force to defend itself in the republics', *New York Times*, 28 Nov. 1990.

[66] Keller, B., 'Gorbachev urged to consider crackdown in republics', *New York Times*, 20 Dec. 1990.

[67] Keller, B., 'Gorbachev given direct authority over his cabinet', *New York Times*, 26 Dec. 1990. See also Keller, B., 'Mourning Soviet reform', *New York Times*, 29 Dec. 1990. On Gorbachev's original proposal, see Keller, B., 'Soviets adopt emergency plan to center power in Gorbachev and leaders of the republics', *New York Times*, 18 Nov. 1990.

viduals in Lithuania, Gorbachev tightened control over the press, reasserted his commitment to preservation of the union, and in February and March increased the central government's military presence and control in Soviet cities.[68]

It appears that as the former centre of the political spectrum evaporated, and demands for political and economic reform folded into demands for sovereignty of the republics, Gorbachev entered into coalition with at least some conservative elements whose outlook he had previously opposed.[69] These conservative elements appear to include, among others: officials in the Communist Party's central bureaucracy; some senior and mid-level military officers; directors of big industry; including those in the military–industrial sector; senior officials in the state security apparatuses of the KGB and the Interior Ministry; part of the Russian Orthodox Church hierarchy; and a parliamentary faction called *Soyuz*, or Union.[70]

However, in the face of a steadily deteriorating economy, a major strike by coal miners, worker resistance to price rises, the increasing militancy and popularity of Boris Yeltsin, head of the Russian Federation, and calls for Gorbachev's resignation from the left and the right, on 23 April 1991, Gorbachev changed tack and surprisingly reached agreement with Yeltsin and the heads of eight other republics to settle unrest in the short-term and to devise a framework to remake the Soviet state in the long-term. Only the three Baltic states and Georgia, Armenia, and Moldavia did not sign the accord. Most significant in the agreement was that change would not be dictated from the centre but in close negotiation with the republics and that the new federal arrangement would involve greater sovereignty and greater power for the republics than Gorbachev had envisioned earlier. By May, Gorbachev and the heads of the republics had agreed that the new union would be named not the Union of Soviet Socialist Republics but the Union of Soviet Sovereign

---

[68] Fein, E. B., 'Gorbachev urges curb on press freedom', *New York Times*, 17 Jan. 1991; Clines, F. X., 'Gorbachev warns of threat to Soviet superpower status', *New York Times*, 7 Feb. 1991; Schmemann, S., 'Gorbachev's offensive: his critics are denounced', *New York Times*, 28 Feb. 1991; Schmemann, S., 'Kremlin's troops to join police on patrol in major Soviet cities', *New York Times*, 26 Jan. 1991; Schmemann, S., 'Gorbachev gives KGB new powers to police economy', *New York Times*, 27 Jan. 1991; Clines, F. X., 'Fighting protests, Gorbachev orders Moscow controls', *New York Times*, 27 Mar. 1991.

[69] On coalitional structure and Soviet foreign policy from Stalin to Gorbachev, see Jack Snyder's ambitious article (note 2), pp. 93–131.

[70] Szporluk, R., 'The Soviet Union has ceased to exist', Editorial in *New York Times*, 23 Jan. 1991; Keller, B., 'Soviet military grows resentful at Gorbachev's policy of change', *New York Times*, 24 Dec. 1990; Keller, B., 'Mourning Soviet reform', *New York Times*, 29 Dec. 1990; Foye, S., Radio Liberty, 'The case for a coup: Gorbachev or the generals?', *Report on the USSR*, no. 2 (11 Jan. 1991), pp. 1–5; Åslund, A., 'Moscow's new power center', Editorial in *New York Times*, 19 Apr. 1991. In addition, important personnel shifts had begun before Shevardnadze's resignation, notably, the replacement in early Dec. of the moderate Vadim V. Bakatin as head of the Interior Ministry by the hard-liner, KGB Maj. Gen. Boris Pugo and the appointment of another hard-liner as his deputy, Army Col. Gen. Boris Gromov. Other important personnel shifts occurred; the departure of two prominently associated with *perestroika*, Aleksandr N. Yakovlev and the economist Stanislav S. Shatalin; and the appointment of the conservative Valentin S. Pavlov as the new prime minister. See Foye, 'The case for a coup' (above); Keller, 'Mourning Soviet reform' (above); and Teague, E., Radio Liberty, 'Gorbachev chooses a new prime minister', *Report on the USSR*, no. 4 (25 Jan. 1991), pp. 21–22. In Feb., Pugo was promoted to the rank of Col. Gen. See Clines, F. X., 'Gorbachev is promoting hard-line police chief', *New York Times*, 5 Feb. 1991.

Republics.[71] On 12 June, the political landscape changed again when Boris Yeltsin became the first democratically elected president in the thousand year history of Russia.[72]

In the midst of these dizzying political changes, and through a process which is not yet well understood by Western analysts, Gorbachev became the first leader in Soviet history to shape the international agenda on arms control rather than simply respond to Western initiatives. Gorbachev proposed far-reaching changes in Soviet military doctrine, announced stunning cuts in Soviet force deployments and made, in Condoleezza Rice's words, 'wildly innovative' arms control proposals. This chapter focuses on Gorbachev's January 1986 proposal to eliminate nuclear weapons, but of more immediate political importance were the following: Soviet concessions regarding force levels and unprecedented on-site inspection procedures that led to the December 1987 INF Treaty; Gorbachev's speech before the United Nations in December 1988 in which he announced plans to unilaterally cut Soviet armed forces by 500 000 men over the next two years, including withdrawing 50 000 Soviet troops from Eastern Europe, along with offensively oriented equipment; and Soviet bargaining positions that made possible the signing of the Conventional Forces in Europe (CFE) Treaty in November, 1990, as well as, by the early summer of 1991, the resolution of most (but not all) outstanding issues in the strategic nuclear arms treaty under negotiation, START.[73]

[71] Schmemann, S., 'Thousands ignore Gorbachev's call for end to unrest', *New York Times*, 11 Apr. 1991; Clines, F. X., 'Yeltsin, criticizing failures, insists that Gorbachev quit', *New York Times*, 20 Feb. 1991; Schmemann, S., 'Huge rally in Moscow calls on Gorbachev to resign', *New York Times*, 11 Mar. 1991; Clines, F. X., '40 000 rally to support Yeltsin against Gorbachev', *New York Times*, 25 Feb. 1991; Schmemann, S., 'Gorbachev and the bear', *New York Times*, 20 Mar. 1991; Schmemann, S., '100 000 join Moscow rally, defying ban by Gorbachev to show support for rival; A gain for Yeltsin', *New York Times*, 29 Mar. 1991; Clines, F. X., 'Gorbachev yields on sharing power and cuts in prices; Yeltsin joins pact', *New York Times*, 25 Apr. 1991; Schmemann, S., 'A cease-fire of chieftains', *New York Times*, 25 Apr. 1991; Schmemann, S., 'Gorbachev offers to resign as Party's chief, but is given a vote of support', *New York Times*, 26 Apr. 1991; Fein, E. B., 'Soviet republics making progress on restructuring and new name', *New York Times*, 26 May 1991; Schmemann, S., 'Soviet price rises ignite big protest', *New York Times*, 5 Apr. 1991; Schmemann, S., 'Yeltsin attains greater powers in his republic', *New York Times*, 6 Apr. 1991; Schmemann, S., 'Soviet slide', *New York Times*; 22 Apr. 1991; 'Braking the Soviet slide', Editorial in *New York Times*, 22 Apr. 1991; Schmemann, S., 'Gorbachev orders republics to halt rebellious moves', *New York Times*, 10 Apr. 1991.

[72] Schmemann, S., 'Yeltsin is handily elected leader of Russian Republic in setback for communists', *New York Times*, 14 June 1991.

[73] On changes in Soviet attitudes towards deterrence, military doctrine, and arms control, see Garthoff, R. L., *Deterrence and the Revolution in Soviet Military Doctrine* (Brookings Institution: Washington, DC, 1990); regarding deterrence, see Shenfield (note 4); on security policy more broadly, see Blacker, C. D., *From Reform to Revolution: Gorbachev and Soviet Security Policy* (Council on Foreign Relations: New York, forthcoming). For the reference to 'wildly innovative' arms control proposals, see Rice (note 49), p. 79; on the Dec. 1988 speech and its broader context, see Holloway, D., 'Gorbachev's new thinking', *Foreign Affairs*, vol. 68, Spec. issue 'America and the World 1988/89', pp. 66–81. After the 1990 CFE Treaty was signed, there were disputes over whether the treaty covered certain equipment assigned to units of the Soviet coast guard, naval infantry, and strategic rocket forces; these disputes were resolved in the spring of 1991. See 'Resolution of the arms impasse', Editorial in *New York Times*, 9 Apr. 1991; Rosenthal, A., 'US–Soviet arms dispute is approaching resolution', *New York Times*, 23 May 1991; Riding, A., 'US and Soviets bridge gap on conventional weapons and plan for summit soon; Bush hails accord', *New York Times*, 2 June 1991; Friedman, T. L., 'NATO–Warsaw Pact arms dispute ends', *New York Times*, 15 June 1991. With the resolution of the CFE Treaty, negotiations were stepped up to complete the draft START Treaty. See Riding (above); Friedman, T. L., 'US and Kremlin fail to close gap on

Clearly, this was not arms control as usual. We may infer from the audacity of the proposals, from the major political reorganizations in which these proposals were embedded and from reports of military opposition to proposals that the process of formulating arms control policy under Gorbachev sharply departed from past practices and that professional military advice was given less weight in the crafting of these and other arms control initiatives (such as the unilateral Soviet moratorium on nuclear testing) than it had been accorded in the past.[74] Were such a trajectory of political reform and arms control initiatives to continue, it is not difficult to imagine intermediate steps—such as the ratification of the CFE Treaty and the completion and ratification of the START Treaty—leading to further Soviet initiatives for, say, very deep cuts in strategic and tactical nuclear weapons, which, once negotiated and implemented, could lead to serious negotiations to eliminate nuclear weapons. But this is only one possible future for the Soviet Union, and it is discussed, along with others, below.

Possible futures

By the summer of 1991, four possible futures could be envisaged for the Soviet Union (see figure 8.1).[75] These are meant to be seen as ideal types; whatever occurs would likely be a variation on one of these possibilities or a combination of more than one. These futures vary, on the one hand, by the degree to which there would be continuity in central state functions (although these functions could be reduced dramatically in specific areas such as economic regulation; in addition, the geographical scope of authority might well be reduced), and on the other hand, by the degree to which the transition to the future would be violent. To the degree that the transition to the future would be violent, democratic outcomes are less likely, although a peaceful transition by no means assures democratic outcomes. Thus, we can imagine four futures, each with somewhat different implications for the possibility of eliminating nuclear weapons. Three, or perhaps all four, of the possible futures represent sharp discontinuities with Gorbachev's agenda for reform of the mid- to late-1980s. Given the uncertainty and fluidity of the situation as of the summer of 1991, I do not speculate on the likelihood of any of these futures, but simply sketch them, discussing preconditions and the implications of each future for the possibility of eliminating nuclear weapons.

nuclear arms', *New York Times*, 8 June 1991; On 17 June 1991, President Bush stated that work on START was '96 percent complete'. See Apple Jr., R.W., 'Victorious Yeltsin due in US today', *New York Times*, 18 June 1991.

[74] Rice (note 49), p. 75; Herspring (note 22), p. 253; Holloway (note 73), p. 75; Blacker (note 73).

[75] I have benefited from the very good systematic analysis of Marc Bennett and Matthew Evangelista, 'Alternative Futures for the Soviet–American Security Relationship', Working Paper, MacArthur Foundation Project on 'Assessing the Future of US–Soviet Relations', Mershon Center, Ohio State University, Feb. 1991. See also the less systematic but very interesting discussion of alternative futures in Pipes (note 46).

	Soviet Union remains largely intact	Soviet Union breaks up into republics
Peaceful/ more likely democratic	reform or radical reform	dissolution and confederation
Violent/ less likely democratic	authoritarian crackdown	civil war

Figure 8.1. Four possible futures for the Soviet Union

In the first case of relative continuity and peaceful reform (upper left cell), the Soviet Union would remain largely intact, considerable central powers would remain regarding foreign and military policy, and a vigorous reform agenda would be resumed for the economy, for domestic political life and for foreign relations.[76] Popular notions of what an evolutionary reform future would look like have changed over time, particularly regarding the geographic definition of the Soviet Union and the relative power of the centre *vis-à-vis* the republics. Before 1990, one might have imagined a wholly intact Soviet Union in which Gorbachev or his successor could have gained sufficient initiative to shape domestic reform from the centre (at the same time maintaining the ability to pull arms control rabbits out of hats). Indeed, until perhaps the summer of 1990, one might have thought such a reformist future not unlikely. However, with the strong popular moves by the republics towards greater autonomy from the central government, and the broad acceptance of those claims by Gorbachev in April 1991, the geographical range of the reconstituted Soviet Union might well include the nine Slavic and Central Asian republics of Russia, Ukraine, Byelorussia, Uzbekistan, Kazakhstan, Azerbaijan, Tadzhikistan, Kirghizia and Turkmenia—and, in addition, perhaps Armenia and Moldavia. It does not appear that it will include the three Baltic republics or Georgia. If agreement can be reached between these nine or eleven republics and the central government on a radical redefinition of the relative powers of the centre and the republics, the result presumably will be a union treaty along federal lines. Key questions to be resolved include: Who will make foreign policy? Who will make military policy? and What will happen to the General Staff?

[76] Reform in these three areas need not coincide. In particular, a Pinochet-like market dictatorship in the absence of political or foreign policy reform could conceivably occur in a future of authoritarian crackdown; for a sceptical view regarding the possibility of achieving a Pinochet market dictatorship, see Åslund (note 70). An analysis disaggregating areas of reform is beyond the scope of this chapter.

It is not possible to predict whether an agreement will be arrived at in collaboration with the centre, but it may well depend on Gorbachev's ability to survive politically, on his vision and skill in negotiating with the republics and the centre, on whether Gorbachev can sponsor an economic reform plan that is sufficiently market-oriented to be able to attract large amounts of foreign economic aid and, closely related, on the willingness of more conservative elements to accept radical economic plans and political agreements.[77]

Were a future in which radical economic and political reforms negotiated between the centre and the republics to occur, one could have some optimism about the political feasibility of eliminating nuclear weapons. One can imagine a world in which continuing warm relations between the United States and Soviet Union could lead to reduction of nuclear weapons to minimum deterrent levels, to the two countries ceasing to target each other with their alert nuclear weapons and to a strengthened international regime to control nuclear weapon proliferation. In such a world, it would not be inconceivable to begin serious discussions on the complete elimination of nuclear weapons. Indeed, one can imagine such an initiative coming from the Soviet Union. And, although we have seen that the Soviet military has had substantial bargaining power, we have also seen that, under Gorbachev, the military has not blocked audacious arms control proposals.

The other predominantly peaceful outcome would be the dissolution of the Soviet Union and the possible confederation of republics (upper right cell). This future is perhaps easiest to imagine as resulting from a breakdown of negotiations for a union treaty between the republics and the centre in which the republics, in Yeltsin's words, would simply conclude the treaty directly, 'without interference from the center'.[78] This second case is actually a rather varied domain of possible futures, which would depend on three things: first, how many republics would be confederated together in some way (we can imagine an almost complete atomization and no confederation, lumpy confederations or unions of republics, or a quite uniform arrangement encompassing virtually all of the republics); second, the degree to which central functions regarding national security and defence (among other functions) would be reconstituted; and, third, the degree to which nuclear weapons would be physically concentrated along with the authority to launch them.

Regarding the issue of nuclear weapons, it seems that the concentration of nuclear weapons is quite high. Although it appears that many Soviet tactical nuclear weapons have been stored outside Russia, there have been reports that the Kremlin has withdrawn at least some nuclear warheads (including short-range missiles and nuclear artillery shells) from the Baltic republics and

---

[77] Friedman, T. L., 'Soviets propose new economic changes', *New York Times*, 30 May 1991; Whitney, C. R., 'Gorbachev moves to fix his credibility', *New York Times*, 16 June 1991; Whitney, C. R., 'Kremlin divided over economic plan', *New York Times*, 18 June 1991.

[78] Schmemann, S., 'Gorbachev agrees, sort of, to negotiate the State of Union', *New York Times*, 28 Apr. 1991.

THE END OF NUCLEAR ARMS CONTROL   195

Transcaucasus region to the Republic of Russia.[79] Regarding Soviet strategic nuclear weapons, ports for sea-based nuclear weapons are located almost entirely in the Russian republic, and mobile missiles and bombers can be moved relatively easily. The major issue is the location of fixed silo-based Soviet ICBMs. According to David Morrison, 'the vast bulk of the Soviet Union's 22 ICBM fields are located inside the Russian republic, in an arc sweeping from European Russia along the Trans-Siberian Railway to the Far East. The exceptions are a brace of missile fields in the Ukraine and another pair in Kazakhstan'.[80] Further, it is not unreasonable to speculate that strategic nuclear weapons might be further concentrated in the future.[81]

Let us follow through only one broad possibility. For the sake of argument, let us assume a non-proliferated future in which nuclear weapons and security policy would be highly concentrated in either a single republic or in a single authority representing those republics possessing nuclear weapons. Let us further assume that the republic or republics possessing nuclear weapons would be relatively democratic. (This is, of course, only one possible future in this domain. It may be that nuclear weapons are more dispersed than I have suggested and/or that those republics possessing nuclear weapons could not agree on a unified policy or would not be democratic. Nevertheless, given the large number of nuclear weapons in the Russian republic, the reform proclivities of Yeltsin's coalition, and the broad democratic mandate Yeltsin gained in June 1991, this is not an unreasonable scenario to explore.)

What implications for the complete elimination of nuclear weapons would there be in a situation in which the Soviet Union as historically constituted had dissolved and in which nuclear weapons and security policy were under a single authority of one or more relatively democratic republics? What kinds of policy preferences might we expect from the militaries in the republic or republics possessing nuclear weapons? I would argue that in a situation of peaceful and very far-reaching state reorganization, radical reform and the elimination of nuclear weapons could be even greater than in the first possible future discussed above. This could be so for two reasons.

First, those involved in formulating military policy in the Russian republic have advocated radical military reform. For example, a group of military reformers in the Congress of People's Deputies, prominent among them former major Vladimir Lopatin, an adviser to Yeltsin on security issues, has proposed the reorganization of the Soviet military from a large standing army based on a draft into a significantly smaller all-volunteer force, with reserve units to be

[79] Rahr, A. and Bryan, R. A., Radio Liberty, 'Concern over security of Soviet nuclear arms', *Report on the USSR*, no. 41 (12 Oct. 1990), pp. 6–7, at 6, citing *The Washington Post*, 28 Sep. 1990 and *Reuters, AP*, 22 June 1990. See also Morrison, D. C., 'Loose Soviet nukes: a mountain or a molehill?', *Arms Control Today*, vol. 21 (Apr. 1991), pp. 15–19, at 18.

[80] Morrison (note 79), p. 16. Morrison's report accords with information from the US Department of Defense that there are silo-based ICBMs in Russia, Ukraine and Kazakhstan, and mobile ICBM bases in Russia and Byelorussia. See the large fold-out map in US Department of Defense, *Soviet Military Power 1990* (Government Printing Office: Washington, DC: Sep. 1990).

[81] Morrison (note 79), p. 16.

formed on a territorial basis. In this formulation, the role of civilian specialists would be increased, and the Communist Party would no longer directly determine national defence policy. The position of such military reformers regarding the future of nuclear weapons is not clear, although it appears that they are open to notions of minimum deterrence.[82] Were radical military reforms carried through in the context of a relatively peaceful dissolution of the Soviet Union, it seems probable that those setting military policy would be far more open than the military leadership under Gorbachev to ideas of radical reductions of nuclear weapons, and to the elimination of nuclear weapons.

Second, the dissolution of the Soviet Union would probably mean a 'downsizing' from former superpower status. Even a geographically large confederation composed of the nine Slavic and Central Asian republics discussed above would probably have a more modest conception of its historical destiny than have had leaders of the Soviet Union and, hence, would not fill the same geopolitical boots that the Soviet Union had. Under such circumstances, it would not be unreasonable to imagine newly sovereign and cash-strapped states extremely interested in friendlier international relations, in economic aid and in being able to end the diversion of domestic resources into military spending. Such newly sovereign states, or a confederation of sovereign states, could be seriously interested in reducing nuclear weapons to minimum deterrent levels, in ceasing to actively target the United States and Europe, in strengthening non-proliferation and in beginning serious discussions to eliminate nuclear weapons.

As with the first case, it is not possible to assign a probability to a future in which a peaceful dissolution of the Soviet Union would lead to confederations of sovereign states. We can, however, state the likely prerequisites. Such a future could be arrived at if negotiations with the centre collapsed, if the republics were able to work out a wide-ranging agreement among themselves and if hard-line elements in the centre did not violently resist the dissolution of their power. Were a peaceful and radical dismantlement of central Soviet power to occur, and were nuclear weapons placed under a single authority representing relatively democratic republics, the dispositions of politicians in the republics and the new historical situation could put radical cuts and even the elimination of nuclear weapons on the international agenda.

The third case of authoritarian crack-down (lower left cell), encompasses a range of possibilities, from retrenchment of reform punctuated by a few violent demonstrations of the centre's determination to maintain the union (in other words, a strategy of limiting the means of popular mobilization and threatening large-scale violent repression), to a virtually complete repression of civil liberties and full-scale violent crushing of sovereignty in the republics, possibly

---

[82] Lopatin is a member of the Soviet Congress of People's Deputies, and the Deputy Chairman of the Committee on the Military and National Security of the Russian Republic's Supreme Soviet. Foye, S., Radio Liberty, 'Radical military reform and "The young turks"', *Report on the USSR*, no. 15 (13 Apr. 1990), pp. 8–10; Foye, S., Radio Liberty, 'Lopatin on Party control of the armed forces', *Report on the USSR*, no. 37 (14 Sep. 1990), pp. 3–5; Seminar with Lopatin, Center for International Security and Arms Control, Stanford University, 2 Oct. 1990.

accompanied by a military coup against civilian authority. A wide-scale use of force against the republics would have implications for the possibility of eliminating nuclear weapons: not only could such state-sponsored violence lead to civil war (the fourth possible future), but it would immediately sour diplomatic relations with the United States and other powers. Were large-scale violence against the republics to occur before ratification of the CFE and START Treaties, not only would it greatly delay (if not foreclose the possibility of) ratification, it would likely make far more difficult the task of negotiating large reductions in nuclear weapons or their elimination.

Perhaps more germane for the purposes of this chapter is that even well short of a large-scale violent crack-down, a resurgence of authoritarianism from the centre would not bode well for the possibility of eliminating nuclear weapons, and not only because of the effect on US foreign policy. More important, the foreign and military policy proclivities of hardliners run counter to the 'new thinking' that provided the dynamic for Soviet foreign and military policy under Gorbachev and Shevardnadze. The underlying argument of the new thinking was that Soviet foreign policy had overestimated the threat from the West—indeed, that the United States no longer constituted a threat—and that in arming against the West, the Soviets had provoked a reaction that made the Soviet Union less secure. Security was to be found in a relaxation of tension with the West and a normalization of relations. Those in this hardline coalition, however, criticize Gorbachev's accomodationist policies. General G. A. Gromov, for example, in early 1990 argued against the notion that the international environment was fundamentally benign and claimed that the Western alliance remained a serious threat. At mid-year even stronger criticism was voiced by Army General Al'bert Makashov, and Minister of Defence Yazov claimed that the United States and NATO were increasing their strength through a policy of nuclear intimidation and direct confrontation. Indeed by the 28th Party Congress in July, the hardliners were debating the question, who lost Eastern Europe?[83] By the end of 1990, high-level accusations of foreign plots against the Soviet Union began to be voiced. KGB Chairman Vladimir Kryuchkov claimed that extremist groups in the Soviet Union were receiving support from abroad and in the new year the new prime minister, Valentin S. Pavlov, argued that in the recent confiscation of currency, the Soviet Government had acted to foil a Western bankers' plot to topple the government by cornering billions in rubles and destabilizing the economy. Further, it appears that both the CFE Treaty and START may have bogged down in the early

---

[83] Foye, S., Radio Liberty, 'Rumblings in the Soviet armed forces', *Report on the USSR*, no. 11 (16 Mar. 1990), pp. 1–3. On Soviet new thinking in security policy, in addition to Foye above, see Parrott, B., 'Soviet national security under Gorbachev', *Problems of Communism*, vol. 37 (Nov.–Dec. 1988), pp. 1–36; Holloway (note 73); and Blacker (note 45). Foye, S., Radio Liberty, 'Military hard-liner condemns "New Thinking" in security policy', *Report on the USSR*, no. 28 (13 July 1990), pp. 4–6. Foye, S., Radio Liberty, 'Defense issues at the Party Congress', *Report on the USSR*, no. 30 (27 July 1990), pp. 1–5. See also Crow (note 64), p. 7.

months of 1991 because of resistance by Soviet hardliners to what they saw as one-sided concessions involved in these agreements.[84]

Therefore, we can only conclude that were there a resurgence or reassertion of right-wing power, whether or not Gorbachev remained in office, the political feasibility of eliminating nuclear weapons would be greatly diminished.

Finally, it is not clear one can say much about the implications for eliminating nuclear weapons in the fourth possible future, civil war (lower right cell). Clearly, in conditions of civil war, political leaders and leadership groups would be utterly absorbed in internal matters and would not have much inclination to focus outwards on visionary arms control initiatives (nor would any leadership group have the authority in the international arena to credibly propose radical arms control initiatives). Further, it seems that in the immediate aftermath of civil war, internal constitution and consolidation of power (whether in a single union or in newly sovereign republics) might be far more the focus of politics than far-reaching foreign policy initiatives. In the longer term, no doubt different outcomes of war would have very different implications for the possibility of eliminating nuclear weapons, but it is quite beyond this author's already cloudy crystal ball to be able to draw out those implications in any meaningful or interesting way.

IV. Assessment of feasibility

Finally, what can we say about the overall political feasibility of eliminating nuclear weapons in the United States and Soviet Union? Given contemporary conditions, the immediate feasibility does not appear to be high. First, even if a sufficient level of trust existed between the United States and the Soviet Union to plan for the elimination of nuclear weapons, a number of other outstanding and interrelated security issues appear to be either very difficult or intractable. Although an issue that previously appeared intractable, the Soviet conventional threat to Europe, has all but disappeared, developing multilateral agreements to inspect, control, reduce or eliminate chemical, biological and nuclear weapons on a world-wide basis seems, at best, extraordinarily difficult. Second, the domestic political prerequisites do not appear to be in place. In neither the United States nor the Soviet Union does the highest level leadership seem determined, possibly at some political risk, to put elimination of nuclear weapons on the immediate arms control agenda. Further, centres of resistance from military and civilian sectors strongly supporting nuclear weapon modernization programmes can be expected in the United States. In the Soviet Union, given the political resurgence of a hard-line position involving military and other conservative elements in the winter and spring of 1990–91, we can postulate similar centres of resistance.

[84] Foye (note 70), p. 4; Clines, F. X., 'Kremlin accuses banks in West of plot', *New York Times*, 13 Feb. 1991; Gordon, M. R., 'Outlook is cloudy for an arms deal by US and Soviets', *New York Times*, 6 Feb. 1991; Friedman, T. L., 'US and Kremlin still deadlocked on arms treaties', *New York Times*, 16 Mar. 1991. On the resolution of CFE and resumption of serious negotiation on START, see note 73 above.

However, the challenge is not simply to assess contemporary conditions but to exercise disciplined imagination to address the following question: Under what conditions might an outcome that appears utopian—the elimination of nuclear weapons—be politically feasible to undertake in the United States and Soviet Union? The trick, of course, is to articulate conditions under which elimination could be feasible without at the same time 'cooking' the analysis by assuming utopian conditions. I have undertaken this analysis by making five assumptions.

First, I have assumed that conditions in the international environment would enable highly motivated political leaders in the Soviet Union and United States to address seriously problems of very deep cuts and then the elimination of nuclear weapons, without assuming that important multilateral problems had already been solved.

Second, I have assumed that change in the international environment would proceed step-by-step, each step having the potential to transform to some degree the world that follows.

Third, I have assumed that changes in the international environment lead in no automatic or determinate way to changes in domestic politics or policy. Rather, events in the external environment are interpreted on the basis of contentious domestic politics. At the same time, claims about external events can be deployed internally to change not only policy, but domestic political process and even political structure.

Fourth, at this historical juncture, domestic political structure and process are stable in the United States, although, within limits, subject to some change. In the Soviet Union, political structure and process are highly unstable.

And, fifth, a proposal to eliminate nuclear weapons would be subjected to domestic processes of approval which broadly resemble the approval process for nuclear arms control agreements. At the same time, a proposal to eliminate nuclear weapons could not be predicated on the old substantive bargain in which nuclear arms control agreements were accompanied by new generations of nuclear arms.

What has emerged in the course of the detailed analysis in this chapter is the importance of the second and third points above, the step-by-step dynamic interplay between conditions in the international environment and conditions in the domestic political environment. As state actions can change international relations, so too can change at the international level affect understandings and competing strategies at the domestic level. Further, and remarkably enough, intentional actions at one level can turn out to be essential, if unintended, prerequisites for action at another. To take a hypothetical example, if the president of the United States undertook a reorganization of the military, partly in response to changed functions resulting from international changes and partly in order to gain better control of the budget, such changes could make far more feasible the elimination of nuclear weapons at some point in the future.

Without making a strong claim that it will be politically feasible to eliminate nuclear weapons in the Soviet Union and United States, we can at least articulate conditions which, if they occurred, would make such a project appear to be both more plausible and more feasible than it does today. Just as the Soviet Union has provided the dynamic force for arms control since the mid-1980s, so too it seems reasonable to assume that a proposal to eliminate nuclear weapons would first be seriously pursued by the Soviet Union, for two reasons. First, Gorbachev has already made such a proposal, and the idea has a familiarity and legitimacy in Soviet politics that it does not in the United States; related, there are others in the Soviet Union besides Gorbachev who could be quite interested in pursuing such a proposal. Second, the instability in Soviet politics provides a dynamism, a potential source for radical political invention, that is not present in the United States. This is not to predict that the Soviets will pursue a proposal to eliminate nuclear weapons; it is simply to say that just as changes in the international environment are already the intended and largely unintended consequences of Soviet strategy, future international relations may very well be largely shaped by how the Soviet state is remade.

The question, then, is this: Under what conditions in the Soviet Union might political leaders pursue vigorously and seriously a proposal to eliminate nuclear weapons, and under what conditions in the United States might political leaders respond favorably to such a proposal? Were the Soviet Union to embark on a course of authoritarian rule, it would not bode well for the prospect of eliminating nuclear weapons. However, were Gorbachev or others to pursue an effective reform agenda, either within a federal structure in which the Soviet Union remained largely intact, or within a confederation of sovereign states, the feasibility of eliminating nuclear weapons could be much greater. In either case, we can imagine dynamic leadership continuing or extending Gorbachev's and Shevardnadze's programme of the mid- to late-1980s, perhaps making further unilateral cuts, and making credible proposals for very deep cuts in nuclear weapons and for the development of an international regime of control and inspection. Were such radical arms control measures implemented successfully, a proposal to eliminate nuclear weapons could likely be next on the international agenda.

In the United States, the fundaments of political process and structure are unlikely to be radically changed. Yet, the potential for change in highly stable institutions might be greater than at first appearance. As threat in the international environment is reinterpreted, and as the budget for the military is put under intense pressure, three developments could make the political feasibility of eliminating nuclear weapons substantially greater than at present: first, the president could commit him- or herself to radical cuts in nuclear weapons and to elimination, with attendant changes in definitions of military missions; second, the military could be reorganized in such a way that advocacy for nuclear missions was severely weakened; and third, the changes already underway in congressional bargaining and coalition structure regarding arms control could continue, thus providing the prerequisites for congressional support to eliminate nuclear weapons.

The occurrence of all of these circumstances—continued dynamic arms control moves in Soviet Union; a US response that would cause, and be made possible by, a partial reshaping of US politics; and, only alluded to in this essay chapter, the beginning of resolution of crucial multilateral security issues regarding weapons of mass destruction—do not seem highly probable. Yet, we have just seen in the onset of historical transformation of European and world politics that the most important events shaping world history are not highly probable, or at least they do not appear to be before they occur. (Which social scientists were predicting that in 1989 and 1990, or even in the decade of the 1990s, the Berlin Wall would fall, Eastern and Central Europe would be transformed, and German reunification would occur?) While on most days it is still not a bad guess that tomorrow will be much like today, the era we have entered clearly shows us how much our faith in such reasoning derives not from the power of the generalization, but simply from having lived in a period of substantial stability. Given the new era we have entered, it becomes incumbent to learn to think more conditionally. This chapter is one effort to do so.

9. Nuclear proliferation and the elimination of nuclear weapons

George H. Quester

I. Introduction

It would be a truism to note that a *denuclearized* international system has never existed. Often, comparisons are made between the system that is known (or is believed to be known) of mutual nuclear deterrence and the real world that was known (or is thought to have been known), the pre-1945 world of confrontations with what are now styled 'conventional' armed forces. Such comparisons induce speculation about whether the invention of nuclear weapons of mass destruction has been entirely bad, or whether their development might have made for fewer wars in Central Europe and Korea, and in other parts of the world. War was assuredly made more horrible by the development of nuclear weapons (if war is to be fought with all available weapons), but, in the process, was war made much more unlikely?[1]

This chapter does *not* seek to compare the world of nuclear weapons of today with the pre-1945 system with all of its balances of power and wars and arms races. Instead, the goal is to compare the post-1945 situation with a world of *deliberate* nuclear disarmament and self-denial, concepts which were perhaps envisaged in the Baruch Plan, a system in which a return to a reliance on nuclear arsenals would always be a possibility.[2]

It is this post-year 2000 nuclear weapon-free world that this chapter addresses, a world about which one can only speculate. In such a world, would there be a conscientious adherence to the elimination of nuclear weapons and a conscientious avoidance of vertical or horizontal proliferation, indeed, of all nuclear weapons? Or would there be rumour upon rumour, and fear upon fear, with these all too quickly becoming self-confirming?

II. Interlocking logic

This chapter examines two parallel, but different, questions: (*a*) What does the process of halting the proliferation of nuclear weapons to date reveal about a

---

[1] For examples of analyses comparing the world of nuclear weapons with a world in which nuclear weapons had not been invented, see Snyder, G., *Deterrence and Defense* (Princeton University Press: Princeton, N.J., 1961); and Mandelbaum, M., *The Nuclear Question* (Cambridge University Press: Cambridge, 1979).

[2] The Baruch Plan is discussed in Hewlett, R. G. and Anderson, O. E., *The New World* (Pennsylvania State University Press: University Park, Penn., 1962), pp. 556–74.

nuclear weapon-free world?; and (*b*) What problems of nuclear proliferation would a nuclear weapon-free world face?

The logical links between these two questions might appear to be fairly clear, but, as is the case with all such politically charged questions, a closer look is in order. A world without nuclear proliferation does not logically require nuclear disarmament, even if the moral sensibilities of the world and of the wording of Article VI of the 1968 Non-Proliferation Treaty (NPT) might indicate that there was a connection.[3] The world could go forward with a finite number of nuclear weapon states (NWS)—indeed it may have to—without that number having to increase decade by decade. But a nuclear weapon-free world conversely *does* imply a successful barrier to nuclear proliferation, for the nth NWS in such a world would be the first of a new array, soon enough to be followed by a second, and so on.

All of this amounts to saying that the existing barriers to nuclear proliferation would be under a much more demanding strain in a nuclear weapon-free world; and that existing strains on the nuclear proliferation regime may suggest pessimism rather than optimism about the achievement of such a world.

More generally, the project, of which this chapter is a part, is focused on *security* in a nuclear weapon free-world. Disarmament, whether nuclear or conventional, may be a means to achieve such security, but it would have to be security, rather than disarmament, that was the end in itself. If disarmament did not contribute to security (i.e., those instances in which it did not reduce the chances of war and fear of aggression, but instead heightened such fears), then it could hardly be so readily accepted as desirable.

Given the emphasis on security, this chapter will often refer to stability, a term which can have many meanings. If stability refers simply to the permanency of the political, social, economic or military status quo, many observers might be reluctant to endorse it. But if stability was taken simply to mean an avoidance of the self-confirming cycles by which rumours of war lead to actual wars (an avoidance of the 'instability' by which pre-emption apparently becomes the best way to respond to the possibilities of an adversary's attack), then many would be readily inclined to favour stability.[4] Again, the key question is whether a nuclear weapon-free world would result in a pre-emptive and mutually reinforcing race to reacquire nuclear weapons, if not in a race to use them.

---

[3] Article VI of the 1968 NPT reads: 'Each of the Parties to the Treaty undertakes to pursue negotiations in good faith on effective measures relating to cessation of the nuclear arms race at an early date and to nuclear disarmament, and on a treaty on general and complete disarmament under strict and effective international control'. Reprinted in Goldblat, J., SIPRI, *Arms Control Agreements: A Handbook* (Praeger: New York, 1982), p. 157.

[4] A very important and seminal work here is Schelling, T. C., *The Reciprocal Fear of Surprise Attack*, RAND Report P-1342 (Santa Monica, Cal., 1958).

III. Conflicting interests

The analysis of our progress to date in slowing nuclear proliferation offers numerous inferences—both of an optimistic and a pessimistic nature—for a world in which the superpowers have drastically reduced, or totally eliminated, their nuclear weapon stockpiles.

On the optimistic side, a remarkable degree of reasonableness and co-operation in the avoidance of further horizontal nuclear weapon proliferation is evident in the world. Although the NPT is sometimes depicted as a sort of Soviet–US *dictat*,[5] amid ritual denunciations of this 'double standard' by Indian and other diplomats at UN gatherings, the great majority of nations have more quietly concluded that the NPT and other barriers to proliferation are actually very much in their own interest, and not just in the interest of the superpowers. Thus nuclear weapons have spread more slowly than almost all of the analysts during the 1960s or 1970s would have predicted, and no nation has seriously threatened to exercise its rights of withdrawal from the NPT. Rather, a sophisticated acknowledgement that nuclear weapons are indeed very different from other weapons has been evident: a recognition that nuclear weapons require different rules and restraints in the exercise of any 'inherent sovereign prerogatives'.[6]

On the negative side, however, a tremendous amount of fissionable material has been produced in the generation of electrical power using nuclear reactors. The on-going production of fissionable material contributes to a continuing disquiet about whether existing inspection arrangements can reliably ensure that one nation or another is not somehow cheating to divert plutonium or enriched uranium to produce nuclear weapons.[7]

Concern about the possibilities of diversion and cheating has been evident even in those cases in which the possible gains of such a diversion are only that a nation becomes the nth NWS with an arsenal that would be vastly outclassed by those of the United States and the Soviet Union. How much more extensive fears and rumour-mongering could we expect if the superpower arsenals were to be eliminated or drastically reduced? After all, the possible gains of becoming an 'instant superpower', or perhaps even possessing a new monopoly of nuclear weapons, would surely appear to be more significant politically than the current possibility of becoming one more possessor of a rudimentary nuclear arsenal.

---

[5] For an interesting example, see Subrahmanyam, K. (ed.), *India and the Nuclear Challenge* (Institute for Defence Studies and Analyses: New Delhi, 1986).

[6] On the global support for halting nuclear proliferation, see Nye, J. S., 'Maintaining a non-proliferation regime', *International Organization*, vol. 35, no. 1 (winter 1982), pp. 15–38.

[7] Worries about the efficacy of IAEA safeguards are outlined in Wohlstetter, A. *et al.*, *Swords from Plowshares* (University of Chicago Press: Chicago, 1977).

IV. The logic of denuclearization and deproliferation

One often hears endorsements of the desirability of the elimination of nuclear weapons. Yet these expressions may involve some leaps of logic and some wishful thinking as the processes by which the transition from one security structure to another have not been worked out.

This is illustrated in the ways that spokesmen for the non-proliferation effort at times try to join forces with the morality of those favouring total nuclear disarmament. When asked whether or not the non-proliferation effort is unfair, they respond that they simply favour having as few NWS in the world as possible, that is they prefer five to six, and they prefer four to five, and three to four, and so on.

One always holds one's breath on whether the mathematical chain will be pursued to its end. Are two NWS preferred over three? Of course they are. However, is *one* NWS preferred over *two*?

This can be written in terms of a mathematical formula (where the '>' sign refers to preferred outcome):

$$0 > 1 > 2 > 3 > 4 > 5 > 6 > 7 > \ldots n$$

Of course, zero NWS is preferable to either only one or two NWS. However, at zero the world's political aversion to 'one' becomes a very serious problem, because any situation of 'zero' may be plagued with continual rumours that one nation or another is trying to sneak back into the position of being the first and only NWS.

Furthermore, it is not clear whether a NWS possessing such a monopoly (as in the case of the United States between 1945 and 1949) would *this time* let the monopoly slip out of its hands, that is, use its nuclear weapons to preclude anyone else from reacquiring such weapons and to impose a sort of hegemony on the world.

Thus, the ordering of our real preferences might rather have to be presented as follows:

$$`0' > 1 < 2 > 3 > 4 > 5 > 6 > 7 > \ldots n$$

with the quotation marks around zero indicating the worry and scepticism about whether the nations of the world can remain free of nuclear weapons.

By this 'realistic' view, the ideal number of NWS would thus probably be two, based on the theory that mutual deterrence ('mutual assured destruction') needs more than one source of destruction, and on an assumption that such mutual deterrence shields not only Moscow from attack by Washington's arsenal, and Washington from attack by Moscow's arsenal, but shields the entire world from attack by either nuclear arsenal. (Hiroshima and Nagasaki may well illustrate what happens when only *one* power in the world has nuclear weapons; but the wars between the UK and Argentina, or the USSR and

Afghanistan, or the USA and North Vietnam, may show how impossible the use of nuclear weapons becomes today, even when 'only one side' of the particular war has such weapons, once another party also possesses a nuclear arsenal.)

The processes by which the Soviet Union and the United States were somehow chosen to be the twin pillars that factor nuclear weapons out of our fears (which have existed ever since nuclear weapons entered the realm of possibility) is open to challenge. Perhaps in 1950 or 1960 Sweden and Yugoslavia would have been chosen to be the sole possessors of nuclear arsenals if these things had been decided by votes rather than by the historical evolution of the arms race. (One might also speculate about what international relations would have been like—and how much, if any, 'nuclear proliferation' there could have been—if a power other than the United States had been the first and only state to acquire nuclear weapons. One need only recall that the urgency of the US effort to develop nuclear weapons came in response to fears that Hitler's Germany might be working to develop them.)[8]

V. Motives for proliferation in the past

The symbolic, political or military motives that have persuaded n countries thus far to acquire nuclear weapons (or simply to acquire all the capabilities for producing such weapons, so that they appear to be on some sort of a 'threshold'), are not easy to sort out. Gains of prestige or image might strike most analysts as very trivial and silly, compared to the enormous risks posed to the world by the development of weapons of mass destruction. Although the prestige of having developed such a capacity may have been great at one time, it is probably less in 1991, with much of the world shrugging off the implicit scientific accomplishment when rumours emerge that North Korea or Pakistan may be closing in on the development of nuclear weapons.

Yet prestige sometimes translates into very material benefits for a nation, even if some of these are difficult to establish. Government leaders around the world may thus still ask themselves whether France would be regarded as important as Germany is today if France did not possess nuclear weapons, or whether the Soviet Union would be deferred to as much as Japan if the Soviet Union did not possess nuclear weapons.

The ties of nuclear weapon possession to military and political interaction, however, can also be real, even when they are difficult to pin down. For example, there may indeed be a number of Frenchmen who, in the wake of German reunification in 1990, now feel grateful on more military grounds for the earlier decisions to invest in nuclear weapons, since this might relieve the fears derived from population totals, and the expansionist drives such totals suggested in the past. And countries like Israel, South Korea and Taiwan may

---

[8] The US motives for pressing forward with the Manhattan Project are discussed in Bundy, McG., *Danger and Survival* (Random House: New York, 1989), chapter 1.

cherish the mere rumours that nuclear weapons were close at hand, for this also reinforces their security.[9]

Much of our analytical problems will indeed be related to the *lessons* the nations of the world think they have learned from their experiences with nuclear weapons. If they draw the lesson that these weapons have been useless (or that their usefulness is now over because of political changes), then the task of keeping proliferation under control, once the existing nuclear powers engage in substantial or total nuclear disarmament, will be easier. If the lesson is instead that such weapons have been quite useful, even if the use is simply so trivial as enhancing a government's domestic appeal and power, then any 'nuclear weapon-free world' may generate much more severe proliferation problems.

Optimistic views

This chapter considers the nature of the nuclear proliferation issues in a world in which the United States and the Soviet Union (and the United Kingdom, France and China, the other nations accepted as having nuclear weapons by the wording of the NPT) had substantially reduced their arsenals of nuclear weapons, with a view towards totally eliminating them.

The optimist might see all the desirable goals of the world moving along together here, as 'horizontal proliferation' was thus abated in the same process which turned around 'vertical proliferation', as the relationship of the existing nuclear powers to the potential nuclear powers was very much one of 'example' being set.[10] When the United States and the Soviet Union engage in a nuclear arms race, and continue to develop new nuclear weapons and 'new strategies' for the fighting of a nuclear war, this (according to such logic) makes nuclear weapons more attractive and legitimate all around the world. When they instead agree on nuclear disarmament, even partially as in the case of the 1987 INF Treaty, and abate their political disagreements, as well as their non-nuclear military preparations (as has indeed been the pattern at the end of the 1980s), the world takes its cue and reduces its own craving for nuclear weapons.

Some evidence of this kind of positive emulation already exists. The Soviet Union and the United States have indeed shown numerous signs of treating nuclear weapons as not just 'ordinary' weapons, by the special command-and-control arrangements which are instituted over such warheads,[11] by the extra psychological tests that are applied to all the officers and enlisted men who will have access to such weapons, and by the way such weapons have been held back out of combat use, ever since they were introduced at Hiroshima and Nagasaki. The reasons that so many nations of the world have been ready to

[9] See Harkavy, R. G., 'Pariah states and nuclear proliferation', in *International Organization* (note 6), pp. 135–64.

[10] For example, Epstein, W., *The Last Chance* (The Free Press: New York, 1976).

[11] On the nuclear command-and-control issue see Bracken, P., *The Command and Control of Nuclear Forces* (Yale University Press: New Haven, Conn., 1983).

sign and ratify the NPT, or to behave as if they were bound by it, even if they had not formally adhered to it, is that they have picked up this signal that nuclear weapons are not just another weapon, but rather something unique in their destructiveness, and therefore unique in their relationship to everything else that is military and political.

The publics of the world, especially (but not exclusively) the publics of the political democracies, attach importance to many of the moral relationships which are behind the logic noted above. When the superpowers seem to be de-emphasizing nuclear weapons and reducing their nuclear arsenals, it would thus be much more difficult for a parliamentary candidate in Japan or Italy or Australia to base a campaign on exploiting his country's national nuclear weapon development option. Conversely, if the nuclear arms race were to heat up again or if extensive new discussions were to be developed of nuclear war-fighting strategies (or if, Heaven forbid, any actual use were to be made of nuclear weapons in a combat situation, even one so free of collateral damage to civilians as, for example, anti-submarine warfare) then these publics might be much more receptive to the idea that nuclear weapons were to be sought after.

As an illustration of some positive possibilities of interaction, it is generally quite plausible that nuclear weapon-free zones (NWFZ) can nicely tie together superpower restraint and non-proliferation.[12] The countries within the specified zone agree not to acquire nuclear weapons (and not to allow other countries to base such weapons on their territory). The NWS conversely supply their part of the agreement by promising not to deploy or use such weapons within the zone. The upshot is a general de-emphasis of the importance or relevance of nuclear weapons, which would be a step, of course, towards a nuclear weapon-free world.

Confidence- and security-building measures (CSBMs)[13] more generally work to reduce the likelihood of war or of great power intimidation of lesser powers, and thus presumably also the likelihood of nuclear proliferation. Any step which makes the conventional military balance less precarious should make nuclear weapons look less necessary or attractive. An emphasis on defence over offence, and on mutual observation and verification to dispel rumours of attack, would thus reinforce peace and denuclearization, even if political disagreements remained just as great as before.

Yet any and all of such generally plausible patterns have also faced some limitations. An NWFZ agreement would work to slow nuclear proliferation for Latin America but in the years when the Federal Republic of Germany so much feared the armoured forces of the Soviet Union and the Warsaw Pact, such an NWFZ would have caused Bonn to sense an end of the US commitment to

---

[12] On the characteristics of such zones, see Sukovic, O., 'The concept of nuclear-weapon free zones', eds. D. Carlton and C. Schaerf, *Perspectives on the Arms Race* (Macmillan: London, 1989), pp. 267–85.

[13] Such measures are analysed in Lynch, A., 'The CDE agreement—achievements and prospects', *Arms Control Today*, vol. 16, no. 8 (Nov. 1986), pp. 13–24.

nuclear escalation, and thus might well have produced a German nuclear weapon programme, rather than discouraging it.

CSBMs are defined by output (rather than by input, as are NWFZs), and it is thus hard to imagine a *successful* example of a CSBM that would not reinforce other desirable outputs. In this instance, the problem may rather be that our inventory of useful ideas and beneficial innovations is not inexhaustible.

Pessimistic views

The counter-perspective—the pessimistic view—maintains that power vacua get filled, that a vacating of the pre-eminent role of superpowers mounting their thermonuclear threats might speedily enough result in another party racing to seize this role. As the United States and the Soviet Union apparently proceed in the direction of nuclear and conventional disarmament, is it reasonable to conclude that there are no admirals or generals or presidents or heads of atomic energy establishments around the world who will suddenly perceive an opportunity to 'take their turn' at steering the world, with all the grandeur or material national benefit that this might bring?

Some of this discussion might strike an observer as too abstract. One view holds that eliminating the first two nuclear powers will induce the others, existing or threshold, also to relinquish nuclear weapons. The opposing abstract view holds that eliminating the first two will prompt one or two others to acquire nuclear weapons, with the world having to pray that it is again *two* and not just *one*. But what is the role of international politics in this instance? Is it not necessary to get past abstract modelling to consider how much political rivalry there would have to be for new rounds of 'nuclear rivalry' to emerge?

If all of the world's pairs of countries were getting along as well as Norway and Sweden, for example, the possibility of the acquisition of nuclear weapons might be shrugged off without enormous worries and rumour-campaigns about the clandestine manufacture of such weapons. If Soviet–US relations continue to improve at the current pace, a similar sort of end to the fascination with military nuclear possibilities might occur.

As anyone now tries to consider the character of a nuclear weapon-free world, he or she will sometimes be integrating the momentous events of 1989, but will inevitably often still be reflecting the scenarios thought plausible up to 1988—even while the real task is to relate all of this to the world as it would most probably be in the 2005. Very few of us can really now have internalized all the jarring changes in premises that might emerge from the dramatic political dissolution of the Warsaw Pact, and from the concomitant changes required for NATO planning, and indeed for planning everywhere else.

Among the questions thus opened for a new dissection are the roles of alliances and ideology and hegemonies in the world that is emerging at the end of the 20th century. Will the conventional balance now make for less recourse to threats of nuclear escalation, as the geopolitically central situation of the

Soviet Union no longer frightens the nations of Western Europe as much? Or will there be new hegemonic threats, as India perhaps looms over its neighbours, or as Germany and Japan are viewed as economic hegemons, amid the very difficult issues of whether economic power can be so easily compared with military power? Analysts will have to reflect on whether hegemonies have always been so threatening through history, or whether some of them have actually served benign purposes, with the hegemon even possibly contributing more to the welfare of the 'weaker' states than vice versa. And they will have to ask whether the spread of democratic institutions will now truly work to reduce the risks of arms race and wars all around the world.

Perhaps we can then look forward to 'an end to history', as the spread of freely elected democratic governments makes for a generally demilitarized world.[14] It was the expectation of Woodrow Wilson, Giuseppe Mazzini, and Immanuel Kant, and other more optimistic political theorists in the past, that international peace might be achieved once all the world was self-governing, once 'government by the consent of the governed' became the norm. If the Soviet Union and all the world's Marxist regimes switch to multi-party electoral systems, and all the rest of the world follows, can nuclear arsenals really retain any role? And can nuclear proliferation remain a problem?

But is the end of such political hostility anywhere in sight between Israel and its Arab neighbours, or even between Pakistan and India? Furthermore, where does one put the current relationship of Argentina and Brazil on this scale? To put the matter most crisply, if there were no other countries in the world that already possessed sizeable nuclear arsenals, could Brazil and Argentina be counted upon to avoid a nuclear weapon race, as Sweden and Norway most probably could?[15]

'Realists' about the international system might intervene here to question even this much optimism. India and Pakistan are both self-governing democracies at the moment, but this hardly eliminates the risk of a conventional war, or a nuclear arms race, or even then of a nuclear war between them. France and the UK came close to war less than 100 years ago, in the Fashoda crisis, when both were already fully developed democracies. If we were to conclude, with justification, that democracies have thus far have shown no record of getting into wars with each other, this might only be the case because the number of such political democracies has been so small, compared to all the other systems of government that have made the decisions on war and peace.[16]

By this more pessimistic kind of reasoning, there could soon enough have been tensions, and the development of mutual nuclear deterrence reasoning,

---

[14] A widely-cited example of this kind of argument is to be found in Fukayama, F., 'The end of history', *The National Interest*, no. 16 (summer 1989), pp. 3–18. See also Doyle, M. W., 'Kant, liberal legacies and foreign affairs', *Philosophy and Public Affairs*, vol. 12 (summer/autumn 1983), pp. 205–35, 323–53.

[15] See the chapter by Harald Müller in this volume.

[16] A basic analysis of the interplay of domestic governmental structure and international factors here can be found in Waltz, K., *Man, the, State and War* (Columbia University Press: New York, 1959).

even between the USA and the UK, if the UK instead of the USSR had become the second country to acquire nuclear weapons (i.e., if the UK had been the first to 'proliferate' after the USA established the category of nuclear weapon state). By this more pessimistic kind of reasoning, the dangers and temptations of the latent possibility of nuclear weapons may never let the world rest in a nuclear weapon-free stance, no matter how many of the world's countries have come to be governed by political democracy.

Why do people run for office in democracies? Is it only for the sense of public service, or is it also importantly for the grandeur and sense of power that comes with winning public applause and elections? One can thus hardly be certain that democratic processes will never generate national leaders who support irredentist sentiments about territory, or who nurture grievances about past national defeats, or who feel a lust for increasing the attention and respect paid their countries at international gatherings. As one looks at the national nuclear decisions and near-decisions of the past, at the 'proliferation' choices made in France or Sweden or the United Kingdom or Australia, the motivations have always included some genuine concerns about national security, but also concerns for national prestige, and concerns also for personal advancement. The heads of atomic energy establishments, even in the most democratic of countries, have not so often run away from the chance of being remembered as 'the father of the bomb'.

VI. Nuclear behaviour which 'realism' would not have predicted

Before one settles into accepting a 'realism' by which the world will always harness technology for international military conflict (this somehow being the 'wisdom of the ages'), some aspects of the existing nuclear confrontation that few, if any, students of international relations would have accepted as a reliable and 'realistic' prediction in 1945 must be noted.

Tens of thousands of nuclear warheads have been produced since Hiroshima and Nagasaki, but none of them have been used in anger. If anyone had predicted in 1945 that so many of this kind of weapon would be built, but would never be used (as each side withheld its own from use as long as its adversary did), he would have been laughed out of the room, assured that 'the world does not work that way', that the historical iron law has been that the weapons which get produced indeed get used.

Similarly, since 1945, a tremendous number of warships have been built, with almost none of them having ever being shot at by the fleets of an adversary. Indeed, the largest ship sunk since 1945 in naval warfare was the the *General Belgrano*, sunk in 1982 during the Falklands War.[17] Who, of the 'realist' school

---

[17] Ironically, the *General Belgrano* (known as the *USS Phoenix* at the time) was a survivor of the Japanese attack on Pearl Harbor. The ship was transferred to the Argentine Navy in 1951. See *Jane's Fighting Ships 1978–79* (Macdonald and Jane's: London, 1978), p. 26.

of thought, would have predicted that the seas would become a sanctuary in almost all the 'limited wars' that were going to be fought? The navies of the world have served often enough as bases for wars that were being fought with great intensity on the ground and in the air over the ground, but have never become targets themselves.

This exemption of the world's fleets from attack never applied in the pre-nuclear period, and it might in fact be causally linked to the existence of nuclear weapons, since the US Navy and the navies of the other NWS have maintained their policies of 'neither confirm or deny', and since anyone attack-ing an aircraft-carrier or other larger ship thus risks discovering that there are nuclear weapons on board, with all the concomitant possibilities of a 'use them or lose them' situation.

Even as things stand, a restraint may emerge on further nuclear proliferation that is analogous to this remarkable restraint on the nuclear weapon states. Each NWS *can* destroy the cities of the others, but will not do so, *as long as* the other NWS does not destroy its cities. Quite parallel to this, it is possible that a num-ber of threshold states *can* produce nuclear weapons quite easily, given the enormous overlap between civilian nuclear technology and the technology required for the production of atomic bombs, but that they will not do so, *as long as* other threshold states do not produce nuclear weapons. Thus, either Washington and Moscow may mutually deter each other from *using* bombs, while other pairs of the countries may mutually deter each other from *making* bombs.

But how much of this mutual deterrence from *making* nuclear bombs is likely in a world in which all existing bombs had been destroyed? Again, the sceptic would point to the enormously greater significance then of a country again being the first-and-only possessor of nuclear weapons, and to the many histor-ical illustrations of the temptations of such a hegemony, or to the fears induced in others by the mere prospect of such a hegemony. The optimist can counter by citing the examples noted above, of mutual restraint and non-traditional behaviour, of patterns of non-use of weapons, and even non-use of capability, for which it would not have been possible to find any historical precedent.

A possible example of this kind of 'mutual deterrence of bomb production' might be the current relationship between Argentina and Brazil.[18] Neither country has signed the NPT, and neither has become finally and firmly bound to the treaty establishing the Latin American nuclear weapon-free zone (the 1967 Treaty of Tlatelolco). Each country has made moves to enhance its nuclear capabilities, actions which have worried those who are concerned about the horizontal spread of nuclear weapons.

Both Argentina and Brazil might thus indeed plausibly like to acquire nuclear weapons, but if and only if it could be alone in introducing such weapons into the Latin American region, for then the gains in national prestige and derived

---

[18] On the Latin American proliferation situation, see Spector, L., *The Undeclared Bomb* (Ballinger: Cambridge, Mass., 1988), chapter 5.

political power might indeed be well worth the cost. Yet each has had to be aware that the other would be quick to follow suit in acquiring nuclear weapons, so that the choice now has become one of neither or both. For two such countries to introduce nuclear weapons would be to dilute the resulting prestige, and it would also serve to introduce new kinds of speculation and worries and risks, all of which one might want very much to avoid.[19] The hope for the region, and for the world, is thus that this logic has come to be very persuasive in Buenos Aires and Brasilia, as each reminds the other that it is quite capable of producing atomic bombs, but as each, in effect, sticks by a posture of 'we won't as long as you won't'.

One can thus indeed find worrisome models for the future, and in particular for our hopeful nuclear weapon-free future, in the nuances of approaches to nuclear proliferation to date. But one can also find some encouraging models. The prospect of a very widespread nuclear proliferation is indeed awful for the world, and it has come to be seen as awful by many other states, and not just by the superpowers. Because it is perceived to be so dreadful, much less nuclear proliferation has occurred than many of us would have predicted.

VII. The model of the Baruch Plan

In the United States, the Baruch Plan is generally remembered as a generous gesture, by which the United States would have given up its monopoly on nuclear weapons (it having already proved its peace-loving nature and generosity by making no moves to use that monopoly), eliminating (under international controls) the entire class of the weapons in which, by definition, it excelled. At the time, many thought that it was Stalin's obtuseness or evil which precluded this plan from being adopted, that is Stalin's rejection of the international controls and safeguards that would have been required to ensure that no country thereafter acquired nuclear weapons.[20]

Perhaps Stalin was hoping to trick the West by opposing the on-site inspection and international management of all peaceful nuclear activities that would have assured outsiders that no particular nation was producing atomic bombs. If the United States and other countries, in face of Soviet resistance, had then retreated to adopting a version of nuclear disarmament without international controls, the USSR could slyly have slipped into a nuclear monopoly of their own, and then dictated terms to the world.

On the other hand, perhaps Stalin was merely fearful of the intrusions into his domestic political and social system that would have come in the wake of the international management of atomic energy activities envisaged by the Baruch

---

[19] See Gamba-Stonehouse, V., 'Argentina and Brazil', ed. R. Cowen Karp, *Security Without Nuclear Weapons: Different Perspectives on National Security* (Oxford University Press: Oxford, 1991), pp. 229–57.

[20] For an interesting discussion of the Baruch Plan, see Herken, G., *The Winning Weapon* (Knopf: New York, 1980).

Plan. Whether the USA wanted this or not, such a foreign presence on Soviet soil could have been extremely destabilizing for Stalin's regime. While this second explanation for the unacceptability of the Baruch Plan refers less to any aggressive Soviet inclinations towards world domination, it would still none the less blame the ensuing nuclear arms race, risks of nuclear war, and nuclear proliferation on the defects of the *Soviet* system.

Yet a third interpretation of the Baruch Plan is more sympathetic to Stalin's situation, and at the same time suggests some more worrisome aspects of our contemporary problem of how to control proliferation in a denuclearized world. If the Baruch Plan had been adopted as proposed, the USA could surely have been counted upon to get rid of its nuclear arsenal (in any event, the USA had quietly allowed its arsenal to wither away to no bombs at all by 1947, as most US nuclear scientists had gone back to their universities),[21] and the USSR would similarly have been reliably free of any nuclear weapons.

But the US scientists of the Manhattan Project would not have forgotten how the bombs had been produced. If there had then been any major international crisis or outbreak of conventional war, with the termination of the Baruch Plan, the USA could always have won the race to be the first to build nuclear bombs again, simply because of its advantage in first-hand bomb-producing experience, an experience from which the USSR was to be totally banned. Furthermore, the mere knowledge of this asymmetry of latent capability to produce nuclear weapons might then have cast a long shadow over all of politics, well before any crises or conventional wars or breakdowns of international nuclear management had occurred. Realists and others who study politics are well aware of how the anticipated is often very immediately real. To have power tomorrow often achieves the possession of power today.

In today's strategic terminology, this might be described as the 'break-out' problem, as each side must consider what the other will be able to do if a treaty is suddenly denounced, or even if some pre-designated period of warning is given for the termination of a treaty. Worries about break-out are not insuperable, anymore than are worries about cheating, but these concerns have none the less been serious and important issues. Indeed, it is almost a truism that such concerns about break-out, about the military application of latent capabilities and memories of past weapon systems, will play a larger and more worrisome role (at least when other factors are held constant), if the current nuclear arsenals are eliminated or even very much reduced.

'Bombs in the basement'

An analogous problem concerns the possibility that South Africa or Israel might one day accede to the NPT and thus accept International Atomic Energy Agency (IAEA) safeguards over all its peaceful nuclear facilities. How could

---

[21] On the size of the US nuclear weapons arsenal in 1946 and 1947, Rosenberg, D. 'The US nuclear stockpile, 1945 to 1950', *Bulletin of the Atomic Scientists*, vol. 38, no. 5 (May 1982), pp. 25–30.

anyone, in retrospect, then be certain that no fissionable materials had been diverted in the years when such safeguard inspections were not in place? To put it another way, how could the problems of 'nuclear archeology' be overcome, as inspectors and others argue about whether all the materials are accounted for, or whether it is instead more plausible that the ingredients for an indisputable nuclear arsenal have been hidden away.[22]

Israel and South Africa have thus posed somewhat of a threat to the current non-proliferation system by their policies. By never having openly claimed to have nuclear weapons and never having detonated any kind of 'peaceful' nuclear explosive device, these two countries (and some others that may be following their pattern, for example, Pakistan) have indeed inflicted less damage than if they had explicitly defied the world by acquiring such weapons. Yet, by refusing to submit to IAEA safeguards and by allowing rumours to circulate that 'bombs in the basement' were indeed being accumulated, such countries have indeed captured for themselves some of the gains (and done some of the damage) that are imputed to nuclear proliferation.

The damage would be greater if the acquisition of nuclear weapons was open and honest. The damage would be less if Israel and South Africa had submitted to full monitoring over what they have been doing. In these cases, it may be too late for such a full monitoring, and, for the rest of our task of producing a non-nuclear world, the implications of being too late may indeed be quite severe.

If the nations that have very openly produced nuclear weapons are now to renounce them, it would necessitate asking the IAEA or some other inspection agency to assay the records of both the civilian nuclear industry, *and* the records of the inventories of the outright nuclear weapons accumulated over the years. Will not the problems in this instance be at least as severe as those pertaining to countries such as South Africa? Will these problems then be too severe for the venture of a nuclear weapon-free world to succeed?

Knowledge and stability

One could aspire to have the total of fissionable material retroactively accounted for, in a world in which all the near-NWS and NWS had decided to co-operate whole-heartedly. Perhaps, if the political groundwork is laid as outlined above, such co-operation might still be possible. Yet, much more difficult to achieve, even with the best of intentions, would be rounding up and eliminating the *knowledge* of how bombs are best made. As noted above, this was part of the problem with the Baruch Plan, as those countries with the experience of actually having carried a bomb-production programme through to fruition would always have the advantage or disadvantage of this knowledge. If international relations ever worsen because political systems begin to diverge and

---

[22] For a general discussion of the problem of nuclear archeology as it relates to accounting for fissionable material, see Von Hippel, F., chapter 7 in this volume; on the Israeli model, see Beres, L. R. (ed.), *Security on Armageddon: Israel's Nuclear Strategy* (D. C. Heath: Lexington, Mass., 1986).

quarrel again or if power disputes even begin to emerge between very similar political regimes, then the fact that one state had possessed nuclear weapons in the past, and the other had not, could be oppressive for the latter, even if all bombs had been dismantled and accounted for, and all fissionable materials had been safeguarded.

President Woodrow Wilson once enjoined his fellow citizens to be impartial in thought as well as in action.[23] Is it reasonable to expect that the world will be non-nuclear in thought as well as in action? If this is too much for anyone to aspire to, a question will remain on whether thoughts in this case would inevitably tend to lead to deeds, producing instabilities on the issue of nuclear arms production or even use.

In this instance, 'zero' is compared with 'mutual assured destruction', but inevitably some of the bedevilling, almost epistemological, questions noted above will have to be faced. How does 'genuine zero' compare with 'near-zero'? Do we have to settle simply for our best effort, 'the nearest we can get to zero'? Is the best effort then to be equated basically to finite deterrence?

Jonathan Schell has put forward a thoughtful vision of a denuclearized world in which there would be 'rearmament parity', as all the erstwhile and former nuclear powers had roughly equal capabilities for a break-out resuming the nuclear arms race if their interests seemed to dictate this.[24] Yet Schell's notion begs a number of questions.

To begin, 'parity' may be just as misleading an indicator here as it is even in today's confrontations of nuclear powers, as the important comparison is most probably not between the number of my bombs and the number of yours, but rather between the number of my bombs and the number of your cities, and vice versa. If there is to be a break-out, each side may be wondering whether it can get back to a position of 'assured destruction' of its adversary, before the adversary gets to the same position in reverse.

Rather than keeping the race even, therefore, our concern must be focused on the avoidance of a race in the first place. This might entail all of the changes of thought and attitude just noted *or* might suggest maintaining nuclear forces in existence, as part of mutual assured destruction, rather than moving into a nuclear weapon-free world that could be so unstable.

Thus the choice might be one of 'bombs on submarines' versus 'bombs in the basement' or 'bombs in the imagination of those who know how to make them in a hurry'; and it is possible that the submarine-based option of existing nuclear weapons would be the most stable of all these situations, the least threatened by nuclear proliferation and the least likely to produce 'a war nobody wanted'.

Analysts of arms control and military strategy sometimes distinguish among three kinds of 'stability': (a) crisis; (b) arms race and (c) deterrence. Each of

---

[23] Link, A. S., *Wilson: The Struggle for Neutrality* (Princeton University Press: Princeton, N.J., 1960), p. 66.

[24] Schell, J., *The Abolition* (Knopf: New York, 1984).

these three concepts of stability is indeed very relevant to the problems and possibilities of a nuclear weapon-free world.[25]

Crisis stability (sometimes also labelled 'strategic stability') might be defined as the impact weapon arrangements have on whether a war will occur, that is on whether weapons actually get *used*. When rumours of war emerge and the perceived possibility of war increases, it would thus be destabilizing to have weapons around that offered any advantages to pre-emptive and first-strike attacks, as compared with weapons which counselled patience and 'wait and see' as the best course to serve the national interest.

Arms race stability refers, in contrast, not to whether weapons come into use, but rather to whether a change in weapon arrangements will cause further weapons to be *procured*. In this case, the problems of nuclear proliferation in a totally or partially denuclearized world are readily apparent. Compared to the world of 1991, what are the linkages that would make the further procurement of nuclear weapons by new nations less likely, and what are the linkages that would make further procurement more likely?

Deterrence stability is a third notion referring more typically to 'extended nuclear deterrence', or the maintenance of classical national security. In effect, the question is posed in terms of whether nuclear weapons, by their presence and existence, have reduced the use of *other* weapons, such as whether the use of tanks in aggression has been deterred by the prospect of nuclear escalation.

What needs to be controlled?

There is one aspect of our current non-proliferation analysis that is of very straightforward use for the grander task of progressing towards a nuclear weapon-free world, for we have certainly already focused a great deal on the issues of 'what needs to be controlled?'[26] One can not make nuclear weapons out of just anything, but rather would be limited for the foreseeable future to the use of enriched uranium or plutonium, or perhaps ^{233}U derived from thorium. As an accessory to the production of fissionable materials, the availability of heavy water can be crucial. The design of thermonuclear weapons brings even a few more crucial elements into play. A well-understood 'trigger list' has been developed over the past two decades of the materials which should generally not be transferred from one country to another without safeguards.

Our problem for the future would thus hardly be one of not knowing *what* must be controlled in the nuclear field, but rather of extending these controls to all the existing NWS, to verify that *they* also are not producing new bombs.

The discussion of the current non-proliferation problem sometimes shifts also to delivery systems, as alarm is expressed whenever a new medium-range mis-

[25] On the distinctions about stability, see Gray, C. S., *Nuclear Strategy and National Style* (Hamilton Press: Lanham, Md., 1986), chapter 5.

[26] On the invocation of safeguards here, see Fischer, D. and Szasz, P., SIPRI, *Safeguarding the Atom: A Critical Appraisal*, ed. J. Goldblat (Taylor & Francis: London, 1985).

sile is tested, or even whenever someone realizes that a contemporary fighter-bomber could carry the weight of a first-generation nth atomic bomb. However, even for the current nuclear proliferation problem, the concern with delivery systems may be misplaced, because the most immediate targets are usually a short distance away, and because so many ways exist of delivering bombs even at longer ranges. Furthermore, there is no reason to conclude that a substantial denuclearization of the world would somehow enhance the supposed advantages of any concentration on constricting delivery systems.

The verification burden

The inspection burden for the IAEA is often depicted, even today, as being too much for the Agency to manage, as engineers and other informed specialists can imagine ways in which some clever country could fool the IAEA inspectors and get away with diverting significant amounts of plutonium or enriched uranium to the production of nuclear weapons. Our predictions of anticipated production of electricity by nuclear power plants translate directly into predictions of the flows of such sensitive fissionable materials, which translate again into numbers of bombs that could be produced: hundreds of bombs in a year for the Federal Republic of Germany, dozens for Taiwan and so on.[27] While the actual installation and operation of such nuclear power plants has been fairly consistently behind the predicted schedule, as problems of safety and cost-effectiveness, and nuclear waste-management have reduced some of the enthusiasm for nuclear power, the actual installation of such reactors has none the less generated a very significant portion of our current nuclear proliferation problem: what seems to make economic sense for civilian needs from country to country offers a very cheap entry into the ranks of possessors of nuclear weapons.

The most important counter to such criticisms of IAEA effectiveness incorporates all the additional political dimensions of the presence of IAEA inspectors, as the safeguards are a constant reminder that the country in question has undertaken a legal obligation not to divert materials to the manufacture of nuclear explosives, and as the continual risk is thus emplaced that an individual scientist or engineer would divulge his country's plans if a violation of the international agreements were under way. The chance that country number 9 might be caught makes country number 10 more relaxed about nuclear proliferation, and hence less likely to move for the bomb itself; and the chance that country number 10 might be caught by the IAEA makes country number 9 more relaxed. In a world where countries numbers 1 and 2 so much dominate the nuclear weapons field to begin with, the existence of IAEA safeguards may thus, by a combination of technical and political considerations,

[27] Estimates of peaceful nuclear activities and the concomitant production of fissionable materials can be found in Potter, W. B., *Nuclear Power and Nonproliferation* (Oelgeschlager, Gun and Hain: Cambridge, Mass., 1982).

work to persuade many of the nth countries to relax about other countries' intentions, and to forego the temptations of sneaking into nuclear weapons themselves.[28]

But what then about the burdens for the IAEA if every country of the world, even the United States, the Soviet Union, the United Kingdom, France and China, have similarly agreed to eliminate nuclear weapons and have submitted to Agency inspections of their peaceful nuclear facilities, inspections intended to assure that no new rounds of nuclear weapons will be built?

In this instance, the current rounds of snide remarks and rumours about IAEA ineffectiveness might be multiplied into a crescendo of serious worries, leading to self-confirming vicious cycles of cheating.

Even the elimination of current stockpiles would be problematic, of course, as trouble-makers and serious analysts on each side may accuse the other of having hidden away some warheads in Siberia or North Dakota, and as the lingering possibility that such charges might be true leads a 'patriotic' officer on one side or the other actually to try to carry out such violations of the disarmament pact.

This may all thus simply be an argument against general and complete disarmament, along the lines of 'you can't get there from here', as the inspection and verification burdens of a *total* global elimination of nuclear weapons would simply be too onerous. Furthermore, this might indeed bring the world closer to nuclear war than anything we have experienced since 1945, because the fears of cheating and the temptations to cheat can translate all too easily into fears and temptations of surprise attack or preventive war.

Perhaps the safest and most attainable end-state would thus leave us instead with five or ten SSBNs (nuclear-powered ballistic missile submarines) in each of two or three or four separate NWS navies, as the final deterrent to any cheating or nuclear sneak attacks, or to any other first-use of nuclear weapons. This might, at least, be required until such enormous waves of political good feeling and co-operation sweep the world, along the lines noted above, such that no one can remember anymore what these SSBNs were intended to do.

It is not our primary task here to debate out the feasibility of general and complete disarmament. Our task would rather be to consider the impact upon horizontal proliferation of either a total, or even a *very substantial,* elimination of the current nuclear arsenals. Even in such a more modified version of a very substantially disarmed world, however, it would be necessary to be prepared for levels of worry and accusation about the adequacy of safeguards far exceeding those of 1991. Various commentators, for tendentious or other reasons, might begin accusing the other superpowers of having more than the agreed maximum of a finite deterrence force, and would thus outline elegant scenarios about how such an illegal increment might make the difference in some

---

[28] A cautiously optimistic interpretation of how IAEA safeguards will work can be found in Scheinman, L., *The International Atomic Energy Agency and World Nuclear Order* (Resources for the Future: Washington, DC, 1987).

'window of vulnerability' for a grand and successful first-strike. And other commentators would be rehearsing the same fears for nations outside this basic nuclear weapon club, seeing much more real possibilities for what Brazil or Germany or Japan or Indonesia might accomplish in a clandestine nuclear weapon programme after the nuclear 'superpowers' had become so much less 'super'.

It goes without saying that even the current non-proliferation effort would have a greater chance of success if the returns on civilian nuclear activities turn out to be less attractive than was envisaged one or two decades ago. The cost-overruns and ecological hazards inflicted by nuclear power plants are a distinct set-back for the economic improvement of the world and a very severe disappointment for the impoverished Third World countries in particular, which have been looking to nuclear-generated electricity as one solution to their energy shortages. Yet these same set-backs for nuclear power have resulted in considerably less of a burden for IAEA safeguards, and less of a worrisome overlap between what might make sense in civilian terms and what is so threatening in the military sphere.

The same holds true, of course, in the nuclear weapon-free world this chapter addresses, when the double task would be to head off nuclear proliferation to nth countries and to achieve a persuasive and reliable *de*proliferation whereby the countries known to possess such weapons also get rid of them. If France continues to rely heavily on nuclear power for the production of electricity, the burdens of achieving a politically convincing nuclear weapon-free world will be greater. If disasters comparable to the Three Mile Island and Chernobyl nuclear power plant accidents should instead burden the French programme and the world's other ambitious nuclear programmes, then the deproliferation component of international security would be easier, even while all the political and military problems of economic disappointment and deferred economic development would be substantially exacerbated.

The systems for verifying a global non-proliferation system, in a world eliminating nuclear weapons more generally, will thus need at least the following (even given the uncertain chances of success no matter what course of action is followed): (*a*) the current IAEA, substantially augmented in manpower and funding (with a global reduction in military spending presumably freeing up such resources readily enough, as long as the political need for this is seen); (*b*) the maintenance and enhancement, and international co-ordination, of national intelligence assets, as various kinds of verification by national technical means, including old-fashioned espionage, are deployed and increasingly dedicated to policing the denuclearization of the world; and (*c*) the enlistment of much of the world's free press and other non-governmental information-gathering systems on the subject of whether a country is cheating on their commitments to forego the acquisition of nuclear weapons. All of this may sound like a pie in the sky prescription for the enforcement of a system needed to preserve the peace; but if this need is sensed widely enough, and if some of the other political changes needed continue to fall into place, it may yet be attainable.

Arguments about economic justice

One argument that is sure to be heard in any plan to eliminate nuclear weapons is that it will, in one direction or another, distort the development and spread of all the new technologies that can enrich civilian life. A country which had made bombs, but makes them no longer, will still be viewed as having an advantage in nuclear energy. Furthermore, any other country moving closer to *de facto* bomb-producing capabilities may offer the rationalization that this was merely to protect its ability to compete in the economic contests of the future.

Issues of monopolization versus considerations of sharing will have some relevance, but they will also often seem like a mask for very disturbing and troublesome narrowings of the threshold to a break-out or reopening of nuclear arms races.[29]

A number of examples of this kind of argument is evident even in the current non-proliferation effort in which (to reiterate) the gains of breaking into the possession of nuclear weapons would be far less major, and in which the fears surrounding possession of nuclear weapons are much less serious for the outside world. Nations moving into sensitive militarily applicable areas of nuclear research now often claim that this is only in the pursuit of pure science, or energy for their national economies, or in anticipation of the possible future international sales of equipment, services or expertise. In an economic world where every nation has to worry about its future balance-of-payments and market-access and prosperity, this scenario is not so far-fetched, but it is worrisome none the less. In a world which has totally renounced nuclear weapons, or has come close to doing so, the list of possible overlaps and accusations and concerns described above will be very real.

Another contemporary analogy is to be found not in the nuclear weapon area, but in the decisions made about conventional weapon production in the NATO alliance. For decades, the analytical observation has been very soundly and persuasively presented that NATO could have achieved a more effective conventional defence, at lower cost, if it had standardized its weapon, communication and logistics systems, rather than maintaining a wasteful competition among alternative producers within the alliance, a competition which has passed up many of the economies of scale in weapon production, and which also has created major problems of inter-operability for any actual battlefield performance by NATO forces.[30]

---

[29] On the inherent overlap of arguments for economic options and weapons options, see Greenwood, T., Rathjens, G. W. and Ruina, J., *Nuclear Power and Weapons Proliferation*, Adelphi Paper no. 130 (Institute for International Strategic Studies: London: 1976).

[30] Such competitions among NATO members are discussed in Pierre, A., *The Global Politics of Arms Sales* (Princeton University Press: Princeton, N. J., 1982).

Yet all of such analyses have been rejected and shrugged off, as each of the major NATO weapon producers has largely continued to go its own way, reducing what could be contributed to current NATO defence (perhaps thereby showing that the fears of Soviet attack have not been at all so imminent), on the plausible grounds that each was thereby retaining its national capability for producing weapons and the related commercial technologies, for its own use or for export, in the future.

Thus even the NATO alliance cannot head off a troublesome form of arms competition among its partners, in which these partners are worried about future balances of payments and future customers. The fear has hardly been that France, Germany, Italy, the UK and the USA have been retaining separate weapon-producing capabilities for possible use against each other, but rather that less-than-maximum defence preparations have thereby resulted against what was seen as the threat of a Warsaw Pact attack. Yet the problem is none the less worrisome, for it illustrates how national considerations of an economic nature can still override considerations of peace and international security. If NATO cannot develop a single weapon-producing monopoly exploiting economies of scale and achieving the military efficiency of standardized weapon systems, is such consolidation in the nuclear field to be expected, in which the international security gain would not be effectiveness against a common enemy, but the avoidance of the return of nuclear confrontations among the partners?

It is indeed possible that the world can only avoid all of the anticipated worries and fears described above by a return to what was proposed in the Baruch Plan, which proposed an actual international operation of the bulk of what passes for peaceful nuclear operations, rather than a mere international verification that such activities are not being diverted to military ventures. This, to begin, might produce much more effective and politically-persuasive verification systems, substantially reducing the rumours of clever ruses by which international visitors were kept from seeing how bombs were being produced in some basement. Beyond this, such an international management might reduce (although it could never eliminate) the invidious international comparisons on who had benefited the most from spin-offs, from the days of weapon production to the harnessing of nuclear technology in a nuclear weapon-free world. Rather than seeing a host of nations investing in worrisome dual-capability areas of nuclear technology, in all or most cases simply because they were hedging against future *commercial* rather than military competition, this might reassure most of the parties concerned that their economies would get a share of the profits and employment opportunities.

But if an international monopoly in the management of nuclear facilities were to be required to achieve meaningful non-proliferation and nuclear disarmament, this might only serve to highlight just how difficult a task this entire venture will be. Given the number of independent countries in the world, there will be enormous resistance to any such attempt to merge the separate national options.

Perhaps, as a compromise, the internationalization of peaceful nuclear industry could be limited simply to the enrichment of uranium and the reprocessing of plutonium, while allowing the separate nation states (under safeguards) to continue to operate their nuclear power plants. If we become globally sensitized to how dangerous nuclear proliferation is, we may also become sensitized then to where the greatest risks of theft and diversion would arise, and (without oppressively overriding the various considerations of independent sovereignty) may control the places where the most trouble was to be expected.

Short of combining all of the current ventures into a single international management scheme, the 'trigger-lists' for controlling sensitive technologies will have to be at least as exhaustive as they are today. Indeed, they will have to be expanded, since the nth countries to be headed off from acquiring nuclear weapons may now include the original five NWS as well.

In any case, therefore, a return to a more modest version of international management may be in order, whereby the world continues to live nervously with many of the current approaches to 'threshold', but where the existing dedicated fissionable materials facilities of the NWS have somehow to be placed under multinational management.

All of this amounts to nothing more than taking the current non-proliferation regime and turning it on its side, in light of the more ambitious goal of a global military denuclearization.

The current system seeks to impose safeguards on all the peaceful facilities outside of the five nuclear weapon powers existing in 1967 (the USA, the USSR, the UK, France and China) and to reduce the availability of some militarily very suspect parts of the nuclear fuel cycle outside these five countries. If the 'double-standard' of the NPT is now somehow to be erased, the safeguards will have to be extended over all the nuclear activities of these first five countries, on a 'full-scope' basis, of course. But what is to be done with the sensitive parts of the nuclear fuel-cycle which are already in full bloom in these five? If, even with IAEA safeguards in place, plutonium-enrichment is too worrisome to be tolerated for Germany or Iraq or Libya, would it not also be too worrisome to be tolerated for France or the Soviet Union, in the nuclear weapon-free world we are contemplating?

The CBW problem

One has to intrude into our discussion of a denuclearized world with at least one other 'proliferation problem', namely that of chemical and biological weapons (CBW). The spread of CBW capabilities may similarly be slowed, or greatly exacerbated, as the world moves away from *nuclear* weapons of mass destruction.

Unfortunately, there are many analogies between nuclear weapon and CBW proliferation. Even more than the nuclear field, the CBW field may plague us with the worrisome overlap between peaceful capabilities and the capacity for producing weapons.[31]

Chemical and biological weapons, being sometimes referred to as 'the poor man's H-bomb', may similarly offer the means for inflicting extremes of death and destruction on an opponent. If the world gets rid of existing nuclear weapons, and if a host of new nations do not slip into the possession of such weapons, will we then simply have to shift our worries to new forms of 'mutual assured destruction'?

Like nuclear weapons, chemical and biological weapons are often touted for their alleged applicability to the battlefield. Some very sensible scepticism has developed about whether the battlefield application can ever be so reliable and predictable on all of its relevant dimensions in the nuclear field: that is, is the offensive or the defensive supported by such weapons, is the larger force or the smaller force supported by the weapons, and can the collateral damage to civilians be contained?[32]

One important (and possibly very worrisome) difference between nuclear and chemical weapons, however, is that the latter sometimes seem to offer *extremely* benign options for warfare. The death and destruction imposed on surrounding civilians, and even on the human beings in the uniform of the opposing armies, could be substantially reduced, perhaps even to zero. Wars might be fought with temporarily incapacitating gases which did no longer-term damage to the soldiers who were knocked out of active combat and which inflicted no collateral damage on innocent civilians.

Such benign possibilities of reducing the costs of war may comply with the traditional sense of morality and with the laws of war, but they can increase the likelihood of war. Certainly, they also increase the chances that this kind of weaponry will be viewed as legitimate and will then proliferate into production and combat use.

VIII. Conclusion: some very general observations

There are some very pessimistic inferences to be made from our efforts to date in halting or slowing nuclear proliferation, as the vastly greater undertaking of achieving a world entirely free of nuclear weapons is contemplated. But there are also some more optimistic inferences.

Where nuclear weapons are treated as 'just another weapon', the outlook becomes gloomy indeed, for other weapons have been difficult to control. But

---

[31] On the dangers of CBW proliferation, see Apt, K. E., *Chemical Warfare Arms Control: Issues and Challenges* (Center for National Security Studies: Los Alamos, N. Mex., 1988).

[32] Examples of a healthy scepticism here can be found in Halperin, M., *Nuclear Fallacy* (Ballinger: Cambridge, Mass., 1987).

the world in the past four decades has decidedly not treated nuclear weapons in the same way as other weapons.

As the dramatic events of 1989 demonstrate, hardly anything in the political sphere can be ruled out, for what seemed 'impossible' (i.e., the elimination of the Berlin Wall) might quickly enough become established fact. Perhaps a new world in which the Machiavellian power politics 'realism' of international anarchy no longer looks so compelling or relevant is not so far fetched. Yet an end to power politics would not be the only 'optimistic' possibility; even against a background of continuing international rivalries, the decisions about the acquisition or the use of nuclear weapons have taken a very different tone from that which applied to all other weapons.

Perhaps if the world becomes democratized and becomes averse to the contests of international power and prestige, a nuclear weapon-free world can develop. If such a global democratization and pacification were to be difficult to attain, however, we have not yet had to resign ourselves to nuclear war, or to endless nuclear proliferation. And we may not even have to resign ourselves to living perpetually under a conscious threat and presence of nuclear weapons.

10. The role of hegemonies and alliances

Harald Müller

I. Introduction

In a world of states security problems abound. The security dilemma is one of the most pertinent features of international politics: given the incalculability of present and future intentions of neighbouring governments in a world system which lacks a supreme authority, states can never be sure whether their existence and survival is, or will be, threatened by powerful and possibly malevolent neighbours. This basic condition exists in nuclear as well as in non-nuclear worlds. States have to cope with this existential fact, and hegemonies and alliances are the result of such efforts to find ways to achieve security.[1]

This chapter reviews the promise of hegemonies and alliances for supplying security to states in nuclear and non-nuclear environments. First, some basic definitions of our main terms are proposed. Then, hegemonies and alliances are reviewed in two separate sections. Each section addresses four questions:

1. What is known from previous theoretical and empirical work about the roles, structures, and dynamics of hegemonies and alliances, respectively?

2. What is the role of nuclear weapons in each structure?

3. How would non-nuclear hegemonies and alliances fare? Here the problem of stability and instability of the structure will be at the centre of consideration.

4. What are the conditions for non-nuclear security?

II. Definitions

Hegemonies and alliances share several attributes. Both are agglomerations of nation-states. Both establish a certain order among states. Both react to the anarchy in the international system, but both go beyond anarchy to create islands of ordered relationships among members of the system. And both, to a certain degree, rely on voluntary compliance rather than on forced submission. In that regard, they are distinct from another form of order, empires or *imperiums*. Resting on strict power-based hierarchy, the dominant state in empires/*imperiums* rules directly in the subject territories. It matters little whether such rule is enforced through puppet regimes, colonial troops, or direct

---

[1] Hertz, J., *International Politics in the Atomic Age* (Columbia University Press: New York, 1959); Buzan, B., *People, States and Fear: The National Security Problem in International Relations* (Wheatsheaf Books: Brighton, UK, 1983); Jervis, R., Cooperation under the security dilemma, *World Politics*, vol. 30, no. 2 (Jan. 1978), pp. 167–214; Waltz, K., *Theory of International Relations* (Random House: New York, 1979).

integration into the core imperial state. What is decisive in empires/*imperiums* is the immediacy of force or threat of force which provides the principle of order among the territories concerned.[2]

This is not the case for either hegemonies or alliances. In hegemonies, there is a well-defined hierarchy based on an asymmetric distribution of resources. The hegemon leads because it is wealthier, more efficient and, after all, more powerful. Alliances, in contrast, may be concluded among equals or they may be asymmetric. The decisive point is voluntary accession and the possibility of secession. Participation is judged on the basis of the security it produces for each single member.[3]

In a hegemony, however, resources are important. The preponderance of the hegemon enters into the cost-benefit calculation of every state in the hegemonic order. Hegemonies comprise a vast continuum. In some types, the hidden possibility of the hegemon's enforcing compliance may border closely at principles of empire. In other types, the hegemon might be happily exploited by the smaller participants in a hegemonic order (see below).

The main difference between hegemonies and alliances in terms of the security supplied is that the former are inclusive while the latter are exclusive. Hegemonies produce security for their members against each other; the efforts of the hegemon, the incentives and disincentives, carrots and sticks provided by its labours, prevent the members of the hegemonic system from getting at each other's throat. An alliance, in contrast, is directed against a party outside the alliance. Security is provided for the members of the alliance not with regard to each other, but against a third party.

III. Hegemonies

What do we know?

Hegemonies[4] emerge among unequals. One state acquires preponderant resources in either a specific issue-area or across all relevant political fields. In the present analysis, the point of interest is security. Hegemons are preponderant in security terms within the environment in which the hegemony operates. That is, they possess a military force strong enough to bolster confidence among all members of the hegemonic system; therefore, no other state could challenge the hegemon successfully. Hegemons may also dispose of additional, particularly economic, resources to offer as incentives for compliance and to be able to threaten deviators with unacceptable costs in case of non-compliance. Beyond that, the diplomatic–communicative resources of the hegemon must be considerable in order to foresee conflicts, to deploy mediators for settlement and to keep balances among competing partners in place.

---

[2] Doyle, M. W., *Empires* (Cornell University Press: Ithaca, N.Y. and London, 1986).

[3] Mares, D. M., Middle powers under regional hegemony: to challenge or acquiesce in hegemonic enforcement, *International Studies Quarterly*, vol. 32, no. 4 (1988), pp. 453–71.

[4] Keohane, R. O., *After Hegemony* (Princeton University Press: Princeton, N.J., 1984).

Security in hegemonies is a public good. It is provided for a certain region and no one inside this region can be excluded from enjoying its fruits. Not everybody, however, is forced to contribute to the common good. Smaller states can escape all obligations to contribute. The hegemon commands superior resources but has also the most to lose; it thus possesses a superior interest in preserving peace and stability in its environment, and is compelled to produce the common good on its own even without the support of others.[5]

The possible costs to the hegemon, however, vary greatly. Theoretical and empirical inquiries in the sphere of the world economy have revealed a rather broad spectrum of possible hegemonic orders. For our purposes it suffices to present two contrasting possibilities: 'benign' and 'malign' hegemonies.

In a benign hegemony, the hegemony gives its efforts for free. Peace and stability are of such great value to the hegemonic state that it does not worry about 'burden sharing' and the like. The smaller members can enjoy peace, without being asked to pay their share for the common good. The hegemon, in other words, is happily exploited by the community of states within the region.

In a malign hegemony, the picture is quite different. As briefly mentioned above, such a system may closely resemble an empire/*imperium* type of structure. Security is certainly provided by the hegemon. But the costs extracted from the participants are high. The hegemon does not give its efforts for free. It employs its power simultaneously to exploit the smaller states in the system. For them, the cost-benefit calculus still advises participation. The hegemon does not need to threaten force, nor does it necessarily consider doing so. On the other hand, consideration of the superior military posture and resources of the mightiest power enters inevitably the decision-making process of the other participants concerning the issue of whether to quit or to continue to participate in the hegemony.[6]

Under these circumstances, benign and malign hegemonies can take considerably different trajectories. Their dynamics, in other words, are not the same.

In a malign hegemony, smaller states have reasons to take precautions against the possibility of the hegemon developing imperialist ambitions. Simultaneously, a situation of exploitation will breed misgivings and resentment among the governments of smaller states as well as within their populations; popular resentment, in turn, will persuade governments to take a more assertive attitude. A malign hegemonic system, thus, engenders an inherent tendency of in-built tension. Over the long run, individual participants, or major groups of them, may try to 'gang up' against the hegemon; the seeds for regional conflict or an arms race are thus laid. Consequently, states may even seek outside assistance to prevent unwanted incursions by the hegemon into their internal affairs. The

[5] Olson, M., *The Logic of Collective Action* (Harvard University Press: Cambridge, Mass., 1965); hegemonic stability theory was first elaborated in political economy, see Kindleberger, C. A., 'Systems of international economic organization', D. Calleo (ed.), *Money and the Coming World Order* (New York University Press: New York, 1976).

[6] Francis, M. J., *The Limits of Hegemony* (University of Notre Dame Press: Notre Dame, Ind., 1979); Mares (note 3).

hegemonic system, thus, breaks up into that of a dominant regional power and a balancing alliance.

The Delian League presents a historical example for such dynamics. It started as a hegemonic alliance (see below) against the threat of a Persian invasion. With the Persian threat receding, it evolved as a regional hegemony, with Athens presiding over a considerable degree of order. However, the Athenian appetite grew with the rising costs of the hegemony, and the emergence of an outside challenge by Sparta to Athens' preponderance. More and more, Athens intervened in local domestic disputes to grant continued governance by its own allies. The hegemony changed from benign to malign. Several allies now looked to Sparta as a counterweight as Athens' hand became ever more heavy. With the seizure of the common treasure, and the forced prevention of several allies seeking exit, it emerged as an *imperium*. Malign hegemonies, it may be concluded, are not particularly stable security arrangements. Stability, in the long run, may come at the cost of considerable suppression and dissatisfaction.[7] Hegemons, as imperial powers, are in a permanent danger of overstretching their resources. As these resources are extended to provide 'peace' to ever greater areas and/or against ever stronger challenges, their capabilities shrink compared to the tasks they are supposed to accomplish; hegemonies then cease to function as security-supplying systems.[8]

What, then, about benign hegemonies? As there is a continuous outflow of 'investment' in security and incentives by the hegemon, stability can only be achieved if the hegemon's resources remain superior. This cannot be taken for granted in the first place; economic, social, political and technological development are unequal across nations across time. Whoever stands at the top at a given time may find himself overtaken some decades later. Moreover, in benign hegemonies, special laws of unequal development apply. As stated, the hegemon is expected to invest considerable value in maintaining the system, while minor powers ride free. Thus, other states are free to invest in those sectors most amenable to spur further development, without the strings and burdens of hegemonic leadership. Unequal development may thus assume a bias against the hegemon. As in the malign variant, the benign hegemon, by over-stretching its own resources to preserve hegemony and peace and stability, causes the decay of the system. Benign hegemonies may last for a while, but from a historical perspective they are likely to represent a phase of history at best and a shorter transitional period in most cases.[9]

The role of nuclear weapons

How do nuclear weapons affect this analysis? First of all, only marginally. By definition, the hegemon is superior in resources. Whether it possesses nuclear

---

[7] See the first chapter of Thucydides, *The History of the Peloponnesian War*, translated with an introduction by R. Warner (Penguin: Harmondsworth, UK, 1968).

[8] Gilpin, R., *War and Change in World Politics* (Cambridge University Press: Cambridge, 1981); Kennedy, P., *The Rise and Fall of the Great Powers* (Random House: New York, 1987).

[9] Francis (note 6).

weapons or not, does not change this situation fundamentally. Nuclear weapons, and threats therewith, are utterly unfit to keep or enforce peace among third parties. If the instruments of persuasion fail, the quick intervention force is far more capable to prevent war in a crisis or to guarantee a cease-fire if war breaks out.

A nuclear threat in any kind of hegemonic system against one of its members would undermine the very rationale of hegemony: voluntary compliance. A challenger so dissatisfied as to provoke a conflict with a vastly superior hegemon can only emerge in hegemonies which already bear signs of decay. If only nuclear weapons can prevent such challenges from emerging, the degree of tension, instability, dissatisfaction and desire for change must be very high. On the other hand, the state threatened by a hegemon's nuclear weapons would inevitably retain the worst possible misgivings and fears of the future. This state could not fail to seek protection against a repetition of such a situation. A hegemony in which nuclear weapons were employed as means to preserve stability and security for the whole, thus, would inevitably degenerate into the malign version, with decay as its very likely near future.

Nuclear weapons may be held as a symbol of preponderance, as the insignia of leadership and achievement. They may also serve to protect the hegemonic area against menaces from outside, but this is not the function of hegemony *per se*. This function falls within the purview of alliance.

However, if more than one nuclear weapon state exists within a hegemonic region, nuclear weapons may contribute to stratification of the system. The internal structure of the North Atlantic Treaty Organization (NATO) is a case in point. NATO is usually regarded as an alliance with justification. However, as Josef Joffe has convincingly argued, NATO has also been a hegemonic system whereby the United States helped to mitigate conflict and to prevent the re-emergence of a pre-1914 pattern among its European allies.[10] Within this hegemony, French and British nuclear weapons have helped to create structures of order. It gave the two minor nuclear weapon states a certain status distinct from the rest, particularly the Federal Republic of Germany. By other means this status would not have existed. The declining French and British empires were a source of pity rather than of status or even admiration by others. The French and British economies were outpaced by that of the FRG. To preserve an intra-European balance (in addition to the Atlantic distribution of power centred on the USA), German economic preponderance was countered, although at a high cost, by French and British nuclear status. Presumably, within hegemonies, this kind of function is the only tangible role nuclear weapons can play.

[10] Joffe, J., 'America: Europe's pacifier', *Foreign Policy*, no. 14 (spring 1984), pp. 64–82

Hegemonies in the present world—a brief overview

In today's world, it is possible to identify one relatively benign regional hegemony, the USA in North America. It plays the same role (in the double-function as a main ally and regional hegemon) in Western Europe. Nigeria in West Africa may fulfil such a role *in nascendo*, although the repeated actions by France would suggest that it is more a theoretical possibility than an actual function by the most resource-rich West African state.

Among these cases, only in Western Europe do nuclear weapons play a visible role in maintaining or modifying hegemony. In North America, the USA would be the preponderant giant anyway. In West Africa, Nigeria of course is a non-nuclear weapon state and is likely to remain one. In Europe, US nuclear strength transfers legitimacy from the alliance to the hegemonic relationship—a rather unique feature. Besides, as discussed, nuclear weapons contribute to the specific stratification of the region. Still, the overall role is limited.

South Africa and South Asia are plagued by what one may call malign hegemonies. The republic of South Africa has managed, by military and economic superiority and the successful application of force, to persuade its neighbours to restrict their adversarial relationship even before the return of Namibia to independence. Compliance by the front-line states with the wishes of the apartheid regime, particularly in the economic sector, was considerable given the harsh anti-apartheid rhetoric and diplomatic efforts by the very same governments. The structure of the region left little other choice than to appease, to a certain degree, Pretoria.

In all this, South Africa's nuclear option appears to have played only a minor role. The resources on which Pretoria could rely were, first, its overwhelming economic superiority, and, second, its better trained and equipped élite forces. The nuclear option was more a bargaining chip towards the Western nations than an instrument of preserving hegemony in the region. Against whom would a threat or even the employment of an uranium fission weapon be considered? For what political purpose? And the front-line states have quite logically although cautiously tried to counterbalance South Africa, first by building ties with the Soviet Union (and, to secure some conventional military aid, with Cuba) and, then, to rebuild relationships with the West. At present, the region is in the course of profound reconstruction; one would hope that the malign hegemony will evolve into a benign hegemony in the years to come, while the nuclear aspect will be safely contained in Non-Proliferation Treaty (NPT) membership for South Africa and all the front-line states.[11]

South Asia is the other place where a struggle emerges from a malign hegemonic system. That India is the major power on the subcontinent goes without saying. India, however, has not used its power in a considerate way. In addition to a good part of the Indian political élite not regarding Pakistan as a legitimate

[11] Fischer, D., 'South Africa', H. Müller (ed.), *A European Nonproliferation Policy: Prospects and Problems* (Oxford University Press: Oxford, 1987), pp. 291–321; Moore, J. D. L., *South Africa and Nuclear Proliferation* (Macmillan: London, 1987).

state, Indian endeavours in Sri Lanka, the refusal to agree to a negotiated regime for the distribution of the waters of the Ganges and the merciless trade war against tiny Nepal in 1989 were political moves not conducive to peaceful coexistence. The relentless buildup of military forces, including the development of a proficient high-tech weapons research, development and production establishment in a situation which outside observers would consider low-threat cannot but add to the fear among India's neighbours that the pattern of the Delian League is going to repeat itself. India has consciously played the nuclear instrument to assert its claim to regional hegemony, only to provoke desperate Pakistan into a high-risk race for nuclear capability. The nuclear option has thus done little to confirm hegemony; rather India risks facing the equalizing role of a nuclear option in a low-stability confrontation. India's non-nuclear resources alone would ensure that there was no serious competitor on the subcontinent. Again, Pakistan has tried to enter counterbalancing alliances, such as with the United States and China simultaneously.[12]

One could discuss the structure in Eastern Europe before the wave of revolutions in terms of hegemony. However, too much has since been revealed to keep this definition of the situation. In hindsight, those who have spoken of a Soviet empire rather than of hegemony were clearly closer to the truth.

Last, there are some potential hegemonic structures which should be quickly reviewed. In Europe, a unified Germany is certainly a possible hegemonic power for the area from the Atlantic Ocean to the Bug river. However, Europe is embedded in the transatlantic relationship, and the nuclear forces of France and Britain serve for the time being as an equalizer countering the foreseeable economic dominance of Germany. Beyond this balance—and this argument is dealt with in the last part of the chapter—the dense institutional network existing as well as emerging in Europe opens the spectre of a non-hegemonic security structure for the future.

In East Asia, Japan rather than China is a giant in the making. Japanese economic sources dwarf those of China, and Beijing's self-imposed politico-economic stagnation does not help to repair this disadvantage. No other state from the Bay of Bengal to the island of Sakhalin emerges as a serious competitor for a power-seeking Japan. Yet hegemony is not being realized. Three counterweights exist in the Soviet Union, China (by way of its small nuclear arsenal) and, first and foremost, the United States. Japan may play a constructive role within the region, and it is incrementally taking over a leading role in the sphere of the political economy of the region. Japan is not likely to emerge as a security supplier, however, as the shadows of the past are as strong in Asia as they are in Europe. The acquisition of nuclear weapons by Japan, if supported by the population and tolerated by the counterweights (both highly

[12] Braun, D. and Ziem, K., 'Die nukleare Komponente eines latenten wie akuten Regionalkonflikts: Indien/Pakistan', D. Senghaas (ed.), *Regionalkonflikte in der Dritten Welt. Autonomie und Fremdbestimmung* (Nomos: Baden-Baden, 1989).

questionable decisions) would not lead to hegemony but to a massive counter-balancing alliance.[13]

Asia harbours one other sleeping giant, Indonesia. If any country is able to set a boundary to Japanese domination (if the above-mentioned conditions were not present), it would be the resource- and population-rich archipelago. Indonesia shows both signs of economic–ecological–demographic stress and indications of the Asian way of development. Within the Association of Southeast Asian Nations (ASEAN) region, it may well become the dominant power. If so, nuclear weapons would play no role. And if Indonesia were ever to renounce its NPT membership, Australia would go a long way to remake ANZUS (Australia–New Zealand–USA) into a highly effective and reliable protecting alliance.

In the Middle East, where at present no hegemony, but rather a precarious and dangerous balance exists, Egypt appears to be the one country with the potential to acquire a hegemonic role in the distant future. Egypt is heading this way with a very pronounced renunciation of nuclear weapons. It plays on its strategic location, size and population, and key role within the Arab world. It tries consciously to make a diplomatic asset out of its non-nuclear status, and to use this asset (within the G-77 members of the NPT as well as *vis-à-vis* Washington) to foster its leading role within the region. Israel, on the other hand, possesses a nuclear arsenal and a proven professionalism in conventional operations, yet it lacks the resources to establish a true hegemony, as no Arab state would voluntarily subject itself to rules defined in either Tel Aviv or Jerusalem.[14]

In South America, Brazil would certainly be the primary candidate for hegemon status. Yet security problems in this part of the world do not abound, at least not between states (but rather within). An over-aspiring Brazil might be the only possibility to upset the region sufficiently to look for any serious security arrangement. The drive towards hegemony, then, would presumably lead immediately to counterbalancing efforts. As for the nuclear component, whatever Brazil does is being and will be neutralized by the nuclear–technological proficiency of its neighbour. Argentina will not permit a nuclear-armed Brazil to achieve a monopoly in South America. At present, collaboration between both countries does speak against the emergence of any clear-cut hegemony; in any event, the Brazilian élites, with the military on top, has displayed a rather unique capability of wasting the country's wealth for either leisure or prestige. This habit, above everything else, bodes ill for achieving hegemony.[15]

This review of present or potential hegemonies in the world confirms the theoretical argument that nuclear weapons do not play a predominant role in the

[13] Mack, A. and Keal, P., *Security and Arms Control in the North Pacific* (Allen and Unwin: Sydney, 1988).
[14] Bhatia, S., *Nuclear Rivals in the Middle East* (London and New York, 1988); Ehteshami, Anoushiravan, *Nuclearisation of the Middle East* (London, 1989); Nashif, T. N., *Nuclear Warfare in the Middle East: Dimensions and Responsibilities* (Princeton, N. J., 1984).
[15] Mares (note 3).

peace-preserving practice of hegemonies. To reiterate, the question here concerns the supply of security for those states inside the hegemony, not the protection of the hegemonic system against threats from abroad (see below). Nuclear weapons or capabilities in present and potential hegemonies may serve to identify the hegemonic power or to establish stratification within the hegemonic system. Those are symbolic order-functions which contribute nothing or only marginally to actual security.

How would non-nuclear conditions affect hegemonies?

At first glance, one should expect that presence or absence of nuclear weapons would not change the picture considerably. This is certainly the case as long as hegemonies remain stable. But, as discussed above, this condition cannot be taken for granted. Internal dynamics of both benign and malign hegemonies suggest that this form of security order will not last forever. This certain lack of stability, in turn, influences the security choices of countries, including considerations to acquire nuclear weapons.

In the middle term, only the benign hegemony is capable of certain stability under non-nuclear conditions: that is, it provides a security environment peaceful enough for its members to forego any nuclear option. As the hegemon is both non-threatening and a reliable supplier of security, there is no need for the member states to strive for alternative instruments of security.

However, to maintain this promising pattern, precautions must be taken for two distant possibilities which, although they may not come to pass, will be in the minds of decision-makers of the minor participants in the hegemonic order.

First, the possibility of the hegemon's turning from benign to malign must be addressed. The domestic political structure of the hegemonic power must display ironclad assurances that such a change of policy can be excluded. It is not completely clear whether any order would provide such clear-cut assurances. Democracy, of course, has the advantages of transparency and inertia. Political changes take place, but they gravitate around the centre and are carried to the extremes only rarely. The larger the state, it appears, the less likely a sudden shift, because the weight of domestic institutions granting inertia is so much stronger. For additional assurances, close relationships between all participants in the system are essential. A network of institutions and organizations would facilitate the buildup of balancing alliances if something went wrong with the hegemon, and it would also permit steps to draw the hegemon into alternative structures of security should it show signs of changing benign behaviour.

The second possibility to take precautions against is, of course, the decay of the hegemonic structure. If the pacifying hegemonic overlay disappears, or is about to disappear, states will be pushed back to an 'anarchic' nation-state world. The instinct to acquire security by self-help, regional alliances, or alliance with an extra-regional power will be strong.[16] If old rivalries reappear, the danger of arms races looms large.

An argument used throughout the rest of the chapter concerns the course of arms races to be expected in an institution-free conflictual relationship. As with any serious security dilemma among states that is not mitigated by hegemony, alliances with a superpower or reliable security regimes, the logic of war as analysed by Clausewitz applies to arms races: left to their own devices, the interaction of nation-states in an arms competition will tend towards the extremes, that is, towards the acquisition of the most powerful and proficient weapons of an age.[17] This course of affairs is impeded by diverse sources of 'friction', most prominently the limits of financial resources, but also techno-logical failure, bureaucratic ineptitude and the idiosyncrasies of the political process. Nevertheless, over the long run the race will approach the outer limit.[18] By implication, this means that in regions where hegemonies are lost and a revival of interstate rivalries occurs, the non-nuclear status of the region will not last forever.

As in the first case, transparency of domestic decision-making processes and the existence of a dense network of interstate relations are the best prerequisites for maintaining security. It is thus not enough to point to the vast superiority of a hegemonic state in order to prove the lasting stability of a non-nuclear secur-ity structure. The domestic as well as the international institutions within and among the participating states are an important ingredient of a hegemonic security system because they represent the assurance for some stability even under conditions of change.[19]

In malign hegemonies, the picture is necessarily bleaker. Smaller states must live in permanent fear that the hegemon may change from hegemonic to imperialist. There is little room to accommodate dissatisfied middle powers, and attempts by some states to improve their positions are likely to be countered by the distrusting hegemon. For these reasons, disturbing moves are to be expected from the smaller powers. First, there is the option of national, self-help armament. As states are facing a hegemon, that is, a more resourceful power by definition, there is a certain likelihood that governments may look for an 'equalizer'. Obviously, nuclear weapons are often ascribed an equalizing effect among states of different size and wealth, be this assumption right or wrong. The hegemon, then, cannot be expected to stand by idly while a smaller

---

[16] Waltz (note 1).

[17] von Clausewitz, C., *Vom Kriege* (Frankfurt, 1980), book 1, chapters 1 and 2, and book 8, chapters 1 and 2.

[18] Buzan, B., *An Introduction to Strategic Studies: Military Technology and International Relations*, (Macmillan: London, 1987); Müller, H., 'Technologie und Sicherheitspolitik. Der Einfluß von technischem Wandel auf Strategie und Rüstungskontrolle', C. Hacke and M. Knapp (ed.), *Friedenssicherung und Rüstungskontrolle in Europa* (Wissenschaft und Politik: Köln, 1989), pp. 173–209.

[19] Keohane, R. O., *International Institutions and State Power* (Westview Press: Boulder, Colo., 1989); Keohane, R. O. and Nye, J. S., 'Power and interdependence revisited', *International Organization*, vol. 41, no. 4 (autumn, 1987), pp. 726–53.

challenger is arming itself with nuclear weapons. South Asia gives us an example for the dynamics of such a process (see above).

Second, the possibility of alliance with external powers must be considered. In a competition between alliances, or between an alliance and a hegemon, the dynamics of arms races in high-threat environments as discussed above apply. Such a race is quite likely to result in a nuclear stalemate over the long run. Again, the malign hegemony is likely not to rest in a non-nuclear status.

Conditions for non-nuclear stability: some conclusions

In light of the above discussion, it is unlikely that a malign hegemony can maintain non-nuclear status for long. Either the hegemony turns into imperialism (to prevent smaller challengers from going nuclear) or there will be a regional or supra-regional arms race towards nuclear capabilities.

In benign hegemonies, the first condition is a vast and lasting superiority of resources on part of the hegemon. In addition, the neighbour's interests must be well presented in the hegemon's political system and properly taken into account in its decision-making process. Ironically, these conditions are not so easily met in a hegemonic democracy. The political system of a hegemonic power must be assumed to be extensive; the amount of domestic demands is thus very large, and a good deal of attention is always turning inwards. Moreover, many requests from abroad will meet competing demands from within, and decision-making processes usually contain an inbuilt bias in favour of domestic demands. While democracy meets two other prerequisites of non-nuclear hegemonic stability rather well—transparency and reliability due to basic inertia—the requirement of responsiveness to foreign countries' demands is not easy to implement. US post-war foreign policy is full of evidence for this assessment.[20]

Trust in the persistent benevolence of the hegemon requires that its behaviour be rule-bound. The existence of rule-making and maintaining institutions is thus necessary. A hegemon will only inspire the trust necessary for long-term nuclear abstention by its friends if it cedes some degree of its sovereignty to regimes or supranational organizations.

Can such a hegemony stand the pressure coming from a hostile world, even a world in which nuclear weapons still exist? This essential question is to be addressed in section V.

IV. Alliances

What do we know?

It is useful to remember that alliances are not necessarily good. Alliances in history have been formed for conquest and booty. The Molotov–Ribbentrop

[20] Czempiel, E.-O., *Amerikanische Außenpolitik. Gesellschaftliche Anforderungen und politische Entscheidungen* (Kohlhammer: Stuttgart, 1979)

Pact is a case in point. For our discussion, this type of 'malign' alliance is not interesting. This chapter examines security structures, and malign alliances do not provide security as its main product, but expansion. Thus, for the rest of the chapter, the focus is on security alliances.

Such alliances have been formed in history to counterbalance a threat. While there are some cases where alliance served a 'bandwagon' function (i.e., where weaker states joined the preponderant power to profit from its superiority), in the overwhelming number of historical cases states joined forces or called in an external helper to balance the power of one or several stronger states in a region.[21]

The internal dynamics of alliances are characterized by the poles of fear of abandonment and entrapment. Allies must be afraid that their friends will leave them in the hour of truth. Many activities in alliance politics are devoted to insuring that abandonment cannot happen. Alliances have developed highly sophisticated symbolic and ritualistic practices to allay these fears, and NATO has been particularly inventive in this regard.

On the other hand, the interests of states differ. Even within an alliance, they will never completely overlap. Thus each ally risks being entangled, by its partners, in conflicts in which it has no tangible interest. Allies thus take precautions to prevent such entanglement from happening. US insistence on the Tropic of Cancer as NATO's outer boundary served as a precaution against entanglement in the colonial struggles of major European powers. The USA was also careful to contain Taiwan's ambitions at reconquest of the Chinese mainland. In turn, the USA's Western European allies proved highly reluctant to give a blank check to US out-of area operations in the 1980s.

Alliances change from the dominance of the problem of entrapment to the dominance of the problem of abandonment. First, the measures taken against each danger exacerbates the partner's fears that the other risk may be realized. Second, depending on events not controlled by the alliance, one or the other of the risks may loom larger. Third, domestic political cycles also cause shifts, as conservatives are usually more abandonment-conscious, while social democrats or left-of-centre liberals take entrapment threats more seriously.[22]

Geographical disparities exacerbate these alliance dynamics automatically. They widen the gap between the geopolitical interests of the allies and cut into the area of overlapping interests. Alliances that span wide geographic areas, therefore, are more subject to shattering entrapment–abandonment disputes than those confined to a range of neighbouring states in a region.[23]

Asymmetries among the allies will also tend to exacerbate alliance dynamics and they are likely to engender some additional difficulties. They aggravate the abandonment-entrapment fears on the part of the weaker allies, because they rely so much more on the protection by a superior power over whose political

[21] Walt, S. M., *The Origins of Alliances* (Cornell University Press: Ithaca, N.Y., 1987); Rothstein, R., *Alliances and Small Powers* (Columbia University Press: New York, 1968).
[22] Snyder, G., 'The security dilemma in alliance politics', *World Politics*, vol. 36, no. 4 (1984).
[23] Boulding, K. A., *Conflict and Defense: A General Theory* (Harper Torchbooks: New York, 1962).

considerations they exert relatively little influence. Smaller allies are keenly aware that their own value to the protector is less than the equivalent of the protector's importance to themselves. As a consequence, they believe that it is easier for the protector to quit if its interest perception changes. The eternal discussions in NATO about 'coupling' and the extraordinary nervousness in South Korea during the Carter years illustrate the degree of concern among smaller allies.

By the same token, entrapment risks are greater for smaller allies tied to a big power. A big power has interests extending beyond the region where the alliance applies. It is not likely to lend too much attention to the opinions of small states on matters beyond the alliance's limits. However, activities in such out-of-area situations may have repercussions on the security of the smaller allies.[24]

Finally, asymmetric alliances face the same public good dilemma as hegemonies. If the threat is the same throughout the alliance, smaller allies will be less inclined to contribute proportionally the same share as the major allies. In a hegemonic alliance, this means that the strongest ally will pay over proportionally for the common security. This is something not easily tolerated by the big ally's domestic constituency. Burden sharing, under these circumstances will be on the agenda permanently. However, as reducing the big ally's burden is a process indistinguishable from the first steps to leaving the alliance altogether, burden-sharing disputes always contain the seeds of an abandonment crisis, even if the fear is completely unsubstantiated. The internal dynamics of an asymmetric alliance with great geographic disparities are therefore complicated and conflictual. NATO is not even worst among these structures in this regard; the US–Israeli and US–Pakistani relationships show how the dynamics work in a higher-threat environment.[25]

The effects of nuclear weapons

In the post-war world, nuclear weapons worked as an essential instrument of counterbalancing supposed regional malign hegemonies or outright imperialism. It does not matter whether or not nuclear weapons, in effect, were needed for this balancing effect. It suffices that, in the minds of the overwhelming number of policy-makers involved in nuclear alliances, they played this role. As the main instruments of balancing, they acquired a special place in the symbolism and ritualism of alliances. For better or worse, nuclear weapons were identified as the main glue that held such alliances together. This worked positively and negatively; in NATO, deployment of new nuclear forces was seen by a majority as an instrument of coupling the United States to Europe. In ANZUS, the sovereign decision by New Zealand not to admit nuclear weapons

[24] Rothstein (note 21).
[25] Olson, M. and Zeckhauser, R., 'An economic theory of alliances', *Review of Economics and Statistics*, vol. 48 (1966), pp. 266–77; Lunn, S., *Burden-Sharing in NATO* (London 1983); Golden, J. R., *NATO Burden-Sharing: Risks and Opportunities* (Washington, DC, 1983).

on its territory and in its ports led to a dissolution of alliance ties. As noted above, the symbolic importance of nuclear arms also served the stratification of NATO.

Nuclear weapons exert an ambiguous effect on the entrapment–abandonment dilemma and the other difficulties plaguing alliances. They bridge geographical gaps and reduce the financial burden which would fall on the protector in a purely conventional high-threat environment. But they exacerbate the perceived effects of geographical difference: for the nuclear-armed protector, the existential threat of nuclear annihilation may exist only because of alliance entanglements. For the protected allies, the willingness of the big power to risk a regional nuclear war because of its possible limitation enhances entrapment fears. And turning this perspective top down, because of the risk of global nuclear war, smaller allies may fear that extended deterrence will not be upheld, while the protector may see the danger of anti-nuclear–pacifist desertion by smaller allies.[26]

Finally, nuclear weapons engender and influence the domestic debates of alliance partners. The debates start from two basic dilemmas of nuclear strategy for alliances comprising nuclear and non-nuclear weapon states. First, it is impossible to devise a strategy which guarantees coupling under all circumstances. The protector will always desire to reserve its final judgement whether, when and where to employ nuclear weapons. No sophisticated deployment scheme and no weapon technology will counteract this very natural political desire. Second, it is equally impossible to devise a strategy which will prevent the risk of the smaller allies becoming the nuclear battlefield—if for no other reasons than because the moves of the 'enemy' are not subject to the alliance's control. As NATO's history shows, an alliance can live with an implausible, unclear and contradictory strategy for a long period of time if it serves basic political purposes. However, domestic debates will inevitably identify the weaknesses and, informed by the partisan biases of domestic power contenders, emphasize one or the other aspect. Thus, nuclear weapons will, in times of crisis and tension, polarize domestic security debates, with the left turning anti-nuclear and the right calling for additional measures for 'coupling'. Faced with such contradictory requests, the alliance then passes through a very difficult period. Nuclear weapons, one can conclude, engender particular and unique problems of alliance legitimacy in domestic publics which, in turn, render consensus within the alliance more difficult to achieve and to maintain.[27]

Effects of a non-nuclear situation

Alliances are the answer of states to a threat. Without a threat—actual or at least potential—states would not feel compelled to counterbalance it. To discuss the possibility of a non-nuclear alliance as a stable guarantor of security

---

[26] Snyder (note 22).

[27] Risse-Kappen, T., *Null-Lösung. Entscheidungsprozesse zu den Mittelstreckenwaffen 1970–1987* (Campus: Frankfurt and New York, 1988).

assumes that at least a potential threat from somewhere is perceived by the actors.

Threats can vary in intensity and actuality across a broad continuum of possibilities. For analytic purposes, this chapter makes a distinction between a low/potential and a high/actual threat. In a low-threat environment, it is very unlikely that a serious challenge will emerge to any state's security. Yet since the basic security dilemma still exists, states feel more comfortable in taking certain precautions. In a high-threat environment, in contrast, conflict abounds, capabilities are available to start offensives, motivations are perceived to exist for aggression, and countermeasures to preserve one's own security are seen as an absolute priority of state policy.

In both threat environments, there is a considerable difference between nuclear and non-nuclear alliances. In a nuclear alliance, the non-nuclear contributions of smaller allies do not change the alliance's posture very much at the margin. Likewise, additions to enemy capabilities in the conventional sector may be disquieting as they can be viewed as a signal of malevolent intentions. However, the actual likelihood of war and aggression is hardly affected by such marginal changes. As the nuclear threat remains a fall-back option projecting the spectre of enormous devastation, the situation is relatively resistant against shifts in alliance postures and, consequently, in the national capabilities of all allies.[28]

In non-nuclear situations, however, the outlook changes considerably. Here, changes at the margin may effectively impact on the balance of forces between the competitors and on the strategic and tactical options available to either. The military capabilities of the alliances are seen more as additive and cumulative. As a result, sudden changes in policies, investments and military capabilities by individual allies may affect systemic security disproportionally. For the alliances themselves, security is far less a 'public good' as in the nuclear situation. There is a greater likelihood for a persistent effort at armaments within all states and, consequently, a harsher arms race between the alliances.

At this point, the low–high threat distinction becomes important. In a low-threat environment, the political mood in most states may provide sufficient inertia to weather the small shocks of individual changes, and to return to a stable and low armament growth security system. In a high-threat environment, the dynamics tend towards an accelerated arms race which will approach absolutes: that is, an arms race will proceed through an aggravated conventional buildup to the creation of standby nuclear capabilities to full-fledged nuclear forces. Non-nuclear alliances in high-threat environments are improbable as stable security arrangements. They are more likely to be transitional stages, tending towards nuclearization.

Low-level threat environments look more promising. Yet they face the problem of reversibility of the situation: by definition, some degree of threat exists.

[28] Jervis, R., *The Meaning of the Nuclear Revolution. Statecraft and the Prospect of Armaggedon*, (Cornell University Press: Ithaca, N. Y., 1989).

There is no guarantee that this threat will not turn, in the future, from low to high. If it does, the process outlined above applies. Even if it does not, some states may regard the risk high enough to take preventive steps; such steps will inevitably precipitate the arms race that could otherwise have been avoided and possibly by itself change the low-threat into a high-threat situation. Thus, while the lower degree of perceived threat is a necessary prerequisite for the maintenance of an alliance's non-nuclear weapon status, it is not in itself a sufficient guarantee for long-term stability.

How will the internal dynamics of an alliance be affected by *denuclearization*? On the positive side, the aggravation of nuclear entrapment fears should be lessened. The problems of inconsistency in strategy will presumably disappear as well. Consequently, domestic polarization and problems of legitimacy of alliance strategy should become less intractable.

On the negative side, the 'glue' effect of nuclear weapons would have to be substituted for by other means. An intensification of a more political level of communication, and the establishment of substitute symbols would be needed. Particular attention must be devoted to the risk of conservative alienation. Conservatives addicted to nuclear deterrence must believe in the status of low threat and must be convinced that precautions were taken against a reversal of the threat situation. Under these conditions, domestic polarization will be ameliorated. If not, a sizeable part of the domestic security community will be alienated from alliance policy, and the emergence of a nationally oriented defence ideology would be likely. This prospect advises approaching denuclearization, should it prove promising and realistic, in incremental steps and with all due precautions in order to preserve a healthy domestic consensus.

Conditions for non-nuclear stability: some conclusions

Non-nuclear alliances in a high-threat environment are not likely to last. First and foremost, then, a condition for non-nuclearism is thus the existence of only a low threat.

In low-threat environments, the crucial issue is that of reversibility. The prospect of a return, or a change, to conditions of high threat must be dealt with both within as well as outside the alliance.

In order to prevent the escalation of low-level threats, measures must be taken to address all open and latent political disputes in the region. Preventive dispute and crisis management procedures must exist, bridging the structures of existing alliances and linking potential enemies. The problem of reversibility must be further addressed by arms control/disarmament measures. The main goal here goes far beyond the production of balance or stability. Arms control, seen in this perspective, must create effective barriers for states to return to threatening postures. Although such barriers can never be absolute as long as considerable decision-making power still rests with the territorial state, they can help to eliminate all reasons for misperception and distrust, and to threaten penalties in case of breach which will automatically enter the deliberations of a government tempted to defect from established rules.

In a low-threat environment, there will be a certain tendency to let remaining military capabilities erode; 'standby' may become 'fall-away', particularly in democracies in which competing claims exist for scarce governmental funds. Yet, as a residual military establishment is widely seen as a necessary symbol of state sovereignty, and as the bureaucratic and status interests of those involved in military careers will struggle to maintain their assets, there exist countervailing powers in a society that tend to prevent or to slow down this path towards zero.

At least for advanced industrialized countries, the considerable resilience of the industrial base should not be underrated. As Buzan has convincingly shown, there is a certain military potential implied in every large, integrated industrial society possessing a high-tech potential.[29] Contrary to most conservative worst-case fears, strategic deception that lulls such a society into a deep sleep while neighbours arm or rearm is largely unlikely. Even in a low-threat environment, states will gather intelligence on the political structures, intentions and activities of each other. Indications for a return from low-threat to high-threat will be collected, evaluated and reacted to. Modern alliances tend to set up special bodies with the main mission of conducting continuing threat analysis. While these special bureaucracies often tend to overshoot in the direction of worst-case analysis, they provide a healthy antidote to the danger of over-complacency.

On the other hand, the residual potential of modern society points to a quite different problem: how can mutual fears be eliminated under such a permanent, if veiled, threat? A state with a well-developed civilian nuclear industry disposes undoubtedly of a basic capability to develop, in due time, nuclear weapons. If industrial activities include the full fuel cycle, enrichment, reprocessing and the recycling of plutonium, the time span required to convert civilian potentials into military assets will be as short as 12 months or even considerably shorter. The answer to this question (see below) lies largely in the creation of international institutions that: (a) create constraints for the unlimited freedom of actions for states to utilize these potentials at will; (b) set agreed rules for the size and specifics of such industrial operations; and (c) seek to establish a maximum of mutual confidence among states concerning the ways their industrial and civilian nuclear potentials are handled. Such institutions must be complemented by national and alliance policies that lend credibility to the claim of peaceful purposes. The combination of both approaches has been largely successful. It is not by chance that countries with high nuclear capabilities such as Canada, Switzerland or Sweden arouse no international concern, while the policies of Pakistan, India or Iraq do.

The second prerequisite is the availability of insurance against the possibility of reversal. It is at this point that the alliance may play its role in a non-nuclear

---

[29] Buzan (note 18).

security system. An alliance can present the framework for insurance, if the threat re-emerges. It gives individual states the option of counterbalancing a threat in the transitional period before the security environment returns to a nuclear status. As argued above, arms races in high-threat environments will tend towards nuclearization. Alliances provide conventional assurances for this transitional process and also serve as a pool of common resources which could be seen as a standby capability for return to a nuclear posture should the need arise. Such a standby capability is easier to achieve for a group of states than for one state alone, although mutual trust even among allies is notoriously compromised when it comes to nuclear guarantees.

V. Security regimes as prerequisites for a non-nuclear world

The above discussion suggests that non-nuclear alliances would not suffice as security systems even under conditions of a low-level threat. What is required is an institutionalized security environment within which the alliance is able to play its residual role. In other words, the alliance must be embedded in security regimes which address grievances, sources of misperception and the military posture of states in the most comprehensive way possible.

Regimes have attracted considerable attention in the academic debate on international co-operation in the past. The bulk of this discussion, however, has focused on the international political economy. Nevertheless, the concept of regime is equally applicable in the security field.

Regimes are international institutions—not organizations—that is, they represent rule-directed patterned behaviour by the actors in a given field of policy. They possess an elaborated structure consisting of: (a) general principles, which define the basic variables in the political field, state the causal relationships between those variables, and note the agreed objectives sought by the regime participants; (b) norms, which contain general prescriptions and tell right from wrong behaviour; and (c) rules, which lay out specific prescriptions and proscriptions for specific situations, and procedures for entry, exit, decision-making, allocation of costs and benefits, consultation, information exchange, verification and the like. This structure may be formal or informal, sanctioned by treaties, based on gentlemen's agreements, or simply rest on a tacit understanding. It may be supported by an international organisation or solely rely on the actions of participating states.

Regimes thus fall somewhere between pure anarchy and world government. States preserve their sovereignty, yet they constrain themselves by entering a regime. Part of their decisions are then bound by their commitment to the rules; in this sense, they move from total to bounded sovereignty, but without renouncing their basic character as nation-states.

Within a network of security regimes, alliances may function as residual suppliers of security; their profile will be far more low-key than in an institution-free, anarchic world. But, of course, it is necessary to bind alliance decisions and behaviour equally strongly as are the decisions and behaviour of states.

Regimes rarely cover a whole area of policy. There are no world economic regimes, but individual, interconnected regimes for monetary relations, trade, telecommunications, shipping, and so on. Similarly, no regime is likely to deal with security at large; the international discussion on security regimes has been misled, unfortunately, by one of the first serious works on the subject endeavouring to identify such an all-encompassing security regime. Rather, security regimes deal with more specific aspects of security; there is a well-developed superpower regime for preventing nuclear war, consisting of more than a dozen individual agreements. There is a well-developed regime for nuclear non-proliferation and a more rudimentary one dealing with strategic nuclear weapons. Since 1975, there has also been a regime on territorial issues in Europe which has worked well and has facilitated maintaining stability despite the breathtaking changes of 1989 and 1990. Thus, there is no security regime but several regimes; the more combinations of such regimes cover the whole area of security, and the better and the more organically they are interconnected, the more stable and reliable the security environment is likely to become.

After all, the fundamental objective of regime-building is to reduce uncertainty in competitive situations, to create stable expectations about the behaviour of the competitors, to reduce the likelihood of unwelcome surprises, to enhance transparency and thereby coincidence and trust, to provide regular channels of communication for routine as well as for crisis exchanges, and to bind national decision-making into a transnational web of norms and rules.

All these functions of regimes help to mitigate our basic problem: reversibility. Security regimes reduce the incentives for changing a non-aggressive policy; they diminish the security dilemma by providing vastly more information; and they establish considerably higher barriers to policy changes by the sheer inertia of institutional entanglements.

In order to function as the proper environment for non-nuclear security policies, the requirements for security regimes are rather high. First of all, they must be comprehensive. All relevant fields of security matters must be covered. Any open gap through which security competition could be pursued in a rule-free way would contribute to enhancing the security dilemma, with the consequences of arms races (or territorial control races) discussed above. Comprehensiveness of the regime network, on the other hand, not only produces the necessary confidence in the security structure, it also directs the behaviour of the whole domestic security establishment towards rule-guided behaviour, and makes them interested in strengthening and upholding these rules.

Second, they must be unambiguous. The practice of leaving open routes of escape, evasion and circumvention, for the sake of securing competitive advantages or to satisfy certain domestic constituencies, which has been so frequent in past arms control agreements, is not tolerable.

Third, participation must be complete. In a given region with common security problems, all states—or at least all major and middle-sized states—must participate (CSCE could operate without the participation of Albania). Free-riders could shatter a regime by deviant behaviour.

As a minimum condition for non-nuclear security structures, the following fields must be covered by regimes: (a) territorial disputes and ways of their settlement; (b) treatment of national minorities; and (c) crisis management.

In addition, the following aspects of a military posture must be addressed: (a) the production of fissile nuclear material; (b) conventional postures (troops, armament levels and arms quality) and conventional arms production; (c) operational practices; (d) military R&D; (e) force planning and military budgeting; and (f) strategy and doctrine.

For such a comprehensive network of overlapping regimes, transparency and trust in deliberate domestic decision-making processes are required.[30] Security regimes of this kind are thus more likely to function in a region of democratic states than in an environment of military or other dictatorships. Breaches of the rules will be exposed to the public by the investigating press and by ever-distrusting peace groups and arms control associations. The competitive political system will automatically expose governments to public criticism by the opposition if they obviate international obligations. The constituency of international agreements within an administration has chances to assert its position in the intra-bureaucratic struggle.

There are two ways to approach the process of regime-building, the systematic way and the way of opportunity. In a systematic way, the main issues at stake would be addressed first. Usually, those are the political quarrels that underlie nuclear arms races. It has been argued correctly that without such underlying disagreements, states would not arm against each other in the first place. While this argument holds merit in theory, it underrates the weight of the security dilemma whereby a mixture of uncertainty and mistrust drives states against each other even in the absence of major quarrels. It is also likely that the main issues at dispute will be far easier to resolve if a certain basis of mutual confidence already exists.

For this reason, it is more promising to start in fields that may be less important but easier to handle, where mutual interests are more obvious and solutions are simple. This history of US–Soviet nuclear arms control gives some hints that this process can work indeed. Regimes for the prevention of accidental nuclear war and for the non-proliferation of nuclear weapons preceded the attempts to curb the unlimited growth of offensive and defensive nuclear weapons. The 'channelling' of the nuclear arms race in the SALT I Treaties, in

[30] Jervis, R., 'Security regimes', *International Organisation*, vol. 36 (1982), pp. 357–78; Nye, J. S., 'Nuclear Learning and the evolution of U.S.–Soviet security competition', G. T. Allison and W. L. Ury (eds), *Windows of Opportunity: From Cold War to Peaceful Competition in U.S.–Soviet Relations*, (Ballinger: Cambridge, Mass., 1989), pp. 131–62.

turn, was the first step on a way towards real limits or even reductions under the INF and START treaties. On the basis of the first regimes, more far-reaching issues such as the territorial integrity of post-war Europe (CSCE) could be addressed, and thereby an issue that was very much at the heart of basic fears existing in the Soviet Union and Eastern Europe. The regime-building between East and West has contributed considerably, through 25 years of ups and downs, to the softening-up of enemy images that helped to produce more decisive changes at the end of the 1980s.

This process may take different forms in other parts of the world. In South Asia, the Pakistani–Indian agreement to abstain from the destruction of each other's nuclear facilities—military as well as civilian—can be seen as the very first step on the road towards mutual confidence. In South America, it started with civilian co-operation agreements between Argentina and Brazil, progressed towards the ritualization of high-level mutual visits to the most sensitive nuclear facilities in both countries, and is presently arriving at a comprehensive regime of bilateral and international safeguarding of these plants.

In this process, the relationship between emerging regimes is undoubtedly interdependent. They support each other by producing an environment of increasing clarity, certainty and thus confidence. The great advantage of the process is, however, that this interdependence does not necessarily mean that the whole building must crumble with the first stone. Regime-building decomposes a complex conflict situation into different, specific fields of policy. These fields remain interdependent, but they can progress at different speeds.[31] Some regimes may suffer setbacks, while others still witness progress. Of course, there are limits to this tolerance, but there is no way to define these limits generally; during the period of the first Reagan Administration, when nuclear arms control was at its lowest point since it earnestly began, co-operation in the field of nuclear non-proliferation still continued, and the 'red line' was even improved in 1983. This shows the resilience of the process of regime-building; but of course, it could not survive a shift in the priorities of one of the partners from co-operation to expansionism, to use an extreme example. It continues throughout to rest on the mutual insight in shared interests.

VI. Global conditions for non-nuclear security systems

Alliances and hegemonies have been discussed for certain regions. This pays tribute to the fact that security issues nowadays are shaped very much in a regional framework.[32] However, it would be a mistake to neglect the influence of extra-regional factors on the specific security area under consideration. First, regional security systems may overlap. Iraq, for example, is part of the near east security system; second, it belongs to the Middle East/Persian Gulf security

---

[31] Rittberger, V. (ed.), *International Regimes in East–West Politics* (London, 1990).
[32] See the examples in Senghaas (note 12); and Senghaas, D., *Konfliktformationen im internationalen System* (Suhrkamp: Frankfurt, 1988)

region where it faces Iran. Iran, in turn, borders Afghanistan and Pakistan, members of the South Asian region. Similarly, the southern European countries are certainly part of the European theatre. At the same time, they face the southern fringe of the Mediterranean; this includes the Near East, one of the most volatile and conflictual regions of the Earth. It also includes the Mahgreb, with its high population growth and inherent instability. Finally, the Soviet Union, with its vast extension over two continents is a European, an East Asian and a Middle Asian power. It impacts on the European security scene, is a main player in the balance that affects China, the Koreas and Japan, and suffers all the uncertainties and potential instabilities emerging from the unruly states of Islam.

These examples have been discussed extensively in order to demonstrate the main argument: the security policy process in neighbouring regions does not necessarily proceed at the same pace and not even in the same direction. A region may be isolated for a while, but not eternally. Exceptions may be regions without natural wealth, strategic minerals, and a geostrategically important location. But such regions are rarely of sufficient interest to hegemons, and few major powers would offer an alliance except when they discover an enemy's presence. For most regions of this interdependent world, however, isolation is not a long-term perspective.

Two conclusions result from this discussion of non-nuclear hegemonies and alliances. Where contact with other conflictual regions imports conflict to a region with a relatively calm setting, stability may be upset. If the countries in a hegemony want to preserve their system, they have to take precautions against undesired intrusions: in other words, the hegemony will become an alliance against the external threat. In this function, it will be subject to the same dynamics as are all alliances. Either the external threat is limited in conventional terms and unlikely to evolve into a proto-nuclear rivalry—maybe for lack of technological proficiency within the bordering region—or certain precautionary measures (such as early warning and greater mobility of conventional forces in direction of the threat) will suffice to preserve the desired degree of security.

An even better alternative would be to apply the model discussed for alliances under the umbrella of a co-operative, security-regime overlay. The old hegemony would then function like the alliance within this model, as a residual insurance against unforeseeable instabilities. Unfortunately, in the real world, the prospect for this scenario is bleak. Cultural differences at the fringes of existing security systems, differentials in the intensity and ferocity of conflicts and, last but not least, a different stage of democratic development make it unlikely that what may appear possible at regional levels will easily transfer to supra-regional conflict spaces.[33]

---

[33] Senghaas (note 30); Mohammed Ayoob, 'The Third World in the system of states: acute schizophrenia or growing pains?', *International Studies Quarterly*, vol. 33, no., 1 (1989), pp. 67–79; Doyle, M. W., 'Liberalism and world politics', *American Political Science Review*, vol. 80, no. 4 (1986); Rittberger, V., 'Zur Friedensfähigkeit von Demokratien', *Politik und Zeitgeschichte*, B44 (1987), pp. 3–12

If we take a slightly different perspective and discuss the security problem for a non-nuclear alliance which exists in a wider security system, a surprising conclusion follows. As the established system promises a higher level of security than the bordering regions, all inhabitants of this system, including those who may still harbour residual fears against each other, share the interest to prevent external incursions into their space of peace. In this sense, the security system comprising sub-alliances to contain troubles from within may emerge as a super-alliance to contain troubles from outside.

This conclusion becomes ever more evident if we change from the assumption of a non-nuclear external security environment to a proto-nuclear or a real nuclear one. It is unlikely that a non-nuclear security space, be it a hegemony or a sub-systemic alliance, can preserve its non-nuclear status for long. If the nuclear capabilities of the outer world are latent, the imperative to maintain a standby capability remains strong. If one or more outside powers are openly armed with nuclear weapons, the alliance, hegemony or security superstructure will sooner or later try to be able to neutralize potential threats from abroad. While regime-governed behaviour may prevent all necessity for nuclear armament within, this serene status may require a deterrent against outside threats, if not in reality then in the minds of government leaders and people of the pacified region.

VII. Conclusions

Alliances and hegemonies are complementary security systems. Hegemonies may work as alliances towards the outside world, and alliances may prevent hegemonies from degenerating into rude imperialism by counterbalancing. Both are unlikely to offer prospects for stable non-nuclear security systems if not complemented and encompassed by other institutions.

In other words, non-nuclear hegemonies function as transitory stages only, and non-nuclear alliances need a framework of reliable security regimes to fulfil their residual functions. Security regimes must rest on a triad of the self-interest of participating states, the weight of agreed norms impacting on decisions and basic orientations of governments, and the anti-nuclear and pacifist ethics of 'watch-dog' élites and mass publics.[34]

Security regimes must contain the inevitable drive by hegemons and alliances to augment relentlessly the instruments of defence. Rule-making must be comprehensive and precise. Procedures must exist to address grievances and to prevent emerging crises from shattering the whole system. Transparency and a low probability of basic reversals are essential for such systems to function. For these reasons, a set of democratic states is more likely to create and maintain such a system than countries with authoritarian or dictatorial rules.

[34] See Müller, H., 'Maintaining non-nuclear weapon status', R. Cowen Karp, (ed.), SIPRI, *Security with Nuclear Weapons: Different Perspectives on National Security* (Oxford University Press: Oxford, 1991), pp. 301–39.

To 'unlearn' the apparent security granted by nuclear weapons, long time spans are probably needed, if it will be possible at all. The average attitude of statesmen in history was not one of confidence in other states. To learn confidence in a system of sovereign or at least partly sovereign states must be a time-consuming endeavour.[35] This augurs for a rather long transitional period in which a build-down to low levels of nuclear deterrence and later on to mere nuclear standby capabilities may prove necessary to keep consensus within societies on principles of security policy, to keep alliances together, and to prevent panic reactions to marginal changes in balances and policies.

How the non-military stratification function of nuclear weapons can be replaced is unclear. Nuclear weapons played a neutralizing role towards economic power in Western Europe and East Asia, and their elimination leaves economic preponderance unchecked. Perhaps economic integration and supranational decision-making on key economic issues, as practiced and foreseen by the European Economic Community, is a sufficient answer to this problem.

The last but decisive conclusion is that a non-nuclear enclave will not survive long in a world of harsh conflict and nuclear arms races. Security considerations shared even by former (and potentially future) enemies suggests the maintenance of standby capabilities or minimum deterrents or whatever the strategic situation is perceived to require. Non-nuclearism, therefore, must encompass the globe, or it will have no future at all.

---

[35] Haas, E. B., 'Why collaborate?', *World Politics*, vol. 32 (Apr. 1980), pp. 357–405; Nye (note 29).

11. Minimum deterrence and nuclear abolition

*Nicholas Wheeler**

I. Introduction

This chapter seeks to explore the value of a policy of minimum deterrence in establishing enhanced security at reduced nuclear force levels between East and West. Beyond this, it also seeks to consider how far minimum deterrent strategies offer the best means of coping with the future spread of nuclear weapons. The problem with viewing minimum deterrence as a remedy for the spread of nuclear weapons is that it overstates the value of deterrence in assuring future global security. The danger here is that a new strategic orthodoxy might build up around the idea of minimum deterrence which will serve to legitimize the possession and proliferation of nuclear weapons in the post-cold war international system.

II. The idea and practice of minimum deterrence

Minimum (sometimes called 'finite') nuclear deterrence has been defined as a 'nuclear strategy in which a nation (or nations) maintains the minimum number of nuclear weapons necessary to inflict unacceptable damage on its adversary even after it has suffered a nuclear attack'.[1] The problem with the idea of minimum nuclear deterrence is that it seems to legitimize whatever level of nuclear capability states consider necessary for their security. Thus, the United Kingdom has defined Trident as a minimum deterrent for Britain, despite the fact that it represents a major increase in nuclear firepower *vis-à-vis* the Polaris force.

Minimum deterrence should be distinguished from what Barry Buzan calls maximum deterrence. He defines the latter as nuclear forces 'capable of fighting, and in some sense winning, nuclear wars across a spectrum of contingencies'.[2] In contrast, minimum deterrence requires 'a secure second-strike force of sufficient size to make threats of AD [assured destruction] credible'.[3] Buzan suggests that we should think in terms of a continuum ranging from pure maximum deterrent policies at one end to pure minimum deterrent polices at

* The author would like to acknowledge his considerable thanks to Ken Booth, Stuart Croft and Tim Huxley for their many helpful comments during the preparation of this chapter.
[1] Hollins, H. B., Powers, A. L. and Sommer, M., *The Conquest of War: Alternative Strategies for Global Security* (Westview Press: Boulder, Colo., 1989), pp. 54–55.
[2] Buzan, B., *Strategic Studies: Military Technology and International Relations* (Macmillan: London, 1987), p. 194.
[3] Buzan (note 2), p. 193.

the other. His contention is that movement away from pure minimum deterrence towards maximum deterrence carries with it the risk of escalating arms competition as states become locked into the 'security dilemma' of matching counterforce capabilities and war-fighting options.[4]

Against this, some writers have suggested that a minimum deterrent strategy is not incompatible with limited nuclear war-fighting options. The argument being that should deterrence fail, states should have limited nuclear options to provide for damage limitation and escalation control/dominance below the level of all out countercity strikes. David Lewis and Lawrence Martin have both suggested that minimum deterrence should include a provision for limited nuclear options, with Martin considering that this should include a deterrent threat of nuclear first use to deter Soviet conventional attack in Europe.[5] However, for David Lewis, what is required is not a deterrent threat of nuclear first use, but a policy of second-strike 'limited' counterforce.[6] This echoes Robert McNamara's nuclear targeting ideas of the early 1960s. As McNamara found out when he tried to fashion such a strategy, however, actions perceived by one side as defensive can all too easily be perceived by the other side as threatening. McNamara did not wish the USA to have a first strike capability, but his doctrine of second-strike counterforce was perceived in Moscow as indicating a clear US intention to achieve such a capability. As a consequence, Moscow responded with its own armaments buildup and any hope of controlling the nuclear arms race in the early 1960s was lost.

As technology became available, the desire of the USA and Soviet Union for war-fighting capabilities led to the adoption of maximum deterrent policies. Neither side has been happy with a pure assured destruction strategy believing that it should maintain nuclear war-fighting capabilities to bolster the credibility of its deterrent, and to provide for nuclear war-fighting options in the event that deterrence failed. However, since the pursuit of military advantage in the nuclear age is illusory, attempts by the USA and the Soviet Union to increase their security unilaterally have led to a decrease in the security of both. If minimum deterrence is to be a model for any future US–Soviet arms reduction regime, both sides will have to eschew the pursuit of unilateral military advantage, accepting that stability and mutual security depends upon each side having secure second-strike retaliatory forces.

Since it is possible to imagine a minimum deterrent strategy, or near-minimum deterrent strategy (second-strike emphasis coupled with limited nuclear options), at anything from a few dozen weapons in the case of the former, to a few thousand weapons in the case of the latter, it is useful to distinguish between minimum deterrence as a particular type of deterrent strategy, and as a force reduction objective of post-START I nuclear arms reductions.

[4] Buzan (note 2), p. 195–96.

[5] See Laurence, M., 'Minimum deterrence', Faraday Discussion Paper no. 8, Council for Arms Control (Jan. 1987).

[6] Lewis, D., 'Finite counterforce', ed. H. Shue, *Nuclear Deterrence and Moral Restraint* (Cambridge University Press: Cambridge, 1989), pp. 51–115.

The framework START I agreement should lead to reductions down to 6000 deliverable warheads (in reality the numbers will be much higher because of START counting rules) but there have been suggestions for a further 50 per cent cut beyond START I down to 3000 warheads, while some analysts have called for even deeper cuts in strategic nuclear forces.[7]

Numerical reductions should not be prized on the grounds that smaller numbers reduce the consequences of a nuclear war, since even the use of a few hundred weapons would lead to unparalleled disaster, especially in terms of 'nuclear winter'. What is more, small nuclear forces that are vulnerable to a first strike will undermine both side's security by creating pressures for nuclear pre-emption in times of crisis. Thus, what is crucial is that reductions enhance mutual security by leading to reductions, if not the eventual elimination, of US–Soviet counterforce capabilities. The draft START I Treaty will reduce counterforce capabilities, but both superpowers will continue to have significant counterforce capabilities, indicating that START I represents only a very small step towards minimum deterrence. Despite this, Presidents Bush and Gorbachev agreed at their July 1990 Washington summit meeting that the goal of post-START nuclear arms reductions ought to be the creation of force postures emphasizing survivability of the nuclear forces of both sides, and that a specific focus should be measures that 'reduce the concentration of warheads on strategic delivery vehicles'.[8]

While a consensus probably exists among US strategic analysts that progress in de-MIRVing should be the goal of the START process, the acceptable level for future nuclear arms reductions remains a matter of considerable debate. Former Carter Administration defence official Walter Slocombe has warned against very deep cuts in post-START reductions. Slocombe has suggested that the task of Western security policy must be to try and take advantage of the promising East–West situation, while 'preserving a long-term buffer against adverse developments'.[9] Slocombe argued that reductions down to 3000–4000 nuclear weapons would strengthen stability, but he warned that 'there are strong arguments against reducing to extremely low levels, say 200 warheads'.[10] Clearly, there is a large range between 3000–4000 warheads and the figure of 200 which Slocombe identifies as a minimum deterrent posture, but the thrust of his argument is that the deeper the cuts in strategic nuclear forces, the greater the risk to strategic stability.

[7] Even before the end of the cold war, former US Defense Secretary Robert McNamara concluded that stable deterrence could be provided for with 500 nuclear warheads on each side. Soviet academics working on post-START arms reductions came very close to concurring with McNamara, considering that 600 nuclear warheads would provide for stability. Others like Frank von Hippel and Frank Feiveson, have suggested that levels of 2000 warheads on each side would be stabilizing, while Richard Garwin suggests that 1000 warheads on each side would be more than adequate. The underlying assumption of all these analysts is that strategic arms reductions should lead to the elimination of counterforce capabilities and the adoption of single-warhead missiles.

[8] US–Soviet Summit Joint Statements on START and START Follow-On Negotiations (June 1990), p. 6.

[9] Slocombe, W. B, 'Strategic stability in a restructured world', *Survival*, vol 32, no. 4 (July/Aug. 1990), p. 302.

[10] Slocombe (note 9).

Slocombe identifies several objections against a stable nuclear balance at low levels. He suggests that if a crisis was to occur, very low numbers would be more tempting targets for pre-emption, while cheating would be a serious problem with very small numbers. Furthermore, small forces would be vulnerable to technological surprise, lacking the 'inherent resistance of multiple basing modes to sudden shifts in technology'.[11] Finally, very low force levels would leave few military options but countercity targeting, and apart from this weakening deterrence against a conventional attack, nuclear war would cause millions to die if weapons were targeted against cities.[12]

The belief that major nuclear reductions will undermine stability seems to reflect the conviction, associated with the realist approach in international relations, that a process of disarmament cannot be expected to change the nature of international politics unless it is part of wider supranational constraints on state behaviour.[13] The argument being that if arms control is pursued in the context of a conflictual relationship, where the threat or use of force is a major factor in relations between states, there is the constant risk of arms control agreements breaking down through mutual suspicion and insecurity. Slocombe's argument then seems to be that nuclear reductions are likely to give rise to the most intense security fears, because the consequences of one side successfully cheating on an arms control agreement could be catastrophic for the other side: the realist prescription is to play it safe and build up positions of military strength, avoiding deterrent strategies that restrict the military options available.

Yet, accepting that a basic precondition for successful arms reductions is a prior relaxation in political tensions (it is impossible to build arms control regimes in a condition of a pure Hobbesian 'state of war'), is there not a role for an arms reduction regime in enhancing security between states that remain mistrustful of each other? Surely, arms control measures that increase confidence and transparency between suspicious states are likely to buttress political co-operation. The experience of US–Soviet arms control in the 1970s does show that arms control cannot survive a collapse in political relations, but that is not to say that the former cannot play a beneficial security role in the context of improving political relations. Additionally, agreements reached in good political times might serve to dampen competitive pressures and arms racing should political relations deteriorate.

The problem with Slocombe's critique of minimum deterrence is that it seems to understate the potential value of an arms reduction process in generating a learning process of security co-operation between mistrustful states. Arms control/reductions depend for their success on a recognition among suspicious governments that they share a common interest in mutual restraint, requiring governments to take into account in their policies the legitimate security con-

---

[11] Slocombe (note 9).
[12] Slocombe (note 9).
[13] See Osgood, R. E. and Tucker, R. W., *Force Order and Justice* (The Johns Hopkins Press: Baltimore, Md., 1971), pp. 335–41.

cerns of others. It was this which was so sorely lacking in the period of *détente* and arms control in the 1970s.

To explore the possible role of a future 'deep cuts' nuclear arms reduction regime in facilitating US–Soviet security co-operation, the next section seeks to rebut the objections (risk of cheating, problem of technological surprise and the inflexibility of small nuclear forces) marshalled by Slocombe against a policy of minimum nuclear deterrence for the superpowers.

III. An examination of the objections to radical nuclear reductions in US–Soviet relations

The problem of cheating

Although states may have a common interest in co-operation, fear and suspicion about the motives of others makes co-operation very difficult. There is always the fear that others might try and cheat on co-operative arrangements in the hope of making unilateral gains. This problem is endemic in an international system which lacks a legal superior, but it is a particularly acute problem in the military security field in which the cost of non-co-operation by others could be loss of national independence. It is the primacy of military security in the hierarchy of state values and the unforgiving nature of the arena which makes co-operation so difficult.[14] Given that the very survival of the state is at stake in the area of nuclear arms reductions, successful cheating carries such a potentially high price that states will be very cautious about agreeing to radical reductions in their nuclear stockpiles.

Historically, disarmament proposals floundered on the Soviet refusal to concede on-site inspection, but Gorbachev's 'new political thinking' in the mid-to-late 1980s led Moscow finally to accept the principle of on-site inspection. The actual experience of 'co-operative verification' in the implementation of the 1987 INF Treaty, and the agreed verification provisions in the draft START Treaty, do provide a good basis for the development of the trust and confidence necessary for the construction of ever more intrusive verification regimes in the future.[15]

Obviously, the closer that the USA and the Soviet Union move towards zero nuclear weapons, the greater the significance attached to the character of their remaining nuclear weapons, and especially their survivability. If de-MIRVing is the centre-piece of a future minimum deterrent regime, effective monitoring of MIRV production facilities will be essential. If this can be achieved, verification will be eased because achieving a decisive military advantage with single-warhead nuclear missiles requires considerably greater cheating than with MIRVed missiles. James Miller also suggests that verification problems

---

[14] Jervis, R., 'Security regimes', *International Organization* , vol. 36, no. 2, Spec. issue (Spring 1982), pp. 174–75.
[15] See the chapter by Patricia Lewis in this volume.

would be eased if nuclear weapon states were not permitted to produce additional nuclear warheads.[16]

The goal of a future strategic arms reduction process should be to create a security regime in which both the USA and the Soviet Union are confident that they face the same lead time in rebuilding nuclear forces in the event of a collapse of the regime: intentions can change and it is prudent to concentrate on actual and potential military capabilities. If a future nuclear arms reduction process collapsed because of a leadership change in the Soviet Union, neither side should be capable of quickly moving into a dominant military position. This depends upon, in Thomas Schelling's words, a 'balance of prudence' such that the 'consequences of transgression are plainly bad—bad for all parties, little dependent on who transgresses first, and not helped by rapid mobilization'.[17]

However, even assuming that a balance of military capabilities can be arrived at by both parties through arms control, what about the risk that one side might still be able to outflank even the most intrusive on-site inspection agreements? The experience of Germany in the interwar period is perhaps not a promising one for those who would argue that a very intrusive on-site inspection regime is a deterrent to violations, since Hitler's Germany was successful in violating the provisions of the Versailles Treaty related to German demilitarization. Against this, Germany's transgressions were detected before it had achieved a decisive military lead. Indeed, the failure of the collective security system in the interwar period was not its inability to detect Hitler's violations of the Versailles Treaty, but its failure, having detected them, to take corrective action against the Nazi regime—a revolutionary regime intent on destroying the existing international order.

The risk of cheating is a serious problem which does become progressively more acute at lower force levels, but it is one which might be overcome through increased transparency and confidence-building measures. If confidence develops between the governments of the USA and Soviet Union that each is interested in common security and not strategic superiority, both might accept progressively higher levels of inspection and intrusion—levels which would have been unthinkable in the cold war era. None the less, the legacy of 40 years of enemy imaging will take years of co-operative behaviour to finally dispel. Vested interests in US and Soviet society have much to gain from a continuation of confrontation, and there is something to the argument that dominant groups in the USA and Soviet Union have connived in using the 'threat' for self-interested purposes. However, it may well be that this connivance was and is unconscious on the part of groups in both societies as the habits and practices of confrontation are deeply ingrained in the culture, values and ideology of the two societies. Given this, the worst-case planners on both sides will be difficult to persuade that the threat has finally disappeared and that the 'other' is now a

---

[16] Miller, J., 'Zero and minimal nuclear weapons', eds J. S. Nye, G. T. Allison and A. Carnesale, *Fateful Visions* (Ballinger Press: Cambridge, Mass., 1988), p. 21.
[17] Schelling, T., *Arms and Influence* (Yale University Press: New Haven, Conn., 1966), p. 259.

partner in the task of managing the global security challenges—including the nuclear challenge—of the late 20th century.

Even if worries about cheating can be addressed through co-operative security policies, what about the risk of a future technological surprise—a unilateral breakthrough in weapons technology which places in jeopardy the assured destruction capabilities of one side?

The problem of continuous weapons innovation

Traditionally, arms control has failed to cope with problems of weapons innovation. The previous experience is that establishing controls over the nuclear arms race simply rechannels it into other areas. Thus, SALT I placed quantitative constraints on the numbers of delivery systems, but this led to a qualitative arms race as the USA, and later the Soviet Union, placed MIRVs on their nuclear forces.

It might be suggested that US and Soviet policy makers have no need to worry about the problem of weapons innovation in the post-cold war era, since the era of competition in nuclear weapons is being consigned to the ash-bin of history. Although this line of argument is quite persuasive at one level, it is important to remember as noted above, that intentions can change, and that as a result it is prudent to guard against both actual and potential military capabilities. Also, if a future 'deep-cuts' regime is to be made acceptable to worst-case planners, it is essential to address their concerns about the strategic consequences of weapons innovation.

There are a number of problems in establishing controls over future weapons innovation. First, while some technological developments are destabilizing such as the introduction of MIRVs, others can actually enhance security by improving the survivability of weapons, as was the case with the introduction of sea-borne strategic nuclear delivery systems. Second, it is impossible to verify a ban on military research which could also have the effect of preventing research that might have important civil applications. This means that any control would have to be exercised at the level of testing and development, but as Stuart Croft notes, by the time a programme reaches the development stage, it is very difficult to stop its deployment.[18] Given that a ban on all strategic weapons development would involve the risk of stopping weapon developments that might enhance both side's security, Croft suggests that selective monitoring by both sides of those weapon systems which might undermine strategic stability is the best role for arms control. Despite this, his approach leads him to question the wisdom of a comprehensive test ban treaty (CTBT) and a ban on missile flight tests, both of which would significantly enhance US and Soviet security, suggesting that total bans in these areas would also serve to prevent future nuclear testing which could be necessary for stockpile confidence, and future weapons development which might enhance

[18] Croft, S., 'Military technological innovation and stability', *Futures*, Oct. 1989, p. 465.

deterrence. He gives the example of the testing of the US mobile single-warhead ICBM whose deployment would arguably enhance stability, but the development of which might be adversely affected by a nuclear and missile flight-test ban. As a result of this, Croft supports 'limited, and not comprehensive, bans on nuclear testing and missile flight-testing . . .'.[19]

Set against this, it might be ventured that a complete ban on nuclear tests and flight-testing would ensure the decay of all nuclear forces, leading to eventual abolition. But, aside from the risk of nuclear accidents, as stockpiles decay it seems that it would be extremely difficult for the USA and Soviet Union to know the rate at which each other's nuclear stockpile was degrading and this even with the most intrusive on-site inspections. Furthermore, as is discussed below, even if at some future point, the USA and Soviet Union no longer have a desire for nuclear weapons *vis-à-vis* each other, they will probably continue to posses nuclear weapons in a nuclear armed world. Thus, even if there are radical nuclear force reductions, some limited testing of weapons might continue to be necessary to ensure the viability of remaining nuclear forces. However, if future US–Soviet testing was conducted within the framework of stringent constraints on general weapons development through on-site inspections of production facilities etc., limited testing for reliability of systems might not undermine a US–Soviet regime of minimum nuclear deterrence.

While major steps towards lasting restraint in the nuclear field lie in tighter controls on nuclear testing, as well as limits on missile flight tests—both of which should help to erode residual confidence in nuclear war-fighting options—strengthening the 1972 Anti-Ballistic Missile (ABM) Treaty has been viewed by many analysts as an essential precondition for movement to very small nuclear forces. The premise that offensive arms reductions depend upon constraints on strategic defences was challenged in the 1980s by the Reagan Administration which argued that radical nuclear arms reductions had to go hand in hand with the deployment of strategic defences. Indeed, it was US–Soviet differences over the role of defences in radical nuclear arms reductions that led to the collapse of the Reykjavik summit meeting in October 1986.

Although limited strategic defence deployments might furnish protection against an accidental or unauthorized nuclear launch, and against the risk of third-party nuclear attack, and additional protection against cheating on a balance of forces at low levels, the risk with even limited defence deployments is that they might afford a near perfect defence against small nuclear arsenals. The problem with strategic defence deployments to enhance stability in the US–Soviet strategic relationship is that if they are necessary to stability, it is very hard to see how the USA and Soviet Union could establish the necessary confidence for a stable transition to a defence-dominant world, or maintain stability even after having arrived at such a condition; but if there is the confidence necessary for a stable transition, it is hard to see why they should be required for stability.

---

[19] Croft (note 18), p. 476.

However, given the spread of weapons of mass destruction and ballistic missiles to the South, the USA and Soviet Union (the latter in terms of geographical proximity to current and future proliferators is more exposed than the USA to these threats) might agree to a limited deployment of defences to afford protection against such threats. The Gulf War heightened US concerns about its growing vulnerability to Third World nuclear risk-takers, and it is possible that the USA might go ahead unilaterally with limited strategic defence deployments in the 1990s. In addition, should the Soviet Union continue to spin further out of control, fears about the custody of Soviet nuclear weapons in a civil-war situation may act as a further spur to unilateral US defence deployments.

The challenge of controlling future technological developments that might threaten either side's assured destruction capabilities is a daunting one. There are many vested interests in the USA and Soviet Union which have a considerable stake in the continuation of weapon research and development, and understandable reluctance on the part of governments to accept limits on technologies that might hold out the promise of an escape from the dilemmas of the nuclear age. These are formidable obstacles to a regime in this area, but in an era of declining East–West threat perceptions, it is likely to be increasingly difficult for the military–industrial complex in both the USA and Soviet Union to secure the resources for new strategic weapon developments. This is especially so in the case of the Soviet Union. The Soviet Union's survival depends upon economic reconstruction at home which probably requires large-scale economic and technical support from the West. It remains to be seen how far the West (including Japan) will be prepared to help the Soviet Union on the path to economic reform and development, but it does seem that the emergence of a market economy in the Soviet Union would change the balance of power in Soviet society away from the military–industrial complex towards groups interested in welfare and consumerism.

A regime of US–Soviet technological restraint must be a goal for the post-START strategic arms reduction process. If this is to be achieved, both sides will have to give up the search for unilateral advantage through the exploitation of new military technologies. The principal motivation behind the search for self-reliance in the security field has been the desire of both sides to escape the fact that their security has depended upon the restraint of the 'other'. This has been extremely difficult for both Moscow and Washington to live with, for it has meant dependence upon an enemy perceived to be the antithesis of its values and beliefs. It was the hope of escaping this dependence which led President Reagan to call for an 'astrodome' defence of the USA in his March 1983 Strategic Defense Initiative (SDI) or 'star wars' speech.

However, if minimum deterrence is to be viable, both sides will have to accept MAD (mutual assured destruction) as a fact of strategic life as well as strategic doctrine. There is a paradox here, for if the basis of mutual security in the nuclear age is acceptance of MAD, it has to be remembered that the latter is predicated on holding the civilian society of each side hostage to its good behaviour. It will be recalled that Slocombe argued that it was this very reliance on countercity targeting which made minimum deterrence unacceptable for both ethical and strategic reasons. But it is this very acceptance of the inflexibility of countercity targeting which is the whole basis of minimum deterrence: MAD as a strategic doctrine is minimum deterrence.

The problem of inflexible forces

The objection that if deterrence failed, very small nuclear forces would, if used, be condemned to a countercity role, and that this is ethically unacceptable, seems to be inescapable. Assuming highly survivable forces—the pre-condition for minimum nuclear deterrence at very low levels—neither side must be militarily capable of destroying the other's strategic forces in a pre-emptive strike. But in a situation where there was only a few hundred nuclear weapons on each side, there would be great reluctance in expending them against so called 'soft' military targets.

At higher levels of nuclear forces which still emphasize second-strike capabilities but which maintained limited nuclear war-fighting options (but below the threshold which threatens force survivability), there might be greater scope for the use of nuclear weapons to signal resolve and willingness to escalate, as well as to try and provide for a measure of damage limitation. Despite this, if the goal is to try and inhibit the use of nuclear weapons, it seems that the more inflexible nuclear forces are, the greater the barrier to crossing the nuclear threshold at all.

Against this, the stock strategic objection to deterrence through the threat of countercity destruction is that such a deterrent posture undermines the credibility of deterrence by encouraging military aggression below the nuclear threshold, and offers no options aside from destruction of cities in the event that deterrence fails. But since like beauty, the credibility of deterrence is in the eye of the beholder, no one knows what is necessary for effective deterrence. Perhaps, as John Mueller contends, war prevention in the post-war era has not depended on nuclear weapons, but on the perceived costs of large-scale conventional conflict.[20] What is more, even if states only have recourse to countercity strikes, an aggressor cannot be sure that conventional conflict will not escalate to this mutually destructive outcome.

In the cold war era, the conventional preponderance of the Red Army provided a clear reminder of the dangers of conventional aggression below the nuclear threshold. However, the Soviet conventional threat is fast disappearing, with the withdrawal of Soviet power from Eastern Europe, and the signing of the 1990 Conventional Armed Forces in Europe (CFE) Treaty. While NATO planners worry about the potential Soviet military threat post-CFE (Moscow will remain the largest military power on the Euro-Asian continent)—a concern

[20] See Mueller, J., *Retreat From Doomsday: The Obsolescence of Major War* (Basic Books: New York, 1989).

not helped by worries about the latter's compliance with the Treaty—the CFE Treaty does provide barriers against rapid Soviet force regeneration. If these barriers are crossed by a future Soviet government, it would be a clear signal of their intent. The best response to continuing worries about the regeneration and reconstitution of Soviet military forces is to extend the CFE process into these areas.

Historically, worries about US extended deterrence to Western Europe have provided a major stimulus to the adoption of maximum deterrent policies, since NATO has sought to persuade Moscow that a European war might escalate to the strategic nuclear level. But it seems that Western reliance on assured destruction would be more acceptable in the context of a diminishing Soviet conventional threat. Some NATO governments would like to see the Alliance continue to have sub-strategic nuclear options in the form of air-delivered stand-off nuclear weapons, but if this proves politically controversial in the 1990s, the Alliance might well have to accept the loss of sub-strategic nuclear options. However, this does not seem to pose high risks to NATO's security in the new era, since a future enemy would have to confront the twin risks that sub-strategic nuclear weapons could be re-deployed to Europe from the USA (much would depend here on the nature of the future US security commitment to Europe) as well as the terrible prospect that war in Europe could escalate to the employment of nuclear weapons against cities.

If then there are good reasons for thinking that the inflexibility of small nuclear forces need not prove a compelling strategic objection to minimum deterrence at low numbers, what of the moral objections to basing East–West security on a policy of MAD? The moral case for MAD as strategic doctrine as well as a fact of life is that it is very unlikely that escalation is controllable, and that attempts to control escalation are likely to undermine rather than strengthen deterrence. Despite this, it can be agreed with Hedley Bull that, 'The preservation of peace . . . by a system in which each threatens to destroy or cripple the civil society of the other . . . reflects the weakness in international society of the sense of common interest'.[21]

To conclude this rebuttal of the criticisms of minimum nuclear deterrence advanced by Slocombe, it seems that there is scope for considerable nuclear reductions beyond START I, although any post-START arms reduction regime must be designed with the goal of stability in mind. The goal here should be to initiate a step by step process of information exchange, confidence-building and transparency which might lead to mutually beneficial nuclear arms reductions. Perhaps, it is utopian to believe that numbers might eventually be reduced down to a few hundred nuclear warheads, let alone a few tens of weapons, but we will only know this if we participate with the Soviet Union in a learning process of nuclear arms reductions. The idea that mistrustful states might learn norms of co-operative behaviour has been explored by security regime theorists in international relations.

---

[21] Bull, H., *The Anarchical Society* (Macmillan: London, 1977), p. 126.

International regimes have been defined as 'principles, rules, norms, and procedures around which expectations can converge in a given area of international relations'.[22] Robert Jervis has argued that US–Soviet relations in the
post-war era have not been characterized by a security regime,[23] although
Joseph Nye has suggested that in the area of nuclear arms control, the USA and
Soviet Union have established a tentative security regime.[24] Nye suggests that
the USA and Soviet Union have gone through a process of evolutionary
'nuclear learning' in the strategic nuclear field. If in the future, this learning
process is to be deepened, the basic norms and rules of a regime will have to be
rejection of nuclear war-fighting policies in favour of a minimum deterrent
strategy predicated on MAD as the basis of common security. Thus, while a
post-START arms reduction regime would in part be an expression of improving US–Soviet relations, it might also play a very important role in sustaining
and strengthening security co-operation by demonstrating in actions as well as
words a US–Soviet commitment to common security.

Yet, if radical nuclear reductions will require the development of common
security practices between East and West, Western governments have tended in
the past to take the view that common security will only be achieved with the
Soviet Union if it develops liberal values and institutions. Gorbachev may have
taken the steps that made possible *détente* (although it is a matter of debate how
far 'new thinking' was compelled by Moscow's economic and political exhaus-
tion in the face of Western political, economic and military strength), but the
key to the new-found spirit of co-operation in the late 1980s was better treatment of human rights in the Soviet Union, and restraint in the Third World,
principles that the West had long since argued for as the basis of any lasting
détente with the Soviet Union. The great claim of common security is that it is
a policy which can be pursued between ideologically opposed states, but the
experience of the past 40 years has not borne this out. It took the processes of
glasnost and the new political thinking to make possible the superpower *détente*
of the late 1980s. It might be argued that Western and Soviet governments
should have been able to develop a security regime in the face of the common
nuclear threat, but agreement on MAD as the basis of common security let
alone the achievement of radical reductions in nuclear stockpiles—proved
beyond the capabilities of East and West in the cold war era. At the beginning
of the 1990s, it seems that US and Soviet civilian policy-makers do now recognize that the only security in the nuclear age is mutual security, but establishing
the confidence necessary for major nuclear reductions beyond START I will be
a process which might well run into decades. Indeed, it does seem that
achieving near-zero force levels will only really be possible—given the level of
transparency and intrusiveness required—in the context of the growth of liberal
values and institutions.

[22] See Keohane, R. and Nye, J., *Power and Interdependence*, 2nd edn (Scott Foresman: Boston, Mass.,
1989), p. 258.
[23] See Jervis (note 14), pp. 187–94.
[24] Nye, J., 'Nuclear learning and US–Soviet security regimes', *International Organization*, vol. 41,
no. 3 (Summer 1987).

If minimum deterrence at near-zero force levels in the East–West relationship is seen as dependent upon the success of the liberal-democratic project in the Soviet Union, the question has to be asked as to whether minimum deterrence could ever lead to the elimination of US and Soviet nuclear arsenals? Jonathan Schell argues that a balance of nuclear terror might exist even without the nuclear weapons themselves—through the mechanism of rearmament parity. However, as discussed in chapter 2 in this volume, this places far too much faith in deterrence as the long-term basis of security. The transition from an interstate relationship in which each party has a few hundred, or even a few tens of weapons, to one in which they have zero nuclear weapons is much more than a technical question of how to get rid of the last few weapons for it involves the vexed philosophical and practical question of how formerly hostile states learn to break down the barriers that divide them thereby extending political community in international relations. In the 1950s Karl Deutsch defined a security community relationship as a situation among states where the threat, or use of force, is not only unacceptable, but also unthinkable.[25] The evidence that a US–Soviet security community had emerged would be Moscow and Washington ceasing to target each other with military forces.

IV. The prospects for a US–Soviet security community

The argument that the triumph of capitalism and liberalism over communism holds out the promise of a benign and co-operative East–West relationship has been most recently advanced by Francis Fukuyama, but his view echoes the long-standing Liberal view of international politics, which sees the path to a global security community as lying in the development of progressive forms of internal government. If it is true that liberal states have an inherent propensity to peaceful relations with each other (but not necessarily with non-liberal states),[26] self-help and the deterrence paradigm would be abolished between liberal states. Western Europe—historically the site of bloody conflict—is often cited as an example of such a pluralistic liberal security community.

If one looks at the history of Western Europe this century, it seems that a remarkable transformation has taken place in the relationships of the West European states, with the threat of force not only delegitimized as an instrument of statecraft, but also virtually unthinkable. Against this, realists have retorted that if Western Europe has experienced peaceful relations, this is a consequence of the bipolarity of the cold war era with the USA providing for Western Europe's security in the face of the Soviet threat. Josef Joffe has argued that the USA has acted as Europe's 'US pacifier' neutralizing the rivalries among European states.[27] However, in contrast to liberal theorists who emphasize that

---

[25] Deutsch, K. W. *et al.*, *Political Community and the North Atlantic Area* (Princeton University Press: Princeton, N.J., 1957).

[26] See Doyle, M. W., 'Kant, liberal legacies and foreign affairs', *Philosophy and Public Affairs*, vol. 12, no. 3, (1983).

[27] Joffe, J., 'Europe's American pacifier', *Survival*, vol 26, no. 4 (July/Aug. 1984), pp. 174–81.

European integration has led to lasting patterns of co-operative behaviour, some realists suggest that with the demise of the cold war order, Europe may experience a revival of long-standing conflicts, leading to the re-emergence of self-help and power politics.[28] While liberal integration theorists point to the marginalization of nuclear weapons in West European security relations, realists like John Mearsheimer point to an increasing role for nuclear weapons in the emerging multipolar strategic environment.[29] The general thesis here is that far from becoming irrelevant as in the security community approach, nuclear weapons should play an increasing role in the provision of intra-European security in the post-cold war era.

However, despite such realist scenarios for an erosion of future European security, it seems that Western Europe has evolved into a security community where there is no expectation of war among its members, and where nuclear weapons are marginal to concerns of intra-European security. Nevertheless, even if it is accepted that Western Europe has evolved into a security community, and that this is a product of liberal democratic institutions and values, is it at all feasible to imagine the extension of liberal values and institutions to Eastern Europe and, eventually to the Soviet Union?

Although positive about the long-term evolution of Eastern Europe into liberal-democratic political systems, Pierre Hassner is very sceptical that the Soviet Union will evolve into a future federation, confederation or even commonwealth arrangement between Russia and its republics, considering that it is more likely that the Soviet Union's current crisis of decolonization, and collapse as a superpower, will lead to increased political violence, if not even general civil war.[30] But it is Hassner's view that while the emergence of repressive military rule in Russia cannot be ruled out, it is not necessarily the case that the choice for the West is between a liberal co-operative relationship, and one where the Soviet Union menaces Western Europe, since it might be 'a hostile yet inner-directed power . . .'.[31] Nevertheless, the risks of instability lead Hassner to believe that it is important for the West to try and hold on to the institution of collective defence in the form of NATO, and to reliance on nuclear deterrence, despite the enormous political difficulties that he sees in trying to legitimize this to Western publics. If nuclear deterrence is seen by Hassner as the ultimate insurance policy, he is well aware, in contrast to Mearsheimer, that nuclear weapons are becoming increasingly marginal to the provision of security in the new Europe. Writing at the birth of the post-cold war era, Hassner commented:

Without even mentioning yet the non-military dimensions of security—economic, social, ecological and so on—it is clear that the dangers of violence in the new Europe come more from the rise of nationalism in the East, from the decay of multi-national

[28] See Mearsheimer, J. J., 'Back to the future: instability in Europe after the cold war', *International Security*, vol. 15, no. 1 (Summer 1990).

[29] Mearsheimer (note 28), p. 30.

[30] Hassner, P., 'Europe beyond partition and unity: disintegration or reconstitution?', *International Affairs*, vol. 66, no. 3 (July 1990), pp. 461–75.

states like the Soviet Union and Yugoslavia, and from the minority and border problems of the Balkans. There is little that NATO (or, for that matter, the French or British national nuclear deterrents) can do about civil war in Yugoslavia, Soviet intervention in the Baltic states or conflict between Romania and Hungary. All these potential domestic or inter-state uses of force have more to do with the problems of pre-war Europe or today's Third World than with the East–West confrontation of the last 45 years.[32]

Yet, while agreeing with Hassner that the post-cold war Europe will see new security challenges which could lead to violent conflicts, these are almost certainly not going to embroil the European powers in general war.

The long-term intentions of a Soviet/Russian state with enormous military power remain uncertain, but the best way to address these concerns is to try and create co-operative security institutions that take into account the legitimate security interests of the Soviet Union in the post-cold war Europe. However, if the Soviet Union behaves in a very repressive way at home, the governments of the West will not wish to extensively co-operate with such a regime, especially in the military security field. As noted earlier, Gorbachev may have made possible the *détente* of the late 1980s, but this reflected a Soviet recognition that the West would only seriously co-operate if Moscow restrained its behaviour in the Third World and engaged in liberalization at home.

However, if the West believes that lasting security with the Soviet Union depends upon the emergence of liberal-democratic institutions and values, should it not be more active in condemning the Gorbachev regime when it shows signs of moving to the right increasing its dependence upon the KGB and military? The difficulty here is trying to decide how the West can best serve the interests of reform in the Soviet Union, for if the West is perceived by the central institutions of the Soviet state to be actively encouraging the breakup of the Union, this might scupper hopes for building common security with the Soviet political and military élite. However, if the West does very little (as is perceived to be the case in some quarters over Soviet repression in the Baltic republics) in the belief that co-operation with a nuclear-armed Soviet Union has to be prior to concerns about human rights and self-determination of the peoples of the Soviet Union, and that in any event public condemnation is likely to make the situation worse and not better, might this not strengthen the hands of those at the centre who argue that Moscow can get away with internal repression? This dilemma was an acute one in the 1970s, but given Gorbachev's desperate need for Western help to bail out the sinking Soviet ship at the beginning of the 1990s, perhaps there is greater scope for the West to drive a hard bargain for any economic reform plan that might be agreed between the Soviet Union, Western governments and international financial institutions. However, should hopes for the 'grand bargain' of economic aid for greater economic and political liberalisation not be realized, and should the Gorbachev leadership find itself more and more dependent upon the KGB and

[31] Hassner (note 30), pp. 473.
[32] Hassner (note 30), pp. 468–69.

military for its power base, Western governments are unlikely to be willing to do serious arms control business with a regime which is repressing its own people. Despite this, the challenge for the West must be to try and build common security with the central government in Moscow, while also seeking to press the centre to devolve greater power down to the republics in the form of a new Union Treaty, since this seems to be the only basis for strengthening liberal values and political forces in the Soviet Union, this in turn being the only basis for a lasting East–West security community.

Although events in Eastern Europe and the Soviet Union remain a source of considerable concern to the West, it is difficult for the West to point to a specific military threat from the East. Indeed, none of the existing nuclear weapon states (NWS) can point to a clearly defined threat against which to justify their continued possession of nuclear weapons. This does not mean that the USA, the USSR, the UK and France will cease to possess nuclear weapons since the latter provide insurance in an uncertain world, as well as the status and prestige perceived to be attached to nuclear weapons. Possessing nuclear weapons as both symbols of great-power status and as the ultimate insurance policy was labelled in chapter 2 of this volume as 'structural nuclearism': the reason for possessing nuclear weapons lies not in the existence of a particular threat, but in the general perception that statehood requires that one cannot afford to be nuclear-free in a nuclear-armed world.

The problem with legitimizing nuclear weapons in this way is that it becomes a charter for global proliferation. If the NWS justify possession of nuclear weapons in terms of security and prestige in an uncertain world, why should other states not wish to acquire them for the same reasons? Radical nuclear reductions on the part of the US and the Soviet government might help the latter in arguing against nuclear proliferation, but for as long as the NWS continue to maintain some level of nuclear weapons, it will be difficult to persuade others that they should forego them in the interests of global security. And while the prospect of radical reductions is not as utopian as might have been thought a few years ago, there is currently a question mark over the willingness of Britain and France to reduce their nuclear arsenals in a US–Soviet post-START arms reduction regime, and uncertainty as to how British and French reluctance might influence the prospects for arms reductions. What is more, there is also uncertainty as to whether China might be persuaded to participate in some future post-START arms reduction process.

V. The medium nuclear powers and strategic arms reductions

After current strategic modernization programmes are completed, it has been estimated that British and French nuclear forces will comprise less than 10 per cent of post-START I forces.[33] The Soviet Union's current official position is

---

[33] See Heisbourg, F., 'The British and French nuclear forces', *Survival*, vol. 31, no. 4 (July/Aug. 1989), p. 312.

that post-START arms reductions must include the other NWS. In the past, the Soviet position has been that since it faces four nuclear-armed adversaries, it should be compensated in arms control talks by being permitted a force level equal to the combined forces of its adversaries. The USA has always rejected this as a charter for Soviet superiority. However, Moscow has not in the past allowed the issue of third-country nuclear forces to block favourable bilateral arms control agreements with the USA.

If the post-cold war era leads to a major change in Soviet threat perceptions, such that the risk of a combined Western nuclear attack is seen to be increasingly incredible in the eyes of Soviet military and political leaders, Moscow might well be prepared to contemplate arms reductions without the participation of the other NWS. Thus, while it is to be expected that there will be strong Soviet pressure for third-country participation in the future, the USA and Soviet Union might agree to reduce their forces further in a purely bilateral START II process. However, reductions down to 500–1000 nuclear warheads would surely require participation by the other medium nuclear powers. But as François Heisbourg notes, if the Soviet Union reduced forces down to 600 warheads as suggested by some Soviet analysts, this would be 'in the vicinity of those corresponding to the level of the British and French force modernizations'.[34] Thus, it seems that if the USA and Soviet Union were to accept a position of near-equality with the two European nuclear powers, Britain and France might be able to join the process accepting a freeze on their nuclear forces, with the question of reductions being considered in a future round of multilateral nuclear arms control.

The opposition Labour Party in Britain is committed to joining a START II process, but is vague as to whether this might include the elimination of British strategic nuclear forces. Although it has stated that a future Labour government will operate Trident with no more than the warhead numbers of the Polaris force. In contrast, the Conservative Government is firmly committed to sustaining a British nuclear capability into the post-cold war era. There is currently no political constituency in France which favours French elimination of nuclear weapons, or the reduction of French nuclear forces in a multilateral arms reduction process. London and Paris both set conditions in the 1980s for possible participation in strategic arms reduction talks, but while conditions such as the elimination of conventional and chemical imbalances in Europe, 'deep-cuts' in superpower arsenals, and a tightening of the ABM Treaty to prevent defence-deployments, were not seen as likely to be achieved in the climate of the early 1980s, all these conditions have been or are very close to being met.[35] But if Paris determines to stay out of any future arms reduction process, London might be less willing to join such an agreement, although much depends here on the character of future British governments. Yet, since the United Kingdom depends upon the USA for its strategic nuclear delivery systems, it might find

[34] Heisbourg (note 33), p. 313.
[35] Heisbourg (note 33), p. 313.

its room for manœuvre considerably more limited than that of France should the USA decide to make major nuclear reductions a priority for the 1990s.

If British and especially French participation is uncertain in any future US–Soviet nuclear arms control/reductions, there is also the question of Chinese participation. China is estimated to possess just under 300 nuclear warheads[36] and probably sees itself as already having a minimum deterrent force. Indeed, all of the three medium nuclear powers would claim that their existing nuclear forces are minimum deterrents, and that any reductions threaten the deterrent value of their forces. Before France and China would even consider cuts in nuclear forces, the USA and Soviet Union would have to massively slash their nuclear forces, a process which would take some time to implement. Despite this, it does seem that there is considerable merit in establishing a dialogue among the five NWS on sensitive issues such as questions of strategic doctrine, command and control, as well as broader objectives of strengthening the norms against nuclear proliferation, since this will be crucial if any future denucle-arization of US–Soviet relations is to act as the vehicle for the development of a global non-nuclear security regime. At the time of writing, there are plans for a meeting of senior officials of the five NWS to discuss controlling the flow of arms to the Middle East, but it remains to be seen whether this meeting heralds the beginnings of a dialogue between the five permanent members of the UN Security Council on nuclear issues and arms control.

The problem with five-power nuclear discussions and any subsequent co-operation is that it might be seen as further institutionalizing the gap between the nuclear 'haves' and the nuclear 'have not' states. As such, it could serve to stiffen the resolve of some regional great powers to join the nuclear club. Against this, there is the optimistic view that co-operation among the five, coupled with radical disarmament by the USA and Soviet Union, will so push nuclear weapons into the background of international relations that governments thinking about acquiring a nuclear capability will desist from doing so. However, this seems to overstate the link between horizontal and vertical proliferation. Also, pessimists would argue that deep reductions in US–Soviet nuclear forces will paradoxically serve to whet the appetite of states to break into the nuclear club. Possession of 50–100 nuclear weapons might be seen as bringing great prestige and political benefits in a world where the USA and Soviet Union only had a few hundred weapons each.

However, the desire on the part of some Third World states to develop nuclear capabilities is a challenge that is with us here and now. How international society might cope with this challenge in the 1990s will be the subject for the remainder of the chapter, starting with an assessment of the value of minimum deterrence in managing the spread of nuclear weapons.

---

[36] See SIPRI, *SIPRI Yearbook 1990: World Armaments And Disarmament* (Oxford University Press: Oxford, 1990), p. 22.

VI. The proliferation problem and minimum deterrence

Although realists and idealists have generally agreed that the spread of nuclear weapons would weaken international order, Kenneth Waltz has challenged this conventional wisdom with his contention that 'the measured spread of nuclear weapons is more to be welcomed than feared'.[37] Waltz's view is that all that is needed to deter even the most crazy of risk-taking states from aggression is a very small survivable stockpile of nuclear weapons—he suggests for third world states a few tens of nuclear weapons might be all that is required. But even if it is accepted that nuclear spread is more likely to induce cautious rather than reckless behaviour (and the problems of applying deterrence rationality in a Third World context have been well-remarked upon), Waltz considerably understates the dangers that the spread of nuclear weapons carries with it: the increased risk of nuclear accidents; and state-sponsored nuclear terrorism and the associated danger of states providing non-state terrorist groups with nuclear devices. Yet, if these perils were not enough, Waltz can be faulted for skipping over the transition problem.

Currently, Brazil, Argentina and North Korea (the latter a party to the 1968 Non-Proliferation Treaty (NPT), although it has not yet accepted International Atomic Energy Authority Safeguards (IAEA) on its nuclear facilities) might be included in the category of 'near-nuclear states', although the two Latin American powers are more advanced in nuclear weapons development than North Korea.[38] Before the Gulf War, Iraq would have been included in the above category, but the destruction of Iraq's nuclear facilities by the US Air Force during the war has significantly slowed down, but not as yet stopped despite UN Security Council Resolution 688, Saddam Hussein's nuclear ambitions.

According to Spector and Smith, a distinction should be made between the 'near-nuclear' states in terms of their potential nuclear capabilities and the '*de facto*' states which they define as those 'that have deployed nuclear weapons or could do so rapidly in times of crisis'.[39] The *de facto* states are Israel, South Africa, India and Pakistan. Israel is by far the most advanced of the *de facto* states. The estimation of its nuclear stockpile varies from 50–200 nuclear weapons.[40] The Jewish state is not in a mutual nuclear deterrent relationship with any of the Arab states, and it is not at all likely to allow any Arab state to acquire such a capability. Although Israel is determined to deny the Arab states the nuclear option, the latter have developed chemical weapons—and their ballistic missile means of delivery in an attempt in part to try and offset Israel's nuclear monopoly.

---

[37] Waltz, K. N., 'The spread of nuclear weapons: more may be better', *Adelphi Paper* no. 171 (International Institute of Strategic Studies: London, 1981), p. 30.

[38] See Spector, L. S. and Smith, J., *Nuclear Ambitions* (Westview Press: Boulder, Colo., 1990).

[39] Spector and Smith (note 38), p. 5.

[40] Spector and Smith (note 38), pp. 150–55.

Thus, a policy of minimum deterrence for the Middle East would only be relevant in a future situation where the Arab states had developed an assured destruction capability against Israel.

However, the risks to regional stability during such a transition are frightening to contemplate. The Indo-Pakistan relationship is the only case among the *de facto* nuclear states where an embryonic relationship of mutual nuclear deterrence might be said to exist. If both India and Pakistan are, as Spector and Smith suggest, intent on expanding nuclear capabilities, confidence-building measures and increased transparency may be important in managing future 'vertical proliferation' in the region. India and Pakistan have already taken a step in this direction with their agreement in December 1988 not to attack each other's nuclear power stations.

Therefore, while it can be agreed with Mitchell Reiss that the 'near-nuclear' and *de facto* nuclear states have tended for political as well as strategic reasons to pursue a policy of diplomatic ambiguity as to their possession of nuclear weapons,[41] there is growing concern that the *de facto* states are intent on the acquisition of ever more advanced nuclear capabilities, and their ballistic missile means of delivery. Reviewing the activities of the *de facto* states in 1990, Spector and Smith commented, 'none of these countries has chosen to "hover" just above the nuclear threshold; all aspire to more advanced capabilities . . . These developments belie the popular notion that emerging nuclear weapon countries slacken their efforts after obtaining a few "bombs in the basement"'.[42]

How then should international society respond to the challenge of both horizontal and vertical proliferation? It has been suggested that without encouraging proliferation, the NWS could offer technical assistance to emergent nuclear powers on the management and handling of their nuclear forces. The problem here is that while this might help ameliorate some of the risks of nuclear spread, it could lend great legitimacy to the acquisition and development of nuclear capabilities. If so, this would run counter to any attempts by the NWS to develop policies that denuclearize international relations. Additionally, since the same level of assistance would presumably have to be given to the *de facto* states, this could pose very difficult political problems, especially if one of the recipients of technical help was perceived as potentially hostile. Imagine for example the United Kingdom's response in the face of any future development of Argentinian nuclear capabilities?

Establishing a stable balance of nuclear terror between regional antagonists might prove vital to future international security if horizontal and vertical proliferation continues in the South, but the problem here goes beyond one of handling nuclear forces since first-generation nuclear delivery systems tend to be very vulnerable to pre-emptive nuclear strikes. Thus, the task of constructing a stable balance of nuclear terror in the world's most contentious regions will

---

[41] Reiss, M., 'Beyond the 1985 NPT Review Conference: learning to live with uncertainty', *Survival*, vol. 27, no. 5 (Sep./Oct. 1985), pp. 226–34.

[42] Spector and Smith (note 38), p. 11.

be an extremely difficult one. Any confidence-building measures reached between hostile states such as not to target each other's nuclear facilities and other vital targets could easily erode in times of severe crisis. As a result, it seems that any movement towards greater nuclear capabilities will, in politically volatile areas like the Middle East and South Asia, only serve to intensify regional security dilemmas compounding the already complex and difficult problems of regional crisis management.

However, there is a caveat here. Whatever the problems in trying to manage the spread of nuclear arms in politically contentious regions, attempts at regulating future regional nuclear arms competition is surely preferable to the spectre of unmanaged regional nuclear arms races. Avoiding the legitimization of nuclear deterrence as the basis of regional security should be the goal of international society, but if nuclear capabilities continue to spread to the South, it does seem that the NWS will have to play some role in seeking to facilitate a stable transition to relationships of mutual assured destruction in regions of high political tension like the Middle East and South Asia. But since the potential consequences of the spread of nuclear weapons for future global security could be catastrophic, it is vital before concluding that minimum deterrence is the only viable strategy for managing the challenge of nuclear proliferation, that analysis be given as to whether international society might prove capable in the post-cold war era of not only containing this global security challenge, but even beginning to reverse it.

VII. Towards global control of weapons of mass destruction

The NPT has been signed by the vast majority of states. It allows states to develop civil nuclear capabilities, but proscribes the development of nuclear weapons. It does seem that most states wish to see the NPT regime survive. Simpson and Howlett consider that 'The NPT remains the cornerstone of the nuclear non-proliferation regime . . . Because of this, the NPT's unique contribution to global security is now increasingly recognized by all parties to the Treaty, including the neutral and non-aligned states'.[43] Thus, the challenge it seems is not one of trying to stop a tide of proliferation in the years ahead, but of strengthening the Treaty in the face of future challenges to the norm of non-proliferation

One of the principal charges against the NPT from non-signatories like Brazil, Argentina, and especially India, is that it is discriminatory because it creates two types of states, nuclear 'haves' and nuclear 'have nots'. Even if the USA and Soviet Union were to cut their nuclear forces down to just a few hundred weapons each, fulfilling a major part of Article VI of the NPT,[44] the regime would still be a discriminatory one. In fact, the only alternative to this

[43] Simpson, J. and Howlett, D., 'The 1990 NPT Review Conference', *Survival,* vol. 32, no. 4 (July/Aug. 1990), p. 358.
[44] The implicit bargain of the Treaty being that the non-nuclear weapon states would give up the nuclear weapon option in return for the nuclear weapon states pursuing nuclear disarmament.

would be a nuclear weapon-free world, or a world where everyone had the bomb. In 1986, India did suggest that the NPT be replaced by a detailed timetable for disarmament by the year 2010, indicating that for India, the goal was a nuclear weapon-free world. [45]

However, the reluctance of a state like India to join the NPT, seems to reflect not only dissatisfaction with the hierarchical principle of the NPT, but also concerns about its vital security.[46] Despite the fact that Pakistan has stated that it will sign the NPT if India does (suggesting that Pakistan's nuclear programme is 'India driven'), New Delhi is worried about threats not only from Pakistan, but also from China. Considerations of national security and the desire for great power status seem to drive the Indian nuclear programme making it reluctant to join the NPT. If India, Pakistan, and China (all non-NPT members) are to be socialized into the norms and rules of the NPT, conflict resolution in South-Asia seems to be a vital pre-requisite.[47] The same conclusion applies to the Middle East.

Here, the aftermath of the Gulf War offers a great opportunity to address the wider question of regional security in the Middle East, including the elimination of weapons of mass destruction from the region. Currently, the Arab states will not sign a global convention banning production and stockpiling of chemical weapons, unless Israel signs the NPT and places its nuclear facility at Dimona under IAEA safeguards.[48] The basic issue is whether the Jewish state would be prepared to countenance this in return for an ending of the state of war and the destruction of its Arab enemies' chemical weapons and ballistic missiles. The Jerusalem Government has not ruled out the idea of a Middle East zone free of weapons of mass destruction, but it is very hard to see Israel giving up its nuclear stockpile—the ultimate guarantee of its security—without cast-iron guarantees for its security; the difficulty here being that Israel is extremely reluctant to rely on others for its security—especially upon global security institutions such as the UN. As Geoffrey Kemp notes

the strategic reality is that none of the key players are going to support curbs on their own arsenals unless and until some semblance of a regional peace accord is in the works . . . no peace arrangements are feasible unless they include iron-clad arms-control agreements; but, equally true, until the fear of military aggression is removed, peace treaties will be illusory.[49]

As such, despite the constant claims of the NNWS in the NPT that a CTBT and radical nuclear disarmament is vital to the continuing viability of the NPT regime, it is illusory to believe that this will be enough to move the world towards a non-nuclear security regime. A CTBT, or at least significant movement in that direction, is important to a strengthening the NPT and to ensuring

[45] Müller, H. and Kokoski, R., SIPRI, *The Non-Proliferation Treaty: Political and Technological Prospects and Dangers in 1990*, SIPRI Research Report (Apr. 1990), p. 50.

[46] Müller and Kokoski (note 45).

[47] Müller and Kokoski (note 45).

[48] Simpson and Howlett (note 45), p. 350.

[49] Kemp, G., 'The Gulf crisis: diplomacy or force?', *Survival*, vol 32, no. 6 (Nov./Dec. 1990), p. 517.

Treaty extension beyond 1995 (although given the hostility of the USA, France and Britain to a CTBT, if it comes to a choice between a CTBT and the NPT Treaty regime at the 1995 NPT Review Conference, most signatories will surely opt for the Treaty regime), but the the real key to a global non-nuclear security regime depends upon breaking down the barriers between hostile states notably in South Asia and the Middle East.

A US–Soviet minimum deterrent security regime would be a clear signal of the determination of the nuclear superpowers to push nuclear weapons further and further into the background of international politics, but for this process to be extended to regional actors which have developed, or are in the process of developing nuclear capabilities, security policies will have to be developed at the regional and global level that address the roots of violent conflict in these regions.

In October 1990, US Secretary of State James Baker indicated in a speech on US–Soviet relations that Moscow and Washington should act as 'joint custodians' of the post-cold war global security order, and that 'regional conflict prevention must become a goal of US–Soviet co-operation'.[50] However, at the same time as working for the settlement of regional conflicts, he suggested that Moscow and Washington should explore 'sanctions, both bilateral and multilateral, that might be imposed against those states that violate international non-proliferation norms or use weapons of mass destruction'.[51]

Currently, the NPT security regime has no powers of legal enforcement. It functions through the IAEA in monitoring state behaviour, seeking to detect any defections from regime rules, but relies for its authority on the voluntary co-operation of member states. However, this requires that states decide that obligation to the norms and rules of the regime is in their national self-interest. However, there are cases where short-run considerations of national self-interest have led to behaviour that challenges the rules and norms of the NPT security regime.

In the past, the NWS (with the exception of the Soviet Union) have not been very effective in restricting the spread of technologies which might have nuclear weapon applications. At the 1990 NPT Review Conference, some 'supplier states made commitments—or confirmed previous commitments—to make all their exports of nuclear supplies conditional on the acceptance by the recipient of 'full-scope safeguards'.[52] However, since there was no final document owing to US refusal to agree to a Mexican proposal for a timetable for negotiations towards a CTBT, the proposed steps to strengthen the NPT lack legal status in the Treaty.[53] Despite this, there is a very strong case for supplier states acting to tighten export controls on transfers of nuclear technology that might have a weapons application as well as closing the loopholes through which nuclear smuggling has taken place.[54]

---

[50] 'US plan to control nuclear weapons', *The Guardian*, 20 Oct. 1990.
[51] Note 50.
[52] *PPNN Newsbrief*, no. 11 (Autumn 1990), p. 2.
[53] Note 52.
[54] See Spector and Smith (note 38), pp. 29–48.

If such a tightening is to take place in the 1990s, it is vital that China exercise greater restraint in this area than has been the case in the past. China is not a party to the NPT, but it did agree in 1984 to place IAEA safeguards on its nuclear exports. In doing so, China implied some acceptance of the rules of the NPT regime, even if it did not accede to the Treaty itself. Despite this, concern has been expressed about Chinese nuclear transfers to Pakistan, India, Argentina and possibly Iraq.[55] Additionally, China's willingness to transfer ballistic missiles further complicates hopes for managing the spread of ballistic missile means of delivery. At the time of writing there is considerable US pressure on China to curtail its missile transfers to the Middle East, but while it has been suggested that the Foreign Ministry may be receptive to the idea of restraint, transfers are under the control of the Army which is eager for hard currency to fund its modernisation programmes. This pressure may be offset in Beijing's overall calculation by its desire to restore better relations with the West, and the growing recognition that economic modernisation would benefit from Western support. However, since a precondition for Western support would probably be increased respect for human rights, a condition which in all probability would be unacceptable to the current Peking leadership, it seems that China will not be easily drawn into future control regimes for weapons of mass destruction.

Although any slowing down of the nuclear weapon programmes of the near-nuclear and *de facto* nuclear states through tighter supplier controls is clearly valuable in the battle against proliferation, there may be little that can be done in the long-term to stop states that wish to do so from developing, or in the case of the *de facto* states, expanding their nuclear weapon capabilities. Therefore, the further question to ask is whether international society might prove ready to consider, as Baker suggested, the application of sanctions against states that flout non-proliferation norms, and if so, which states would be prepared to enforce these norms upon others?

In the early 1960s, British Labour MP John Strachey had written that a 'concert of the world' offered the best hope of preventing nuclear proliferation. For Strachey, international order required that the 'nuclear super-powers arrange humanity's affairs amongst themselves (and no doubt to suit themselves) and for that purpose keep the rest of the world in order, using the United Nations as their instrument'.[56] He envisaged a 'world nuclear authority' based around the superstates of the day, which would 'bind themselves to prevent any further nation states from acquiring nuclear capability'.[57] Strachey believed that if there was a collective will among the great powers to prevent further nuclear proliferation, if necessary by the use of military force, nuclear proliferation could be controlled. To his credit he recognized that such policing might, in the final analysis, even require the use of nuclear force, although he went to great

---

[55] Spector and Smith (note 38), p. 43.
[56] Strachey, J., *On the Prevention of War* (Macmillan, London, 1962), p. 297.
[57] Strachey (note 56), p. 298.

pains to discount the perverse possibility that nuclear weapons might be employed to stop nuclear proliferation.[58]

Believing that the balance of nuclear terror was too perilous a foundation for a lasting international order, because of the risks of nuclear proliferation, Strachey placed his hopes in an order where the superstates of international society set themselves up as the guardians of order and justice. Strachey hoped a concert of the great nuclear powers would evolve into a global political order, providing for order and justice among humankind. Yet, in seeing order as requiring global nuclear policing by the great powers, Strachey suggests that the only realistic prospect is not nuclear abolition, but control by the great powers of small nuclear forces which serve as the ultimate police power in international society. He did hope that great-power coercion would not be the sole basis of order and that, over time, states might come to behave in a community minded fashion. However, he neglected to consider that a great-power concert which had to threaten, or even employ force, to maintain its nuclear hegemony would be one which would not be seen as very legitimate in the eyes of the rest of international society.

It is important in considering Strachey's vision to remember the cold war context in which he floated these ideas. Strachey's prescriptions for international order, depending as they did upon a recognition among the USA and Soviet Union of a common interest in policing the nuclear peace, offered a vision of escape from the perils of nuclear war at a time when there was great concern at the dangers of a US–Soviet conflict. In the 1960s, Strachey's hope for a concert of the nuclear states was utopian, but in the 1990s, with the end of the cold war, and new hope being invested in the UN Security Council as a consequence of its reactions to Iraq's invasion of Kuwait, does Strachey's vision of great power co-operation have a greater chance of being realized?

Rejecting a policy of minimum deterrence as a charter for global nuclear proliferation, Professor Joseph Rotblat proposed in 1989 a small nuclear force under UN control to serve as a guarantee for the world community against the risk of deviant or law-breaking states acquiring nuclear weapons.[59] This idea has also been suggested by some Soviet analysts as the long-term goal of the nuclear disarmament process.[60] However, the basic problem with all such 'global policing' ideas of this kind, as with Strachey's proposals in the 1960s, is that they assume a world where there is a basic consensus on global community norms and values, and where threats to global order are seen by the world community as arising from those it labels as 'law-breaking' states. In such a world, a small UN nuclear police-force might be both feasible and desirable, but this is not the world of contemporary international society.

The UN Security Council enforced international law against Iraq in 1990–91 because there was a consensus among the great powers, but how far this will

[58] Strachey (note 56), p. 314.

[59] Professor Rotblat's comments were made at a Scientific Congress in London in Dec. 1988. See Shenfield, S., 'Minimum nuclear deterrence: the debate among Soviet civilian analysts', Center For Foreign Policy Development, Brown University, 1989, p. 21.

[60] Note 59.

lead to a new world order based upon respect for the rule of law in international relations, or how far it reflects the USA and its allies pursuing self-interest under the cover of morality and international law—the 'old world order'—will be revealed in UN responses to future challenges to international peace and security. The USA may be the only power capable of 'global policing' but if this is not to be viewed by the South as a Western or Northern 'imperialism' designed to protect access to vital economic resources, and to prevent Southern states from acquiring weapons of mass destruction, the North will have to draw the Southern states, especially China, into the management of global security problems. As noted earlier, drawing India and China into the NPT regime is crucial to its long-term future, but both these states flout non-proliferation norms—norms seen by the North as vital to global order—but viewed by India and China as no more than rationalisations by the North to cover its desire to maintain its nuclear hegemony.

Robert Tucker in his book *The Inequality of Nations* argued over a decade ago that attempts by the North to co-opt the South were flawed and that this would just whet the appetite of the Southern states for more and more power. Tucker contended that the challenge from the South would express itself in the form of an increasing spread of nuclear weapons, and that this would in turn lead to an erosion of Northern strategic dominance.[61] More recently, Stephen Krasner has suggested there can be no lasting accommodation between North and South, since what is at stake is the North's political, economic and military dominance.[62] If the 1990 Gulf crisis cautions against casting future conflict in North–South terms, with the Arab world fundamentally divided, it also demonstrates the risks that attend the diffusion of advanced military capabilities to states hostile to Western interests and values.

If Tucker saw the co-option of the South as a recipe for global disorder, Hedley Bull viewed it as vital to the provision of global order. For Bull, the North–South divide has led to a weakening of the element of society in international relations. This erosion carries with it the danger that force will be promoted as the basis for settling conflicts in international relations. Bull believed that it was not only necessary for the North to engage in a fundamental redistribution of wealth from North to South, so that poverty and injustice in the South might begin to be tackled, but also that Southern political and diplomatic élites accord greater respect to human rights and to protection of the environment. Bull hoped such a North–South accommodation might make possible the reconciliation of the provision of order with the achievement of justice in global international society.[63] The North cannot solve the problems of the South, but a shift of wealth and power from North to South, coupled with

[61] Tucker, R., *The Inequality of Nations* (Basic Books: New York, 1977), pp. 198–201.

[62] See Krasner, S., *Structural Conflict* (University of California Press: Berkeley, Calif., 1985).

[63] See Bull, H., 'Order and Justice in International Relations', Hagey Lectures, University of Waterloo, Ontario, 1983. Also, see Vincent, R. J., 'Order in international politics', eds J. D. B. Miller and R. J. Vincent, , *Order and Violence: Hedley Bull and International Relations* (Oxford University Press: Oxford, 1990), pp. 38–64; and Linklater, A., *Beyond Realism and Marxism: Critical Theory and International Relations* (Macmillan: London, 1989), pp. 19–20.

greater liberalization in the South, might help tackle the roots of violent conflict in the Third World.

The link between global military expenditure and the problems of development in the South have been well remarked upon, but if Southern diplomatic and political élites are to be prevailed upon to pursue arms control and disarmament, it will surely depend not only upon greater support from the West in helping the South to cope with the interrelated global crises of debt, development and ecological degradation, but also upon such assistance being made conditional upon reductions in defence budgets and protection for human rights. Third World élites want economic development in order to secure political legitimacy, but for the most part they do not want to see the growth of genuinely liberal-democratic political processes (as distinct from the emergence of 'democratic' populist forces which might be directed against outsiders) since this might threaten their rule by coercion. If a new world order is to be built on the basis of a new North–South bargain, it is important that new security arrangements increase protection for human rights, but since Third World élites are the most jealous defenders of state sovereignty, it may well be necessary for international society to consider whether certain states should not be denied protection of the norms of sovereignty and non-intervention if their behaviour threatens international peace and security and/or violates the humanitarian codes of what some would see as an emergent global political community. This could mean international action to protect basic human rights; to stop national governments from destroying the global environment; and even action as Strachey hoped in the 1960s to prevent the spread of nuclear weapons.

Against this, Bull himself was sceptical that global security challenges would lead states to act as 'local agents of a world common good',[64] considering that states were 'notoriously self-serving',[65] Bull realized that police power in international society depended upon the great powers, but he hoped that they would act as joint custodians of the international order taking into account the legitimate aspirations of international society for justice. Despite this, the realist in him remained very doubtful that the great powers would be able to rise above parochial and particular interests. Bull was not happy with the argument made by E. H. Carr that claims of morality and law in international relations were solely a cover for the pursuit of self-interest by the dominant powers (Carr himself did not always put it as starkly as this), but he was unable to offer any other basis for order and justice than an appeal to the enlightened self-interest and morality of the great powers—a position which as he recognized is vulnerable to the indictment that morality will be what is left when power has had its due.[66]

Less sceptical than Bull, neo-Kantian theorists of international relations not only see the path to a global security community and nuclear abolition as lying in the universalization of liberal values and institutions, but consider that this project is at work in contemporary international relations. It does seem that

[64] Bull (note 63), p. 14.
[65] Bull (note 63), p. 14.

threats of force do not characterize relations between liberal-democratic states. As such, self-help and war seems to be abolished among liberal states. Despite this, Timothy Garton Ash cautions that we should have 'Kant in one hand, but the deterrent in the other',[67] since even if liberal states have peaceful relations with each other, there may always be some states which will lie beyond the liberal security community. Given this, liberal–democratic states will probably continue to possess nuclear weapons for as long as there are 'others' lying beyond the liberal zone of peace which in Jonathan Schell's term possess 'nuclear knowledge'—that is the potential capacity to make nuclear weapons.

VIII. Conclusion

Despite the ambiguities surrounding the concept of minimum deterrence, especially with regard to what level of nuclear forces should be deemed minimum, it does seem that a policy of minimum deterrence would greatly strengthen stability in US–Soviet relations. In this, it offers substantial improvements on maximum nuclear deterrence. Accepting that the basic pre-condition for a successful arms control/reduction regime is that the parties place a common value on mutual security, it has been argued here that a long-term process of co-operation in the strategic nuclear arms control field might serve as both symbol and substance of improving US–Soviet political relations. This hope proved illusory in the 1970s as SALT became the victim of the collapse of *détente*. If arms control is to be successful, hostile states have to accept that they share a common interest in restraint. It was the failure of both sides to do this which wrecked *détente* and arms control in the 1970s. Future arms reductions beyond START I will depend upon both sides acting on the principle that the only security in the nuclear age is mutual security.

Détente failed in the 1970s because the USA did not believe it could have a lasting co-operative relationship with its ideological foe. Henry Kissinger's *détente* strategy which sought to separate out Soviet internal conduct from its external behaviour failed to secure policy legitimacy in the eyes of a US body-politic which believed that the way a government treated its own people was an important indication of how it would behave on the world stage. This remains the case today. A return to repression in the Soviet Union in the 1990s could easily scupper hopes for future East–West security co-operation and arms reductions. If the Soviet Union does return to 'hard line' policies, limited security co-operation on arms control and proliferation issues might be acceptable to Washington on pragmatic grounds, although Congress might as in the 1970s bulk at dealing with a Soviet regime which is repressive at home. However, it is very unlikely that Washington would consider extensive nuclear arms reductions beyond START I (stabilizing measures which were in both side's interest might be agreed) with a regime which was violating human rights at home.

[66] For an excellent discussion of Bull's thinking on these points, see Vincent, R. J., 'Order in international politics', eds J. D. B. Miller and R. J. Vincent (note 63), pp. 45–46.

[67] Ash, T. G., 'Kant in one hand, deterrence in the other', *The Independent*, 10 May 1990.

The argument made by Kissinger for pursuing *détente* and arms control with the ideological enemy was that the moral imperative of the nuclear age was to avoid nuclear war. Kissinger and others may have been too timid in their assessment of the dangers of a more confrontational policy which championed human rights *vis-à-vis* the ideological foe; this remains a matter for historians of the cold war to argue over. However, in thinking about how to achieve stabilizing radical reductions in the post-cold war era, it does seem that given the level of intrusiveness required for verifying very small nuclear force levels, and the risks of cheating on a balance at very low numbers, establishing the confidence necessary for this will only be possible among liberal societies. Stabilizing the nuclear competition and achieving START I reductions should be possible with today's Soviet Union, but radical cuts in nuclear stockpiles have to go hand in hand with the entrenchment of human rights and liberal-democratic values in the Soviet Union.

Even if the Soviet Union does gradually evolve into a more liberal polity, it will probably take some time for a security community relationship to develop. Today in Western Europe, historic enmities may have died away, but there remains a legacy from the past which still exerts a powerful influence over the thinking of governments in Western Europe. In the case of relations between the West and an emerging liberal Soviet Union, fear and mistrust would probably be a feature of relations for many years to come, especially since the Soviet Union would remain in possession of significant military capabilities, including nuclear forces. Western and Soviet nuclear forces would come to be justified as an insurance policy against new threats beyond the frontiers of what would be an enlarged liberal security community. Yet, Soviet and Western policy-makers would probably also privately justify possession of nuclear weapons in terms of their deterrent value *vis-à-vis* the old enemy. Despite this, as with the Franco-German relationship, it is to be hoped that habits and practices of mutual co-operation would develop between governments and peoples which would create a web of links and ties such that an ant-nuclear non-violent conflict culture (see chapter one) would emerge among the former enemies of East and West as has been the case in the Western half of the continent.

The eventual emergence of a security community which stretched from Vancouver to Vladivostok would mark an unprecedented extension of political community in international relations, but while nuclear weapons would cease to play a role in intra-East–West relations in such a security community, the question of how to cope with nuclear challengers on the outside would remain? It has been argued here that while minimum deterrence offers positive security benefits in the East–West context, it is not a desirable strategy for managing the spread of nuclear weapons. Rather, it has been argued here that the problems of managing a transition among the *de facto* nuclear states to a balance of assured destruction capabilities, as well as the uncertainties of applying deterrence rationality in a politically volatile Third World context, point to severe problems with any policy of trying to construct future regional balances of nuclear terror.

The best alternative strategy is to try and work towards the establishment of regional security regimes, and beyond that to a world of regional security communities on the West European model. The USA and the Soviet Union maybe finally ready to play the role of 'nuclear trustees' for humankind (although what role the Soviet Union can really play in building a new world order remains one of the major issues at the beginning of the 1990s), but if there is to be real progress towards the control and abolition of weapons of mass destruction, there will have to be a serious effort made by Western governments to try and help regional actors to arrive at processes of non-violent conflict resolution in international relations, especially in areas like the Middle East and South Asia. The problem here is that it remains very difficult to see how to achieve co-operative security institutions, and an amelioration of the 'security dilemma', in the Hobbesian 'state of war' that shapes interstate relations in both the Middle East and South Asia.

The best long-term hope for controlling and reversing nuclear proliferation seems to lie in strengthening those processes that marginalize the role of nuclear weapons in international politics. In this, it can be agreed with Hedley Bull that 'the best course is to work against all nuclear proliferation, that which has already taken place as well as that which may occur in the future, however difficult this might be. This requires us to take every opportunity to push nuclear weapons—and the doctrines and practices of nuclear deterrence associated with them—as far into the background of international political relationships as possible'.[68] Minimum deterrence is an important step towards this goal in the US–Soviet context, but since it is a policy rooted in the self-help/deterrence paradigm, it should be viewed as a transitional strategy, and not as a desirable end-point in itself. The challenge then is to encourage political, social and economic and ecological processes in international politics that lead to the delegitimization of force in relations between states, since it is only in the fostering of such processes that humankind will be able to move beyond a negative peace based on deterrence to a positive peace based on community norms and values.

Andrew Linklater suggests that the modern international society is in a period of transition from a world order based on sovereignty, power politics, and self-help to a 'post-sovereign international politics' which looks to the extension of justice and community in world politics. The 'post-sovereign' world has a Kantian basis since 'Kant argued that the purpose of foreign policy was to replace force with order and, subsequently, to move beyond order to justice, and to do so incrementally, mindful of the constraints'.[69] Yet, the realists might ask, why should they believe late 20th century expressions of Kantian optimism when the message has proved a premature one so often in the past? For realists,

---

[68] Bull, H., 'Future Conditions of Strategic Deterrence', ed. C. Bertram, *The Future of Strategic Deterrence* (International Institute of Strategic Studies: London, 1981), p. 16.
[69] Bull (note 68).

international anarchy generates self-help behaviour which today, as much as in the past, can lead to interstate violence, including for those states that possess nuclear weapons, or have the capacity to make them—the risk of nuclear conflict: for realists, anarchy, self-help and recourse to force provide the recurrent theme of international politics across the centuries. However, to accept the pure realist view is to end up with moral despair at the inability of states to escape the consequences of power politics and self-help, finding order in the nuclear age in the civilization threatening perils of a balance of nuclear terror.

Some realists do attempt to try and escape a hard-nosed power politics with its rejection of the possibilities of co-operation and the extension of community in international relations, but they end up with the problem of how to reconcile the opposites of power and morality.[70] Accepting that a proper realist foreign policy should be one which looked to the achievement of common interests and a common morality, Stanley Hoffmann considered that states 'ought not to give up the hope of a future world community . . . but cannot act as if it already existed'. How can statesman, he asks, 'fight for the particular interest of the nation so as not to jeopardize the eventual reconciliation of national interests, without which no "international community" could ever emerge'?[71]

More optimistically than Hoffmann, John Strachey put well the necessity for humankind to act as though there can be an eventual escape from the cynicism and barrenness of a pure Realism. 'We must believe that one day our descendants will scale and possess the Holy Mountain of peace. For us it is too distant and too high. Yet we can see its peak. If we were to loose sight of it we should wander for ever in the wilderness'.[72] If we recognize this as the real challenge, we will have realized the enormity of achieving nuclear abolition, but also made the first step to its possible achievement. Schell believed the Kantian project could follow nuclear abolition: the real conclusion is that nuclear abolition will only be achieved as part of the realization of the Kantian ideal of a universal community of humankind.

[70] See Clark, I., *The Hierarchy of States* (Cambridge University Press: Cambridge, 1989), pp. 82–84.

[71] Hoffmann, S., *The State of War: Essays on the Theory and Practice of International Politics* (Praeger: New York, 1965), p. 86.

[72] Strachey (note 56), p. 329.

About the contributors

Ken Booth (United Kingdom) holds a Personal Chair in the Department of International Politics, University of Wales, Aberystwyth. He has been Scholar-in-Residence at the US Naval War College and Senior Research Fellow at Dalhousie University, Canada. In 1992–93 he will be Visiting Fellow at Clare Hall, Cambridge University. His books include *Navies and Foreign Policy* (1977), *Strategy and Ethnocentrism* (1979), *Law, Force and Diplomacy at Sea* (1985), *Britain, NATO and Nuclear Weapons* (with John Baylis) (1989) and *New Thinking about Strategy and International Security* (1991).

Regina Cowen Karp (Germany) is Senior Researcher and leader of the SIPRI Security Without Nuclear Weapons? project. Previously she was a Resident Fellow at the Institute for East–West Security Studies in New York. She is a co-editor (with Walther Stützle and Bhupendra Jasani) of *The ABM Treaty: To Defend or Not to Defend?* (1987) and editor of *Security With Nuclear Weapons? Different Perspectives on National Security* (1991). She is a contributor to a number of books and journals, writing on nuclear weapon, arms control and European security issues.

Julie Dahlitz (Australia), Ph.D., LL M, is a Barrister and Solicitor who is a specialist in the legal aspects of arms limitation. While Research Fellow at a number of institutes, Political Affairs Officer at the United Nations in New York and Senior Researcher with the United Nations Institute for Disarmament Research, she has published widely on this subject. Her attributed publications include the book *Nuclear Arms Control* (1984) and the Peace Research Institute Oslo monograph *Co-operative Deterrence* (1989). She is co-editor of the United Nations book, *The International Law of Arms Control and Disarmament* (1991).

Lynn Eden (USA) is Senior Research Scholar at the Center for International Security and Arms Control at Stanford University, and Lecturer in the Sociology Department at Stanford. Before coming to Stanford, she taught at Carnegie Mellon University in the Department of History. She is co-editor (with Steven E. Miller) and contributor to *Nuclear Arguments: Understanding the Strategic Nuclear Arms and Arms Control Debates* (1989). She has written on US foreign policy of the early cold war period and is working on a book on the social construction of US nuclear targeting. She currently serves on the editorial board of *International Security*.

Nicholas J. Wheeler (United Kingdom) is a lecturer in Politics at the University of Hull where he teaches International Relations theory and Security Studies. His is co-author (with Ian Clark) of *The British Origins of Nuclear Strategy 1945–55* (1989) and a chapter (with Ken Booth) in John Baylis and N. Rengger (eds) *Dilemmas of World Politics: International Issues in a Changing World* (1992). He has also written on European security in the post-cold war era, and is currently working on the policing role of the United Nations Security Council in protecting humanitarian values after the end of cold war.

Patrick J. Garrity (USA) is on the staff of the Center for National Security Studies at Los Alamos National Laboratory. He holds a Ph.D. in Government from Claremont Graduate School. He has served on the faculty of the Naval Postgraduate School in Monterey, California, and has been a Research Fellow at the Center for Strategic and International Studies in Washington. His research interests include US nuclear weapon policy, nuclear arms control and international space policy. He is co-editor (with Jeffrey Larsen) of the volume, *The Future of Nuclear Weapons in Europe* (1991) and co-editor (with Steven A. Maaranen) of *Nuclear Weapons in a Changing World: Perspectives from Europe, Asia and North America* (1992).

Frank von Hippel (USA), a physicist, is chairman of the research arm of the Federation of American Scientists, and Professor of Public and International Affairs at Princeton University. He is co-editor (with Roald Z. Sagdeev) of *Reversing the Arms Race: How to Achieve and Verify Deep Reductions in the Nuclear Arsenals*.

Erwin Häckel (Germany) is Professor of Political Science at the University of Konstanz and Research Fellow with the Deutsche Gesellschaft für Auswärtige Politik, Bonn. His publications include *Die Bundesrepublik Deutschland und der Atomwaffensperrvertrag* (1989) and numerous articles on nuclear weapons proliferation, international energy policy, and German foreign and security policies.

Patricia M. Lewis (United Kingdom) is Director of the Verification Technology Information Centre in London. In 1988–89 she undertook a consultancy study, commissioned by the British Foreign and Commonwealth Office, on the verification of a conventional armed forces in Europe treaty. She is the British expert to the 1989–90 United Nations study on the role of the UN in verification.

Harald Müller (Germany) is Director of International Programs at the Peace Research Institute Frankfurt (PRIF). He is the author of *Nuclear Proliferation: Facing Reality* (1984) and *Strategic Defences: The End of the Alliance Strategy?* (1987), and the co-author (with David Fischer) of *Nonproliferation*

Beyond the 1985 Review (1985) and (with Richard Kokoski) of *The Non-Proliferation Treaty: Political and Technological Prospects and Dangers in 1990* (1990).

Robert E. Pendley (USA) is on the staff of the Center for National Security Studies at Los Alamos National Laboratory. He holds a Ph.D. in political science from Northwestern University, as well as degrees in physics from the University of California at Berkeley and the University of Oregon. He has taught at Rice University and the University of Hawaii, consulted on international security affairs, and served in the National Science Foundation. At Los Alamos, he has held staff and program management positions in arms control, verification and international security policy, and has served as Deputy Director of the Center for National Security Studies. He is co-editor (with Joseph F. Pilat) of *Beyond 1995: The Future of the NPT Regime* (1990).

George H. Quester (USA) is Professor of Government and Politics at the University of Maryland. He has taught at Harvard and Cornell Universities, the University of California at Los Angeles and the National War College, Washington, DC. He is the author of *Deterrence Before Hiroshima* (1966), *Nuclear Diplomacy: The First Twenty-Five Years* (1970), *The Politics of Nuclear Proliferation* (1973), *Offense and Defense in the International System* (1976), *The Future of Nuclear Deterrence* (1984) and *The International Politics of Television* (1990).

Paul C. White (USA) is the Division Leader of the Applied Theoretical Physics Division at Los Alamos National Laboratory. He received his Ph.D. in physics from the University of Texas in Austin, and joined Los Alamos in 1975 after teaching for five years on the faculty at St. Edward's University. He has been the Laboratory Program Manager for Advanced Nuclear Weapons Design, and before assuming his present position, he served as Deputy Director, and later as Acting Director of the Laboratory's Center for National Security Studies. He was a technical advisor to the Nuclear Testing Talks in Geneva, and has written a number of papers on the relationships between technology and national security policy.

Index

ABM (Anti-Ballistic Missile) Treaty (1972) 90, 91, 257
Abolition, The (Schell) 32, 33, 34, 36–39, 41
Absolute Weapon, The (Brodie) 32–33
Adelman, Kenneth 129fn.
adjudication 82
Afghanistan 69, 247
aircraft 72, 111
Akhromeyev, Marshal Sergey 186
Alfonsín, President Raúl 159fn.
alliances:
  abandonment and 237, 238, 239
  asymmetries in 237, 238
  definition 226
  denuclearization 241
  domestic debates and 239
  entrapment and 237, 239, 241
  hegemony and 227, 238, 248
  nature of 236–38
  non-nuclear situation and 239–41
  nuclear weapons and 238–39
  role of 209
  security and 237
  security regimes and 243, 244, 247
  threats and 240, 241
  see also hegemonies
America *see* United States of America
Amin, Idi 58
Antarctic Treaty (1959) 83, 88, 89
anti-nuclear non-violent conflict culture 43–5, 46, 51, 52, 54, 55
ANZUS 233, 238
Arab League 101
arbitration 82
Argentina:
  Brazil and 212, 233, 246
  nuclear capacity 59, 159fn.
  see also Falklands/Malvinas War
'armaments-first approach' 40
Armenia 190, 193
armour 114
Arms and Influence (Schelling) 32
arms control:
  bargaining chips 181
  politics and 253

  prospects for, improving 50
  see also nuclear weapon elimination
arms race, conventional 31, 235, 236
arms trade 50
ASEAN (Association of South–East Asian Nations) 101, 233
Ash, Timothy Garton 277
Athens 229
'atomic escapism' 23
'Atoms for Peace' 59, 72
Australia 233
Azerbaijan 193

B-1 bomber 177
B-2 bomber 178, 181
B-17 bomber 113
Bakatin, Vadim V. 190fn.
Baker, James 153fn.
ballistic missile defence 257 *see also* Strategic Defense Initiative
Baruch Plan 202, 213–24
battlefield:
  information systems and 127
  management 111, 127
  nuclear weapons and 96
Belgium 58
Berlin Wall 24, 201, 224
biological weapons 31, 104, 111, 223–24
biotechnology 111
bombers 67 *see also designations of*
bombs, smart 113
Boulding, K. 44fn., 54
bracketing 167
Brazil:
  Argentina and 212, 233, 246
  nuclear capacity 59, 159
breeder reactors 157
Brezhnev, President Leonid 184, 185
'brilliant' weapons 113, 121
Brodie, Bernard 23, 24, 32–33, 54
Brownlie, Ian 86
Bulgaria 133fn.
Bull, Hedley 260, 275, 276, 279
Bunn, George 165fn., 174
Burt, Richard 116
Bush, President George 134fn., 252